The Globalization of Ethics
Religious and Secular Perspectives

The Globalization of Ethics seeks to provide an alternative to post-9/11 pessimism about the ability of serious ethical dialogue to resolve disagreements and conflict across national, religious, and cultural differences. It begins by acknowledging the gravity of the problem: On our tightly interconnected planet, entire populations look for moral guidance to a variety of religious and cultural traditions, and these often stiffen, rather than soften, opposing moral perceptions. How, then, to set minimal standards for the treatment of persons while developing moral bases for coexistence and cooperation across different ethical traditions?

   This volume argues for a tempered optimism in approaching these questions. Its distinguished contributors report on some of the most globally influential traditions of ethical thought – both religious traditions such as Islam, Christianity, Buddhism, Judaism, and Confucianism, and the secular ethics of international law, liberalism, and feminism – in order to identify the resources within each tradition for working toward consensus and accommodation among the ethical traditions that shape the contemporary world.

William M. Sullivan is Senior Scholar at the Carnegie Foundation for the Advancement of Teaching and was Professor of Philosophy at La Salle University, where he is now Associate Faculty. He is the co-author of *Habits of the Heart* and the author of *Reconstructing Public Philosophy* and *Work and Integrity: The Crisis and Promise of Professionalism in America*, second edition.

Will Kymlicka is Canada Research Chair in Political Philosophy at Queen's University and Visiting Professor at the Central European University in Budapest. He has written and edited many titles, including *Contemporary Political Philosophy* and *Multiculturalism in Asia*. He is a Fellow of the Royal Society of Canada and of the Canadian Institute for Advanced Research, and current President of the American Society for Political and Legal Philosophy.

The Ethikon Series in Comparative Ethics

The Ethikon Series publishes studies on ethical issues of current importance. By bringing scholars representing a diversity of moral viewpoints into structured dialogue, the series aims to broaden the scope of ethical discourse and to identify commonalities and differences between alternative views.

TITLES IN THE SERIES

Brian Barry and Robert E. Goodin, eds., *Free Movement: Ethical Issues in the Transnational Migration of People and Money*

Chris Brown, ed., *Political Restructuring in Europe: Ethical Perspectives*

Terry Nardin, ed., *The Ethics of War and Peace: Religious and Secular Perspectives*

David R. Mapel and Terry Nardin, eds., *International Society: Diverse Ethical Perspectives*

David Miller and Sohail H. Hashmi, eds., *Boundaries and Justice: Diverse Ethical Perspectives*

Simone Chambers and Will Kymlicka, eds., *Alternative Conceptions of Civil Society*

Nancy L. Rosenblum and Robert Post, eds., *Civil Society and Government*

Sohail Hashmi, ed., Foreword by Jack Miles, *Islamic Political Ethics: Civil Society, Pluralism, and Conflict*

Richard Madsen and Tracy B. Strong, eds., *The Many and the One: Ethical Pluralism in the Modern World*

Allen Buchanan and Margaret Moore, eds., *States, Nations, and Borders: The Ethics of Making Boundaries*

Sohail H. Hashmi and Steven P. Lee, eds., *Ethics and Weapons of Mass Destruction: Religious and Secular Perspectives*

Michael Walzer, ed., *Law, Politics, and Morality in Judaism*

William M. Sullivan and Will Kymlicka, eds., *The Globalization of Ethics: Religious and Secular Perspectives*

The Globalization of Ethics

Religious and Secular Perspectives

Edited by

WILLIAM M. SULLIVAN

Carnegie Foundation for the Advancement of Teaching

WILL KYMLICKA

Queen's University

CAMBRIDGE
UNIVERSITY PRESS

CAMBRIDGE UNIVERSITY PRESS

Cambridge, New York, Melbourne, Madrid, Cape Town, Singapore, São Paulo, Delhi

Cambridge University Press
32 Avenue of the Americas, New York, NY 10013-2473, USA

www.cambridge.org
Information on this title: www.cambridge.org/9780521700214

First published 2007
Reprinted 2008

Printed in the United States of America

A catalog record for this publication is available from the British Library.

Library of Congress Cataloging in Publication Data

The globalization of ethics : religious and secular perspectives / [edited by]
William M. Sullivan, Will Kymlicka.
p.   cm. – (The Ethikon series in comparative ethics)
Includes bibliographical references and index.
ISBN-13: 978-0-521-87335-2 (hardback)
ISBN-13: 978-0-521-70021-4 (pbk.)
1. Ethics.   2. Globalization – Moral and ethical aspects.   I. Sullivan, William M.
II. Kymlicka, Will.   III. Title.   IV. Series.
BJ21.G56   2007
170 – dc22   2006035659

ISBN 978-0-521-87335-2 hardback
ISBN 978-0-521-70021-4 paperback

Contents

Contributors

Chris Brown is professor of international relations at the London School of Economics and past chair of the British International Studies Association. He has published widely in classical and modern international political theory and international ethics. He is the author of *Understanding International Relations* (which is in its third edition and has been translated into three languages) and *Sovereignty, Rights, and Justice* and co-editor (with Terry Nardin and N. J. Rengger) of *International Relations in Political Thought: Texts from the Greeks to the First World War.*

Kimberly Hutchings is reader in international relations at the London School of Economics. She is the author of *Kant, Critique and Politics; International Political Theory: Rethinking Ethics in a Global Era;* and *Hegel and Feminist Philosophy* and co-editor (with Roland Dannreuther) of *Cosmopolitan Citizenship.* She is a founding editor of the journal *Contemporary Political Theory* and currently associate editor of the *European Journal of International Relations.* Her interests range across the fields of Continental and feminist philosophy, international ethics, and international political theory.

Will Kymlicka is professor of philosophy at Queen's University and a frequent visiting professor at the Central European University. He is the author of *Liberalism, Community, and Culture; Contemporary Political Philosophy; Politics in the Vernacular: Nationalism, Multiculturalism, Citizenship; Multiculturalism in Asia;* and *Multicultural Citizenship,* which was awarded the Macpherson Prize by the Canadian Political Science Association and the Bunche Award by the American Political Science Association. He is also the editor of *Justice in Political Philosophy* and *The Rights of Minority Cultures* and co-editor of *Alternative Conceptions of Civil Society* (with Simone Chambers), *Ethnicity and Group Rights* (with Ian Shapiro), and *Citizenship in Diverse Societies* (with Wayne Norman). His works have been translated into thirty languages.

Richard Madsen is professor and chair of the sociology department at the University of California, San Diego, and a co-author (with Robert Bellah et al.) of *The Good Society* and *Habits of the Heart*, which received the *Los Angeles Times* Book Award and was nominated for the Pulitzer Prize. He is a former Maryknoll missionary and has authored or co-authored five books on China, including *Morality and Power in a Chinese Village*, for which he received the C. Wright Mills Award; *China's Catholics: Tragedy and Hope in an Emerging Civil Society*; and *China and the American Dream*. He also co-edited (with Tracy B. Strong) *The Many and the One: Religious and Secular Perspectives on Ethical Pluralism in the Modern World*.

Muhammad Khalid Masud is a student of religion, law, and social change in Muslim societies. Formerly academic director of the International Institute for the Study of Islam in the Modern World (Leiden, The Netherlands), he is presently chairing the Council of Islamic Ideology, Government of Pakistan, Islamabad. He is the author of *Shabiti's Philosophy of Islamic Law*; *Iqbal's Reconstruction of Ijtihad*; and *Muslim Jurists' Quest for the Normative Basis of Shar'ia*; editor of *Islamic Laws and Women in the Modern World* and *Travelers in Faith: Studies on Tablighi Jama'at as Transnational Movement for the Renewal of Faith*; and co-editor (with Brinkley Messick and David Powers) of *Islamic Legal Interpretation: The Muftis and Their Fatwas* and (with David Powers and Ruud Peters) *Dispensing Justice in Islam*.

Mark C. Murphy is professor of philosophy at Georgetown University. He is the author of *Natural Law and Practical Rationality*; *An Essay on Divine Authority*; *Natural Law in Jurisprudence and Politics*; and *Philosophy of Law: The Fundamentals* and the editor of *Alasdair MacIntyre*. His research interests include the history of early modern philosophy and moral, political, and legal philosophy, with special emphasis on natural law theory, both in its historical manifestations and as a live option for jurisprudence and the theory of practical reasoning.

Peter Nosco is professor and head of Asian Studies at the University of British Columbia. A specialist in the intellectual and social history of early modern Japan, he is the author of *Remembering Paradise: Nativism and Nostalgia in 18th Century Japan*; the editor of *Confucianism and Tokugawa Culture* and *Japanese Identity: Cultural Analyses;* and translator of Ihara Saikaku's *Some Final Words of Advice*. He has also been a guest editor of *The Japanese Journal of Religious Studies* and *Philosophy: East and West*. He is currently working on the construction of individual identity in Tokugawa (1600–1868) Japan.

Daniel Philpott is associate professor in the Department of Political Science and the Joan B. Kroc Institute for International Peace Studies at the University of Notre Dame. He is the author of *Revolutions in Sovereignty: How Ideas Shaped Modern International Relations* and a number of journal articles on national self-determination, religious freedom, and related topics. His major current interests include reconciliation and transitional justice. He is a senior associate at the International Center for Religion and Diplomacy and travels regularly to Kashmir to train leaders in faith-based diplomacy. He is also collaborating on a Harvard-based study of religion in global politics.

Max L. Stackhouse is the Rimmer and Ruth de Vries Professor of Reformed Theology and Public Life, Princeton Theological Seminary. He is the author or editor of twelve books, including *Creeds, Society, and Human Rights: A Study in Three Cultures; Covenant and Commitments: Faith, Family and Economic Lift; On Moral Business: Classical and Contemporary Resources for Ethics in Economic Life; Christian Social Ethics in a Global Era; Public Theology and Political Economy;* and *God and Globalization,* 3 vols. (the last volume is forthcoming). His books and essays have been translated into Korean, Japanese, and Chinese, and he is a frequent lecturer at conferences and universities in India and China. He is an ordained minister in the United Church of Christ.

William M. Sullivan is senior scholar at the Carnegie Foundation for the Advancement of Teaching. He is co-author (with Robert Bellah et al.) of *The Good Society* and *Habits of the Heart,* which received the *Los Angeles Times* Book Award and was nominated for the Pulitzer Prize. He is the author of *Reconstructing Public Philosophy* and, most recently, *Work and Integrity: The Crisis and Promise of Professionalism in American Life.*

Michael Walzer is a member of the School of Social Science at the Institute for Advanced Study, Princeton. He is the author of *The Revolution of the Saints, Just and Unjust Wars, Spheres of Justice, On Toleration,* and *Politics and Passion;* co-editor of *The Jewish Political Tradition* and *Dissent;* a contributing editor of *The New Republic;* and a member of the editorial board of The Ethikon Series in Comparative Ethics.

Acknowledgments

This book is the result of a dialogue project organized by the Ethikon Institute in collaboration with the Dominican Lay Scholars Community. The trustees of the Ethikon Institute join with Philip Valera, president, and Carole Pateman, series editor, in thanking all who contributed to the success of this project.

We are especially indebted to the late Joan Palevsky and the Sidney Stern Memorial Trust for their enabling financial support and to the Carnegie Foundation for the Advancement of Teaching for its assistance in preparing the manuscript for publication.

Special thanks are due to William M. Sullivan and Will Kymlicka for taking on the challenging task of editing this book and to William A. Galston for his key role in facilitating the dialogue that resulted in this volume. We are also grateful to Uzma Jamil and Sohail Hashmi for providing helpful advice and assistance, as well as to Laura Ostenso for valuable technical support. We also wish to thank Ronald Cohen, whose editing of the manuscript sharpened the prose and helped us to avoid errors.

Finally, we wish to express our thanks to Beatrice Rehl, our editor at Cambridge University Press, for her encouragement, valuable guidance, and support.

The Ethikon Institute

The Ethikon Institute, a nonprofit organization, is concerned with the social implications of ethical pluralism. Its dialogue-publication projects are designed to explore a diversity of moral outlooks, secular and religious, and to clarify areas of consensus and divergence among them. By encouraging a systematic exchange of ideas, the Institute aims to advance the prospects for agreement and to facilitate the peaceful accommodation of irreducible differences. The Ethikon Institute takes no position on issues that may divide its participants, serving not as an arbiter but as a neutral forum for the cooperative exploration of diverse and sometimes opposing views.

The Dominican Lay Scholars Community

The Dominican Lay Scholars Community is an ecumenical organization that promotes both interreligious contact and carefully structured dialogue between religious scholars and professional scholars in other intellectual disciplines. Among its other objectives, the DLSC encourages a systematic and impartial search for common intellectual ground among secular and religious outlooks on a wide range of important issues.

Introduction

The Globalization of Ethics

Will Kymlicka

A great deal has been written lately about the ethics of globalization, under-stood as the intensification of interactions across national boundaries, partic-ularly in the areas of trade and investment, but also the transfer of technology, the movement of peoples, and the global diffusion of a Western consumer lifestyle embodied in products such as Hollywood movies and McDonald's. There have been many impassioned ethical debates about the benefits and costs of these processes of globalization, including their effect on inequality both within and between societies, their consequences for the environment, and the way they are uprooting and displacing traditional ways of life.

One striking aspect of these ethical debates about globalization is that they are themselves globalized. These debates take place across national bound-aries, bringing together activists, academics, and government officials from all parts of the world, who must therefore find a common vocabulary to dis-cuss their ethical concerns about globalization. People from Western liberal societies must find a way to discuss ethical issues with people from Buddhist societies in Southeast Asia or from indigenous communities in Latin America. Such transnational debates about ethics are increasingly unavoidable, given the intensity of interaction amongst the world's cultures. As globalization increases, ethics must itself become globalized.

Our aim in this volume is to explore the globalization of ethics, which is a surprisingly neglected phenomenon. In particular, we examine how some of the world's most influential ethical traditions think about the task of construct-ing moral conversations and moral norms at a global level. What intellectual resources are available within Christianity, Islam, Judaism, Buddhism, liberal-ism, natural law, Confucianism, and feminism when confronted with the need to engage in a globalized ethics?

It is difficult to overstate the gravity and difficulty of this task. We live in a world where entire populations and blocs of nations look for moral guid-ance to different religious and cultural traditions. And while these different moral traditions all contain elements that allow and encourage cooperation across religious, cultural and national lines, they also may mandate conflicting norms and incompatible social arrangements that render cooperation difficult. Conflicts can arise between the adherents of different traditions, not because people suspend their ethical sensitivities when dealing with outsiders, but precisely because of their ethical sensitivities. Indeed, conflicts rooted in rival perceptions of good and evil may be more destructive and intractable than conflicts rooted in conflicting material interests. Such ethically based conflicts can arise over such issues as the status of women, religious tolerance, forms of punishment, models of governance, and the use of public space.

Yet, despite these important sources of potential conflict, there are also grounds for consensus amongst diverse ethical traditions. Indeed, these areas of consensus arguably outweigh the areas of disagreement. Unfortunately, the scope for convergence has too often been obscured by different modes of expression, historical grievances and resentments, and the absence of appropriate forums for open dialogue. It is one of our aims in this volume to promote a dialogue across ethical traditions to help clarify the real points of agreement and disagreement, to identify and broaden areas of possible consensus, and to consider ways of accommodating enduring differences.

We can imagine a range of possible responses to the challenge of globalized ethics. One option would be to start with an existing moral tradition and to attempt to impose it as the single legitimate framework for global ethical discourse. Throughout much of recent history, particularly in the era of colonialism, many people around the world have criticized Western powers for doing just this, whether in the form of imposing Christian religious values or secular liberal values. Obviously this option is only feasible in a context of massive inequalities in power, and for just this reason attempts to impose a particular ethical tradition are likely be perceived by others as an exercise of unjust power, not as an attempt to construct a genuine global ethical community.

Indeed, as the following chapters make clear, it is widely recognized by most traditions today that the attempt to impose one's values on others is both illegitimate and unrealistic. While each tradition harbours the hope and expectation that others will come to share its values and perspectives through the force of example and persuasion, this is seen as the desired outcome of an ethical conversation, not as its starting point.

Another option would be to try to define an entirely new ethical vocabulary that is not drawn exclusively from one of the historical ethical traditions, but rather is built specifically for the purpose of engaging in cross-cultural debates. This, of course, is one of the aims of the vocabulary of "international human rights" articulated by the United Nations. This approach has developed to the point where it too can now be seen as an "ethical tradition," or at least as the ethical core of the larger tradition of international law. Like any tradition, it has its own "canonical texts" – particularly the 1948 Universal Declaration of Human Rights and the two International Covenants on human rights adopted in 1966. But these canonical texts are supposed to be free-standing, available to (and agreed upon by) all of the world's major ethical and religious traditions, not tied to any one historical tradition.

The remarkable global diffusion of the idea of "human rights" since 1948 shows that there is indeed great potential in this approach. People from all regions of the world, and all religious and cultural backgrounds, have been able to appropriate the language of human rights, and use it to articulate their ethical concerns. In many ways, it has come to serve as the "gold standard" of international moral debates.

Yet the idea that human rights can function as an adequate basis for a globalized ethics is controversial. For some people, the human rights framework is a lightly disguised form of Western liberalism. It purports to be the product of an international consensus, but in fact reflects distinctly Western ideas about the individual as a rights-bearing agent who needs protection from society and the state. (It is important to remember that the 1948 Universal Declaration was adopted before the era of decolonization, so that most of the world's non-Western societies were not in fact part of the negotiation over the original definition of human rights.)

For others, the idea of human rights, even if it has universal resonance, is nonetheless insufficient to discuss many of the ethical issues raised by globalization, such as the effect on the environment, or on local communities, or on families. International human rights must therefore be supplemented by other ethical norms and principles, including norms of collective responsibilities. However, there does not appear to be any consensus on how to fill in these gaps. For example, feminists and Confucians may well disagree about what sorts of measures are needed to protect the family, or indeed about how to define the family in the first place. Indigenous peoples and European settlers may well disagree about what sorts of property rights are compatible with protecting the environment, or indeed about whether ideas of "property" and "ownership" are appropriate at all in regards to the natural environment.

In principle, one could imagine trying to build up the international discourse of human rights so that it can address all of these issues in a way that can be endorsed by all of the different traditions. But it's not clear that this is feasible, given the diversity of the world's ethical traditions, or even desirable. After all, each of the world's major ethical traditions carries with it centuries of experience, argument, and example, and as such is a repository of potential moral resources from which we can learn. In this respect, the fact that the discourse of international human rights is "self-standing," not rooted in any historical religious or ethical tradition, is both its strength and its weakness. Insisting that everyone use a constructed discourse of human rights helps to ensure a degree of consensus and mutual understanding, but it comes at the expense of cutting us off from the wisdom embodied in older ethical traditions, which often can only be expressed in the tradition's own vocabulary. Indigenous ideas of "stewardship" of the land, for example, cannot readily be translated into human rights terminology, but it would be a mistake to therefore exclude them from our globalized ethical discourse. So too with Catholic natural law's ideas of "subsidiarity." Indigenous ideas of stewardship, or Roman Catholic ideas of subsidiarity, have positively influenced ethical debates about how to protect communities from the more pernicious effects of globalization, but only because our ethical debates are not confined to the constructed discourse of human rights.

A third option, therefore, is to think about global ethics as a two-level phenomenon. At one level, we have a self-standing international discourse, such as human rights, that seeks to define a minimum set of standards agreeable to all. At the second level, we have a multiplicity of different ethical traditions, each of which has its own account of what more, or what else, is needed above and beyond human rights. Any convergence at this second level will be the result of learning, mutual exchange, and inspiration, which is likely to be a slow and uneven process. Room must be provided for such learning and persuasion to take place through the articulation and propagation of different ethical views. History shows clearly that the members of different cultures are indeed able and willing to learn from each other, not just with respect to issues of technology, but also with respect to basic ethical values. A crucial task of a globalized ethics, therefore, is to think about the conditions under which such interchange can take place, without presupposing or imposing a single ethical perspective, and without limiting ethical debate to the thin and minimal discourse of international human rights.

Most ethical traditions today endorse some version of this two-level view. As we will see, all of the ethical traditions discussed in this volume disavow a "crusader mentality" that seeks to impose their own ethical views on others. Instead, they seek to show that (1) they can endorse and support a doctrine of international human rights constructed on a cross-cultural basis, and (2) insofar as they seek to propagate their views globally, they do so through open and constructive dialogue, not coercion.

Indeed, this disavowal of the crusader mentality is clearly a point of pride, as well as a point of principle, for many ethical traditions. Many traditions believe themselves to have been uniquely resistant to the temptation to use violence and coercion to promote their views. For example, according to Kimberly Hutchings, of all the traditions surveyed in this volume, feminism is the "most reluctant" to use violence to promote its ends. Peter Nosco claims that Buddhism is unique in its commitment to the principle of "conquest by righteousness" as opposed to "conquest by force." Richard Madsen argues that Confucianism is distinguished by the absence of a Crusader mentality in its history and canonical texts, and its commitment to spreading Confucian values through free debate. According to Michael Walzer, while Jews have always seen themselves as a "light unto the nations," they seek to achieve this ethical leadership through the force of example, not through the force of arms. Mark Murphy argues that Catholic natural law doctrine rests on respect for the rational nature of human beings, and hence privileges reasoned debate over coercion for the resolution of moral disagreements.

Historians may question whether these traditions have always been as committed to peaceful relations and free debate as they are presented in some of the chapters of the book. The widespread support today for persuasion over coercion arguably reflects distinctly modern ideas about the rights and dignity of all human beings and the repudiation of older ideologies of ethnic and racial hierarchies, as well as a reaction against the horrors committed by crusading and colonizing powers in the name of morality.[1] We could say that the narratives provided in these chapters reflect a distinctly post-colonial attitude, highlighting those aspects of each ethical tradition that privilege free and equal deliberation with the members of other cultures, and downplaying those aspects that legitimize acts of coercion. While the contemporary doctrine of universal human rights was built upon the shared values of the world's ethical traditions, that doctrine has in turn exercised a profound influence back upon those traditions, reshaping how they interpret their texts and practices in a more egalitarian and post-colonial direction.

And yet it would be a mistake to imply that the two-level view based on universal minimum standards and voluntary debate and conversion is entirely a modern invention. We can find examples of it far back in history. As Michael Walzer notes, the Jewish tradition has always distinguished a minimal set of norms binding on all groups and accessible to all rational humans (the "Noahide" laws, articulated in the Ten Commandments) from the thicker set of laws given by revelation to the Jews (the 613 "Mosaic" laws). The latter are seen as a higher moral code, and it is hoped and expected that non-Jews will come to see the code's merits and voluntarily subscribe to it, but so long as other societies respect the minimal standards of the Noahide laws, they must be respected. This is a very ancient example of the two-level view.

However, the line between the coercive crusading approach and the two-level view is not always clear. Consider, for example, the way the Spanish conquerors justified their treatment of the indigenous peoples of the Americas. The way in which coercion was used to propagate Catholicism, and the sorts of abuses and atrocities this gave rise to, is now widely seen as a textbook example of the problems of a crusading moral imperialism. Yet this is a potentially

---

[1] That such a "post-colonial" change has taken place within Western traditions, religious or secular, is clear enough when we recall the near-universal support in the nineteenth-century amongst both liberals and Christians for European colonization. But I would argue that a similar change has also taken place amongst many of the other ethical traditions. For example, there is considerable evidence that Buddhist kingdoms in Southeast Asia were historically quite willing to forcibly conquer and convert the "barbarians" on their borders. See the discussion of Laos, Vietnam, and Thailand in *Multiculturalism in Asia* (Kymlicka & He, 2005). For the persistence of such ideas into the modern era, in Buddhist, Confucian, and Muslim-majority societies, see *Civilizing the Margins: Southeast Asian Government Policies for the Development of Minorities* (Duncan, 2004).

misleading account. Many influential officials in the Spanish court and Catholic Church did not claim that they had a right to coercively impose Catholicism on non-believers.[2] Instead, they too endorsed a version of the two-level view according to which:

There are certain minimal standards that are accessible to every competent and rational person, even without the benefit of divine revelation, canonical texts, or a particular history of moral teaching. Any society that falls to meet these standards is either composed of people who lack rationality, or is barbaric and corrupt. Intervention can be justified to enforce these universal minimal standards – for example, by suppressing certain "barbaric" indigenous practices, such as human sacrifice.

Catholicism is a higher moral code whose virtues will be made clear through force of example and persuasion, so long as Catholics are allowed to live their exemplary lives, and to discuss its merits with non-believers. Therefore, intervention can be justified to enable Catholics to freely share their knowledge and experience – for example, by forcing indigenous communities to allow Spanish missionaries to preach.

Put this way, their view was not all that different from many contemporary views, at least in its basic structure. The position was that coercion was justified, not to impose Catholicism directly, but rather (1) to ensure that indigenous peoples respected universal minimum standards available to all rational beings, and (2) to ensure the conditions for people to freely witness and discuss the merits of the Catholic religion. On the surface, this does not seem vastly different from any number of contemporary views that insist on the twin goals of respect for universal human rights, combined with the freedom to propagate one's views in peaceful dialogue.

Why then has the Spanish treatment of indigenous peoples come to be seen as a paradigm of a crusading and intolerant approach? Part of the answer is that the actual behavior of the Spanish colonizers went far beyond what was justified by the official pronouncements of government and Church. Coercion was used not only to prohibit allegedly barbaric practices and to permit peaceful evangelism, but also to dispossess Indians of their land, and indeed to enslave and murder them in appalling numbers. Many Catholic missionaries were horrified by this brutality, and fought bravely against abuses that were committed in the name of Catholicism.

---

[2] There was in fact a broad range of views amongst sixteenth-century Spanish officials and Church thinkers regarding how to treat indigenous peoples in the Americas. Some (for example, Sepulveda) assumed that Indians were incapable of rational thought, and hence incapable of being converted to Christianity, and were therefore fit for slavery, in accordance with Aristotle's theory of natural slavery. Others (for example, Las Casas) believed that Indians were rational, and therefore would freely convert to Christianity given the opportunity, so that forced conversion was unnecessary and unjustified, although using force to enable missionaries to freely travel and preach was justified. For a good overview of these debates see *The Spanish Struggle for Justice in the Conquest of America* (Hanke, 1965) and *The Fall of Natural Man: The American Indian and the Origin of Comparative Ethnology* (Pagden, 1982).

But for our purposes, let us set aside the abuses, and focus instead on the official justifications for coercion, in order to see how a two-level view can edge closer to the crusading view. Consider the Spanish claim that indigenous peoples failed to respect certain universal minimal standards that should be apparent to all rational human beings. A powerful example concerns the Aztec practice of human sacrifice. Few people today are likely to criticize the Spanish conquistadores and missionaries for suppressing this practice. But the Spanish also intervened in indigenous communities that did not practice human sacrifice. To justify those interventions, the Spanish relied on a much broader list of "barbaric" practices that included idolatry, "promiscuous" sexual relations, and matrilineal kinship.

These practices shocked the conscience of the Spaniards, almost as much as human sacrifice, and hence were all labeled as practices that violate natural reason and natural law. Yet, viewed from today's perspective, this is a curious list, lumping together truly horrific practices with harmless variations in cultural mores. The Spanish appealed to the idea of universal minimal standards that are accessible to all rational human beings, but their account of these standards is strangely parochial, based on very localized sixteenth-century European norms about "proper" family relations. To put it charitably, the Spanish did not make much effort to see whether other peoples around the world shared their sense of what is "universally" abhorred. If a practice shocked their conscience, they simply assumed it would shock the conscience of all humanity, without bothering to test whether other peoples shared their reactions or reasons. Any account of universal minimum standards that is defined in this unilateral way runs the risk of becoming a coercive moral crusade.

A similar problem arises with the Spanish account of the conditions of dialogue and debate about religion. The Spanish justified the colonization of indigenous lands on the grounds that this was needed to permit Catholic missionaries to peacefully evangelize. The freedom to engage in missionary work was said to be a "natural right" that could be enforced against indigenous communities that threatened to expel or kill the missionaries. Yet, at precisely the same time the Spanish were forcing indigenous peoples to allow Catholic missionaries to preach, they were restricting the religious liberties of Jews and Muslims in Spain itself, and were engaged in the ruthless suppression of Christians suspected of heresy. (This was, after all, the heyday of the Spanish Inquisition). In other words, the Spanish insisted that they had a right to freely propagate their religion to non-believers in the Americas, but no one had a reciprocal right to attempt to convert Catholics within Spain.

Viewed from today's perspective, this is a remarkably hypocritical account of the conditions under which religious beliefs should be expressed and debated. The Spanish wanted the freedom to convert others, but did not want to run the risk of losing any of their own members, and hence they put in place various measures to prevent any backsliding. They wanted dialogue, but only under "winning conditions."

This problem of what we might call "asymmetrical" accounts of the freedom to propagate one's views is not unique to sixteenth-century Spain. In most countries with a Muslim majority, for example, Muslims have historically been allowed to attempt to convert Christians and Jews, but the latter were not allowed to proselytize amongst Muslims. Muslim men could marry non-Muslim women, on the assumption that women will follow the religion of their husband, but Muslim women were not allowed to marry Christian or Jewish men, since they would then be lost to the faith. More generally, conversion to Islam was permitted, even encouraged, but apostasy from Islam was discouraged, in some cases legally prohibited, and in a few countries was (and remains) subject to the death penalty.

In both these cases, conversion to either Catholicism or Islam was seen as voluntary. In theory, no one was forced to convert. In that sense, there is a commitment to the idea that conversion should be the result of example and persuasion. Yet, for members of other religious or secular traditions, this is hardly an acceptable account of "free debate" or the "free exercise of reason." It is a biased and asymmetrical idea of freedom, in which only one side can hope to benefit. Any account of the freedom to propagate one's faith that is so one-sided runs the risk of becoming a coercive crusade.

In these (and other) ways, the two-level view endorsed by some Spanish colonial officials is difficult to distinguish from a coercive crusader mentality. Of course, we have come a long way from sixteenth-century colonization of the Americas. No one today is likely to endorse the blatantly biased and arbitrary moral reasoning of the Spanish colonizers, and the Catholic Church itself has over time become a dedicated defender of the principle of freedom of conscience as a universal human right, applicable to all religions.

Yet this case raises some important methodological challenges that remain with us. For example, how can we be sure that our own assumptions about what is "barbaric" are any less parochial than the Spanish colonizers? Consider questions of punishment. Many people in the West are appalled by the practice of spearing in some Aboriginal communities in Australia, or the cutting off of hands in Iran. Yet many people around the world would find it barbaric to lock someone up in a tiny jail cell for long periods of time. There are many things about the world that we find shocking and appalling, but which of these reactions is rooted in parochial cultural assumptions and which is rooted in universal human reasoning? How do we distinguish them?

Similarly, how can we be sure that our account of the conditions under which people should be free to propagate their faith is truly impartial? One could argue that most ethical traditions today still seek to stack the deck, demanding greater freedom to convert others while setting obstacles to the propagation of other views, often in the name of "public order," countering "blasphemy," or "national security." The United States today actively pressures countries to allow greater access to evangelical Protestant missionaries, as a condition of aid or preferential trade status, while making it more difficult for Muslim religious leaders to enter the United States. Is this a faint echo of earlier Spanish views? Many liberals would argue that they have overcome this problem, given that they defend freedom of speech for critics as well as defenders of liberalism. Yet liberals typically seek to put in place constitutional restrictions that protect liberal values from possible rejection. Liberals hope and expect that others will come to see the merits of liberalism in a free and open debate, but in the event that liberals lose some of these debates, they also want constitutional guarantees that prevent the electorate from backsliding from liberalism. Critics of liberalism have suggested that this too is a biased account of "free debate."

All of this suggests that there are many unresolved challenges facing the globalization of ethics. Living as we do in a post-colonial era, everyone today is at pains to repudiate the crusader mentality and to disavow the right to forcibly impose one's values on others. Instead, people accept the idea that the propagation of one's views should occur through voluntary conversion and free dialogue. Force should only be used to protect universally acknowledged minimum standards, defined through international negotiations and consensus reflecting the shared values of many ethical traditions. These have almost become platitudes in the contemporary literature.

This is certainly progress compared with the ethnocentric and arrogant attitude of earlier times. Yet these platitudes raise as many questions as they answer. How are these universal minimal standards set? How are the terms of debate and interaction amongst ethical traditions to be defined?

Our goal in this volume is to explore these challenges to the globalization of ethics. Our approach, which is employed in all of the volumes in the Ethikon Series in Comparative Ethics,[3] is to invite each author to address these issues from the perspective of a particular ethical tradition. Authors serve as "reporters" on the tradition, exploring its main lines of thought, while also identifying what they take to be the most promising lines of development within it.

As with all Ethikon volumes, we have brought together a mixture of religious and secular ethical traditions, chosen either for their historical significance in shaping the world's ethical perspectives (such as the major monotheistic world religions), and/or for their influential role in contemporary debates about human rights and globalization (such as international law and feminism).

---

[3] For other volumes in the series, see *The Ethics of War and Peace: Religious and Secular Perspectives* (Nardin, 1996); *International Society: Diverse Ethical Perspectives* (Mapel & Nardin, 1998); *Boundaries and Justice: Diverse Ethical Perspectives* (Miller & Hashmi, 2001); *Alternative Conceptions of Civil Society* (Chambers & Kymlicka, 2002); *Civil Society and Government* (Rosenblum & Post, 2002); *The Many and the One: Religious and Secular Perspectives on Ethical Pluralism in the Modern World* (Madsen & Strong, 2003); *States, Nations, and Boundaries: The Ethics of Making Boundaries* (Buchanan & Moore, 2003); *Ethics and Weapons of Mass Destruction: Religious and Secular Perspectives* (Hashmi & Lee, 2004).

In each case, we have asked our authors to explain how, from the perspective of the tradition they are reporting on, certain crucial questions about the globalization of ethics are addressed. These include:

1. The basis on which universal minimal standards are defined, and the legitimate scope for coercion in enforcing these universal norms. What sorts of issues should be seen as matters of universal norms, and what sorts of issues can be seen as a matter of legitimate variation? To what extent should these universal norms be made legally binding, and coercively enforceable?

2. The desirability of constructing a new and self-standing cross-cultural vocabulary or framework for debating global ethics (such as universal human rights) that is not rooted in any particular ethical tradition. How would such a new vocabulary relate to older ethical traditions? What role does each play, on what sorts of issues?

3. The appropriate ways of seeking to propagate one's moral views. Insofar as coercion is ruled out, and persuasion and example is relied on, how should dialogue amongst ethical traditions be conducted? Is it appropriate to pressure other societies to enter into the sort of debate that might lead to conversion? Is there a right to engage in proselytization even in societies that do not wish it?

Not all of these questions have the same application or relevance for all traditions. However, as the chapters show, these questions have been a source of concern, and sometimes anguish, to many of the best minds within these traditions. There is often a striking diversity of answers within each tradition, as well as across the traditions. There are also some surprising gaps and omissions. Our hope is that this volume will encourage greater reflection on these issues within these traditions, and inspire new lines of debate and exchange across them.

Structure of the Volume

As noted earlier, contemporary debates over the globalization of ethics typically involve at least two elements: (1) the attempt to construct a common self-standing international discourse, such as the discourse of universal human rights, that can be accepted by adherents of different ethical traditions, and can be used to define a set of minimal standards; and (2) the attempt to promote dialogue amongst defenders of different ethical traditions, each explaining and defending their distinctive concepts and norms, in order to identify areas of disagreement, grounds for mutual learning, and possibilities for accommodating differences. These two elements – the construction of a shared ethical discourse and the exploration of diverse ethical discourses – are closely linked. On the one hand, the new international discourse of human rights has been continually challenged to show that it is indeed acceptable to the world's diverse ethical traditions. On the other hand, as the discourse of human rights grows stronger, the world's major religious and secular traditions are increasingly challenged to show that they can accept and uphold this new global discourse.

In order to explore these complex dynamics, we begin the volume with the international law tradition and its influential attempt to build a new globalized ethical vocabulary through the language of human rights. In Chapter 2, Daniel Philpott explores the history of this tradition and the way it has attempted to build and strengthen a global consensus on certain moral values. While international law is of course a form of law, rooted in modes of legal reasoning and interpretation, Philpott emphasizes that proponents of international law have also seen it as an ethical project. It is seen as a moral achievement that more and more countries have subscribed to international law norms, covering an ever-wider range of issues. But this task of gaining global consensus is complicated by the fact that the international law tradition has its roots in particular ethical traditions, including versions of consent theory, natural law, and liberalism, that are not always universally shared. There have always been ethical traditions that disagree with some of the intellectual foundations and moral norms of international law. Using the example of freedom of religion, Philpott describes how a process of dialogue and re-interpretation has enabled some of these potential ethical disagreements to be resolved.

We then consider how a range of religious and secular ethical traditions have understood the task of developing a globalized ethics, both historically and in today's era of universal human rights. We first look at some of the major religious perspectives on these issues. In Chapter 3 on the Jewish tradition, Michael Walzer explores the basis for distinguishing the minimal Noahide laws (applicable to all) and the more ethically demanding Mosaic laws (applicable in the first instance to Jews). He then considers debates within the tradition about whether or how Jews should attempt either to (1) enforce compliance with the Noahide laws, and/or (2) actively propagate the Mosaic moral code. He distinguishes a particularistic "orthodox" strand within the tradition from a more universalistic "missionist" strand, with the latter supporting a more activist approach to promoting Jewish ethical values. While the former strand has often been stronger within Judaism – of the major world religions, Judaism has been least inclined to proselytization – the distinctive Jewish history of exile and holocaust has also provided powerful motivation to pursue global norms about rights to asylum and protection from genocide. For this and other reasons, Jews have been active participants in the international human rights movement.

In Chapter 4 on the Christian tradition, Max Stackhouse examines debates within the tradition about the implications of globalization for Christian ethics. He distinguishes a pessimistic strand, which views globalization as "another Fall" whose evils Christians must bear witness to and/or resist, from a more optimistic strand that views globalization as a form of God's "providential grace," and as an opportunity to spread distinctly Christian values across the world. According to this latter view, many aspects of globalization, from the spread of markets and technology to the diffusion of human rights, can be seen as spreading a distinctly Christian ethos and as preparing the grounds for successful Christian proselytization. On this view, globalization may appear on the surface as a matter of secular economic and political reforms, but is in fact "a new form of mission" for which Christians must be prepared and accept ethical responsibility.

Interestingly, a similar attitude towards globalization and ethics can be found within contemporary Buddhism, as discussed by Peter Nosco in Chapter 5. According to Nosco, Buddhism has proven surprisingly resilient and successful in the new global marketplace of ideas, in part because many of its core ideas reflect the defining conditions and needs of the modern era. Its emphasis on the interdependence of all creatures fits well with modern environmental sensibilities. Its emphasis on achieving mastery over one's self fits well with modern ideas of autonomy. Its emphasis on the importance of compassion, as the core of morality, fits well with modern ideas of humanitarian obligation, just as its commitment to peace fits well with modern ideas of human rights and international law. Although none of these ideas is unique to Buddhism, it articulates these ideals in a non-theistic way that fits comfortably with modern science and technology, and without requiring potential adherents to subscribe to "superstitious" beliefs about a supernatural divinity. Nosco suggests that this has enabled Buddhism to play a much larger role in shaping the terms of contemporary debates about global ethics, including debates on human rights, than one might expect.

For both Stackhouse and Nosco, therefore, globalization in general, and human rights in particular, are not only consonant with the distinctive values of the Christian and Buddhist traditions, but provide a vehicle for their further peaceful propagation. In contrast to this confident attitude, it is often said that Muslims have responded defensively to globalization and to human rights norms, and view them as a destabilizing threat to their values and ways of life. While acknowledging that some Muslims have responded this way, Muhammad Khalid Masud in Chapter 6 offers a more nuanced account of contemporary Muslim thinking on global ethics. He surveys a range of responses by Muslim organizations and intellectuals to international human rights norms, as well as Muslim critiques of other recent attempts to draft a global ethic, such as the "Declaration Towards a Global Ethic" drafted by Hans Küng and adopted by the Parliament of World Religions in 1993.[4] According to Masud, while many Muslims have objected to the way that human rights are invoked selectively and instrumentally by Western powers to advance their geopolitical interests, and while many Muslims have also expressed concern about the secularist presuppositions of human rights discourse, there is widespread support

---

[4] See Appendix D.

amongst Muslims for the general idea of a global ethic, and for many of the substantive values enshrined in current human rights norms. He distinguishes three strands within contemporary Muslim thinking – "neo-conservative," "Islamic modernist," and "progressive" – and argues that they differ not only on substantive issues (for example, gender equality or punishment), but also on methodology (for example, the relationship between reason and revelation), with implications for their attitude towards emerging international human rights norms.

In Chapter 7, Richard Madsen examines the Confucian tradition. As Madsen notes, there are no authoritative spokespersons or organizations for disseminating Confucianism, and no state defines itself as Confucian. But Confucianism exercises a pervasive if implicit influence on many thinkers and rulers in East Asia, and can be seen as shaping a distinctive approach to the issue of global ethics. Its distinctiveness lies not such much in its substantive moral values – Madsen suggests that Confucians can accept all of the basic values of dignity and freedom underlying contemporary human rights documents – but rather in its ideas about how to promote these values. In particular, the Confucian tradition has emphasized the cultivation of personal virtue rather than the application of impersonal law, and the pursuit of harmony through rituals of proper relationships rather than the assertion of individualized "rights" enforced through adversarial procedures. It has also emphasized the importance of moral elites and of state-guided moral efforts. These views are obviously at odds not only with the practices of Western societies, but also with the current structure of international law, which is legalistic and "rights-based." While adherents of these Confucian views typically view them as of universal validity, and as superior to the atomized and individualistic practices of Western liberal societies, they also recognize that there is little likelihood of pushing either the West or the international community in a more Confucian direction. Rather than seeking to push global ethics in a more Confucian direction, therefore, they have instead sought greater latitude to adopt their own more virtue-based and ritual-based procedures for pursuing universal values of freedom and dignity. Madsen suggests that an echo of this Confucian view can be found in the 1993 "Bangkok Declaration on Human Rights," which affirms the universality of human rights, but pleads for greater context-sensitivity in their promotion.

In Chapter 8, Mark C. Murphy examines the natural law tradition, as exemplified by the work of Thomas Aquinas. As we noted earlier, natural law is one of the intellectual antecedents of contemporary human rights discourse, and the proponents of natural law have always presented it as a universal ethic, accessible to all rational human beings. It is often assumed, therefore, that the natural law tradition is inhospitable to diversity in ethical norms and practices, and committed to encouraging (or compelling) all societies and cultures to engage in identical patterns of moral life. As Murphy shows, however, this is not true. There are many reasons, within the natural law tradition, why one would expect and tolerate diversity in what he calls the "de facto moral systems" found in societies around the world. While natural law identifies certain universal goods (and universal bads), societies will always face choices about how to set priorities for these goods. These choices will legitimately vary from society to society (and from time to time), both because these goods are of incommensurable value (and hence cannot be given a determinate ranking) and because the relative difficulty of achieving different goods will vary from one context to another. Even when societies are acting in ways that clearly violate natural law, and hence have "defective" moral systems, there are often good reasons, within the tradition, for avoiding the use of coercion to enforce conformity to natural law. These include norms of subsidiarity, reciprocity, and a commitment to the ideal of rational interaction. Hence, in the natural law tradition, as in the other traditions discussed in this volume, the pursuit of a common global ethic operates alongside the toleration and accommodation of ethical diversity.

Amongst modern secular ideologies, the liberal tradition is often seen as most closely aligned with contemporary human rights norms. Indeed, as we noted earlier, some critics have suggested that the modern ideology of universal human rights is a thinly veiled form of Western liberalism. In Chapter 9, Chris Brown explores the way the liberal tradition has understood the universality of its values, and the scope for legitimate ethical diversity. He distinguishes two strands of liberal thought – a "cosmopolitan" strand and a "communitarian" strand. Both adopt a universal conception of human nature, which attributes certain basic core interests and capacities to all human beings and which invokes these common human attributes to support the idea of universal human rights. However, they differ on the extent to which human freedom and well-being is seen as tied up with membership in particular communities and cultures, and hence on the value that should be ascribed to the political autonomy of such communities. For the more "communitarian" liberals, in order to respect the communal dimensions of a free society, external coercion should only be used to protect a modest set of human rights, leaving communities free to decide amongst themselves how and when to pursue a more robust set of human rights. The "cosmopolitans," by contrast, support a much stronger list of universal human rights, and are sceptical of appeals to the ideals of community and culture as a justification for not upholding such rights.

In Chapter 10, Kimberly Hutchings examines the feminist tradition, which emerged out of the liberal tradition. Hutchings distinguishes three strands of contemporary feminist ethics, which she calls "enlightenment feminism," "care feminism," and "post-colonial feminism." The first is most clearly aligned with the liberal tradition, and shares its commitments to the ideals of universal human rights and democracy. The second and third, however, have a more critical stance on some aspects of the current discourse of global ethics.

Proponents of care feminism typically view their approach as of universal relevance, but feel that the ethics of care cannot be formalized in a list of universal rights, and instead requires strengthening our sense of responsibility to promote peace, the environment and human well-being. (In this respect, it shares some characteristics with Confucianism, with its commitment to pursuing universal values through a more contextual virtue-based and responsibility-based approach). Post-colonial feminism is perhaps even more sceptical of the idea of a global ethics, which it views as inevitably contaminated by power inequalities between North and South and between men and women. On this view, a truly global ethics could only emerge through a much more inclusive dialogue than currently exists (or indeed than may currently be possible).

Finally, in Chapter 11, William Sullivan provides a concluding overview that summarizes some of the key themes that emerge in the chapters, and draws out some important lessons from this exercise in comparative ethics. In particular, he argues that the various chapters reveal, in their own way, the extent to which all moral thinking is deeply embedded in particular contexts and traditions, even when it appears on the surface to be using or constructing a common global ethical discourse. Failing to attend to the way that ethical thinking is embedded in traditions, he suggests, can lead to serious misinterpretations and to exaggerated hopes for the possibility of "constructivism" in global ethics. In his view, given the diversity of ethical views within and across the different traditions surveyed in this volume, the best hope for developing a viable form of global ethics is through the exercise of "practical rationality," focused on specific issues in particular contexts, rather than the exercise of theoretical rationality in constructing a new abstract theory of the foundations and principles of global ethics.

Finally, we have included in the appendix some of the key documents that are referred to by the authors and which exemplify some of the most important contemporary efforts to address the challenge of the globalization of ethics. The main document, of course, is the UN's 1948 "Universal Declaration of Human Rights," which is the foundational text for the contemporary discourse of universal human rights. But this document, by itself, may give a misleading impression of the nature of that global discourse. The international human rights framework has developed in the half-century since the UDHR was adopted, and many of these developments have been driven by the concerns of non-Western societies. When the 1948 Universal Declaration was adopted, much of the world was still under colonial rule, and so did not have a full voice in its formulation or adoption. But subsequent human rights declarations, adopted after the era of decolonization, have been the result of a more truly global process of negotiation and dialogue.

To give a sense of the way that these subsequent developments have broadened the scope of the international human rights discourse, we have included the International Covenant on Civil and Political Rights and the International

Covenant on Economic, Social and Cultural Rights. These two Covenants, adopted in 1966, have dramatically expanded the range of issues and norms that are considered part of the global human rights framework.

For many defenders of human rights, the development of this expanded framework through a more inclusive process of global dialogue shows that the discourse of international human rights can serve as the basis for a truly universal ethic, accessible to members of different cultures, religions, and ethical traditions. Critics argue, however, that the international human rights framework, even in its expanded form, still reflects a distinctively Western conception of ethics, rooted either in liberalism and/or Christianity and/or secularism. And so various attempts have been made to formulate charters of human rights that are more sensitive to the diversity of the world's traditions.

We have included five of the most important such attempts: "The Universal Islamic Declaration of Human Rights" (1981), "The Cairo Declaration of Human Rights in Islam" (1990), "The Bangkok Declaration on Human Rights" (1993), "The Asian Human Rights Charter: A People's Charter" (1998), and the "Declaration of a Global Ethics" adopted by the Parliament of World Religions (1993).

We hope that the inclusion of these documents will help readers understand and assess the issues and arguments raised by the authors, as well as serving as a resource for persons interested in the issue.

2

Global Ethics and the International Law Tradition

Daniel Philpott

Is a universal ethic, one extending to all corners of the planet, a worthy aspiration? The international law tradition responds summarily: A planetary ethic is the very point of the tradition. That is, the international law tradition is dedicated to extending to the entire globe a set of commitments to which states give their active assent – through covenants, charters, conventions, declarations, treaties, and even customary law governing war, commerce, human rights, refugees, the environment, the making of treaties, membership in international organizations, and many other affairs. The tradition is dedicated to widening this ethic so that more and more states make such commitments. It is dedicated to deepening this ethic so that among the states that have signed on, an ever-increasing proportion of their leaders and citizens come to accept international law as legitimate, not simply as a set of norms to be endorsed for instrumental purposes. And the tradition is committed to broadening this ethic, so that more numerous categories of people and attributes come under the law's protection.

Although many of the traditions in this volume also propound a universal ethic – and some more than others – these others focus far more on justifications for claims about truth, goodness, justice, and the general character of law and institutions, and relatively less on creating, spreading, and defining the practice of legal norms. To be sure, proponents of the international law tradition regard their commitments to global legal norms as ethical ones, and may well seek to justify them according to philosophical and religious frameworks. But no legal norm – no treaty, no law, no covenant – explicitly requires such grounding. The tradition concentrates rather on developing the internal standards and precedents that govern how laws are to be applied, practiced, prioritized, adjudicated, and enforced, and it relies upon a community of judges, lawyers, scholars, and officials to perform this work. It is indeed these norms, these standards, and this community that merits the label of tradition for international law. It is a tradition in the sense that Alasdair MacIntyre famously defined the concept: "an historically extended, socially embodied argument, and an argument precisely in part about the goods that constitute that tradition" (1981, p. 222).

Virtually all members of this tradition desire to see its norms universalized in this way – that is, in the consensus and practice of states. Some will be explicitly written, some recognized as customary law, and some as *jus cogens*, or broadly accepted norms. Of course, they will debate the extent and manner of this universalization: Should there be an International Criminal Court? Does the doctrine of universal jurisdiction have merit? Should the law be expanded into new areas, say more robust conceptions of women's rights or stronger international environmental agreements? Some will favor a rapid advance in international law to cover new areas, thus broadening it. Others will favor a more conservative course: Better to have a "thinner" but stronger consensus that is broader and wider agreement on fewer norms than to risk eroding this consensus through too rapid an attempt to deepen it. But whatever their views on the speed of change, members of the tradition will commonly aspire to a planetary ethic that states agree to and uphold. It is an ethic that accrues strength to the degree that it elicits compliance, gains the assent of more and more states, and wins wider and wider adherence among these states' populations. It is one that is enfeebled when states violate it or when they contest its legitimacy.

It is this sort of globalization of this sort of ethic that frames the central dilemma of the globalization of ethics for the international law tradition. This dilemma comes in two versions. The first embodies the conflict between the expansion of international legal norms and states that demur from these norms because of their dissenting cultural and religious commitments. They may be Islamic states where *Shari'a* forbids religious freedom as it is spelled out by international covenants, where punishment by amputation persists, contrary to international human rights agreements, or states whose cultural traditions demand the permissibility of female genital mutilation.

The second version of the dilemma arises from states that have already signed on to international covenants but then come to dissent from them, also for religious and cultural reasons. In August 1990, the Organization of the Islamic Conference, meeting in Cairo, promulgated a document, "Human Rights in Islam," asserting that human rights could only be endorsed in concurrence with and interpreted according to Islamic law. Where human rights law and Islamic law conflict, it maintained, Islamic law must be held superior. Prior to the United Nations Conference on Human Rights in Vienna in June 1993, a large coalition of Asian, African, and Muslim states signed the Bangkok Declaration, in which they criticized Western states for imposing their values on the rest of the world. In states whose cultures are comparatively communal and where the imperative of economic development is relatively stronger, the argument ran, Western civil and political rights are less meaningful and important.

Expressed in both of these ways, the common dilemma is this: How to reconcile the universalizing aspirations of the international law tradition with cultures and religions that dissent from it, or at least from certain parts of it? Can an accommodation be reached that will allow legal norms to broaden and deepen? Or must the tradition settle for a "thinner" consensus in which a more minimal set of standards will unite the world's states? The dilemma has grown in recent years.

As they are described here, this dilemma and this definition of international law rest upon certain assumptions about what law is. These assumptions are contested, of course, and evoke ongoing philosophical and jurisprudential arguments about the nature of law. Command theory positivists, who believe that authentic law must have behind it the force of coercive sanctions, for instance, dispute that international law is law at all.[1] Others will deny such a requirement and stress consent, international judicial determinations, natural reason, or some combination of these as the proper criteria of law. Such controversies are not pursued here. The analysis, rather, rests on a concept of international law that corresponds broadly to how the people who make up the tradition view it. It is broadly the set of treaties, covenants, charters, customary laws, and *jus cogens* norms to which states have committed themselves, and which they in fact regard as law. They call each other to account for living up to these commitments with the understanding that they are binding. Even more so, it is a set of commitments that enjoy the support of the communities of people who interpret, adjudicate, apply, and call for the enforcement of these commitments. It is this conception of law whose universalization is most debated by states and citizens.[2]

The dilemmas attending pluralism and the globalization of ethics are not, of course, the only dilemmas that international law faces. Equally difficult, both today and historically, is the problem of how law is to be robustly practiced in an anarchic world of sovereign states, one where violators often go unpunished, where states regularly interpret law according to their interests in power and wealth, and where international relations scholars routinely ask whether law is a mere epiphenomenon of power. But the present collection of essays is about the globalization of ethics. In this realm, it is the conflict between universalism and pluralism that poses the most difficult dilemma.

The Growth of a Uniform Global Ethic of International Law

Again, the international law tradition makes the development of a uniform global code its quintessential goal. It seeks the broadening of legal norms to include more subject matters and jurisdictions, the deepening of such norms in the hearts and minds of populations, and the widening of these norms to more

---

[1] See *Leviathan* (Hobbes, 1968); and *The Province of Jurisprudence Determined and the Uses of the Study of Jurisprudence* (Austin, 1965).
[2] It is a conception that corresponds closely to what Terry Nardin calls "rule of law positivism." See Terry Nardin (1998), "Legal Positivism As a Theory of International Society."

and more states. The tradition's proponents hope that states that dissent from these norms will eventually be brought into the fold. What inspires this hope and confidence in the expansion of international law is, to a significant degree, its own historical development. Over the past three and a half centuries, this development has followed a path similar to that by which political philosopher John Rawls has described the growth of modern liberalism – namely, one from a *modus vivendi*, an agreement based on a temporary balance of forces, to a deep consensus on constitutional principles (Rawls, 1993). For international law, this consensus has grown dramatically especially during the twentieth century, reflected in the proliferation of international legal instruments and their spread to a great number of states all across the globe.

The international system began very much as a *modus vivendi*, through a peace settlement that brought to a close the most cataclysmic struggle in Europe prior to the twentieth century, one that historians estimate killed from one-quarter to one-third of the population of Germany (Philpott, 2001, p. 96). At the Peace of Westphalia of 1648, virtually all of Europe was for the first time organized according to the principle of sovereignty, by which a single holder of authority enjoys supremacy within a bounded territory. A continent full of polities of this sort, juxtaposed astride one another, fighting, allying, trading, and making peace in the absence of a superior authority, constitutes a system of sovereign states.[3]

Westphalia consummated the centuries-long fracture of medieval Christendom, a society in which European Christians shared a rich set of laws and morals, anchored in the Catholic Church. Though Europe-wide norms coexisted with local customs and feudal law, they nevertheless elicited a level of uniformity that Europe would not begin to recover until after World War II. The *Respublica Christiana* reached its apex in the High Middle Ages, roughly between 1100 and 1300 AD. After 1300, fragmentation began to set in as England, France, and not long thereafter, Sweden evolved into polities much like sovereign states, independent of outside claims on their authority. Westphalia was hardly history's inevitable destination. Europe seemed to be amalgamating anew as late as 1519, when Charles V was crowned Holy Roman Emperor only two years after he had become King of Spain, these developments placing him in control of most of modern Spain and the Netherlands, tying him closely to the possessions of the Habsburg family, including Austria and parts of Burgundy and Italy, and rendering him the enforcer of Catholic orthodoxy throughout central Europe.

---

[3] Westphalia's status as the origin of the modern international system is controversial among historians and political scientists. For skepticism toward the claim, see Stephen D. Krasner (1993, 1996), *Westphalia and All That,* and *Compromising Westphalia.* My own defense of this status appears in *Revolutions in Sovereignty: How Ideas Shaped Modern International Relations* (2001). For further discussion, see also Andreas Osiander (1994), *The States System of Europe, 1640–1990.*

What sundered Europe devastatingly and enduringly was the onset of widespread ethical pluralism over one of the deepest questions of political authority – the role of the state in promoting religious faith. Behind this thoroughgoing fracture was the Protestant Reformation, which began in 1517, just as Charles V was consolidating his powers. Virtually all Protestants, whether they were of the "magisterial Reformation" of Martin Luther, John Calvin, John Knox, or Anglicanism, or one of the many other sects – Mennonites, Puritans, and the like – opposed on deep theological grounds not only the ecclesiastical powers of Popes and Catholic bishops, but also the Church's temporal powers, its vast holdings of land and wealth, the prerogatives of its bishops, who often held political office, and, most of all, the Church's powers to enforce Catholic orthodoxy by the sword.

In response to Martin Luther's protests of 1517 and to all of the Protestants who followed him in breaking away from the Catholic Church's authority, Charles V sent his quelling armies. Over the next 130 years, Europeans who held exclusive and uncompromising notions of authority – Catholics who would brook no less than a restored Christendom, Protestants who were willing to fight to the death to resist it – fought ferocious war on a continental scale. A temporary truce was reached in 1555 with the Treaty of Augsburg, which established in the Holy Roman Empire the principle *cuius regio, eius religio* ("whose the region, his the religion"), allowing every prince to determine the religious makeup of his own territory. But Augsburg did not last. Throughout the Empire, disputes about this or that provision of the treaty erupted into skirmishes, then war, expanding finally into the continental Thirty Years War, which ended finally at the Peace of Westphalia.

Sovereignty was the set of terms on which Westphalia settled the wars of religion. This was not explicitly the case, for sovereignty appears nowhere in the text of the two treaties that comprise the settlement. Westphalia was not even an explicit victory for *cuius region, eius religio,* for the treaties required princes and nobles within the Holy Roman Empire to permit certain proportions of religions to live and worship within specified territories. But in practice, princes were sovereign. One analysts of the settlement discovered the principles of equality and autonomy running as leitmotifs through the treaties.[4] The practice of intervening in other princes' territories in order to alter the religious makeup of their realm all but ceased. Though the Holy Roman Empire continued to exist until 1806, it did little to compromise the authority that holders of sovereignty exercised within their own territories.

A system of sovereign states in which each state generally respects the autonomy of other states to govern their inhabitants as they see fit and to abide by a code of conduct that comprises minimal general obligations, exceeded only by the pacts that states make with each other – this is a uniform set of norms, but a very thin one. At the time of Westphalia, even this concept of a system of

---

[4] Krasner (op. cit.).

sovereign states was deeply controversial. Protestants, of course, were happy that they could finally practice their faith, at least in certain regions, without having to fight to the death for it. Pope Innocent X, though, did not accept the sovereign states system as legitimate, calling the Westphalia settlement, "null, void, invalid, iniquitous, unjust, damnable, reprobate, inane, empty of meaning and effect for all time" (Maland, 1966, p. 16). The Catholic Church indeed persisted in its skepticism of the sovereign states system well into the nineteenth century, when it banned the writings of Hugo Grotius, often considered the father of international law, and condemned international law as a Protestant science. The source of this skepticism was the Church's allegiance to the unity of medieval Christendom. During early modern Europe, certain philosophers, Catholic and Protestant alike – Francisco Suarez, Franciscus de Victoria, Alberico Gentili, Hubert Languet, and Hugo Grotius – had hoped that even as states were gaining prominence, echoes of Christendom would persist, that sovereign rulers would acknowledge and practice a robust set of universal obligations to the common good. They advocated, for instance, a practice similar to contemporary humanitarian intervention. But no such norms developed. Instead, the state emerged as a carapace under which rulers could govern as they pleased, as long as they respected other states' rights to do the same. This was the concept that emerged as the standard practice of states in the eighteenth and nineteenth centuries. In the eighteenth century, when Emmerich de Vattel outlined a law of nations, the equality and autonomy of states and non-intervention were central norms. International law amounted to a positivist conception in which states were obligated by little but the terms they agreed to with one another.

After two and a half centuries of stagnation, a renaissance of international law and norms reversed the international system's historical momentum in the twentieth century. It occurred despite, but also because of, some of the most egregious departures from standards of civilization since Westphalia – the two world wars and genocides in Cambodia, Bangladesh, Rwanda, and elsewhere.

This renaissance occurred through several episodes and trends.[5] Even prior to World War I, several inter-American conferences and two international conferences for peace in the Hague in 1899 and 1907 began to develop standards for the arbitration of disputes. But it was after the war, through the Covenant of the League of Nations, that legal innovations proliferated and states came to adopt common standards for conflict resolution, the conduct of war, labor conditions, minority rights, and self-determination. During the interwar period, certain habits and machinery for consultation and dispute resolution emerged through the League system, particularly in the areas of minority rights and self-determination. Meanwhile, in Latin America, a strong set of norms was developing, too.

---

[5] An excellent account of this development, on which I rely here, is Dorothy V. Jones (1989), *Code of Peace: Ethics and Security in the World of Warlord States.*

Following the notorious failures of the League to stop aggression in the 1930s, international law again began to expand as World War II came to a close. Most famously, the United Nations Charter put forth collective security mechanisms that were meant to give great powers more authority to respond to aggression. Human rights norms also flowered after World War II, particularly in response to the Holocaust. In the Universal Declaration of Human Rights of 1948, most of the world's existing states declared their principled agreement to over thirty categories of rights. As an episode in the strengthening of the international law tradition in the face of global pluralism, the Universal Declaration stands as a landmark achievement. One of the central breakthroughs in its negotiation was the securing of agreement between representatives of a wide variety of religious and cultural traditions.[6] Later, in the 1960s, two United Nations Covenants – one on Civil and Political Rights, one on Economic, Social, and Cultural rights – gave human rights a legal status. Other international legal instruments expanded rights to new categories of people and classes of attributes, including religious freedom, women, new areas of labor, and refugees. War conventions expanded, too, to cover genocide and crimes against humanity.

Dorothy Jones, in her impressive study of the development of an international "code of peace" over the course of the twentieth century, estimated that by 1989, states had created over seventy-nine major legal instruments though which they committed themselves to common principles of international conduct. Nine major principles are included therein: (1) the sovereign equality of states; (2) territorial integrity and political independence; (3) equal rights and self-determination of peoples; (4) non-intervention in the internal affairs of states; (5) peaceful settlement of disputes between states; (6) abstention from the threat or use of force; (7) fulfillment in good faith of international obligations; (8) cooperation with other states; and (9) respect for human rights and fundamental freedoms. Jones also proposes two principles that have arisen in international instruments since World War II, but have not gained as much consensus as the other nine: (1) creation of an equitable international economic order, and (2) protection of the environment.[7]

Since the end of the Cold War, some of the most significant developments in international law and norms have involved the consensual circumscription of sovereignty – historically, a poignant set of developments, given the hardening of state sovereignty that occurred when the international system was consolidating at the time of Westphalia. In the emergence of internationally sanctioned intervention, the early modern philosophers's dream of a set of norms that would permit states to intervene in other states' affairs in cases of massive humanitarian suffering is now being realized. It is through precedent

---

[6] See Mary Ann Glendon (2001), *A World Made New: Eleanor Roosevelt and the Universal Declaration of Human Rights*.

[7] Ibid. (p. xii).

and consensual practice – arguably, a case of emerging customary law – that intervention is gaining legitimacy, at least under certain circumstances. In several locales – Iraq (until 1998), Somalia, Bosnia, Kosovo, Rwanda, Haiti, and elsewhere – international bodies such as the UN, the European Union, NATO, and the Organization of American States have approved of the use of military force that would have failed to gain approval in the same bodies during the Cold War and earlier. Unlike United Nations peacekeeping operations during the Cold War, intervening parties here acted without the consent of their target state's government or of the parties to a conflict, thus violating this state's sovereignty. The interventions have involved several ends, including the delivery of vital supplies in times of war and famine, the ending of active shooting, the enforcement of peace, the rebuilding of state institutions, the overthrow of governments that thwart human rights and democracy, the furtherance of democratic elections, and the arrest and trial of war criminals.[8]

The power of the trend should not be overstated. That an intervention takes place does not mean that it is successful; many of the cases just mentioned were mixed successes at best. Even if internationally sanctioned, many of the interventions have been unilaterally carried out. Many of them have been the subject of important disputes among great powers. The 1999 intervention in Kosovo failed to win the approval of the UN Security Council, though it was approved by NATO. The 2003 war against Iraq led by the United States also failed to win the approval of the Security Council. Yet, the cooperation of the Security Council in most of the post-Cold War interventions, along with its approval of other sorts of unprecedented curtailments of sovereignty that did not strictly involve intervention in locales such as Cambodia and Namibia, is nonetheless historically remarkable. Even China, whose protests of others' infringement upon its sovereignty are a regular feature of its message to the world, overtly opposed intervention only in the cases of Kosovo and the Iraq war of 2003. In other cases, it abstained from Security Council votes at worst. Islamic states often strongly supported intervention as well. Indeed, Pakistan and Bangladesh have ranked among the leading contributors of troops to UN peacekeeping and observer missions. The development of a norm of intervention, though far from spotless, is still quite significant.

Through other developments, too, international laws and norms have delimited sovereignty since the end of the Cold War. The creation of an International Criminal Court by the Treaty of Rome in 1998 enables the prosecution of individuals who commit war crimes, sometimes in opposition to the legal

---

[8] For the legal precedents of humanitarian intervention, particularly with regard to sovereignty, see Jarat Chopra and Thomas G. Weiss (1992), "Sovereignty Is No Longer Sacrosanct: Codifying Humanitarian Intervention"; David Scheffer (1992), "Toward a Modern Doctrine of Humanitarian Intervention"; Lori Fisler Damrosch (1993), *Enforcing Restraint: Collective Intervention in Internal Conflicts*; Anthony Clark Arend and Robert J. Beck (1993), *International Law and the Use of Force: Beyond the UN Charter*.

procedures of the states in which they are citizens. Though the opposition of the United States strongly detracts from its efficacy, this court nevertheless enjoys the support of well over sixty states. The expansion of European integration continues what is perhaps the most dramatic compromise of norms of sovereignty since World War II. Here, states have "pooled" some of their sovereign powers into a supranational organization for the first time since the creation of the Holy Roman Empire. Since the end of the Cold War, integration has continued through the 1991 Maastricht Treaty, which created the European Union, through the more recent creation of a constitution for the Union, through the expansion of its foreign policy and defense prerogatives, and through the accession of Scandinavian and Central, Eastern, and Southeastern European states.

The past century, then, has been one of growth towards a unified global code of law and ethics, despite the huge obstacles and enormous violations of this code that have taken place. The consensus around the code dramatically expanded through the "revolution of colonial independence" of 1945 to 1970, when over seventy colonies gained their independence and subsequently signed on to most of the various international legal instruments. The growth of international law, then, has involved a widening, a deepening, and a broadening of norms. As international law now extends to states of diverse cultures, sizes, and economic circumstances, this growth is impressive.

Challenges to the Achievement of Uniformity

The rise and fall of uniformity and diversity in ethical systems is in part the story of historical tides, sometimes swelling, sometimes receding, sometimes running in opposite directions. Just as Charles V was seeking to tie the ligaments of European unity, the Protestant Reformation was generating its fissiparous momentum. So, too, at the end of a century when international law has expanded dramatically, new forms of deep pluralism have arisen to challenge the universality of its norms. This challenge has manifested itself in the Bangkok Declaration of 1993, in the 1990 Cairo document of the Organization of the Islamic Conference, at the Beijing Conference on Women's Rights in 1995, and in many other forums.

The challenge posed for the international law tradition is not that of states that simply violate international law, but of states whose deep culture and values give rise to dissent from important norms found in the international legal documents. Proponents of the tradition are pressed to answer: How to preserve and continue the project of broadening, widening, and deepening in the face of these challenges? Should the tradition insist that where there are conflicts, dissenting states be encouraged, if not pressured, to conform to the claims embedded in the legal instruments? Should only those states that have actually signed the instruments be encouraged to conform? Or should non-signatory states also be encouraged or pressured? Or should the tradition favor a more accommodationist approach? If so, what is the minimal core that should be maintained without compromise? What rights and obligations are truly universal? What practices can never be tolerated? These questions may be summarized as the dilemmas of pluralism.

The sharpest dissent from the international law tradition arises from groups whose religious commitments lead them to reject thoroughly the basic tenets of the Westphalian sovereign states system. A strand of Islam, aptly termed "Radical Islamic Revivalism," embodies this thinking best. Al Qaeda is its best-known representative. Convinced that Islam has fallen into a state of *jahilliya*, or pre-Mohammedan barbarism, over preceding centuries, Radical Islamic Revivalism envisions the recovery of a social order in which the entire body of Muslims, the *umma*, is governed by Muslim law, or *Shari'a*, under a common head. Radical Islamic Revivalism challenges the Westphalian order in fundamental ways. It disputes the notion that the sovereign state is the legitimate form of polity. Revivalist organizations are not themselves states, but rather a religiously constituted actor that claims to exercise authority in the name of a group that extends far wider than any state – namely, the *umma*, in whatever state its members may reside. Contrary to the Westphalian norm of non-intervention, particularly with respect to matters of religion, Radical Islamic Revivalists make it their central aim to cross borders in order to alter the way in which other states treat religion, particularly when they defile Islam. Revivalists also dissent from another of modernity's signatures, one advanced at Westphalia – the differentiation of religious and temporal authority. They envision religious authorities exercising far more influence on temporal authorities, and state officials promoting *Shari'a* far more assiduously, than is the case in modern secular states. They make scant provision for the freedom of non-Muslims.

Al Qaeda and other revivalists pose the sharpest religiously based challenge to the terms of the international legal order. Yet they remain a tiny portion of Islam and find little sympathy with the vast majority of Muslim clerics and scholars. Al Qaeda is particularly regarded as an outlaw organization, its attack on the World Trade Center of September 11, 2001, condemned unanimously by the Organization of the Islamic Conference. What is far more widespread in Islam is a notion of politics that accepts the basic terms of the Westphalian order, that admits in principle almost every one of the consensual norms of international conduct summarized by Dorothy Jones, yet dissents sharply from specific planks in the international legal instruments, particularly certain human rights. This dissent has emanated from a global "Islamic Resurgence" over the past three or four decades through which most of the world's majority Islamic states have become more strongly and traditionally Muslim in their orientation. There are many reasons for this – a commitment to the revival of Islam, a more moderate commitment than that of radical revivalism, to be sure, but strong nevertheless; the perception of being threatened by the relentless spread of Western civilization; maltreatment by populations in which

Muslims are minorities or immigrants, as in Western European states; and economic and demographic factors such as rapid population growth, unemployment, and social dislocation. The agonistic results have included tensions over weapons proliferation, Islamic migration into Western societies, the control of oil, the role of the West in conflicts involving Muslims such as Bosnia, and, most importantly for the international legal tradition, the universality of certain human rights.

In scrutinizing any plank in the international legal order, including human rights, orthodox Muslims draw upon their distinctive sources of moral guidance. When they accept the state as a legitimate form of polity, or certain norms of international conduct as legitimate principles, they do so because they judge them compatible with *Shari'a*. Abdullah An-Na'im writes that "it would be heretical for a Muslim who believes that *Shariah* is the final and ultimate formulation of the law of God to maintain that any aspect of that law is open to revision and reformulation by mere mortal and fallible human beings."[9] So, as Ann Elizabeth Mayer concludes, "whenever there is conflict between Islamic and international law [of human rights], Muslims are bound to follow their religious law."[10] Resulting from these obligations are Islamic legal documents with titles that may at first seem self-contradictory, such as the 1981 Universal Islamic Declaration of Human Rights. For Muslims, of course, Islam is universal, as are notions of human rights that emanate from Islam. The Declaration's Preamble, then, proclaims that "Islam gave to mankind an ideal code of human rights fourteen centuries ago." A Pakistani politician interprets these words: "When Muslims speak about human rights in Islam, they mean rights bestowed by Allah the exalted in the Holy Koran; rights that are divine, eternal, universal, and absolute; rights that are guaranteed and protected through the Shariah."[11]

Viewing human rights from the standpoint of their grounding in *Shari'a* law, Muslim authorities arrive at a different understanding of particular human rights from what is expressed in the international legal tradition. Differences will show up in highly publicized forums such as the 1994 United Nations International Conference on Population and Development in Cairo, where Muslim states allied with the Catholic Church in clashing with international human rights activists over abortion and artificial contraception as methods

---

9 Abdullahi A. An-Na'im, "Religious Minorities Under Islamic Law and the Limits of Cultural Relativism," *Human Rights Quarterly* 9 (1987): 10, quoted in Johan D. van der Vyver, "Introduction," in *Religious Human Rights in Global Perspective*, eds. Johan D. van der Vyver and John Witte, Jr. (The Hague: Martinus Nijhoff Publishers, 1996), xxx.

10 Ann Elizabeth Mayer, "Current Muslim Thinking on Human Rights," in *Human Rights in Africa*, eds. Abdullahi Ahmed An-Na'im and Francis M. Deng (Washington, D.C.: The Brookings Institution, 1990), 133, 136, quoted in ibid., xxxi.

11 Khan Bahadur Khan, "The World of Islam," in *Proceedings of the Third World Congress on Religious Liberty* (International Religions Liberty Association Press, 1989), 33, quoted in ibid., xxx.

of family planning and population control. They show up, too, in declarations such as "Human Rights in Islam," mentioned earlier, emanating from the 1990 Cairo meeting of the Organization of the Islamic Conference. Asserting the superiority of *Shari'a* to international human rights law, the declaration maintains that fulfillment of *Shari'a* requires restrictions on speech and the emancipation of women.

The differences also show up in divergent interpretations of specific human rights. Two areas of human rights law evince, but do not exhaust, the claim: women and religious freedom. Contrary to the spirit and letter of the Convention on the Elimination of All Forms of Discrimination Against Women (1979) are several provisions of traditional *Shari'a* that govern marriage and property law. For instance, a Muslim man is permitted to marry a Christian or Jewish woman, but a Muslim woman is not permitted to marry a man of another faith. A Muslim man may be married to up to four wives at once, whereas a Muslim woman may only be married to one man at a time. In divorce law, a Muslim man may divorce his wife (or wives) through *talaq*, or a unilateral release, whereas a Muslim woman may be granted a divorce only with the permission of her husband or by a judicial decree that is granted only for prescribed reasons such as the inability or unwillingness of a husband to provide for his wife.[12] Whether it is true, as some Muslim scholars claim, that such inequalities are not intrinsic to Islam and not grounded in the Qur'an, and that Islam in fact makes women equal to men, the current status of women in many Islamic countries does not match the standards posed by international human rights conventions.

A broad consensus of interpreters of *Shari'a* also holds that full religious freedom, as spelled out in the United Nations Declaration on the Elimination of All Forms of Intolerance and of Discrimination Based on Religion or Belief, is contrary to divine law. The most extreme form of denial occurs in Saudi Arabia, Yemen, Sudan, Indonesia, Pakistan, Iran, Iraq, Egypt, and Oman, where governments restrict and often persecute dissidents, converts away from Islam, and religious minorities. Even those Muslim scholars and religious officials who are broadly sympathetic to a wide set of universal human rights will object to the right to exercise certain forms of religious liberty, especially to a Muslim's conversion to another religion and a non-Muslim's practice of his faith in all of its fullness. Admittedly, a long Islamic tradition of respect for the religious practice of "people of the book" – Christians and Jews – attests to a history of tolerance, but in practice, this tolerance has often been shaky, and certainly does not amount to a right to full religious freedom for individuals. Again, what *Shari'a* requires and what international legal covenants demand are far from consonant.[13]

---

[12] See Abdullahi Ahmed An-Na'im (1990), *Toward an Islamic Reformation: Civil Liberties, Human Rights, and International Law* (p. 176).

[13] For an expert treatment of Islamic law and religious freedom, see Donna E. Arzt (1996) "The Treatment of Religious Dissidents Under Classical and Contemporary Islamic Law."

Several Asian states, acting in the name of an "Asian Way," also dissent openly from the international legal tradition. During the 1990s, this dissent turned into open disputes with the West, especially the United States. In response to American criticism of Asian compromises of civil and political rights, sometimes accompanied by threats of economic sanctions, Asian intellectuals and politicians such as former Singapore President Lee Kuan Yew argue that such rights must be curtailed in order to achieve other values – namely, cultural solidarity, the strength of the family, and economic development. It was Asian states, acting in alliance with Islamic states, that led the coalition that blocked a strong declaration of universal human rights at the 1993 United Nations World Conference on Human Rights in Vienna. It was in anticipation of this conference that they issued the Bangkok Declaration condemning the Western particularism of the "universal human rights regime" and asserting instead the principles of national sovereignty, non-intervention, and territorial integrity.

These are illustrations of how cultures and religions pose challenges to the international legal tradition. The degree of challenge will depend on the power of dissent within cultures and religions, both in public opinion and in the stances of influential elites. Other challenges could also be mentioned – the legitimacy of female genital mutilation in some traditional cultures, punishment by severance of limbs in other cultures, and the like. What is important here are not the full details of such beliefs and practices, but rather the dilemma of pluralism that they pose for the international law tradition: To what degree ought it tolerate cultural practices that diverge from it?

Answers to the Dilemma of Pluralism

For the international law tradition, this dilemma is an ethical one. Proponents of the tradition, after all, regard the strengthening and extension of international law as a moral achievement for all of humanity. Though the law itself comes with no particular philosophical justification attached – one could endorse it from a variety of philosophical and religious standpoints – the belief that international law is an ethical achievement leads proponents of the tradition to want to see it broadened, deepened, and widened to include all people under its authority.

Such is the ethical standpoint from which the international law tradition approaches the dilemma of pluralism. Again, there are two versions of the dilemma – states that refuse to sign onto international law conventions out of religious and cultural dissent and states that have signed but now dissent. But the tradition's commitment to the strength of the law does not alone answer this dilemma. What is the solution to conflicts between the law and individual systems of ethics? Should the project of broadening, deepening, and widening be suspended when such conflicts exist? Or is such an abeyance ethically inadequate, deferring all too much to dissenting cultures? Or should the law seek to fortify itself by assertively incorporating dissenting cultures into its system of obligations? If so, does the tradition provide ethical guidance as to how this might be done? What sorts of answers are available to this problem?

One answer lies in a consent theory version of legal positivism that claims that states are obligated only by those legal conventions to which they have explicitly signed on.[14] Such an approach provides ready answers to the two versions of the dilemma of pluralism. States that have already agreed to conventions are still bound, even if they have come to dissent, while states that have not yet signed on are not bound. Consent theory positivism also stresses a commitment embedded in the very character of international law as a collection of public documents – the central importance of explicit, active approval. The international law tradition, after all, does not simply demand that its hearers perceive the truth of certain rules of international conduct, but that states actually sign on to them. What the tradition is likely to find inadequate in consent theory positivism, however, is its preference for the status quo. While it affirms the obligation of states to adhere to what they have agreed upon, consent theory positivism provides little guidance as to how the sphere of this obligation may be extended. It says little about how proponents of the international law tradition ought to proceed when they encounter dissenting cultures, and fails to support the tradition's aspiration for broadening, deepening, and widening international law.

Another potential answer to this dilemma appears to offer a far stronger basis for extending the reach of international law – namely, one rooted in a universalistic theory of morality that itself comports with aspirations of the international law tradition. Imagine, say, a modern version of natural law theory that endorses virtually every existing legally embodied human right, including those that are controversial among cultures, such as religious freedom and the treatment of women as equals in marriage and divorce law. It is not clear that any such theory exists, though there are certainly contemporary versions of natural law that are quite friendly to modern human rights, including religious freedom.[15] The proponents of such a theory, regarding its arguments as philosophically grounded in natural reason, would first approach dissenters with arguments about the truth about human rights, hoping to demonstrate that the dissenters' tradition is at least partially mistaken or that the true meaning of their tradition requires adherence to the disputed human rights.

But if arguments can trump dissent from certain human rights, it remains unclear how, if arguments fail to persuade, dissenters can be brought to endorse human rights. Most natural law theories recognize the importance of positive law for effecting social justice and cooperation and call for the positive law to

---

[14] For a description of this point of view, see Nardin (1998), "Legal Positivism as a Theory of International Society."

[15] See, for instance, the work of "new natural law theorists" such as John Finnis, Germain Grisez, and Joseph Boyle. A primer is John Finnis (1980), *Natural Law and Natural Rights*.

be as consistent with natural law as possible. The same goes for international law. The natural law perspective desires that positive law that promotes what natural law prescribes (or at least that portion of it that is appropriate to promote publicly) be created, adhered to, strengthened, and widened among states. But what does natural law say about an instance in which a state dissents from one of those human rights that natural law teaches and that international law prescribes, but in which the dissenting state has not signed onto the positive law or else had once signed on to it but now no longer adheres to it? Should an outside state enforce the law? Does any state have such authority to do so? Would it be acting as a vigilante? Is such behavior justifiable?

Natural law's commitment to the validity of positive law seems to suggest that law ought not to be enforced upon one who does not fall explicitly under its authority. Such enforcement would violate its own concept of right authority. At the same time, though, there are some sorts of violations of international human rights law – especially horrific sorts such as genocide – that "shock the conscience of mankind" and demand the remedial action of outsiders, whether or not the perpetrators have consented to the positive law. This was, of course, a central operative principle at the Nuremberg Trials of Nazi war criminals after World War II, and a principle that natural law is well equipped to support, given that such law exists prior to and apart from the positive law.

Which way ought states to act? It is not an easy question for a natural law ethic to decide. Such an ethic respects positive law and wants to extend it to protect the natural law as fully as possible. It may also affirm the Nuremberg principle that some levels and kinds of crime are subject to legal judgment, even if they were not explicitly outlawed. But it offers no easy answer as to how the positive law ought to be extended to peoples whose philosophical or religious conception rejects what the natural law demands. Similarly, the international law tradition also wants the law to be extended. But its advocates may well worry about the effects of enforcing or imposing it on those with divergent conceptions. If states can act outside the positive law whenever they so desire, the credibility of the law is damaged. And if this credibility is damaged, then so too is the consensus and legitimacy that allows it to be broadened, deepened, and widened.

The desiderata of both a universal reach and consensus among divergent cultures point the way to yet a third answer to the dilemma of pluralism, an alternative to consent theories and natural law. This is the approach of political philosopher John Rawls in his book, *The Law of Peoples*. Rawls seeks to extend to the international level his project of developing a principled defense of liberal institutions that can gain assent in societies where there are divergent "comprehensive conceptions of the good" – that is, philosophical and religious systems.[16] Addressing relations between states and peoples, he seeks to find principles of justice that apply to a world characterized by "diversity among

---

[16] See John Rawls (1971, 1993), *A Theory of Justice* and *Political Liberalism*.

reasonable peoples with their different cultures and traditions of thought, both religious and nonreligious"(Rawls, 1999a, p. 11).

Where may such principles be found? Rawls is emphatic about what ought not to be the public basis for the international order – a particular comprehensive conception of the good. He repeatedly returns to the religious wars of early modern Europe – cruel and unrestrained as they were – to show the consequences of seeking to impose a comprehensive conception of the good in a society where a diversity of such competing conceptions exists. Like the international law tradition, he claims that the law does not depend upon or demand adherence to any particular conception.

But neither is Rawls content with Westphalia. A law of peoples must be more than a *modus vivendi*, and should offer a set of standards to which states agree in principle. To discover consensual principles, Rawls envisions an international version of his famous device for eliciting principles of justice in the domestic realm, the original position. Here, the parties are states, ones that arrive at common principles of justice behind a "veil of ignorance" that blinds them to their wealth, power, status, and comprehensive conception.

The principles that states choose govern not only their relations with one another – treaties, war, intervention, and the like – but also their treatment of their own people. Rawls, though, does not want to demand that all states adhere to a full-blown conception of Western liberalism, with all of its rights, notions of equality, and standards of economic justice. He also wants to include non-Western societies whose conceptions of justice are not primarily liberal democratic ones as members in good standing of international society. But they must respect certain standards, ones that make them "decent hierarchical societies." They must be governed by the rule of law and involve a mechanism of consultation that allows bodies within society to participate in their governance.

The principles that unite both liberal and non-liberal societies in a common law of peoples are as follows: "1. Peoples are free and independent, and their freedom and independence are to be respected by other peoples. 2. Peoples are to observe treaties and undertakings. 3. Peoples are equal and are parties to the agreements that bind them. 4. Peoples are to observe a duty of non-intervention. 5. Peoples have the right of self-defense but not the right to instigate war for reasons other than self-defense. 6. Peoples are to honor human rights. 7. Peoples are to observe certain specified restrictions in the conduct of war. 8. Peoples have a duty to assist other peoples living under unfavorable conditions that prevent their having a just or decent political and social regime" (Rawls, 1993, p. 37). Many of these are familiar, as they are ensconced in the United Nations system. Many will be contested, though – human rights, for example. The human rights that Rawls (1999a) expects all societies to uphold include the right to life, to liberty, which he defines as "freedom from slavery, serfdom, and forced occupation, and a sufficient measure of liberty of conscience to endure freedom of religion and thought," and to formal equality before the law (p. 65). But there are other rights that appear in the Universal Declaration and other international legal instruments that he does not include – freedom of expression, full freedom of speech, freedom of assembly, minimal economic standards, women's rights, and full religious freedom. Rawls (1999a) envisions that a decent hierarchical society might have an established religion and curtail the full religious freedom of its citizens.

Why does Rawls include some rights but not others in his law of peoples? Some rights are necessary for any decent system of social cooperation, he argues, no matter what the culture. Thus, they are chosen in the original position. Why not ask for more? Why not demand that all societies adhere to a full conception of political liberalism? Here, Rawls appeals to the virtue of respect. We can hope that all societies move towards political liberalism, he writes. But to pressure them into accepting it or to seek to impose it would be to fail to respect them.

Many features of Rawls' project echo the commitments of the international law tradition – his desire to find a set of principles with universal reach that can be endorsed by diverse cultures, his restraint from presenting the law as an expression of a particular comprehensive conception, and his desire that the law be more than a *modus vivendi*, but a principled agreement. Yet in several respects, proponents of the tradition who want to see international law flourish and grow will likely remain unsatisfied with Rawls' law of peoples.[17]

Most importantly, the set of human rights that Rawls sets forth actually regresses from the accomplishments of current legal instruments. Of twenty-eight rights outlined in the Universal Declaration of Human Rights, Rawls leaves out twelve. Other rights in the documentary heritage he also omits. Committed to expanding international protections for human rights, the tradition is unlikely to welcome a turning back of the clock.

Another assumption that will not sit well with advocates of extending human rights law is Rawls' construal of decent hierarchical societies as unitary, uniform bodies. Rawls' deference to non-liberal societies, they will argue, ignores the presence of individuals in these societies who depart from the hierarchical conception. Often, actual "hierarchical societies" are in fact divided between traditionalists and pro-Western parties that may well have more in common with outsiders than with their own people. It is not clear why Rawls' minimal set of rights ought to trump the more maximal standards of those who wish to see their societies' systems of law conform more closely with the international instruments. If respect is the reason for deference, then why is

---

[17] Examples of these critics include Allen Buchanan (2000), "Rawls' 'Law of Peoples' Rules for a Vanished Westphalian World"; Kok-Chor Tan (1998), "Liberal Toleration in Rawls' Law of Peoples,"; Andrew Kuper (2000), "Rawlsian Global Justice: Beyond the Law of Peoples to a Cosmopolitan Law of Persons"; and Colleen Gilg (2002), "The Dilemma of Promoting Human Rights in a World of Deep Diversity: A Critical Examination of the Approach of John Rawls."

respect accorded to traditionalists but not to those who aspire to international legal standards?

Still less is it clear, the international law tradition will argue, why hierarchical societies, even if we assume their uniformity, ought to be taken as unchanging social realities. It does not make one a relativist or historicist to point out that all societies are constantly revising their laws to achieve greater justice, whether slowly or swiftly, through increments or revolutions. If this is the case, then should not hierarchical societies be encouraged to develop towards the international legal standards? Advocates of these standards may point out that this development need not involve coercive imposition or sanctions, but might be approached discursively, through the exchange of ideas.

Finally, the international law tradition will object to Rawls' unwillingness to insist on the universality of one particularly important right for achieving justice – unfettered freedom of expression. Without freedom of expression, the kinds of activities that are likely to lead to a development in standards of justice – the participation of dissenters, a societal conversation about legal norms, and the reasons behind them – become sharply limited. The lack of such a right only reinforces the status quo bias embedded in the law of peoples.[18]

The international law tradition, then, with its commitments to widening, deepening, and broadening, will likely conclude that Rawls' law of peoples unduly suppresses possibilities for expanding international law. In this respect, it will find Rawls' answer to the problem of pluralism an inadequate one. Yet, there is one feature of Rawls' thought that it is likely to welcome – his concern for consensus. If the law is to be expanded so that it is not only widened to a larger number of peoples, but is also deepened so as to enjoy legitimacy among them, then it must win their assent, not just their instrumental endorsement.

The Solution of Dialogue

The solution to the dilemma of pluralism, as the international law tradition views it – essentially the problem of expanding consensus – can only be found in a change of perspectives, on the part of traditions that dissent from the tenets of international law, on the part of proponents of the international law tradition, or both. This change of perspective, in turn, might come about through an internal evolution, or more likely, from both internal and external factors. For the change to come deliberately, one of the most fruitful avenues is dialogue. It might occur between the international law tradition and cultures that object to some of its provisions, among the opposing perspectives within a particular culture, traditionalist and modern, or between cultures that have different views of the controversial questions in the law. Along these lines, in recent years, Pope John Paul II and President Khatemi of Iran have proposed a "dialogue between civilizations" involving Christianity and Islam. In order to

---

[18] Ibid. (Rawls, note 17).

achieve success in strengthening the international law tradition, this dialogue, which may occur over decades or even longer, must result in dissenting traditions coming to re-evaluate their stance towards international human rights in light of their enduring beliefs, and in the international law tradition making efforts to enunciate rights in ways that are more consonant with the claims of multiple traditions. Only in this way can a meeting of the minds occur.

In this dialogue, the participants and representatives of each side accord each other the full dignity of an interlocutor. Only reasons count, not differentials in power, authority, or status. The particular culture and religion at issue must be faithful to its beliefs about enduring truth. Yet dialogue is based on the possibility that over time, culture and religions may come to interpret their enduring doctrines in new ways, to undergo an evolution in understanding that yields a new synthesis of their beliefs, or to adapt these beliefs to new circumstances.

Something like this kind of evolution occurred during the twentieth century within the Catholic Church with respect to the issue of religious freedom. During early modern Europe, the Church and temporal rulers acting to promote its authority fought Protestants to the death out of the conviction that the Protestants' decision to leave the Church and challenge its temporal powers could not be tolerated. Since the Middle Ages, the Church had taught that a Catholic society was one in which the Catholic Church would be established as the official religion and heresies would enjoy no legal right to be practiced and expressed. The Church continued to teach this doctrine well into the twentieth century. An ideal society was still one where the Catholic faith was authoritative for the realm and where dissent from its truths was entitled to no rights. If the Church found itself in a state where it did not enjoy this supremacy, then it could accept a pluralistic order, but only on provisional, prudential grounds. This was its attitude towards the Peace of Westphalia, which, as Pope Innocent X's condemnation reveals, the Church considered far from ideal. During the nineteenth century, Popes continued to reject religious freedom and to uphold the old integralist ideal. Pope Gregory XVI labeled freedom of conscience "an absurd and erroneous opinion" in 1832, while Pope Pius IX condemned religious freedom and the separation of Church and state alike in his famous *Syllabus of Errors* of 1864.

The contrast between this ideal and the Church's teachings at the Second Vatican Council is a significant one. In 1965, the Council promulgated *Dignitatis Humanae*, declaring that religious freedom is a fundamental human right, rooted in the dignity of the person. Though the Church had always claimed that faith could not be coerced, it had to come to affirm that individuals enjoyed a right to pursue truth without interference from others, including state authorities. The Church made it clear that it was in no way compromising its historic, dogmatic teachings about faith and morals, allowing a "right to error," or embracing Enlightenment individualism, but rather was forbidding the restriction of the search for truth. It insisted, then, upon the possibility presently asserted: that a tradition might evolve significantly without compromising what it deems as essential.

This dramatic evolution was the result of a dialectic between Catholic philosophers and the modern world of liberal democratic rights and institutions. It was two philosophers in particular who paved the way for the Church's acceptance of religious freedom – Jacques Maritain and John Courtney Murray. Maritain's contribution was to develop a defense of human rights and democracy in the Thomist natural law tradition. Murray focused much more on religious liberty. An American Jesuit priest, he was strongly influenced by the American founding and viewed the U.S. political regime as one where Catholicism was not only tolerated, but could flourish, even under laws preventing establishment and mandating religious freedom. Murray then became a major influence behind the development of *Dignitatis Humanae* at the Second Vatican Council.[19]

The Catholic Church's gradual embrace of religious freedom is an example of how a tradition can evolve so as to come to accept new understandings of political forms and institutions while being true to its core commitments. The Catholic Church, of course, is not the only religious tradition to evolve. The continued maturation of international law will depend on other traditions evolving in their own understandings. Some such evolution is now evident in Islam, in which a circle of scholars has, through both its own internal dynamics as well as dialogue with outsiders, embraced an understanding of law and politics that is consistent with norms of liberal democratic constitutionalism, including religious freedom.[20] At this point, these scholars are still a minority within Islam, but their influence is growing. Other traditions, too, evince a pluralism in which voices of modernity compete with voices of tradition.

It would be a mistake, however, to think that progress in international law is solely the result of "pre-modern" traditions coming to accommodate "modern" understandings of rights and obligations. Change must be mutual; dialogue is a two-way street. The rapprochement between Catholicism and the modern tradition of rights, including religious freedom, for instance, required not just an evolution of Catholic doctrine, but a growth in European liberal republicanism away from its hostile anti-clericalism of the nineteenth century

[19] For an account of the influence of Maritain and Murray, see John T. McGreevy (2003), *Catholicism and American Freedom*.

[20] Abdulaziz Abdulhussein Sachedina, *The Islamic Roots of Democratic Pluralism* (New York: Oxford University Press, 2001); Abdullahi Ahmed An-Na'im, *Toward an Islamic Reformation: Civil Liberties, Human Rights, and International Law* (Syracuse, NY: Syracuse University Press, 1990); David Little, John Kelsay, and Abdulaziz Sachedina, *Human Rights and the Conflicts of Culture: Western and Islamic Perspectives on Religious Liberty* (Columbia, SC: University of South Carolina Press, 1988); Abdullahi Ahmed An-Na'im and Francis M. Deng, *Human Rights in Africa: Cross-Cultural Perspectives* (Washington, D.C.: The Brookings Institution, 1990); Robin Wright, "Islam and Liberal Democracy: Two Visions of Reformation," *Journal of Democracy* 7 (April 1996).

and towards an acceptance of religious freedom and the participation of religious parties – Christian Democratic ones, for instance. Indeed, it was only once it felt secure in the political participation of Catholics that the Catholic Church was willing to endorse religious freedom and embrace human rights.

Not only does a consensus around principles of international law also require secular traditions to evolve, but at times, religious traditions have contributed directly and proactively to the development of international law. John Nurser has shown how an ecumenical coalition of Protestant leaders, in alliance with Catholic bishops and Catholic lay intellectuals such as Jacques Maritain, was crucial in establishing the Commission on Human Rights in the United Nations in 1945, and, later, the Universal Declaration of Human Rights in 1948, which was, of course, a milestone in the incorporation of human rights into international law (Nurser, 2005). In more recent decades, Protestant churches and, following the Second Vatican Council, Catholic churches, have kept the torch of human rights burning under authoritarian regimes – in Poland, Lithuania, Chile, Brazil, Nicaragua, El Salvador, the Philippines, Kenya, Malawi, South Africa, East Timor, South Korea, and many other sites – leading to the overthrow of these regimes and thus to the lodging of human rights in domestic constitutions all over the world.[21]

Developments in international law, then, will be propelled by many communities. These developments, the progress of dialogue and normative evolution, are likely to be slow and gradual, not deliberate, structured, and final, but carried on over decades, through multiple writings, conversations, and public forums. Proponents of the international law tradition might hope for something more speedy and deliberate. But as such conversations must eventually elicit the assessment not just of the involved participants, but of a much wider swath of voices in a tradition, the results are not likely to be immediate or dramatic. But for the international law tradition, this broad avenue, replete with its slow traffic, is the one that promises most to achieve the broadening, widening, and deepening that the tradition envisions.

[21] See Daniel Philpott (2004), "The Catholic Wave."

3

Morality and Universality in Jewish Thought

Michael Walzer

Two Kinds of Universalism

With regard to many of the standard ethical/philosophical questions, Jewish views are both complex and contested. But with regard to the universality of moral rules, there is general agreement on one simple proposition: all human beings live "under the commandments." They don't all live under the same commandments: the 613 laws of the Torah are "laws" only for the people of Israel. They are a particularist code, but the particularism is limited to religious matters – rituals, holidays, physical purity, sacrifices, and so on – and then to specific legal elaborations and sometimes expansions of the moral rules. (Actually, the particularism extends also to the narrative in which the rules are embedded, but I will postpone that issue until later in my argument.) The moral rules themselves are common to humankind, and they have the same form as the religious code; they are divine commandments. There are Jewish writers who believe that morality is "natural" – that is, accessible to all rational beings. If the moral rules had not been revealed and commanded, they argue, we would have found them or constructed them for ourselves: "These are matters written in the Torah which, even if they had not been written there, reason would have required that they be written."[1] But it is a central feature of the Jewish tradition that the rules were in fact written; they were revealed and commanded – first to the "sons of Noah" (that is, to all humanity) and then to the people of Israel. The moral world, on this view, is a world of requirements, laws, to which all men and women are subject.

Western liberals (a category that includes large numbers of Jews) generally oppose subjection. Liberals set a very high value on individual autonomy, and rightly so. The choices we make shape our lives to a very large extent, and there

---

[1] Quoted in David Novak, *Natural Law in Judaism* (Cambridge: Cambridge University Press, 1998), p. 73, from *Sifra* (Aharei Mot); see also Babylonian Talmud, Yoma 67b, in Michael Walzer, et al. editors, *The Jewish Political Tradition*, vol. 1, *Authority* (New Haven: Yale University Press, 2000), pp. 52–53, with commentary by Noam Zohar, pp. 53–54.

are many things that we have to choose. In democratic politics, for example, the idea of consent is central, and consent is a choice: citizens choose the people who govern them, and they help choose the policies of their government. And in the same way, in everyday life, we choose spouses, friends, projects, careers, professions, and all the organizations and associations that we join (or leave) in the course of our lives. Most liberals would say that choice is crucial to the good life; some would say that we literally determine the meaning of our lives by the choices we make.

But there are also things we don't choose: most importantly, we don't choose our morality. When we live a moral life, we are living in accordance with values and principles that are commonly expressed as injunctions – the Jewish version is: "Thou shalt not . . . " In the biblical story (as understood by the rabbis), the injunctions are God-given, and they are agreed to by the recipients: both the sons of Noah and the people of Israel "accepted the commandments upon themselves." Unfortunately, there is no historical record of the first of these acceptances to set alongside the Sinai event, but the rabbis assumed it; acceptance, in fact, was morally obligatory in both cases. Neither the value nor the force of the rules depends on consent, and men and women can refuse the rules only in the same way that they can subsequently violate them. Exactly what the covenants of Noahides and Israelites with God add to the meaning of morality is a matter for philosophical and theological debate; I won't address that issue here. It is enough to say that the moral rules are understood as actual commandments, delivered in historical time; after that, they are inherited within a tradition. We don't make them up for ourselves or by ourselves. We can join in an ongoing process of interpretation and even revision, but the moral world is not subject to our will; we are its subjects. We incur obligations by making promises, but when the Noahides and the Israelites promised not to murder, or lie, or rob, they were responding to a prior obligation. It simply is the case that all men and women are bound not to do those things, and other things too.

I don't think that this sense of living under commandment, this sense of morality as an overhanging presence, is peculiarly Jewish, but it is profoundly Jewish; it resonates through every aspect of Jewish life. The role of interpretation in Jewish law, for example, is determined by the absolute givenness of the rules – and also, of course, by the identity of the giver. But givenness is a general feature of moral life, even when no "giver" is recognized. Consider contemporary arguments about human rights: the idea that all of us have rights simply by virtue of being human, rights not to be killed, or enslaved, or tortured, implies that all of us also have obligations not to kill or enslave or torture. And it doesn't matter that we never voluntarily accepted these obligations; we know or should know that we are obligated. Doesn't it follow that if we disagree about the meaning or reach of our obligations, we are disagreeing about the interpretation of human rights? Don't rights have the same givenness as commandments, even though they are not divinely revealed? Even if rights are "social constructions," as I believe, they are not constructed by individual men and women; they are constructed collectively over long periods of time, and each generation lives "under" the constructions of past generations, just as if they lived "under the commandments."

But in the Jewish account, there are different sets of commandments for different people, and these differences give the moral universe its particular shape. The first set chronologically, according to the rabbis of the talmudic period, is the Noahide code. Most of the code is creatively "derived" from a biblical verse relating to Adam, but its historical setting is the immediate aftermath of the flood, when Noah's progeny are commanded not to shed human blood. There are seven laws in the code, each of them actually a category of law, subject to expansion, and variously expanded by later Jewish writers.[2] The first of them is positive, requiring the establishment of a judicial system in society; the remaining six are negative, like most of Sinai's Ten, prohibiting blasphemy, idolatry, murder, sexual acts taken to be perverse or impure (adultery, incest, homosexuality, and bestiality), robbery, and finally – this is, along with murder, the only prohibition explicitly "given" to the sons of Noah – eating a limb torn from a living animal (Maimonides reads this last prohibition as a ban on cruelty). Some such original code is necessary, in the rabbinic view, to explain or justify pre-Sinaitic events such as the destruction of Sodom: how could its people have been punished if they had never been warned of what God required of them? There must be a moral law that precedes and defines human immorality. So the sons of Noah were commanded, and they "accepted" the commandments – even though, much like Israel later on, they didn't always live by them.[3]

One possible understanding of this Jewish argument is that the laws given to the Noahides are subsequently folded into the laws given at Sinai to the people of Israel – and then they are similarly incorporated, though without the benefit of divine revelation, in other (that is, non-Jewish) moral and legal systems. This view is put forward with great clarity by Jacob Anatoli in his *Ha-Malamed* (1249), but it has a talmudic basis (Sanhedrin 56b). Anatoli (Lichtenstein, 1981) writes that when

the Noahides were enjoined concerning justice, they were put under obligation to create legal arrangements. . . . It is incumbent on the judges to draw up rules of equity that shall be appropriate for that particular country, as exemplified by the manner is which this matter is handled currently by the nations severally. Likewise, it is incumbent upon merchants and upon the members of the trades to establish regulations for themselves . . . and whatever emerges as the law in this manner is law as much as that which is written in the Bible. (p. 43)

---

[2] The fullest discussion is in BT Sanhedrin 56a-59a; see *The Jewish Political Tradition*, M. Walzer et al. (eds.), vol. 2, *Membership* (New Haven: Yale University Press, 2003), pp. 455–461.

[3] See BT Avodah Zarah 2a-3b, in *The Jewish Political Tradition*, 2, pp. 20–23, with commentary by Moshe Halbertal, pp. 23–29. Cf. BT Hullin 92a, where there are thirteen commandments that the sons of Noah "took upon themselves."

So there is a universal code, and many (better and worse) elaborations of this code – and these may well co-exist for all time. It was never the standard Jewish view that when the messiah comes, at "the end of days," all humanity will be converted to Judaism. Instead, Israel and the nations will continue to live side by side; Israel will live fully in accordance with its law and the nations fully in accordance with theirs – that is, with the Noahide code in its various elaborations. Insofar as the messiah is imagined as a king, he will presumably enforce, not one universal law, but these two (overlapping) laws. It is only because the Noahide code bans blasphemy and idolatry that the prophet Zephaniah's words will come true: "On that day, the Lord shall be one, and his name shall be one." But the names of the nations will not be one; they will never be replaced by a single universal nation. This is probably the dominant orthodox view; it suggests the characteristic Jewish mix of universality and particularism.

But this "mix" can be shifted significantly in the direction of universality. For it is also a common Jewish view that the version of the moral law delivered at Sinai is the best possible one (different reasons can be given for this claim) and that the "mission" of the Jews is to teach that morality to the world. This mission is in fact one of the theological or world-historical explanations for the exile and dispersal of the Jewish people: we were dispersed so that we could carry the Torah to the four corners of the earth.[4] The Moroccan-Italian rabbi, Elijah Benamozegh, made a missionist argument based on the Noahide code (it was published by a French disciple in 1914, fourteen years after Benamozegh's death, under the title *Israel et l'humanité*),[5] but Jewish writers more often take the Torah as a whole or the moral criticism of the prophets as the Jewish exemplification of universal morality. It is not just the seven original laws, delivered to Adam and Noah or discovered by reason, but the specifically Jewish elaborations of these laws – the commandments relating to morality that figure in the 613 and the prophetic account of what these commandments mean in everyday social life, summed up in the nineteenth century as "ethical monotheism" – that the people of Israel carry through the centuries and teach to "the nations."

Isaiah's description of Israel as "a light unto the nations" invites the missionist interpretation it has commonly received (though that may not be its original meaning). It doesn't, however, suggest or call for active missionizing. Israel has only to sit in its own place, living in accordance with God's commandments, and its light will blaze forth. Ahad Ha-am (1970), though a committed secularist, got the classic religious position exactly right when he wrote:

The Prophets no doubt gave utterance to the hope that Judaism would exert an influence for good on ... the other nations; but their idea was that this result would follow naturally from the existence among the Jews of the highest type of morality,

4 The classic text is BT Pesahim, 87b.
5 See the English version: *Israel and Humanity* (1995).

not that the Jews existed solely for the purpose of striving to exert this influence. It is the nations who are to say, "Come ye and let us go up to the mountain of the Lord.... and He will teach us of his ways..." We do not find that Israel is to say, "Come, let us go out to the nations and teach them the ways of the Lord...." (p. 231)

In exile, it is much harder for Israel's light to blaze forth, but exilic Jews were supposed to exemplify goodness and justice in their individual lives and their local communities. This was the standard view of nineteenth-century religious reformers and enlightened philosophers: the Jews had a vocation for morality. Other nations with other vocations were presumed to be capable of responding to Jewish moral teaching – that is, they were capable of seeing the light. This is a stronger universalism than the orthodox view, since it asks more of the sons of Noah than, for example, Jacob Anatoli asked. It does allow for the religious particularism of the Jews and presumably of Christians, Muslims, and other monotheists too; it doesn't allow for moral particularism. The biblical maxim "Justice, justice shalt thou pursue" is given a singular and universal meaning. Perhaps nineteenth-century reformers thought that this universalism was the particularism of the Jews – but this was so only until it became genuinely universal.

The Noahide Code

I want now to describe in greater detail the orthodox view of the Noahide code and to suggest some of its possible interpretations (and then do the same in the next section for the enlightenment and reform view of Israel's mission). The dominant understanding is that the laws delivered to the sons of Noah represent a minimal morality, designed by God for humanity in general, but also, more specifically, for non-Jews. Thus Moses Isserles, interpreting the talmudic discussion of the Noahide code in Sanhedrin 56a, describes one rabbinic argument (attributed to Rabbi Yohanan): "a Noahide is only obligated to maintain civic norms [*minhag ha-medina*] and to adjudicate equitably 'between any man and his fellow or a stranger' (Deuteronomy 1:16)."[6] With the Jews, by contrast, God is far more demanding: the Torah is a maximal code. In the talmudic period, no Jewish writers acknowledged the existence of alternative maximal moralities. Most of the world, as seen by the Jews, was idolatrous, and it is virtually axiomatic to the Jewish account of idolatry that idolaters recognize no moral restraint. If they violate the commandment not to worship idols, they are sure to violate all the other commandments – above all, they are prone to violence and murder. It isn't unique to the Jews to insist that morality requires a commitment to monotheism (see John Locke's "Letter on Toleration"), nor is it unique to the Jews to ignore empirical evidence about the moral

---

[6] Moses Isserles, Responsa 10, in "The Jewish Political Tradition," 2, pp. 463–465; see also the discussion in Lichtenstein, "Seven Laws," p. 43.

conduct of real-idolaters-in-the-world. Still, the Noahide code is probably the first example of a "natural" or rational morality grounded on a religious precept.

Since this is Judaism's foundational precept – "the Lord is one" – the code is, in effect, a Jewish law for non-Jews. Hence it is very much like the earliest form of *jus gentium*, which, as David Novak reminds us, was a version of Roman law designed for non-Romans living or traveling in the empire. The rabbis conceived the Noahide code similarly, as a set of rules that would be imposed on non-Jews in a Jewish state.[7] So it was a way of tolerating the "others." You don't have to convert to Judaism, they would be told, but you must observe this minimal set of rules if you want to live among us. Some scholars have suggested that the code must therefore have been worked out in Hasmonean times, when Jewish rule extended over a number of non-Jewish nations. But some of these nations, like the Idumeans, were forcibly converted – which suggests that adherence to the code was not yet available as an alternative to conversion. Probably the code is a later creation; perhaps it was designed for the "God-fearers" of Roman times, men and women drawn to the Jewish version of monotheism, but not ready for the 613 commandments. Or perhaps it was designed for the messianic age, when some set of laws, short of the 613, would be universally enforced or universally accepted – a code for "the nations," wherever they lived.

There were some Jewish writers, indeed, who argued that Jews should enforce the code themselves, without waiting for the messiah, whenever and wherever they were able to do so. This can easily become an argument for holy war, a religious crusade against idolatry; I don't think it was ever a common argument, but it is the subject of a famous disagreement between Maimonides and Nahmanides in which Maimonides, codifying the law in his *Mishneh Torah*, argues for Jewish enforcement. His prooftext is the biblical story of the rape of Dinah and the subsequent killing of the inhabitants of Shechem by the sons of Jacob (Genesis 34): "A Noahide who violates any of the seven commandments is executed by decapitation with the sword. Therefore all the citizens of Shechem were liable for the death penalty because Shechem (that is, the prince) had been guilty of [rape]. They saw it and knew it, and failed to bring him to justice."[8]

In his commentary on the book of Genesis, Nahmanides (1981) writes that "these words do not seem to me to be correct" and goes on to argue that law enforcement is a matter for the Noahides themselves – not only in the first instance, as Maimonides also says, but in every instance; they don't need Jewish interference or, better, the Jews are not obligated to interfere: "it was not the responsibility of Jacob and his sons to bring them (the citizens of Shechem) to justice"(1971, pp. 417–419). In any case, there has hardly been a time in

---

[7] See *The Code of Maimonides, Book Fourteen, The Book of Judges* (Hershman, 1949, p. 237).
[8] Ibid., p. 234.

Jewish history when it would not have been foolhardy to attempt the enforcement that Maimonides advocates. (I can imagine arguing for "humanitarian
intervention" out of these texts, but this would be a radically secularized version of what Maimonides intended, and it would not encompass what Jacob's
sons actually did.)

But even if enforcement (whether in religious or secular versions) was
impossible for diaspora Jews, they could still refuse to cooperate with nations,
or groups of people, that violated the moral law. Refusal is, in fact, enjoined in
the Talmud. Since idolators are assumed to violate the law, "It is prohibited to
sell them weapons or weapons' accessories, or to sharpen weapons for them;
and it is prohibited to sell them stocks, [iron] collars, fetters, or iron chains."
This rule is discussed at length in the tractate Avodah Zarah (Idolatry), where,
as Noam Zohar has demonstrated in an illuminating essay, all the contemporary questions about boycotts and embargoes are raised: Are defensive as well
as offensive weapons subject to the prohibition? What about sales to middle-
men? What about materials that aren't weapons but might be used to make
weapons or to facilitate their use? But the rabbis are not writing here in the
hope of stopping the violence of idolators. "They knew full well," as Zohar
(1993) says, "that... prospective clients would find other sources of supply"
(pp. 45–49). Their concern was only to keep Jewish hands clean.[9]

Once Christianity and Islam had replaced the idolatrous religions of the
ancient world, it was possible to understand the Noahide code simply as the
established law of the Noahides – their actual moral/legal systems, which didn't
depend on either Jewish or messianic enforcement. This view is less the product of theological reflection or textual interpretation than of everyday experience. Exilic Jewry had no powers of enforcement, yet in all the countries
of the exile, the code was more or less effectively enforced by the Noahides
(that is, the gentiles) themselves. So here is a set of commandments or laws,
revealed to humankind in the days of Adam and Noah, knowable by reason,
and visibly established in the world. And not only established but fully elab-
orated: thus Nahmanides claims, according to Lichtenstein's interpretation of
his argument, "that just as the Israelite code has a definite ruling for each civil
dispute, similarly the Noahide tradition has a definite – but not identical – ruling" (Lichtenstein, 1981, p. 37). Taking the Noahide code to be the actual law
of the gentile nations is a way of recognizing what Novak calls the "normativity" of the others. One can see the full extent of the recognition in the famous
statement by Menachem Meiri, a fourteenth-century talmudic commentator
living in Provence, that "every Noahide whom we see, who accepts upon himself the seven commandments, is one of the saints of the nations of the world,

---

[9] Noam J. Zohar, "Boycott, Crime, and Sin: Ethical and Talmudic Responses to Injustice
   Abroad," in *Ethics and International Affairs*, vol. 7, 1993, pp. 45–49, commenting on BT
   Avodah Zarah, 15b-176a.

and is in the category of the religious, and has a portion in the world-to-come"
(Novak, 1983, p. 351).[10]

And even though the normativity of the Noahides is not the same as "ours,"
it might still be possible for "us" to learn from "them." The validation of gentile law provides a comparative standard for Jewish law. Look and see: they
are stricter here, we are stricter there; they do things this way, we do things that
way. I don't want to suggest that comparative law was ever a central feature
of Jewish scholarship. Until very recently, it certainly wasn't. Indeed, curios-
ity about the others is barely visible in the classical Jewish texts. But some
sort of comparison was made necessary by the talmudic maxim that "There
is nothing permitted to Jews that is prohibited to gentiles" (Sanhedrin 59a).
It would have been illogical and wrong, so the rabbis thought, if Jewish law
on any subject were more permissive than Noahide law. And this comparative
impulse could extend beyond the Noahide code as it was understood by the
rabbis to any of its gentile elaborations – or, indeed, to any gentile moral or
religious practice that seemed to cast Jewish law or practice in a bad light. A
bad light in whose eyes? Obviously, in the eyes of the gentiles, whose "normativity" is thus given extraordinary force. One of the crucial modifications
of Jewish law, the abolition of polygamy (despite its biblical sanction) some-
time around the year 1000, is probably best explained in these comparative
terms. When Rabbi Gershom and his colleagues in the Rhineland forbade
marriage to more than one woman, they acted, writes Robert Gordis (1990),
because "they found it intolerable for Jews to maintain an attitude toward
marriage . . . that set women on a lower social and ethical plane than did their
monogamous Christian neighbors" (p. 143).

Still, comparisons of this sort were not all that common, and they were
never intended to lead to the formation of a single law for Jews and gentiles
alike – not even, as we have seen, in messianic times. Nor was the distinction
of social morality and religious law, and the focus on morality in the Noahide
code, meant to suggest the greater importance of the moral law – as a modern
reader might expect. For Judah Halevi, moral laws are merely "the preamble
to the divine religious law, [preceding] it both in nature and in time. They are
indispensable for governing any group of human beings [no matter what it may
be], so that even a band of robbers cannot avoid adhering to justice in what
is [simply] between them" (Halevi, forthcoming). Religious law is far more
important because its delivery to Israel is a sign of the special bond between
Israel and God, which is sustained by ritual observance. Of course, both the
Noahide code and the Torah are a mix of religious and moral precepts, but,
again, the code is the minimal version, the Torah, so to speak, the real thing.

---

[10] Quoted in David Novak, *The Image of the Non-Jew in Judaism: An Historical and Constructive Study of the Noahide Laws*. Toronto Studies in Theology, vol. 14 (Toronto: Edwin Mellen
Press, 1983), p. 351.

This duality, the code and the Torah, is as permanent as the duality of "the nations" and Israel. It will never be transcended. Jewish monism relates only to God, not to humankind. If one believes in a pluralist universe, then this everlasting duality can be seen as the great advantage of Jewish "tribalism." Even in the best of times, even in the end of days, even when "God's name shall be one," there will still be many nations, many religious communities (though none of them idolatrous), and many versions of the moral law. In contemporary language, morality has a common core and then a wide range of historical and cultural variations; it is at once universalist and multiculturalist.

The Missionist Argument

The stronger universalism of nineteenth- and twentieth-century Jewish reformers, and then of several generations of secular radicals, has biblical and rabbinic antecedents, but I will focus on its modern versions. Some of these are theological, some philosophical, some overtly political, but they have in common a selective (but not, I think, a distorted) reading of biblical and talmudic texts that emphasize the centrality of justice. It is certainly possible to construct a full-scale ethical doctrine – duties and virtues, the right and the good – out of the classical Jewish books. Moritz Lazarus attempts this in *The Ethics of Judaism* (1898), and Hermann Cohen does something similar in *Religion of Reason* (1919). Still, the emphasis of modern writers, these two included, falls on the special Jewish commitment to justice. Lazarus explains the commitment not only with reference to "the ethical consciousness of the Jews," but also with reference to the "severe trials" they endured. "Like all . . . persecuted minorities," Lazarus writes, "the Jews developed ethical cohesion, a feeling of mutual responsibility, to a great degree. The thought, which . . . lies at the substructure of our oldest legislation, that all ethics, by reason of its primary impelling force and its highest aim, is social ethics, more and more gained ground in actual life" (pp. 103–104).[11]

This is a little odd, since the "oldest legislation," as well as the prophetic critique that is often explicitly based on it, is already closely involved with "actual life." Still, the point is clear: if the Jews have a vocation for morality, this is specifically the morality of social and economic life. The treatment of strangers, the wages of workers, the protection of widows and orphans, shelter for the homeless, the practice of lending money, rich and poor in the courtroom, individual responsibility, the integrity of witnesses and judges: these are its classic subjects. In the nineteenth and twentieth centuries, the impact of this account of Jewish ethics was to push people who took it seriously toward the left side of the political spectrum. This was so whether they focused on the legislation of Exodus and Deuteronomy or on the criticism of Amos and Isaiah.

---

[11] Moritz Lazarus, *The Ethics of Judaism*, trans. Henrietta Szold (Philadelphia: Jewish Publication Society, 1900), I, pp. 103–104.

Hermann Cohen's "principle of justice," culled from a wide range of biblical books, "has as its consequence the relativity of the principle of property – this bulwark of egotism ... " (Cohen, 1995, p. 430). Hence, as Cohen writes in his chapter on "The Idea of the Messiah and Mankind," the centerpiece of *Religion of Reason*, ethical monotheism generates "ethical socialism" (9. 259). Though he explicitly repudiated Marxist versions of socialism, Mordecai Kaplan made a similar argument in the United States just fifteen years after Cohen's book appeared. He writes in his *Judaism as a Civilization* (1934) that "There has never been such vindication as there is today of the impassioned warnings sounded by the great Prophets of Israel, that any social order which is based upon exploitation of the weak, the helpless and the simple, by the strong, the resourceful and the cunning, is bound to be wrecked" (pp. 472–473). It turned out that the Jews also had a vocation for radical politics, which is another universalizing enterprise.

For all the philosophers and reformers, Jewish justice was a universal project; it wasn't narrowly connected to the collective life of the Jews, even if it was supposed to be manifest there. "The fundamental idea of the Hebrew Prophets," Ahad Ha-am (1970) argued in his essay "Priest and Prophet," "was the universal dominion of absolute justice" (p. 133). This is also the central theme of Lazarus' book, which is concerned throughout to rebut charges of Jewish parochialism. He writes (1900), "The fate of the Israelitish people and the conduct of the surrounding heathen, especially their idolatry and its immoral practices, had necessitated laying stress upon national segregation. But the ideal visions of the future conceived by the most exalted of the Prophets were luminous and forceful in conveying their universal point of view" (p. 199). Jewish particularism is re-described here as a purely defensive maneuver, temporarily necessary, never valued in itself. "The purpose of ... Israel's election," Lazarus writes, "is not confined to Israel; it is realizable only through the whole of mankind" (p. 205).

Hermann Cohen's account of Jewish messianism provides the strongest possible argument for Israel's universalizing mission – extended now from teaching humanity about the one and only God to teaching the "nations" a more political singularity. Cohen is writing in part against Zionism, of which he was a fierce opponent, but I want to stress here his more positive, and equally fierce, commitment to the unity of humankind and the uniformity of the moral law. Israel, in Cohen's conception, was something like Lenin's proletarian vanguard, whose historic task was to make itself unnecessary and then disappear. Once Israel's mission is accomplished, the Israelite nation will have no further purpose: so "national limitations are abandoned for the sake of Messianism." (Cohen, 1995, p. 259). But first, of course, the messiah himself, who on the standard account is an Israelite king, has to be abandoned: "The ideality of the Messiah," Cohen writes, "his significance as an idea, is shown in the overcoming of the person of the Messiah ... in the dissolution of the personal image in the pure notion of time ...."(p. 249). The messiah is replaced by the messianic age, when there won't be any kings in Israel or anywhere else. And then "Israel, as a nation, is nothing other than the ... symbol for the desired unity of mankind." This unity is literal in Cohen's conception; it involves the end of all political divisions – he takes this to be the natural consequence of monotheism: one God, one humanity. "The total liberation from national patriotism ... upon which the rule of social power groups is based, is to be attributed to the ethical rigor [that is] the consequence of the ... religious one-sidedness of monotheism" (p. 261).

So there is a single uniform and rigorous ethical code for all men and women, to which, one day, they will all conform. Rather than a common core and a range of cultural variation, what is envisioned here is a general convergence on a thick set of moral norms. These norms are still expressed as commandments; the prophets, after all, deliver the word of God in the imperative mode. But they can be translated into a doctrine of human rights – and translated, as David Novak has argued, without theological loss. Novak's account is too complex to be summarized here; I want only to suggest the moral simplicity of the translation, while avoiding for now its theoretical difficulties. Consider, for example, the first principle of economic morality: "That the poor of the community have a right to ... provision," Novak (2003) writes, "is emphasized by the fact that charity is not left to ... individual discretion" (p. 193). If individuals are bound to contribute to the Poor Fund, then the poor have a right to the contributions. Obligations entail rights, whether or not rights are specified in the law. The Jewish poor did not need to learn "rights-talk" in order to assert a sense of entitlement. The brazenness of the *schnorrer* (beggar) in Jewish folklore, where it is usually admired, suggests that a command morality is not all that far from a morality of rights. Still, orthodox Jews would defend a pluralist version of this morality: the rights that follow from God's commands to Israel are different from the rights that follow from the Noahide code or, as Novak says, from "the general order of justice at work in the universe." Reformers and liberal philosophers, on the other hand, would insist that it is the mission of Israel to raise the "general order" to the level of the covenantal community.

The task of Israel here and now (unlike the task of Lenin's vanguard) is to exemplify this higher order, not to enforce or even actively promote it. With regard to the moral minimalism of the Noahide code, it was possible to think about enforcement; Maimonides, as we have seen, endorses the use of force to maintain the seven laws, but he would not compel obedience to the whole of Torah law. Nor did any of the missionists imagine a Jewish role in enforcing the maximal ethic that they believed humanity would one day accept. Secular Jewish radicals joined parties and social movements that aimed at enforcement, but religious Jews, even religious reformers, generally didn't. To be sure, many Reform congregations in America today have "social action" committees that address issues of public policy and sometimes call for coercive action by the state. It is probably true that Jews as a whole have been more ready to defend state action for the sake of justice than the average citizen of Western democracies, and this presumably has something to do with the teachings of the tradition. But the role assigned to the Jews in the standard missionist arguments is educational, not actively political.

The missionist view of the universal morality of the future represents what I have elsewhere called a "high-flying" universalism.[12] It doesn't involve any close engagement with the actual terrain of moral and political life. It abolishes difference with a philosophical or theological wave of the hand. Oddly, the biblical prophets, who are a central source of missionist arguments, are much more closely engaged. Consider one of the most famous prophetic texts, Isaiah's vision of the "days to come" (cited earlier by Ahad Ha-am), when

> The Mount of the Lord's House
> Shall stand firm above the mountains
> And tower above the hills,
> And all the nations
> Shall gaze on it with joy.
> And the many peoples shall go and say:
> "Come,
> Let us go up to the Mount of the Lord,
> To the House of the God of Jacob,
> That He may instruct us in His ways,
> And that we may walk in His paths."
> For instruction shall come forth from Zion,
> The word of the Lord from Jerusalem,
> Thus He will judge among the nations
> And arbitrate for the many peoples,
> And they shall beat their swords into plowshares.... (2:2–4)

This prophecy is sometimes taken to point toward a world state, with its capital in Jerusalem. But I believe that it suggests a more distinctive form of universalism. The prophet's universe is not composed, like the world of modern reformers and philosophers, of individual men and women who have somehow escaped their "national limitations," transcended their differences, and become citizens of the world. They have only stopped fighting about their differences. Nations and peoples still exist, and what is more telling, they still find themselves in conflict; they are different, and they differ. Even though they all aspire to "walk in His paths," they still need judgment and arbitration – which they seek from God himself, not from some Jewish king sitting in Jerusalem. I take this to mean that the common paths are more like a minimal than a maximal morality. Isaiah represents a "low-flying" universalism, which acknowledges the actually existing landmarks and demarcations of the social terrain. This vision is closer than the vision of reformers and philosophers to what we might think of as classic Judaism. I don't want to say that "low-flying"

---

[12] "Universalism and Jewish Values," Twentieth Morgenthau Memorial Lecture, Carnegie Council on Ethics and International Affairs (New York, 2001).

universalism is more authentically Jewish, for monotheistic faith presses all believers toward some version of moral transcendence. But it is nonetheless more characteristically Jewish.

The Sinai Story

This simultaneous commitment to monotheism and pluralism is supported by the narrative structure of Jewish morality. As I have already said, the moral law is delivered in historical time. More important, the specifically Jewish version of the moral law is delivered at a specific time: after the liberation from Egyptian slavery. The timing is not accidental; it provides the moral and emotional grounding for the Torah's account of justice. We are not to act justly just because God commands it, but also because we remember what it was like to be treated unjustly. "You shall not oppress a stranger, for you know the feelings of the stranger, having yourselves been strangers in the land of Egypt" (Exodus 23:9). The celebration of Passover is designed to sustain this knowledge, and therefore this motivation, across generations: "In every generation, let each person look on himself as if he came forth out of Egypt ... [for] it was not only our fathers that the Holy One, blessed be he, redeemed but us as well did he redeem along with them."[13]

But what about people who don't "remember" the exodus, who don't join in the celebration, and who are not taught each year to think of themselves as slaves and strangers? How can a morality that is so historically focused be given universal force? The Noahide code may appeal to reason, but it has no similar grip on the feelings of the people it binds. Hence one account of Jewish pluralism: all men and women are required to obey the moral law, but the Jews have been given both a more detailed version of the law and a deeper understanding of why it is binding. Maimonides may have some philosophical version of this account in mind when he writes that only a gentile who accepts the Noahide laws "because the Holy One ... commanded them in the Law and made known, through Moses, our teacher, that the observance thereof had been enjoined...." has a place in the world-to-come. "But if his observance thereof is based upon a reasoned conclusion, he is not deemed ... one of the pious of the gentiles, but one of their wise men."[14] Maimonides is probably not interested in what is today called "narrativity," but he is focused on the Sinai event: historical revelation is more important than ahistorical reason. And there is only one historical revelation. (Needless to say, Maimonides' argument outraged all the Jewish universalists, beginning with Spinoza; Moses Mendelssohn and Hermann Cohen also wrote famous protests. The protesters

---

[13] This is from the Passover Haggadah, but the text is very old; it first appears in the Mishnah, Pesahim 10:5.

[14] Hershman, op. cit., p. 230.

actually seem closer to the tradition, which is probably well represented by the passage from Menachem Meiri quoted earlier.)

There is, however, another possibility latent in the Jewish narrative, which is developed, so far as I know, only in the prophetic writings of Amos. In an extraordinary passage, the prophet denies the uniqueness of the exodus from Egypt. That liberation, indeed, liberated only the people of Israel, but there have been others: "Are ye not as the children of the Ethiopians unto me, o children of Israel? . . . Have I not brought Israel out of the land of Egypt, And the Philistines from Caphtor, And the Syrians from Kir?" (Amos 9:7)

While there is only one liberator, there are many different liberations from different "houses" of bondage. Amos doesn't say, and presumably he didn't believe, that the Philistines and the Syrians also had their own moment at Sinai (or its equivalent) and their own covenant with God; he doesn't say that God revealed to each of them their own torah. But his argument invites that further step, and if we take it, then we have another version of low-flying universalism – engaged this time with the historical rather than the political landscape. Imagine a reiterative history: repeated experiences of oppression, liberation, covenant, and moral legislation. Each experience might be different but also recognizably similar; the moral codes of the different peoples would not be the same, but they would overlap in significant ways, even if the narrative in which the code was embedded and the emotions it generated were specific to each case. So Amos' suggestion allows us to retain the particularism of the exodus experience but also point the way to its possible universalization.

This isn't a universalization that anyone could enforce from the outside; nor could anyone determine its precise outcome. Even divine deliverance is, in practice, a form of self-determination – since Israel's God is committed to mediate deliverance through the free will of human beings in the world. Each collective self determines itself differently. But the outcomes can still be judged by any or all of us, at least with reference to something like Novak's "general order of justice" – an order that is not itself the product of self-determination. And Jewish prophets (but others too) can criticize violations of the general order, as Jonah denounced the crimes of the non-Jewish city of Nineveh.

How much is included in the general order, how extensive the seven laws of the Noahide code really are, how wide the range of prophetic criticism is – there are many discussions of these questions in Jewish writing, but none that has become authoritative. Until recent times, Jews have not been sufficiently engaged in the politics of the others; the questions have not been urgent. Now that they are urgent, most Jews, at least, most American Jews, are likely to respond to them as liberal universalists; they will respond in the style of Moritz Lazarus, Cohen, Kaplan, and Ahad Ha-am, and they will believe, most of them, that this is the characteristic Jewish response. It is, indeed, one Jewish response, a very important one, but perhaps not the one that is closest to the classic Jewish understanding of the moral universe.

The Experience of Massacre

Those same liberal Jews, however, would also be drawn to a contemporary restatement of the classic understanding. In addition to the exodus story, there is another Jewish story that can be, and obviously has been, reiterated among "the nations" – the story of persecution and mass murder. And so it is possible to construct a specifically Jewish argument, not only in favor of clean hands, but also in favor of the universal enforcement of human rights, above all, of the rights to life and liberty. Consider the case of Rwanda, where there was no enforcement at all and almost a million people died. Phillip Gourevitch has written a book about the Rwandan massacres, memorably entitled *We Wish to Inform You that Tomorrow We Will be Killed with Our Families* (1998). The Jewish argument for intervening to stop the killing and punish the killers would start from that sentence, and it would paraphrase the line about strangers from the book of Exodus that I have already quoted: "You shall hurry to rescue those who are waiting to be killed, for you know the feelings of those who are waiting to be killed, having waited yourselves in the years of Nazi tyranny." This is a characteristically particularist argument with a universal conclusion: all those who wait to be killed should be rescued. In the years of the Yugoslav civil wars, and of Rwanda, and of East Timor, and of Sudan, many Jews felt an obligation to make this argument (as Elie Wiesel famously did in an encounter with President Clinton), speaking with the moral authority that comes from the experience of suffering. But anyone who speaks this way must recognize that others too have the same authority. It isn't only Jews who have endured the slaughter of the innocent. This experience sets an absolute limit on what can be tolerated in the society of nations – and here the sons of Noah and the people of Israel have exactly the same obligations: they have been commanded, we might say, not only to respect the human rights to life and liberty, the laws against murder and cruelty, but to enforce them whenever they need to be, and whenever they can be, enforced. We all live "under" this commandment, whether or not we remember when or how we "accepted" it upon ourselves.

4

Globalization and Christian Ethics

Max L. Stackhouse

There is no single attitude or program, statement, or orientation that articulates a Christian approach to the globalization of ethics, or, for that matter, to global trends in society, economics, culture, technology, law, or politics, which are often the carriers of religiously rooted ethical principles and ends. That is in part because there are competing definitions of what globalization is, its sources, range, and effects, and in part because there are several alternative understandings of what the most important features of Christian ethics are. Neither the biblical resources nor the classical traditions present Christians with a monolithic perspective. Although there is one Christ, he is portrayed in the Gospels by many authors, and although there is one God, that unity is held to be constituted by a trinitarian set of "persons" in interactive relationship.

In ethics as well as in theology, which is always a companion to ethics in the Christian tradition, several key modes of normative discourse have been joined in various ways in various parts of the tradition. Thus, in order to focus the discussion, so that it does not sprawl in all directions, I shall proceed in four steps. First, I will describe what I take to be the major modes of Christian moral discourse needed to address this question of the globalization of ethics. Second, after setting out these modes of moral discourse, and emphasizing how they necessarily interrelate in all actual Christian moral judgments, I will use this approach to evaluate the relative merits of two major, antithetical, understandings of globalization in debate among Christians today. Third, I will indicate what I think the most faithful and compelling Christian perspective on a global ethic might be. I will conclude by noting how the pluralism among Christian ethical perspectives emphasizes the value of conversation on this issue with other traditions of ethical thinking.

In a widely read book, *The Responsible Self* (1963), H. Richard Niebuhr reviews the classic traditions of philosophical and theological ethics and applies them to an understanding of personal morality. He states that ethics has been usually treated in term of two major modes of moral discourse: one deontological, the other teleological. The first investigates the question of whether there

are law-like principles that are knowable and binding on humans, principles
that identify universal standards of right and wrong. In this mode, every person
is held to be a cosmopolitan citizen, living under a divinely given natural law.
This deontic sense that there is a moral law that humans did not construct,
but have to interpret and apply, is sometimes identified with key elements
of the Platonic and Stoic understandings of justice in antiquity, with Locke's
"self-evident truths" or Kant's "categorical imperatives" in early modernity,
and with "universal human rights" in contemporary life. In Christian thought,
these laws are held to exist in the mind or character of God, and are written into
the hearts of all who bear the "image of God," and the paradigmatic biblical
summaries of these laws are the Ten Commandments and the commands to
love God and the "other."[1] Indeed, the philosophical forms of deontology are
viewed as attempts to show that these laws can be reasonably known.[2]

   The second mode of moral discourse studies whether we can know the
basic ends that we should pursue, and if so what we should intend, hope
for, and live toward, and thus what evils we should avoid or constrain. In
this mode, humans are seen as agents of proximate or ultimate purposes, to
enhance the well-being of persons, to enhance the common good of the community, or to actualize God's purposes for humanity for souls and societies.
Humanity and human institutions are to be agents of and for what is good.
While this telic sense that we can and should commit our lives to that which is
good in itself is identified (1) with Aristotle or Thomas and the cultivation of
virtue in pre-modern traditions, (2) with Mill or Dewey in modern form, and
(3) with the spread of democratic government and open economies by many
in contemporary life, the classic promise of teleological ends can be found in
the "blessings" of the Reign of God as they indicate the parabolic coming of
"a new heaven and a new earth" and with the promise of a "New Jerusalem,"
beyond history. Indeed, many views of the good and especially the common
good can be seen as intimations of what is signaled in the Sermon on the
Mount and parallel statements of the coming eschatological possibilities that
God intends for all peoples.[3]

---

[1] See, for example, Paul G. Kuntz (2004), *The Ten Commandments in History: Mosaic Paradigms
    for a Well-Ordered Society*; Jean Porter (1995), *Natural and Divine Law: Reclaiming the
    Tradition for Christian Ethics*; and Walter Harrison (1997), *The Ten Commandments and
    Human Rights*, rev. ed.
[2] Not only philosophies, but also various religions. Hans Küng was the primary author of the
    "Declaration Toward a Global Ethic," passed by the Parliament of the World's Religions in
    1993. The core of this Declaration rather obviously echoes the Ten Commandments, and the
    subscription to them by many signatories suggests that some religious particularities may in
    fact bear within them universalistic principles that can be affirmed by all. See *A Global Ethic*
    (1995).
[3] See, for example, Dennis McCann & Patrick Miller, eds., *In Search of the Common Good*
    (Harrisburg, PA: Trinity Press International, 2005) for representative Catholic and Protestant
    views in dialogue with each other and a number of non-theological views. However, in this

But in light of the fact that Christianity is a historically oriented religion that has evoked a dramatic sense of existence, and the impact of Christianity on cultures has often induced radical social change, Niebuhr argues for a third kind of moral discourse, one that interprets vital dynamics of life in a way that enables us to respond creatively and fittingly. In making this argument, he touches on a view that most Christians endorse: the Lord of history shapes all the contexts in which we live. This is so even if it is also the case that humans are ever disposed to corrupt the moral contexts of life, the "ethos," that sustain us, and even if "the powers" – those psycho- and socio-spiritual forces of human relational and institutional life that tend to capture our loyalties and sometimes go out of control – become self-idolatrous, pursue their own ends, and make social life incapable of being genuinely responsive, and thus unfit for human habitation. These "powers," which can become demonic in effect, are variously called, in scripture, the "principalities, authorities, thrones and dominions."[4]

Yet, many Christians view history in a way that sees God's repeated and providential reformation of those relationships and institutions in such a way that "the powers" can, in some measure, be drawn into associations of disciplined moral service under God's laws and for God's intended purposes and thereby better serve rather than only disrupt human flourishing.[5] The "spirit" or "mentality" or "ethos" of a community can be transformed and renewed. Thus, a social theology of history, studied by what some call "ethology," enables us to read the dynamic ethos as it undergoes rapid social change, and see what possibilities there are to contain a plunge toward destruction or for cultivating its potentials. This approach is also taken to be a mode of ethical reflection. Behind this, according to Christians, is the belief that there is a master narrative lurking at the depths of human history. Every social development can be seen as under "the powers" (such as Mammon or Mars) in various degrees, or more or less constrained or guided by grace. H. Richard Niebuhr, to be sure, saw this as particularly pertinent to issues involving personal responsibility,

---

area, world religions and philosophies seldom agree in the long run, even if they can largely agree on deontological matters and can find overlapping similarities in regard to the analysis of the contexts of life, which we shall come to shortly. This eschatological difference has been clearly argued in Mark Heim, *Salvations* (Maryknoll, NY: Orbis Press, 1995), in which he sees the fundamental difference between religions in the ultimate end that they see as the goal of life. The Buddhist nirvana, for example, is simply different from the Islamic paradise, the Confucian harmony of heaven, earth, and society, the Marxist perfect classless society, or the Christian New Jerusalem, and these ultimate ends, when deeply believed, shape all proximate and penultimate ends that we think we ought to pursue.

4 See G. B. Caird (1956), *Principalities and Powers*, now a classic on these terms; and Walter Wink's trilogy (1984, 1986, 1992) *Naming the Powers, Unmasking the Powers, and Engaging the Powers* reflects further study of the social political implications of these biblical terms.

5 For this reason, Christians often debate with great intensity the moral shape of family life, of polity in church and society, of rights and duties in politics, of economic systems, and of the procedures of decision making in all areas of life.

while others, from Augustine (in his City of God) to Niebuhr's brother, Reinhold, sought to interpret social history in ethical and theological terms, without losing sight of the moral law, a vision of God's ultimate destiny for humankind, or the real wrongs and evils that abound. One thinks not only of the great reformers of the church, but others from the Dutch neo-Calvinist Abraham Kuyper, to the German Lutheran martyr Dietrich Bonhoeffer, to the remarkable "Social Encyclicals" of the twentieth-century Roman Catholic popes, to Martin Luther King, Jr., to the new generation of Christian leaders arising in the developing countries.

I think it is true that all profound traditions of ethics must contain all three elements in some juxtaposition, and that Christian ethics has done this in distinctive ways with various accents on various modes at different times. This implies that every ethical judgment, polity, or program is inevitably synthetic – an integrative effort to grasp both the historical particularities of a changing and changeable ethos, and to engage that dynamic ethos on the basis of the universal absolutes of deontic principles and a vision of the ultimate ends that we hold to be sacred. Thus, paralleling the doctrine of the Trinity at the level of fundamental Christian beliefs, a basic triunity of reference points constitutes, together, the primary way of understanding how to do ethics.

Christians have engaged ethical issues in particular ways that may nevertheless have general implications, especially in regard to globalization, for it demands a catholic, reforming, and ecumenical outlook. Indeed, it is likely that catholic, reformed, and ecumenical Christian influences over the centuries helped generate globalization, that it cannot be understood without reference to these influences, and that any modification of it may require further theologically guided alteration of the "powers" in the institutions and behaviors of globalizing activities.[6]

Reading our Globalizing Ethos

Today, the most disputed area of ethics has to do with competing attempts to discern what is going on morally and spiritually in globalization, and how to relate that dramatic development to the first principles or ultimate ends that Christians endorse. Clearly the contexts of life in which increasing percentages of the world's population live are undergoing transformations, and these changes are creating a wider context that comprehends and modifies all local social and cultural contexts. This dynamic change has many implications for the world as a bio-physical planet, for the world as an interdependent cluster

---

[6] Without the interaction of these reference points, an ethic, including that of Christianity, tends to become perilous. If ethics is understood solely as universal principles, moralism or legalism tends to ensue. If only an eschatological vision becomes the focus, millennial dreams or militant utopianism tempt us. And if the focus is only on the historical situation, ethics becomes little more than journalism or, at best, a sociological commentary.

of societies, and the world as a philosophical, theological and ethical concept.[7] While Christianity and other religions have had world-comprehending perspectives for centuries, the extent and rapidity of current change demands a reassessment of those influences that have contributed to the expansive ethos that is now disrupting and changing every cultural, political, and economic order, but also potentially leading humanity toward a new encompassing world civilization, one of greater complexity, pluralism, diversity, and inclusiveness than the world has yet seen.

People from various backgrounds have very strong views about these issues. Many are locally affected by the changes and are not unwilling to project local experiences and interests onto a global screen. Kofi Annan, Secretary-General of the United Nations, pointed out some time ago that many see "globalization" less as "a term describing objective reality" about the creation of a new civilizational possibility than as "an ideology of predatory capitalism," which they experience as a kind of "siege." Against it, they join a "backlash" that takes at least three major forms (Annan, 1999). One is a growing nationalism (often using religious identity as a cement to form an otherwise failing sense of solidarity), threatening multi-ethnic states. The second, more troubling in view of the history of the twentieth century, is the call for strong, often authoritarian, leaders who seek to mobilize popular sentiment against "foreign" influences. And the third is the attempt to use globalization as a scapegoat for all the ills that in fact "have domestic roots" of a local political and social nature. To many who hold these views, "globalization" has little to do with religion, theology, or ethics except the threatening of the folkways in which they used to live. They do not know how to resist it, control it, or to join it; they view it as the actions of some powerful "them" disrupting their traditions and imposing "secular" or "materialistic" alien forms of corrupted morality. They resist this by appealing to a hostile and defensive form of piety – often by reasserting (or reinventing) local traditions in fundamentalist form. Thus, they resist the contemporary globalization of the ethics born by many global trends.

What many note about globalization above all is the emergence of global business, especially as conducted by trans- or multi-national corporations using modern technologies that alter older ecological and social systems. Thus, many tend to identify globalization primarily with the increase of power and economic privilege on the part of some and the corresponding decline of power and status on the part of others, even if most gain materially in some measure.[8] This economistic view is very widespread among advocates for the poorer segments of the world's population, but it appears to be based more in cultural

---

[7] I draw many of the following themes, as well as some of the methodological points treated above, from the first three volumes of Stackhouse's *God and Globalization* (2000, 2001, 2002). Motifs from this chapter will appear in the fourth and final volume, forthcoming.

[8] This is the view, as I understand it, of my friend I. J. M. Razu (2001), *Transnational corporations as Agents of Dehumanization.*

and religious perspectives than on compelling economic evidence.[9] Further, while both the anti-government libertarian and the anti-market socialist voices are today muted, and very few advocate either a totally free market or a totally state-run economy, the echoes of older capitalist vs. socialist debates still resound in the rhetoric of many economistic arguments – including those found in Christian circles.[10] Often, these views are combined in various ways and incorporated into one of several representative social theologies of history by which globalization is interpreted and to which the first principles of right and wrong and the varying views of good and evil ends are applied. We can sketch these, in typological fashion, recognizing that there are nuanced variations of all of them.

Globalization as "Another Fall"

This perspective sees social history in terms of political economy and its succession of lapses from the kind and quality of life that God intended and Christ called for. The first fall, of course, is portrayed in a mythic story of the generic human departure from a primal harmony that God intended for humanity and nature. In post-mythic history, humanity lives in a world of tempting desires, distorting deception, bloody competition, and pretentious arrogance, and in tension with the forces of the ecosphere. Judgment was rendered against human civilization by paradigmatic events – natural disaster (Noah), cultural division (Babel), and social enslavement (Pharaoh). God, to be sure, raised up first Abraham and later Moses to lead the people to a city that has foundations and to a mountain where a divine law was disclosed. But the people kept wandering after false gods, in spite of the warnings of prophets and sages, who faithfully kept alive the hope for a coming messiah who would fulfill the law and inaugurate a new age.

Christians hold that the good news of the Gospel is that the Messiah has come in Jesus Christ and formed a new kind of community, based in faith, love, and hope made present in him. In the "another fall" view, however, this cluster of commitments is essentially alien to the institutions of the common life. They demand a counter-cultural form of discipleship and organization. In the Roman Catholic and Eastern Orthodox churches, this impulse took

---

[9] These economistic assumptions are challenged by the data gathered by Martin Wolf (2002), *Why Globalization Works*, on strictly economic data grounds, and by the studies assembled by Peter Berger, et al. (2002), *Many Globalizations: Cultural Diversity and the Contemporary World*, on comparative sociological grounds. The latter documents the ways that religions and cultures shape globalizing influences when people embrace them and adapt them to their traditions and their traditions to them.

[10] See, for example, the several documents of the World Council of Churches on economic globalization at http://www.wcc-coe.org/wcc/what/jpc. Cf. Rob van Drimmelen, *Faith in the Global Economy* (Geneva: World Council of Churches, 1998) and Peter Heslam, ed., *Globalization and the Good* (London: SPCK, 2004).

shape in the great monastic traditions, emblems in a sinful and broken world of an entirely other order of reality, demanding an alternative lifestyle that eventually became articulate in the vows of poverty, chastity, and obedience (to this alternative reality as manifest in the discipline of their order, and thus not to any earthly social order). Laity were expected to be economically engaged, to be married, and to serve an earthly "lord" in battle as necessary; but this involvement with wealth, sex, and power entailed a lower spiritual status.

However, over the centuries, the church became wedded to imperial power when Constantine not only demanded toleration for but also supported the establishment of the faith. This brought with it economic privileges and a changed attitude toward the use of force, with teachings (later known as the "Just War Doctrine") that made distinctions between just and unjust use of coercive power.[11] In the perspective of this first view as it took root over the centuries, this Constantinian development was seen as another "fall," now of the "official" churches insofar as their embrace of and by political power led, as some say, directly to crusades, inquisitions, religious wars, colonialism, and the Holocaust. Against this captivity of the established churches to the idol of Mars, we need a recovery of the Gospel for the faithful, confessing church, standing as an alternative witness to the powers of the world and against a faith that has compromised both the law of love and the peaceful purposes of God's reign.

This "confessing" sectarian type of Christianity is not the only example of the notion of an alternative believing community. Other Christians, often tied with populist movements, are more "radical" in their sense of Christian alienation from the structures and powers of society, and they have taken their convictions in a more militant direction. They have seen it to be a sacred duty to confront "the powers" that be, in reality the artifices of power elites. To set things right, they are willing to use force in "just revolutions." Thus, they chart a Christian way of open dissent, opposition, and, in some cases, revolt, willingly accepting the role of martyr at the hands of established power. A famous hymn by James Russell Lowell states this mood in poetic terms:

> Though the cause of evil prosper, Yet 'tis truth alone is strong;
> Though her portion be the scaffold, And upon the throne is wrong.
> Yet that scaffold sways the future, And behind the dim unknown,
> Standeth God within the shadow, Keeping watch above his own.

---

[11] This is one of the key doctrinal developments in the early Catholic tradition, one that now informs most of the Christian traditions. Although a minority defend pacifism, and it is presumed by all that we should ordinarily live with our neighbors in peace, it is also recognized that Christian participation in politics depends on the view that ethical principles can apply to all areas of life, including the use of military and police forces to ensure the defense of the neighbor, to prevent the disruption of civility, and to contribute to a just society. The Peace, Catholic, and Main-line Protestant churches generally agree, however, that Just War criteria have not always been used by Christian leaders, and that some wars, even if they were justifiable, might well have been differently conducted had they done so.

Here too is a counter-cultural vision, in continuity in some ways with the early Manichaeans, the Peasant Revolts of the late Middle Ages, the Diggers and Levellers of the Puritan period, and some slave uprisings. The vision persists into the present among some liberation theologies: to be faithful means to be in radical solidarity with people's revolutions when they arise, for they experience the violation of first principles in society most directly and they see the promise of a redemptive reversal of good and evil most clearly.

However, for many in these two wings of the Christian tradition, a further fall is lurking, if not already here. During the period that we now call the Enlightenment, many intellectuals turned to humanistic philosophies and scientific methods in efforts to overcome the dogmas that, they said, had caused violence and wars. Their project, however, had unintended consequences. Out of their repudiation of theology as a mode of public discourse and resource for ethics, a hyper-modernist set of secular ideologies developed that accepted the techno-scientific view of nature with its utilitarian view of reason, fomented the industrial revolution that displaced millions of people (and is doing so still in developing countries), fostered "Manchesterism" (now called "Neoliberalism"), and unleashed human greed. This generated a capitalist economic system that has little regard for (1) faith, (2) the moral law "written on the heart," (3) an eschatological vision that portrays another dimension of reality, (4) the character of traditional communities, or (5) the intrinsic worth of the earth. Everything becomes a commodity, marketed for gain, and "the good" is reduced to "more." In globalization, we face the consequences of these developments, terrors of imperialism again, now less from the geo-politics of iron and blood than from the geo-economics of markets and profit.[12]

Aided in many respects by the rise of the modern nation-state and its tendency to dominate all of society, and later by the trenchant criticism of free-market capitalism by Karl Marx, even if political prescriptions of his disciple, Lenin, turned out to be disastrous, it was possible for a time to regulate the emerging power of the technocratic corporation. However, the development of the corporation in its multi-national or trans-national forms made it possible for the capitalist system to escape the control of political and legal constraints. Thus Mammon became the functional deity of post- modernity – the driving force of a globalization that chews up all in its rationalized, calculating, neo-colonial path. This is the primary reality of the globalization that is engulfing the world and impoverishing the peoples of the world while benefitting those in command of the new world economy, the corporate and financial hidden

[12] I draw this typological sketch from one of its leading theological advocates, Ulrich Duchrow. See his *Global Economy: A Confessional Issue for the Churches* (1987); and his *Alternatives to Global Capitalism* (1995) as well as from parallel sources, some of which he cites: R. H. Tawney, *Religion and the Rise of Capitalism* (1926); Karl Polanyi, *The Great Transformation* (1944); David Korten, *When Corporations Rule the World* (1995); F. J. Hinkelammert, *The Ideological Weapons of Death: A Theological Critique of Capitalism* (1986); and, in some ways, Walter Wink, *Naming the Powers; Unmasking the Powers; Engaging the Powers*, op. cit.

elites who are served not only by the armies of the great powers, but also by their new international inventions, the IMF, World Bank, and WTO.[13] These together are crucifying the weaker peoples of the world and destroying the ecological systems that make life possible.[14] Against this, many say, believers must raise their voice in prophetic protest by becoming again a confessing or a radical church. They must again reassert that God is Lord, support solidarity with various people's movements, seek to overcome the rampant individualism and materialism of modern life, and oppose those who are engaged with Mammon as well as Mars.

The "Providential Grace" View

A second theology of history is held, in various versions, by a large percentage of the world's Christians who believe that the dynamics of the common life, personal and social, can only be grasped and interpreted at its deeper levels theologically – although it has only rarely, so far, been so articulated in regard to contemporary globalization.[15] This second view of the globalizing ethos also

[13] In fact, the creation of these new international institutions, like that of the United Nations in politics, can be seen as the nascent, if still weak and under-developed efforts to bring world economic interactions under agreed upon principles of just law after the end of colonialism, with its imposition of national laws on many regions, and for purposes such as aiding poorer countries and aiding development.

[14] In his new book, Columbia University economist Jagdish Bhagwati takes up these charges one by one and summarizes the data of the many studies that have (some reluctantly, others enthusiastically) refuted them. See his *In Defense of Globalization* (2004). In brief, where the dynamics of globalization are embraced, as in China, India, Brazil, Peru, and so on, they dramatically raise the standards of living more pervasively and rapidly than at any other time in history. Further, they create new middle classes at astounding rates, the most remarkable economic result of globalization, although it is also true that they create (at least temporarily) greater ranges of inequality between those who benefit greatly and those who do less. Those parts of the world that remain in poverty usually do not have the kind of ethos that fosters change, the formation of a civil society distinct from kinship and one-party political institutions. The ethical issue this data raises is whether the reduction of poverty can and should override the ethical ideal of local communal or national identity, and thus whether agents of globalization should continue to introduce those religious, ethical, and material options that bring with them transformation, the prospect of participation in the global community, and increased opportunity for many, even if not for all.

[15] This view is more often held by believing, modernized laity than by clergy, but a few theologians have seriously grappled with these issues in a systematic way. Among the new, creative works in this area, see especially: David Hollenbach, S. J., *The Global Face of Public Faith: Politics, Human Rights, and Christian Ethics* (2003), who is in dialogue with official Catholic and ecumenical statements; William Schweiker (2004), *Theological Ethics and Global Dynamics*, who is in dialogue with contemporary philosophy and hermeneutics; Amos Yong & P. G. Heltzel (2004), *Theology in a Global Context*, which is in dialogue with the philosophy or religion; and Leonardo Boff (2005), *Global Civilization: Challenges to Society and Christianity*, who is in dialogue with the liberationist movements of Latin America. My own perspective is also influenced by dialogue with the sociology of religion.

recognizes the centrality of Creation, Fall, and Redemption, but it sees them in another aspect. This view is alert to the fact that humans inevitably distort the gifts that God gives humanity. In fact, it may take the doctrine of sin more seriously than the confessional and the radical positions mentioned earlier, for it sees life as fraught with the kind of struggle for survival that Darwin identified.[16] Thus, it recognizes globalization's obvious ambiguities. Yet it sees the chief forms of sin not in the use of legitimate coercive power by political authority, nor in the development of instrumental reason in advanced, modern technology, nor in the operations of a market-oriented economic system, nor in the organization of corporations, but in the wanton violence, ignorance, scarcity, poverty, and mistrust that occurs when these are not present or not guided by a religiously and ethically shaped civil society, a regulated system of just law, and a hope for a better world beyond the wrongs and evils of history. And in spite of the fact that politics, technology, and economy are sometimes distorted and misused, this view sees society and history as also influenced by moral and spiritual realities so that we can rejoice when the frequency and severity of wrong is reduced, some persistent evils are at least partly overcome, and some measure of good is done. Further, while believing that in Christ a new age has begun that points toward Redemption, most of social life is lived in the midst of conditions that remain sinful, broken, and distorted, from which neither confessing churches nor radical movements are exempt. Thus, most of ethics has to do with how to live in the "in-between" times, where providential grace sustains civilized life in ways that reduce drudgery, want, pain, suffering, injustice, and premature death.[17] And one of the tasks of theology is to work with philosophy, science, and social analysis to form and sustain the moral architecture for civil society.

The ever-present evils are mitigated when humans are enabled to use the gifts they are given: the story of creation tells us that humanity is stamped with the divine image, commanded to have dominion over the earth, and given the

---

[16] Many Christians who are inclined to accept this second view doubt that Darwinism is ultimately valid. It is not that they reject evolution, as do some fundamentalists, but that they see the "bloody law of tooth and claw" logic it implies as the law of life as only true at some levels of existence. In fact, these Christians can be said to view Darwinism in much the same way that classical Christians doubted earlier forms of "fatalism," or the rule of life by blind material forces. Instead, they believe both that existence has a deeper ontological dimension, and that history is ultimately, if not always proximately, governed by more profound moral and spiritual dynamics that modulate the struggles and grace all areas of life. See Luis Lugo (2000) *Religion, Pluralism, and Public Life*; Lawrence Harrison, et al. (2000), *Culture Matters: How Values Shape Human Progress*; and James Skillen, *In Pursuit of Justice* (2004).

[17] This view is often called "Christian Realism" and was articulated by Reinhold Niebuhr in the crisis of the mid-twentieth century when both the neo-pagan Nazis and the militantly secular Communists threatened the world and neither confessional nor radical Christian stances were able to challenge them effectively on the ground. See especially Niebuhr's *The Nature and Destiny of Man* (1939–41, vol. 2). There is a current revival of his thought today.

capabilities that allow the cultivation of its incomplete possibilities. The residual capacities to reason, choose, and care (*intellectus*, *voluntas*, and *caritas*) remain part of each person's potential and can be nurtured by a sound faith so as to make the quest for truth, the principles of freedom, and the relative possibilities of justice more actual in the common life. Moreover, this view holds that God, the source and object of that faith, is ultimately the Lord of history, and God's expansive, providential grace anchors human existence in covenanted communities and vocational commitments. The church particularly is called on to preach, teach, and cultivate this grace, so that all can live in a viable ethos able to sustain a viable civilization and create the possibilities of a more abundant and just "modernized" society. And although it recognizes that some modernizers repudiate religion or theology, it views them as a modern form of "flat earth" thinking, plagued by an incapacity to imagine the heights and depths of mind, heart, and passion.[18]

This view draws on the Bible and religiously sympathetic social theory to identify those paradigmatic events and developments that allow us to interpret contemporary history.[19] When applied to an understanding of globalization, this view reminds us that when Greek cultural influence, Roman political rule, and vast networks of trade connected Europe to both Asia and Africa, the first proto-globalized civilization was formed. In God's providence, that is when the Christian movement was formed and began to expand, extending once-tribal boundaries of covenantal bonding, renewing the understanding of the universal moral law, and offering a new vision of God's salvific purposes, now open to all the peoples of the world. The life, teaching, death, and resurrection of Jesus were taken as evidence that God's Kingdom was inaugurated, providentially working in the hearts of persons and in the very fabric of social history. It oriented then, and it orients now, all who would attend to the vision of a complex, comprehending and holy civilization, a New Jerusalem on the far side of history to which all nations could bring their gifts – the divinely intended end for humanity to which all may contribute (Goudzwaard, et al. 2001). Christianity formed on this basis not only affirms a universal moral law, it transforms the inner structure of every person and society it encounters and orients all of

---

[18] See William F. Storrar, et al. (2004), *Public Theology for the 21st Century*.

[19] This view tends to draw more from Max Weber than from Karl Marx. It does so because Weber took religion seriously as a causative factor in social, political, and economic ethics, and not only as a product of social forces, magic, myth, or interests. Moreover, he studied the major religions and ideologies on a comparative basis and held that they were, more or less, rational systems. Yet he held that different ones had differing effects on social life because the assumptions behind their rationality and the constituencies to which they appealed shaped the way reason was deployed. It is true that he thought modernity toward which Protestantism led inclined us to secularism, but he also foresaw the possible resurgence of religion – as now seems to be the case around the world. In one sense, it can be said that many theologians and Christian ethicists studying globalization take key elements from Weber in much the same way as earlier parts of the tradition selectively adopted and baptized Aristotle.

life toward a new, trans-natural telos. Until that ultimate promise is fulfilled, personal meaning and human society is sustained by providential grace, even in the face of wrong and evil.

In such a view of history, it is possible to see the impetus for several ethical dynamics that became decisive in forming the moral and spiritual bases of today's globalization. For one thing, these developments substantively shaped other parts of the world – the early Greek church shaped all of Eastern Orthodoxy, and through it Slavic civilization, as the Roman tradition shaped Catholic Europe and Latin America, and as the Reformation did much of Northern Europe and America. Beyond the West, various missionary movements not only converted souls and planted churches, they spread modern education, medical care, ideas of the equality of men and women and all races before God (and gradually also in church and society),[20] and the notion of inalienable rights (which also entailed the freedom of religion, and the rights of speech, assembly, and association), constitutional democracy, technology, and economy opportunity – all taken by those who hold to this theology of history as signs of God's continuing and expansive grace.[21] These, after many centuries of slow and widely resisted development, formed a new ethos by providing the moral and spiritual architecture for the complex and dynamic civilizational transformations now on the horizon.[22] Some leaders of other religions (some Muslims, Hindus, and tribalists, for example) who are hostile to the effects of modernization and globalization on their own society are not entirely wrong when they blame it on Christianity and its ethics. The implication of this brief sketch of Christianity's influence on societies, often

---

[20] See, in terms of the contemporary implications of these movements in global developments, for example, Robert W. Hefner (1995), *Conversion to Christianity* (with special focus on the Islamic world in Malaysia/Indonesia). Cf. David Martin (1990), *Tongues of Fire: The Explosion of Protestantism in Latin America*; Philip Jenkins (2002), *The Next Christendom: The Coming of Global Christianity* regarding Africa; and David Aikman (2003), *Jesus in Beijing: How Christianity is Transforming China and Changing the Balance of Power in the World.*

[21] I traced the historical background of many of these developments in my book *Creeds, Society, and Human Rights, A Study in Three Cultures* (1984) in comparison with developments in Eastern Europe and South Asia. For a new, compelling study of how direct the influence of Christian ideas were, see John Nurser (2005), *For All Peoples and All Nations: The Ecumenical Church and Human Rights*, which traces in great detail the ways in which the development of the United Nations Declaration of Human Rights was essentially driven by Christian thinkers with Jewish support, drawing on deep traditions, supported by parachurch NGOs working behind the scenes from the 1930s on. And recently, with Lawrence Stratton, I have written a bibliographical essay calling attention to the growing body of research that challenges the conventional secular views of these developments and documents the theological influences on them: *Capitalism, Civil Society, Religion and the Poor* (2002).

[22] See John Witte, Jr., et al. (1999), *Sharing the Book: Religious Perspectives on the Rights and Wrongs of Proselytism*. Cf. Lalsangkima Pachuau, et al. (forthcoming), *News of Boundless Riches: Interrogating and Reconstructing Missions in a Global Era.*

unintentionally, is that once we become aware of unintended consequences of the faith, that faith may have to take upon itself the responsibility of forming and informing an emergent global civilization ethically in an intentional way with a new consciousness of its encounter with other religions and cultures.

The deeper historical evidence suggests that the classic Roman Catholic, Reformation, and now the newer Evangelical and Pentecostal traditions tend to generate an ethos that foments modernization, a fact that is arguably traceable to a basic attitude toward the duty to convert souls and societies and gain stewardly dominion over the ecosphere in a fallen world. However, for this to take place, people must be free to change or modify their religion, their culture, their society, their environment. To insist that one must remain in the context of the ethnic group into which one is born, or be obedient to fixed social ontocracy, or to a pre-given cultural, political, or racial pattern of life leads to a lie in the soul, a repression of the capacities to reason, choose, and form affectional bonds, and often to the formation of new fundamentalist movements to secure local and static identity.[23] If conversion is successful, it forms new associations and creates the social space for a civil society wherein people develop their own institutions and leadership, seek to influence the hearts of others, reform the ethics of public institutions, and openly debate the truth and relevance of the first principles of justice and the ultimate ends of life.

The development of a pluralist civil society was aided in the West by the little-known history behind the development of the modern corporation. The formation of ecclesiastical organizations that fought for and eventually won the rights to hold property and engage in production and trade outside the control of the patriarchs of the family and the grasp of the princes established the precedents for both non-profit and business corporations.[24] In a long history, these have become the primary organizational home of complex social and economic activities in modern and now global life. They took root first in the European cities of the Middle Ages and the Renaissance/Reformation periods, as a wide variety of autocephalous bodies were formed.[25] Some became universities or hospitals, some took the form of proto-democratic organizations (elected town governments and populist lay movements), and some evolved into limited liability, trustee-guided, for-profit economic organizations.[26] These supported concepts of basic rights, governance under law, and

---

[23] See the multi-volumed series edited by Martin Marty and Scott Appleby, as a part of the cross-cultural studies "The Fundamentalism Project." The overview volume is *Fundamentalism Comprehended*. (Chicago: University of Chicago Press, 2004). It is argued that Fundamentalism is much the same in all the world's religions and frequently forms itself in resistance to historical change and cultural or ethnic pluralism.

[24] See, especially, H. J. Berman (2003), *Law and Revolution*.

[25] This development was earlier (c.1914) charted by Max Weber (1968) in "The City," in a way that Berman thinks needs revision.

[26] See my "The Moral Roots of the Corporation" *Theology and Public Policy* (1993).

the cultivation of civic virtues. They evoked wider reflections on the doctrines of covenant and vocation, and applied them to daily life.[27]

Moreover, the impetus to change the world by the use of the "mechanical arts" gave rise to modern technology. That impetus came from the doctrines of protology and eschatology, but became a part of providential thought. Nature was interpreted as fallen, needing repair and development to be what God intended it to be. The intention in religiously cultivating these arts was, however, not only the restoration of basic "original design," corrupted in the fall; it became also (especially under the influence of the Joachite movement) the formation of a more just and abundant society, one that reduced the drudgery of the many, and pointed toward, even if it could not attain, the hoped-for vision of the New Jerusalem.[28] While every civilization has had its scientists and philosophers of nature, it is essentially in a Christian environment, driven by these concerns, that technology in its modern forms was theologically driven, and that it not only shaped the Industrial Revolution, but altered communications, medicine, production, education, and transportation, and produced, more recently, bio-engineering and geo-engineering.[29] The ethical consequence of these developments is that many in Christian-influenced cultures see it as a moral mandate to form pluralistic societies with many kinds of institutional spheres, to establish and defend constitutional democracies with guarantees of human rights, and to develop open market economies and the technological capacity to produce wealth and manage the ecosphere.

There have been frighteningly ambiguous effects of each one of these developments, all of which, cumulatively, are the progenitors of globalization. The frightening possibilities appear, many Christians say, when humans begin to think that they are sovereign over life and do not see the capacities to develop these possibilities as under God's laws and for Godly purposes. While reforms, constraints, and limits must be put on a number of them, they are, at bottom, seen in this view as a manifestation of the expansive, providential grace that needs to be shared with those presently left out, helping them become prepared for these dynamic changes and inviting them to bring resources from their own traditions and cultures to enrich and refine them. Constitutional

---

[27] For the historical impact of the Biblical concept of covenant over the centuries, see Daniel J. Elazar (1995–2000), *The Covenant Tradition in Politics.* For a summary of the ethical implications of the doctrine of vocation, see my "Vocation," *Oxford Handbook of Theological Ethics* (2004).

[28] On this see note 11, especially David Noble, *The Religion of Technology: The Divinity of Man and the Spirit of Invention,* op. cit. Some of his interpretations are controversial, but the work contains a suggestive review of historic sources on this thesis. For a similar argument from a cross-cultural point of view, see Toby Huff, *The Rise of Early Modern Science: Islam, China, and the West* (New York: Cambridge University Press, 1993).

[29] These themes are artfully summarized in Brad Allenby (2002), *Observations on the Philosophic Implications of Earth Systems Engineering and Management.* See also David Landes (1983), *Revolution in Time.*

democracy, human rights, the corporation as part of civil society, and technology are among the contemporary worldly carriers of the secondary, often unintended, effects of the Christian ethical vision, socially incarnated.[30]

Indeed, globalization fed by these developments may well be a new form of missions, a mandate for our time to invite all the peoples of the world to become participants in a global civil society that is marked by the empowerment of the people in these ways. The church and its leadership will probably have to recover its memory in these areas, critically evaluate where these developments have gone wrong as a result of distorted theological and ethical influences or the arrogant denial of them, and take responsibility for the consequences of its own doctrines and actions insofar as this is so. Further, it may have to consciously prepare the people in the pews to face and become partners in the moral guidance of new developments in these areas. These are all basically consistent with the expectation that there can be, in these areas, under God's providence, degrees of progress in humanity's increasingly common history. The fact that globalizing developments have been shaped by Christian theological roots means that they probably cannot be understood, modified, resisted, or ethically extended on a global scale without seeing them as in need of continuous theological and ethical critique and guidance.[31]

There are dangerous misunderstandings of the view of providential grace as just outlined. One is often called "theocracy," but it should more accurately be called "hierarchy," in the specific sense of rule by clergy, so that "religious experts" determine all public policies according to doctrinal formulas and enforce obedience to their faith and policies by use of the coercive power of the political magistracy. This tendency can be found in not only in some of the Catholic Popes and Protestant preachers who turned political, but also in the world religions – for example in attempts to rule, at various times and places, by Hindu Brahmans, Tibetan Buddhist Llamas, or by Islamic Ayatollahs. A second peril is "Erastianism," found among those who subordinate faith and religion to political rule. Some developments in Russian Orthodoxy, Lutheranism, Anglicanism, and some American forms of Evangelicalism tend in this direction, as do some wings of Theravada Buddhism and Confucianism. When religion becomes essentially political, or politics becomes essentially religious, something of the integrity of each can be lost. The result can be triumphalistic, messianic politics, celebrating the empire or nation-state as the direct agent of the Gospel, and its leaders as the saviors of the world. This politicalization of the faith has a terrible record in the West, from the Crusades, the Wars of Religion, and colonialism, to the complicity of many believers in the support of Hitler, Stalin, slavery, and apartheid, and the tradition of "Manifest Destiny" in the United States. In these cases, what becomes important is either

---

[30] One of the pioneering arguments along this line was made by Arend T. van Leewen (in contrast to the anti-modern works of Jacques Ellul) in his *Christianity in World History* (1964).

[31] See John Atherton (2000), *Public Theology for Changing Times*.

an imperialistic impulse to use religion to impose political domination on all who resist it, or the triumphalistic attempt by religion to use political means to make the world bow down to the doctrines of the hierarchy.

This is not to say that Christianity is without political implications. While it has adapted itself to Caesar, to feudal lords, to "Holy Roman Emperors," and to modern nationalism, its deeper theological impetus is toward a constitutional republic with a separation of church and state, a defense of the freedom of religion, guarantees of human rights, and constitutional government under just laws.[32] We can see this in ancient but decisive battles between rulers and bishops, the formation of ecumenical councils and representative synods able to challenge popes and emperors, the development of constitutional government out of canon law, and the formation of congregations, orders, and sects that gradually won the right to exist, to elect their own leaders, and to advocate their own ideas. Religion, in other words, fomented social movements in which convinced people began to take independent actions in all spheres of life, including politics and economics, to shape the common ethos and to filter out both imperialism and triumphalism. This is what has built the inner foundations of democracy from the center out, from the bottom up, and around the world, and not from the top down. This view of the indirect but highly influential political implications of the faith is supported by the fact that theories of "subsidiarity" have modulated hierarchy, and "federations" of particular groups have linked once-exclusive "covenantal" societies. Indeed, over the centuries, these two models of social order – hierarchical/subsidiary and federal/covenantal – have become the two major Christian forms of social theory with deep roots and long-range implications.[33]

On the whole, I think the weight of evidence presses us to see the Providential Grace view as the most realistic and most faithful theology of history,

---

[32] The current state of the discussion on this matter can be found in John Witte, Jr. (1993), *Christianity & Democracy in Global Context*; Daniel Philpott (2001), *Revolutions in Sovereignty*; and J. D. Carlson & E. C. Owens (2003), *The Sacred and the Sovereign*. For the most part, the understanding of Christianity as fomenting a democratic republic stands in partial conflict with the French revolutionary (and Russian and Chinese revolutionary) understanding of democracy, which repudiates the influence of religion.

[33] This, I think, has become a part of Catholic teaching in the Social Encyclicals of the twentieth century, and is in many documents of Vatican II and the teachings of Pope John Paul II's encyclicals on faith and social issues that bear on globalization. In *Centesimus Annus* and *Veritatis Splendor*, as well as in shorter statements and letters, such as his "Address to the United Nations General Assembly" (1982), he embraces democracy and capitalism, in ways that fit the emerging doctrine of "subsidiary" view of society. Further, he gives "unconditional" support to ideas of human rights as parts of the Christian approach to society and the quest for peace, while clearly holding that these must be guided by a profound theological rootage that is shaped by grace. Protestant theologies of society that include accents on human rights and a transforming ecumenical vision more often draw on the federal/covenantal perspective than the hierarchical/subsidiary one, but there are increasing areas of overlap. See, for example, James Skillen, et al. (1991), *Political Order and the Plural Structure of Society*.

although those of us who hold it have not abolished sin, and need the constant reminders of the perils and difficulties that attend great civilizational shifts. Those who hold the view of "another fall" can thus, be seen as specialized vocational "orders" in the whole catholic faith, warning lest the faith in its engagement with culture lose itself in enculturated loyalties. They remind the core, ecumenical faith that the burden of change often falls on the weaker segments of the population, and that the bearers of a transformative ethic must attend to the damage done among them. Further, it contributes the institutional insight that there must be a separation between church and state (and, for that matter, mosque and state, temple and state, Caesar and God), even if precisely that institutional separation allows ethical influence to flow from religious community into the fabric of civil society and from there into public polity and policy. In this regard, the Another Fall view stands as a resident critic, issuing the prophetic warnings that must be taken seriously, but not embraced as the whole picture, since it has no reconstructive theory of society as a whole. To put this point in the classical language of the theological tradition, that prophetic role must be supplemented and complemented by those who recognize that Christ, who is the norm of Prophecy, is also the norm of Priest and King. In other words, the task of the church is not only to condemn wrong and warn against evil, but to minister to the needy and to cultivate among the laity the responsibilities and skills of participation in the governance of all the public institutions of society. All believers, in short, must be loving neighbors to all whom they encounter by becoming faithful and hopeful prophets, priests, and political actors in all the spheres of life in a global civil society.

There is no reversing the tides of history, especially if one thinks that God's providential grace is more powerful and significant than the human sinful betrayals of that grace that rightly demand repentance and reform. Political democracy, human rights, and an open economy cannot save humanity ultimately, and their presence does not mean that the New Jerusalem is at hand; but if they are ordered in a subsidiary or covenantal way, they are likely to providentially grace life in the foreseeable future. This view suggests that it may be possible to influence and channel the energy of this massive civilizational shift called "globalization," and not only to critique or resist it. If so, we must all recover and re-invigorate the attention to first principles of right and wrong that we all, more or less, know, engage in debate about what the ultimate ends are that we should seek, and consciously seek to plow these into the flow and structures of history. Thus, in concert with the whole tradition, we turn again to reflection on the Ten Commandments and the Beatitudes.[34]

---

[34] In times of transition, the classic traditions have turned and found fresh ethical guidance from these sources. As examples, I cite Augustine, *De perfectione justitiae...*; Thomas, *Summa Theol.* **I**, II, 91; Luther, *The Shorter Catechism* and Calvin, *The Institutes...*, II, viii. Also, see note 2.

Back to the Basics

The Ten Commandments (Ex. 20) have been interpreted by Christians through the prism of Christ's commands to love God, the neighbor, and the stranger, the outcaste, and the enemy. Thus, they are not only seen as negative limits to behavior ("Thou shalt not ... !"), but a summary of the law of life, the inner core of the exterior principles of justice that give a vertebrate, binding shape to the common life. It represents the kind of morality that is universalistic in principle and "written on the hearts" of all (Isaiah and Paul).[35]

However, these principles also have to be "published," as the tradition says, so that each generation can learn them and not let them fall into obscurity. Thus, they can be "emblazoned" on the heart and made prominent in every ethos, shaping the institutions and patterns of social activity. This does not so much mean that every local official should post them on the wall or every school teacher make the students learn them by rote; but it does mean that those most concerned with justice and the right may have Moses and the Commandments (with Hammurabi, Solon, Mencius, Manu, Justinian, Gratian, Mohammed, and Jesus, and so on) hovering over them – just as they are symbolically carved into the chiaroscuro over the Supreme Court, where these matters are debated. No society can long survive without a legal system, and all the legal systems of history are known to be under a higher law toward that these religious ethicists pointed to, even if they did not fully agree or understand all of what they pointed to. Some version of the ultimate principles must govern every righteous person and people, and, in a globalizing era, we must seek to clarify and publish anew these principles as they bear on the dynamic new conditions we face, and assess whether the current political, economic, technological, and military policies are in accord with them and the most profound theology of history. Blessed are those who delight in the law and meditate on it, while the unprincipled drift away with the next wind (Psalms 1)

These principles can become living guides in the spheres of life where people live, for they cover not only duties to God but duties to fellow humans in all the basic spheres of historical life – on the practice of religion, on cultural arts and language, on work and leisure, on marriage and the family, on earning a living, and on doing business and living in a community. They begin with a focus on the divine and, end with the matter of the disposition of human desires. Christians, like Jews, believe that "not only with our forebears did the Lord make this covenant, but with all of us alive here this day" (Deut. 5:3).

---

[35] This leads to the doctrines of a God-given "natural law" (preferred by most Catholic thinkers) or "common grace" (preferred by most Protestant ones), and the basis of "self-evident truths" (as in Locke) or "categorical imperatives" (as in Kant). Many Christians see the latter two as residual, but unacknowledged, results of theological influence, but suspect that their views can only be sustained with a theistic metaethic). See Michael Cromartie (1997), *A Preserving Grace: Protestants, Catholics and Natural Law*; and Russell Hittinger (2004), *The First Grace: Rediscovering Natural Law in a Post-Christian World*.

These principles are not temporal constructs, even if our interpretations of them are; they stand outside history and allow us to assess what we think and do in history (Miller, 1990).[36] Moreover, these principles are also not local in pertinence; they are universal and compatible with the moral truths that exist in all major traditions.[37]

The Beatitudes also have a trans-historical dimension. If ethics in the Christian tradition demands an interpretation of the ethological contexts of life, which requires a theology of history and social theory, and demands attention to divinely given universal absolutes that limit and guide behavior in all human contexts, as the Ten Commandments represent, it also requires a sense of what basic moral dispositions are to be cultivated as we face an indeterminate future. The Beatitudes of the Sermon on the Mount parallel, in certain respects, the promises made to those to whom the covenant was made at Sinai: If you remember what God has done for you over the centuries, and if you follow the Commandments, God will bless you and your lives will be fulfilled. If you do not, you will be cursed and beset by many woes. In terms of ethical methods, they thus articulate a teleology; they point toward the good and specifies how to avoid evil in personal life and, in society toward the common good, as noted.[38]

But Beatitudes also turn the ordinary ethical logic of teleology around. In Christ, it is held, the telos is begun; the end has broken into the midst of history in ways that we could not attain if we only sought to move history to our desired ends. No legal system can bring humanity to perfect righteousness, and no good intention can guarantee virtue. Yet, the blessings of happiness begin to flow even now, in hope, and a certain reversal of priorities begins to take place. The poor, and the poor in spirit, are blessed![39] So are those who mourn, and the meek, and those who hunger and thirst for righteousness,

---

[36] For a series of commentaries on the Commandments by scholars who are more convinced that "modernity" is essentially "fallen," and not related to "providential grace" see Carl Braaten and C. R. Seitz (2004), *I Am the Lord Your God: Christian Reflections on the Ten Commandments*.

[37] Comparative religionist Diane Obenchain has argued that all religions share something like these principles, that it is because there is a moral "logos" scripted into the nature of human existence, and that this is what makes possible cross-cultural and inter-religious commonality at this level of ethical discourse. See her "The Study of Religion and the Coming Global Generation," in *God and Globalization*, vol 3. op. cit. This makes possible commonalities such as those found by Hans Küng's *A Global Ethic for Global Politics and Economics* (New York: Oxford University Press, 1998) and the efforts of UNESCO to identify common principles and virtues for a world ethic. See also Yersu Kim, "Prospects for a Universal Ethic," in *God and Globalization,* Vol. 1., op. cit., and Peter Paris, "Moral Exemplars in Global Community" in *God and Globalization,* Vol. 2, op. cit.

[38] See D. McCann & P. Miller, eds., *The Common Good*, op. cit.

[39] Luke, of course, says "the poor" in contrast to "the rich," who will see only woes; while Matthew identifies the "poor in spirit" as those to see God. Compare Luke 6:20 with Matthew 5:3.

and the merciful and the pure in heart. They can rejoice, for the kingdom of heaven is with them so that they shall be comforted and satisfied, and they shall obtain mercy and come to know the divine life. But not only the humble, so also those who have the power to be peacemakers and use it, and those who, like the prophets and sages, are reviled for their faith. Together, these are likened to a city on a hill, a witness to the New Jerusalem that is not yet.[40]

This does not mean that the law is voided, and whoever says it is shall be judged, as the scriptures says, but it does mean that the law can be interpreted, universalized, and applied in new ways, as Christ does (Matthew 5: 17–48). If love is revealed to be the law of life, it evokes a hermeneutic of trust beyond the ordinary hermeneutic of suspicion, and it thus bonds people into communities of conviction that are able to more nearly approximate right reason and good will. Above all, it means that we can live with an ultimately hopeful expectation, even if we are properly penultimately realistic about the reality of death and destruction, wars and rumors of war, the fragility of natural harmonies, and the mixed motives on which humans act.

In short, Christianity has four motifs that are pertinent to the globalization of ethics:

1. The created world is good, although creation and all in it has become distorted and broken.
2. History is lived in the tension between the way things are and both the first principles of right and the ultimate ends that God intends for humanity and the world that we can come to know.
3. In that context, Christians interpret historical developments and civilizational shifts in terms of successive "falls" into error and sin, but more profoundly in terms of God's providential grace.
4. We can understand that globalization involves both error and sin, and prospects for a better world, one that anticipates in some modest measure our ultimate destiny symbolized as an inclusive heavenly city, the image of a complex and holy civilization that comes to us by grace.

Those who grasp this vision may be called to become agents of God's Reign in all areas of the common life, and channel all the powers of life toward the new possibilities, which are even now breaking into time, by drawing them into covenanted communities of commitment. A dynamic Christian ethics, inevitably synthetic and in need of reformation is being globalized in manifest ways. Such a vision is part of the faith and a manifestation of God's love for the world.

---

[40] In every area of the world where people embrace globalization, we find new bursts of Evangelical, Pentecostal, or Charismatic piety that celebrate the new possibilities of life they have discovered. See note 23.

Conclusion

Because of Christianity's powerful formative role in the history of Europe and its colonies, and the impact it is now having in Africa and Asia (especially Korea and China), the several branches of the Christian tradition stand in a particularly intimate and complex relationship to the globalizing currents of our time. As advocates of the "providential grace" understanding point out, many of the key elements of the global order such as human rights are either directly related to Biblical insights or can be seen as valid ethical developments from them. At the same time, the very intimacy of these relationships between religion and Western culture can, according to critics who see globalization as "Another Fall," make it difficult to differentiate Christian ethical perspectives from global political and economic developments. This may be especially so when the situation is viewed from the standpoint of other religions, or when Christians outside the West are reshaping the tradition by creating new syntheses of faith and society by drawing on key elements of their indigenous culture. These tensions have been a source of both conflict and urgency in spurring creative Christian thinking about what is at stake in taking up a stance toward various aspects of globalization.

For these reasons, it is particularly important to emphasize all three dimensions of Christian ethical judgment described earlier in the chapter. As we have seen, Christian thinkers differ profoundly on the interpretive dimension of judgment concerning the dynamics of the ethos of the emerging global order. Christians today embrace both critical and affirmative stances toward engagement with globalization, and the debate is far from finished. The disagreements arise out of the very breadth and complexity of Christianity's view of the world as well as out of the particular contexts from which the disputants perceive the driving dynamics of globalization. On the one hand, the critics of globalization should seek to discern where Christian influences have constructively shaped global developments. At the same time, the powerful arguments of those Christians who see globalization as consonant with "providential grace" must temper any inclination toward wholesale rejection of the perspectives of those convinced that globalizing modernity represents "another fall."

To be authentically Christian, ethical judgment always demands attention to the transcendent dimension. Christian ethical judgment must not only interpret the present from the vantage point of universal moral principles. It also must struggle to be faithful to the ultimate ends embodied in the symbol of the New Jerusalem. Since these ends are both sacred and trans-temporal, the practice of Christian judgment demands a degree of detachment from immediate perspectives in order to open the present to prophetic questioning. At the same time, because Christians believe that God's redemptive power is at work in the very fabric of the common life, even in the midst of wrong and evil, Christian judgment requires an engaged participation in the formation of new, promising possibilities of a more inclusive and humane civilization.

The challenge of global ethical pluralism can perhaps be seen by all Christians as providential in at least this sense. In spite of the complexity and difficulty of moral judgment, globalized conditions make more salient the tradition's insistence upon clarifying for our times the transcendent principles and purposes that can frame our moral reflections. At the same time, the dynamics of change demand that we give attention to concrete new conditions and contexts to which the transcendent principles and purposes must be applied, or in which they can be found to be operating almost anonymously. This should serve to restrain the crusading moralism that has sometimes marred Christian evangelization, even as it prompts a renewed sense of mission that would enable Christians to participate as moral agents in the common effort to shape the emerging globalized world into a more just, compassionate and sustainable civilization.

5

Buddhism and the Globalization of Ethics

Peter Nosco

In late April 2004, His Holiness the Dalai Lama visited Vancouver and the University of British Columbia. He came to lecture and teach, to receive an honorary degree, and to participate in a roundtable dialogue titled "Balancing Educating the Mind with Educating the Heart." More than a year in advance, preparations were already in high gear, and at times the level of publicity and celebrity attached to this event seemed scarcely credible – for example, one heard of tickets to his largest public teaching being auctioned on e-Bay for $1,000 each. There were also times when it all seemed a bit surreal, as when an email to participants in the related Conference on Tibet in the Contemporary World showed itself to come from "HHDL Info," and under the rubric "Conference Extras" noted that "Specially designed conference T-shirts and monk's bags will be available for purchase at the conference."

One could only empathize with the other scheduled distinguished honorary degree recipients and participants in the roundtable dialogue – fellow Nobel Laureates Professor Shirin Ebadi, His Excellency Vaclav Havel (who was unable for medical reasons to be present), and His Excellency The Most Reverend Desmond Tutu – none of whom were invited to deliver a keynote address, or even had their own individual posters (the Dalai Lama had no fewer than two in conjunction with the events at UBC). In this august company, other honorary degree recipients such as Dr. Jo-Ann Archibald of UBC representing local aboriginal First Nations communities, and Rabbi Zalman Schacter-Shalomi, seemed almost like afterthoughts, but only prior to the dialogue itself, where both distinguished themselves brilliantly.

All this of course begs the question as to what makes this fourteenth Dalai Lama (b. 1935) so special. Surely it is not simply that he is the spiritual leader of some 6 to 7 million Tibetans, most of whom live outside the Tibetan Autonomous Region, since they represent no more than 2 percent of the world's 325 million Buddhists, and would be dwarfed by the world's 2 billion Christians or 1.2 billion Muslims, and even outnumbered by the comparably mistreated 6.4 million Baha'is (Wright, 1997, pp. 498–500). The fact of the Dalai Lama's political exile and the genocidal oppression of those for whom he continues to serve as spiritual leader are surely fundamental to the world's fascination with him, and the Chinese government's obvious ongoing irritation with his activities continues to generate generous and sympathetic reporting of those very same activities. For his believers, he is the fully realized incarnation of Avalokiteśvara, the bodhisattva of compassion, known as Guan-yin in China and Kannon in Japan. Still, one senses that the reasons that explain why the Dalai Lama attracts such a wide following and enjoys such near-universal admiration lie in something more than this.

During the keynote address he presented at UBC, the Dalai Lama spoke of the need for universally governing principles around which we all can unite.[1] He asserted that we are all fundamentally good, and that evil is thus an aberration. He invoked his Tibetan heritage's traditional concern with compassion as a foundational value on which to build contemporary cross-cultural and inter-faith dialog on a global level. Later in his address, he expanded upon compassion's importance by asserting a universal need for unbiased infinite compassion. He also promoted an understanding of religious harmony whereby one acknowledges that differences exist, while still recognizing that we all share a common message of love, compassion, commitment, and self-discipline. He emphasized the extent to which such seemingly disparate practitioners as Buddhist thinkers and theoretical physicists can learn much from one another. He also spoke of his personal moral mission summed up in his favorite prayer adapted from the eighth-century saint Shantideva, "For so long as space endures and suffering remains, then I too remain to serve."[2] In interviews after the ceremony at UBC, many spoke of the honorary degree ceremony and keynote address as events of personal life-changing and perhaps even globally epochal significance.

If we examine the phenomenon of the Dalai Lama's celebrity and following in the light of these teachings, we will find helpful clues in our quest for the meaning and implications of the globalization of ethics in general, as well as Buddhism's perspective on and role in this, itself an enormous topic that by far exceeds the attention I will give it in this chapter. It is surely obvious, but nonetheless good to affirm at the outset, that the Buddhist world is at least as variegated as Christendom, and so for every proffered generalization in the pages that follow, one can invariably think of exceptions. Further, for an individual Buddhist, the ethical considerations that devolve from one's commitment are ultimately driven less by abstract principles, such as those

[1] An excellent summary of the Dalai Lama's Buddhist teachings can be found in his *The Meaning of Life from a Buddhist Perspective* (Johns Hopkins University Press, 1992).

[2] The full text of the prayer follows. "With the wish to free all beings, I shall always go for refuge to the Buddha, Dharma and Sangha until I reach full enlightenment. Enthused by compassion and wisdom, today in Buddha's presence I generate the mind for enlightenment for the sake of all sentient beings. For as long as space endures, and as long as sentient beings remain, until then may I abide too to dispel the misery of the world."

discussed in this chapter, than by the challenge of reconciling one's actions in a constantly changing world with those ideally unchanging vows and spiritual commitments that punctuate one's progress along the Buddhist path.

In this sense, the dilemma for the individual Buddhist is not unlike that of the individual Christian – how can one remain faithful to the essentials of one's creed without detaching oneself from the world of which one remains an integral part, and this precisely so that one can leave one's world a better place? Again like the Christian, the Buddhist is understood to be engaged in a spiritual path of self-transformation in the direction of a moral absolute, which in Buddhism is understood as a process of becoming a fully "realized" creature. And still again like Christians, Buddhists will acknowledge a certain "thick tradition" that binds them to other Buddhists despite relatively thin but nonetheless important denominational differences. The core principles of this essentialized Buddhism or Christianity then form the basis for the capacity of these traditions to accommodate differences with neighbors, both near and far. However, since there is room for considerable disagreement as to what these core Buddhist principles might be, we begin with a discussion of them, and only then turn to the questions of this volume's topics. At times along the way, we shall invoke the Dalai Lama as be our guide and interpreter. We also return to him in conclusion, when we examine Buddhism in terms of the current competition for hearts and minds, the dueling propositions represented by the globalization of ethics.

Some General Buddhist Principles

If Buddhism can be said to have a cardinal virtue, it would be compassion, and this compassion stems from Buddhism's view of the cosmos as an integrated and organic whole within which all causes and effects, all phenomena, every movement of dust or even stirring of the consciousness contribute to a grandly orchestrated harmonic. The conductor of this orchestra, the orchestrator, is the dharma, the impersonal, abstract and eternal law of the universe, which is as much moral law as it is natural law. This conductor is good in the dual senses of being morally just and practically skilled – that is, its operation in the world is by its very nature salutary, working for the good of all, and it is at the same time goodness itself. Further, dharma courses through both the world of non-living objects and the complex multiple realms of all sentient creatures – that is, creatures with consciousness that share a potential for progress on this spiritual path.

Most Buddhists believe that dharma has an analog within human beings and other sentient creatures in the form of a Buddha-nature, a bit of the dharma within, which is what universalizes the potential for enlightenment. Recognizing that we share a common nature in turn deepens our sense of universal fraternity with other sentient creatures, and this translates into not just radical tolerance for others' differences, but also a profound empathy that forms the basis for our compassionate engagement of the world. Because of the integration of ourselves into the morally governed harmonic of the cosmos, we find that it is impossible to separate our own interests and consequences from those of others, and our fates are thus one-and-all intertwined. Buddhism powerfully reinforces this sense of mutuality, and the sufferings and hardship of others ultimately become inseparable from one's own suffering and hardship, just as the saving of others becomes a way of saving oneself. By identifying with the hardship and suffering of others, one deepens one's own compassion, dedicating oneself to the bodhisattva's goal of returning again and again to this world until all have achieved complete liberation from its strictures.

Buddhism teaches that there are many levels of existence beyond the human that thus necessarily concern us, from the celestial and blissful realms above, down through our own complex realm of human frailties, and further below to animals and their instincts, and eventually all the way down to the depraved abominations of the lowest nether realms. Buddhism asserts that it is incumbent upon us to familiarize ourselves with these diverse realms – those below as much as those above – for they are each as much components of the cosmic harmonic as we ourselves are and thus represent potentialities inherent in each of us at every moment. Again, this awakening to the infinite possibilities constantly confronting us can be understood as both reinforcing and representing an outgrowth of one's compassion.

It is the human realm that most concerns both us and Buddhism, and like the cosmos itself, this human realm is a decidedly mixed bag. Ignorance, confusion, greed, instincts, and passions are all obstacles that have to be overcome if one is to escape the cycle of birth, old age, death, and new birth. Giving in to these mostly mental obstacles, one generates karma, with soteriological consequences that proceed in an altogether impersonal and mechanical fashion. The law of karma is believed to take into account a deed, its consequences (or fruit), and most importantly the intention behind the deed. In simple terms, the ethic of Buddhism dictates that what goes around must eventually come around. One's good deeds will be rewarded if not in this life, then surely in some subsequent existence, just as one's wickedness will likewise have consequences. When evaluating the ethical and moral worth of a deed, however, the deed itself and its consequences are ultimately of less import than the intention that initially inspired the deed. This, in turn, suggests that if one could only learn how to act instinctively in perfect and spontaneous accord with the dharma, then one would be liberated from both karma and rebirth. This liberation or release is what is meant by enlightenment, though it is not the acquisition of something new so much as the realization of that with which one has all along been endowed. Indeed, some Buddhist interpretations have even suggested that we all are in fact born possessing original enlightenment but have mostly not yet "realized" it.[3]

---

[3] See Jacqueline Stone (1999), *Original Enlightenment and the Transformation of Medieval Japanese Buddhism*.

If we revisit our original obstacles – ignorance, confusion, greed, instincts, and passions – we find that the solution lies less in a path of conduct, though conduct to be sure is important, and more in gaining control over one's mind. One's thoughts, predispositions, and consciousness are what Buddhism calls upon us to master, and we begin with the quest for objective knowledge about ourselves and the world, or with what Buddhism calls seeing things as they really are. The third-century author Matercheta described this insight as follows: "Buddhas do not wash away sins with water, they do not heal suffering by laying on of hands, and they do not transmit their understanding into others' minds; they introduce beings to freedom by educating them about reality."[4]

Buddhism regards reality as constantly changing and contingent, neither fully real nor unreal, and it represents this reality as emptiness. Negotiating here, as elsewhere, a Middle Path between opposing extremes, Buddhism maintains that there is in the world sufficient reality for the purposes of everyday experience, but no more, and we are accordingly instructed to avoid the extremes of either clinging vainly to reality (materialism) or rejecting it utterly (nihilism). This understanding of emptiness has several profound implications for us as well. First, we humans are just as empty as the world of objects, but this emptiness is precisely what enables us to vicariously absorb the suffering of others, and thereby to demonstrate our compassion. Second, this inner emptiness is what provides a space to be filled by the light of Buddhist knowledge. And third, recognizing our own emptiness undermines the ever-attractive illusion of a permanent self or soul, and thus helps us to avoid this dangerous folly.

From this insight regarding emptiness, one learns that the key to interacting with reality is learning how to control the mind, for which there are many techniques that endeavor variously to bring the mind to a single point and to hold it steady there, so that distractions no longer intrude and a kind of bliss is attained. Thereafter, as one becomes more enlightened, one becomes more attuned to the dharma until one is in spontaneous conformity to its every dictate. And one thus becomes a realized being.

Buddhism is not indifferent to statecraft or rulership, and has throughout its history had certain model rulers, of whom none is more prominent than the third-century B.C. King Aśoka, a convert who promoted Buddhism while allowing others faiths and creeds alongside. In this, Aśoka established a model for Buddhist accommodation of a non-Buddhist world, and he is perhaps best known for his goal of conquest by righteousness (*dharmavijaya*) rather than conquest by force (*digvijaya*) – a concept that resonates through much Confucian thought as well – whereby one politically wins over others through the moral force of one's example. Within his kingdom, Aśoka used edicts inscribed on steles to promote good deeds, kindness, liberality, truthfulness, and purity, while he forbade the slaughter of animals within his capital, pardoned

---

4 Quoted in Robert A. F. Thurman, *Essential Tibetan Buddhism* (New Delhi: Harper Collins Publishers India, 1996), p. 12.

criminals, and generally promoted compassion and mercy. He did not, however, altogether relinquish military aggression or abolish capital punishment, to which we will return later.

Indeed, each tradition and region within Buddhism has had its model monarchs, such as the pious Shōmu (701–756 A.D.) in Japan, and Trisong Detsen (c. 741–797 A.D.) in Tibet, but Buddhist theocratic states on the Tibetan model have been the exception rather than the rule. Buddhism has more often asserted itself as the protector of different national polities, as during China's T'ang dynasty, or for centuries following Japan's Nara period.

Buddhism has frequently championed egalitarian principles within otherwise highly stratified social environments – perhaps the best example is the Buddha's opening of his spiritual community to those from all castes, including outcastes – and in this sense it has historically appealed to social reformers. But otherwise Buddhism's embrace of highly stratified cosmologies with many levels of spiritual existence provided a rationale for comparable social stratification and inequities in the terrestrial realm, and Buddhist societies have for most of Buddhism's history generally been steeply hierarchical. Note, however, that despite the potential for nationalistic expression as evidenced at times in Japan, Buddhism's universalistic tendencies have generally supported transnational perspectives on such global issues as environmentalism, pacifism, and so on. Further, at least in medieval Asia, Buddhism was the only truly international religion.[5]

Issues such as pacifism and humanitarianism have largely defined contemporary Buddhists' engagement of the world around them, and in this sense have been fundamental to what is often styled Engaged Buddhism. Here, Buddhism has been consistent with its earliest ideals when it championed social institutions such as orphanages and infirmaries in regions where none had exited previously. On gender-related issues, Buddhism's record has been more mixed. Many Buddhist denominations taught until modern times that a woman's first step toward liberation was to be reborn as a male. Similarly ambivalent has been Buddhism's attitude toward abortion, which has been traditionally condemned even while some Buddhist temples have profited through assuagement of abortion-related remorse.

Alternatives

The question of whether Buddhism would advocate our aiming for a uniform planetary ethic, a global accommodation of conflicting ethical differences, or some combination of uniformity and particularism certainly articulates the range of most Buddhist responses, and as with all doctrines that make truth claims, Buddhism's answers have historically been colored by how much exclusivity and distinctiveness individual Buddhists attach to their own

---

[5] I am indebted to my colleague Jinhua Chen for this important insight.

denominational claims. It has often been observed that Buddhism has never engaged in Crusades, Jihad, or Holy Wars, and of the world's major religions, Buddhism appears to be alone in its ability to make this claim. Buddhist countries have of course engaged in conflict, just as non-Buddhist countries have, and one finds doctrines of a "just war" in Buddhist and Abrahamic traditions alike. The principal difference appears to be that where matters of theology are concerned, Buddhism has preferred persuasion to coercion, and tolerance to intolerance. The absence of contemporary Buddhist theocratic states is striking, and suggests that the effort to find areas of compromise between religious and secular authorities may be more prominent in traditionally Buddhist realms than elsewhere.

Buddhism has throughout its history had important devotional elements, where salvific consequences devolved from the adoration of and/or faith in individual Buddhas and bodhisattvas. But even such devotional movements nowadays tend to represent themselves as acknowledging a set of core precepts that appear at least as "philosophic" – that is, metaphysical, ethical, ontological, and epistemological, as "religious" in the sense of devotional, ritualistic, soteriological, and symbolic. These philosophic and intellectual precepts form Buddhism's core or "thick" truths and include:

- Understanding the lessons of change, emptiness, and contingent reality, and the consequences of this for the individual person as this person engages the world.
- Acknowledging that life is characterized by hardships of various sorts, and seeing how this hardship or suffering is linked to various forms of desire and craving.
- Ethical teachings regarding the consequences of one's every thought, word and deed, and the importance of intention.
- The claim to teach one to see things as they really are and thus to know truth.
- The argument that through knowledge one can overcome the spiritual consequences of ignorance and be liberated from its shackles.
- Accepting that there is no permanent self or soul.

Buddhism in all its setting has also traditionally made claims concerning what constitute honorable ways in which to make a living, how to care for one's body, dietary laws, and so on, though these have varied from region to region and seem a "thinner" tradition. Buddhism's traditional accommodation of local preferences in such less fundamental issues as vocation can be seen in the fact that despite their proscription in the earliest Buddhist teachings, astrologers and practitioners of other forms of divination have traditionally flourished in Japan while retaining a loosely constructed Buddhist identification.

Buddhism would thus likely assert that even though its core claims are all equally true, and hence all equally appropriate constituents of a uniform planetary ethic, they are not equally essential to Buddhism's goal of facilitating

one's escape from the bonds of this world's hardship. This is a difficult conces-
sion for Buddhism to make, since it prides itself on the logical coherence of its
teachings, and so exempting even one precept has serious implications for the
entire edifice. Nonetheless, what is perhaps most striking about Buddhism's
core truth-claims is how they are in most ways compatible with the precepts and
creeds of other major religions. Hence, one frequently finds Buddhism and its
spokespersons at the forefront of much interfaith dialog – and especially that
with the Abrahamic traditions – when soteriological issues and the problem
of the soul are left unaddressed. Indeed, in such teachings as the inescapable
nature of change, the problem of attachment to the self, the problematic nature
of possessions, the importance of respect for the physical environment, ecology, and so on, Buddhism often appears in the guise of providing intellectual
argument in support of the theological premises of other creeds. Thus, one can
easily imagine Buddhism contributing substantially to a uniform planetary
ethic even without actively seeking to shape it.

Of the various alternatives available to any doctrine's response to the globalization of ethics, the most likely for Buddhism is endorsement of a global
accommodation of conflicting particular ethical differences and other less fundamental issues, even while aspiring to consensus around its more metaphysical teachings. This accommodation goes beyond the mere domestication of an
originally foreign religion, as when traditional holidays are absorbed into a new
church calendar. This dynamic in the United States might be seen in Buddhist
denominational celebration of both U.S. secular and non-Buddhist religious
holidays, such as the celebration of Thanksgiving, including much of its traditional meal, with an emphasis on gratitude for the blessings one has received;
and Christmas, with its emphasis on hope and renewal. The accommodation of
difference, of course, is consistent with Buddhism's historical role of seeking
to win others over through the persuasive force of its arguments, even using
such expedient means as compromise whenever necessary to achieve desirable
ends. In this sense – that is, in its appreciation of expediency as a global spiritual strategy – it is easy to imagine Buddhism affirming that various degrees
of the globalization of ethics are morally acceptable, even if unequal in value.

Uniformity

It is the issue of uniformity that forces us to refine these broad strokes. Let us
begin with the obvious by asking the following: Is there a creed anywhere that
would not welcome having its own premises become universally and uniformly
embraced? Buddhism, like any of the propositions under consideration in this
volume, regards its own premises as absolutely true. It recognizes points of
congruence with other teachings and celebrates those points as corroboration
of initially Buddhist truths. And it embraces the optimistic proposition that
one day the world as a whole will be won over by the force of the dharma.
But the issue of uniformity ironically posits an equally problematic Buddhist

essentialism, and even within the Buddhist world, it is difficult to see whose Buddhism might be construed as representative of all or pan-Buddhism. It is in this respect important to note that the Dalai Lama probably enjoys a higher regard outside the Buddhist world as a spokesman for Buddhism than he does within that world. One reason for this may be his emphasis on a thicker and more intellectual tradition that shares numerous assumptions widely embraced in contemporary literate circles, and his diplomatic affirmation that many paths can bring one to the truth.

Several models are at work here. Recall that the historical model within Buddhism's past for dealing with alternative thought systems is that of King Aśoka whose *dharmavijaya*, or moral force of ideas and example, was apparently sufficient to win others over without resort to force. As an evangelist, by contrast, the great example remains Nāgasena, who converted the second-century B.C. Greek monarch Menander (Milinda) to Buddhism through the intellectual vigor and clarity of his arguments, which reduced complex metaphysical principles to easily understood everyday examples. In turn, many, both within and outside Buddhism, continue to embrace an image of Buddhism, in the words of Alfred North Whitehead, as "the most colossal example in history of applied metaphysics . . . , a metaphysic generating a religion."[6] These different apologetics expand upon a root-branch metaphor by imagining Buddhism as comprised of a fundamentally intellectual core, its root surrounded by a spiritual efflorescence – that is, its branches, and it is this model of Buddhism that is perhaps most compatible with other religious systems including the monotheistic Abrahamic traditions. This is essentially the model that the Dalai Lama prescribed during his visit to Vancouver – that is, a secular ethic that promotes good-heartedness without a theological superstructure, and this in part explains the powerful widespread appeal of his teachings.

The Buddhist answer to the question of how to deal with others who, to varying degrees, embrace symbol and belief systems that differ from one's own has always been through the empirical evidence of the truth of one's core beliefs regarding change, suffering, the problem of the self and desires, and the principle of absolute interrelatedness. From the beginning, Buddhism has invited believers and potential believers alike to measure and test its teachings against the evidence of the senses and empirical observation, never seeing itself in conflict with science, and it is evident that Buddhism has historically done well in the competition for hearts and minds, perhaps never more so than in the present. Buddhism can boast, for example, that with considerable support from the world of contemporary science including psychology and theoretical physics, it has from the beginning asserted what are nowadays regarded widely as essentially true propositions regarding change, emptiness, the problem of attachment and desires and their connection to suffering, and

[6] William Theodore de Bary, ed., *The Buddhist Tradition in India, China and Japan* (New York: Vintage Books, 1972), p. xvi.

the principle of interconnectedness, all of which are central to its teachings. Generally speaking, in the Buddhist world, one would find near-universal assent to the importance of these propositions even if they might not be central to a specific denomination or movement's interpretations, and one can thus easily imagine a hypothetical global ethic coalescing around propositions with which Buddhism would likely find little to quarrel. This is especially so if the Abrahamic traditions are imagined to provide the likeliest alternative propositions in the world arena of ideas, since Buddhism has already enjoyed impressive success in drawing these traditions into dialog with itself, and this dialog has been conducted largely on Buddhism's own terms.

Diversity

All would prefer that their own worldviews became the world's views, but recognizing the improbability of this over the near term, the question arises as to what is acceptable to a particular tradition, and what is not. In the late sixteenth century in Japan, a newly centralized state had begun to emerge, a state that for the first time in centuries successfully asserted the priority of the "King's [secular] law" (*Ōbō*) over "Buddhist [dharma] law" (*Buppō*). The hegemon at that time, Toyotomi Hideyoshi (1536–1598), had disarmed arms-owning peasantry, thereby separating the samurai into a distinct and exclusively arms-bearing class, and he appointed Maeda Gen'i (1539–1602) as civil magistrate with authority over shrines and temples. Hideyoshi ordered the confiscated swords of disarmed agriculturalists to be melted down and recast into a gigantic statue of the Buddha to be housed at the temple Myōhōin and completed in 1595. Maeda Gen'i later that same year ordered each of the so-called "ten denominations" of Japanese Buddhism to send one hundred of its monks to participate in monthly services at the Myōhōin honoring Hideyoshi's ancestors (especially his beloved late mother), and to share a meal there.

This posed a problem for one of the denominations, the Nichiren (or Lotus), which contained a movement styled *fujufuse*, meaning "neither to receive nor to give" alms. With extremists basing their principles on a narrow reading of passages in the writings of the founder Nichiren (1222–1282), the *fujufuse* issue revolved around the correct attitude and behavior of believers toward a non-believing world. Anyone who did not acknowledge the primacy of the Lotus Sutra was, according to this view, a "dharma slanderer" (*hōbō*) with whom association of any kind was questionable, even as an expedient to draw someone into the Buddhist fold. Association with non-believers was thus to be avoided at all cost as part of a broader strategy of *shakubuku*, the effort to "break and suppress" devils and other opponents of true Buddhism along with their heresies. The *fujufuse* principle was so strongly held by some within the Nichiren denomination that they refused under any circumstances to partici-pate in the memorial services at the Myōhōin, resulting in a schism within the denomination, and in the state's formal proscription of the *fujufuse* principle some decades later.[7]

Refusing to share a meal with fellow Buddhist clergy from different denominations with different emphases is not the familiar model of Buddhist tolerance that has prevailed at most times and in most places within the Buddhist world, and yet it represents one important extreme evident within the Buddhist tradition when truth-claims compete. Nowadays, one of Japan's most popular new religions, the Sōka Gakkai, claims the mantle of Nichiren Buddhism, including the *shakubuku* principle for which it was roundly condemned in the 1960s. The Sōka Gakkai also sponsors a political party, the Kōmeitō, which advocates the establishment of a Buddhist theocratic state in Japan. Nonetheless, and despite Sōka Gakkai's claim to have 12 million followers internationally,[8] most of them both within and outside Buddhism's embrace would likely reject such exclusivity and isolationism, especially when used as a strategy for winning others over to one's views and creed, leading one to ask the question anew as to what practices and/or social arrangements are acceptable from a Buddhist perspective, and what points of view are generally unacceptable.

Among the latter, the extremes of both materialism and nihilism would be especially problematic. Clinging to the notion of a static reality in which material things have enduring and abiding reality is folly from a Buddhist perspective, and this perspective challenges the celebrity and materialism on which much contemporary popular culture rests. Buddhism likewise rejects the opposite extreme of proposing that the world is simply an illusion that one need not engage. The tradition of spiritually charged individuals who retreat into isolation has been prominent within Buddhism, but raises obvious political concerns as well. Particularly in its modern transformation, Buddhism has instead sought to represent itself as intellectually and socially engaged with the world's problems and concerns, and as actively participating in the pursuit of solutions.

In terms of social philosophies, one would expect Buddhism to be sympathetic to liberal democracies, and in fact the Dalai Lama made frequent reference to democracy during his recent 2004 travels through Canada. The notion of using the state's resources to address such social needs as those of orphans, or the sick and infirm, and so on is a theme among Buddhism's model monarchs, and represents the kind of fruitful cooperation between Buddhist church and state that again represent a certain ideal model for such collaboration. Furthermore, one would expect Buddhism these days to be an advocate for feminism, understood here as equality in both rights and opportunity, though

---

[7] See Miyazaki Eishû (1969), *Fujufuseha no genryû to tenkai*; and Jeffrey Robert Hunter (1969), "The *fujufuse* Controversy in Nichiren Buddhism: The Debate between Nichiô and Jakushôin Nichiken."

[8] On the following of Sōka Gakkai International, see http://www.sgi.org/English/SGI/history.htm.

Buddhism's past, like its present, represents a tale of uneven progress, and we are reminded of traditional Buddhism's unfortunate insistence that before she could experience full enlightenment, a female first had to be reborn as a male.

It is good for all these reasons to remind ourselves that Buddhism originates in the recognition of and acknowledgement of life's fundamental hardship, a perspective that has made Buddhism uneasily compatible with authoritarian and other morally problematic regimes throughout its history. Thus the question of what might make a particular regime's policies and/or social practices intolerable is more likely to be answered in terms of degree rather than in terms of specific proscriptions. For example, it is unimaginable that Buddhism would condone the exploitation of children or their labor, but Buddhism has through much of its past tacitly accepted varying degrees of such exploitation in its local environments, and even within its monastic fold.

One would expect that Buddhism's issues with the monotheistic Abrahamic traditions would be the most intractable, because of the latter's exclusivity, making the success of its inter-faith dialogues with Christianity, Judaism, and Islam all the more striking. Buddhism has had considerable success in representing itself in these dialogues and elsewhere as a non-theistic spiritual complement to monotheism, and especially the patriarchal monotheism of Abrahamic creeds. In other words, by veiling its own devotional theistic traditions, contemporary Buddhism has succeeded in reconstituting itself along its foundational lines of more than two millennia ago – that is, as a set of fundamentally physical, metaphysical, and psychological propositions that are empirically verifiable and thus pose no challenge to any theological tradition that accepts the splendor of knowledge.

Mix of Universal Principles and Particular Practices

It is a challenging exercise to try to distinguish between these norms and practices on which Buddhism, generally speaking, would insist upon universal acceptance, and these on which it would accept and accommodate particular differences. Even though they might not be central to the teachings of one or another denomination, the following three assumptions, which Buddhism asserts as fact, would most likely be the core: that all things are constantly changing, and there is no static moment in life; that life is characterized fundamentally by sorrow and suffering; and that there is no permanent self or soul.

Life's ineluctable change is a necessary part of a Buddhist worldview, since Buddhism does not deny that life can have its pleasures. Buddhism, however, insists that those moments are not representative, which they would be (at least for some) if matters could somehow be kept from changing. To demonstrate this truth of change, Buddhism explains that all things are composite – that is, they are comprised of smaller units styled *aggregates*, which themselves deteriorate, whether or not, we wish them to, rather like the tires on one's car, or for that matter the car itself. Though the change may not be evident from one moment to the next, the long-term fact of change is unarguable, and so change, even if small, is assured over even the shortest interval of time.

So, too, with suffering, most Buddhists would agree. Birth, toil, sickness, old age, and death are as inescapable as change, and each of these developmental changes involves its own forms of pain, sorrow, disappointment, sadness, or suffering. With an almost mathematical precision, Buddhists typically conclude that since the sum total of human desires will inevitably exceed the sum total of things in the world to satisfy those desires, the solution to the problem of this inevitable disappointment lies in learning how to control the mind, and specifically learning how to rein in one's desires. In the process, Buddhism also teaches one how not to confuse the impure and impermanent with the pure and permanent.

Of Buddhism's core teachings, however, surely the one that encounters the most resistance from those outside the fold is the teaching that there is no permanent self or soul. The importance of this teaching within Buddhism lies in the following: Buddhism argues that if one believes in a permanent self or soul, then one cannot but be drawn to this soul and wish to perpetuate it through all eternity, which would represent both a dangerous folly and an unhealthy generation of karma tying one ever further to the sorrowful cycle of repeated births. If instead one can detach oneself from this misplaced confidence in a soul, one can then further detach oneself from the world, with salutary consequences for the hereafter.

Much of this begs the question of whether the assumptions regarding change and suffering are not in fact demonstrably true. Buddhism has become an ally for those who seek to rectify social ills globally, no less for those who seek to make advances in theoretical physics. Who would not agree that the things of this world are comprised of smaller things, among which particle physicists seem to discover even-smaller things all the time? Who would disagree that Buddhist practice and insights can be of therapeutic value for some psychological disorders in some individuals? And who would quarrel with the proposition that it behooves one in an age of globalized awareness to see one's self-interest and well-being intertwined with the interests and well-being of others?

The core principles of Buddhism coexist comfortably with a broad range of competing propositions, and virtually everywhere it has arrived in modern times, Buddhism has found ways to reconcile itself to local belief systems, from the animism of Japanese Shinto, Tibetan Bon, and Chinese folk religion, to the specific insights of today's physicists and psychoanalysts. Even what I have styled Buddhism's core insistence that there is no permanent self or soul has been compromised within East Asian Buddhism by the construction of traditions, such as the Pure Land, promising paradisiac consequences as a reward for a life of faith. In all of this, the student of comparative religion would see the dynamic interplay between universalizing traditions and local particularism.

One needs to restate here the problem expressed at the outset that Buddhism is an exceptionally elastic tradition. It has not had an apostolic succession or other similar mechanism to promote orthodoxy, nor has it had authorized supra-denominational seminaries that would represent authorized teachings produced by authentic interpreters, and it has no tradition of ordaining Buddhist clergy in anything but a specific denomination. This, in turn, may make our hypothetical construction of a pan-Buddhist set of assumptions even more difficult than for some of the other traditions represented in this volume.

Propagation

Any discussion of the ethics of propagation necessarily begins with an examination of the nature of the truth-claims that one is making. How confident is one that the truths one espouses are in fact truly independent of the contexts of time and place? Do these claims represent secular or contingent truth, rather like a law of gravity that is essentially and practically true for everyday life, but nonetheless lacks absolute truth? And what are the consequences of both knowing and not knowing these truths. One assumes that possession of the truth represents a boon, if not in this life then surely in the next, but does ignorance of this truth carry an inverse proportionately negative price, and if so, how great is this liability? The answers to these questions largely shape and determine one's attitude toward broader questions of one's ethical responsibility to those outside the fold.

Buddhism's model for propagation has rarely embraced the use of force of any kind to introduce its values to another society, the Nichiren denomination's embrace of *shakubuku* (break and subdue) techniques representing an important exception. Buddhism has also benefited from its well-deserved reputation for tolerance and pacifism, recalling the example of Aśoka's tolerance for other creeds and embrace of the goal of conquest by force of the dharma rather than conquest by force of human arms.

The historical spread of Buddhism two millennia and more ago, however, tells another set of stories. Buddhism's initial spread across the deserts of central Asia and into China for the first time benefited from its reputation for assuaging sickness and worshiping a deity with such supernatural powers as flight. During its spread through China, Buddhism benefited from its thaumaturgic associations and exotic new understandings of space and time, which eventually helped it to overcome local distrust of its alien origins. Later, in its spread from China to Korea and then to Japan, Buddhism again benefited from its identification with advanced civilizational sources, which themselves offered new concepts of monarchy and statecraft on the one hand, and the cosmos on the other. It is said that in early Japan, those who promoted the initial spread of Buddhism were actually more interested in advancing Chinese concepts of centralized monarchy and bureaucratic administration than Buddhist truths *per se*, but it is also evident that the one converged with the other.

As a result, those whose interests were challenged by the centralization of power in Japan initially opposed Buddhism as one part of a larger potentially threatening package of ideas.

But it is difficult to imagine a Crusade, Holy War, or Jihad in Buddhism, even if coercive strategies at times surface in aberrant ways, like *shakubuku*. There is, to be sure, a lively literature within Buddhism using parables such as that of the burning house, in which a father tells his children lies in order to get them to escape from a house that they do not realize (or believe) is aflame. Buddhism recognizes such lies as expedient means intended to bring about a greater good, such as the saving of one's (after)life.

The matter of whether from a Buddhist perspective a cross-societal display of one's values through globalized media would constitute a coercive form of propaganda is difficult to address because of the question of what constitutes a value. How should Buddhism respond to the media assault by multi-national global corporations that daily promotes consumption-oriented and unsustainable excesses? The answer is probably to be found in the historical response of Buddhism to ignorance of any kind, which has been to seek to educate. But generally, and as we have observed, those Buddhist movements that seek to educate through active proselytizing have been the exception.

The question of whether Buddhism's preferences regarding accommodation of moral and ethical pluralism should be sanctioned by law cuts to the heart of Buddhism's historically ambiguous relationship regarding the state. As we also have observed, the historical pattern of Buddhism in East Asia has been to place itself at the service of different governments and states by promising to protect the interests of their rulers. In this sense, Buddhism has traditionally represented itself as an ally of the state, with which it has from time to time found itself in an uneasy equilibrium, as in China during the eighth and ninth centuries and in Japan during the fifteenth and sixteenth centuries. This may help to explain why denominations such as the Pure Land and Ch'an (Zen) continued to flourish in China, where they were perceived as less political than most of their alternatives, and why in Japan the road to political unification in the seventeenth century ran through the major temples and their formidable armies formed during the sixteenth century.[9]

During the twentieth and twenty-first centuries, Buddhism emerged as an international champion of human rights, and much of this concern with rights is rooted in Buddhism's traditional principles such as the universal human potential for spiritual advancement and the interrelatedness and attendant interdependence of all sentient creatures. But some of these rights would likely be more important – that is, more closely connected to Buddhism's philosophical and theological premises – than others. For example, one would expect Buddhism to champion notions of equality of dignity and rights, without

---

[9] See Peter Nosco (1996), "Keeping the Faith: Bakuhan Policy towards Religions in Seventeenth-Century Japan."

distinctions based on race, ethnicity, gender, social status, wealth, or other consideration, even if Buddhism's own record on some of these issues has been mixed. Buddhists have also been at the forefront of contemporary efforts to reject torture, capital punishment, and other inhuman or degrading forms of punishment, and to ensure freedom of thought, conscience, and religion, even while acknowledging that from the time of Aśoka, its past has at times embraced alternative paths.

However, it is difficult to imagine the world of Buddhism becoming exercised over rights of jurisprudence, privacy, employment, nationality, marriage, access to public service, and so on, all of which figure prominently in some discussions of human rights.[10] Here it is difficult to say why Buddhists have embraced some causes and not others. The answer may lie in the fact that Buddhism can no longer be regarded as a principally Asian religion, and as it has done many times in the past, it is once again accommodating itself to the needs, interests, and causes of a new world.

Conclusion

The globalization of ethics is a competition of ideas. The most basic ethical pronouncements – not killing, stealing, or lying – can all be thought of as socially generated, since it is difficult to imagine a society that would condone acts that challenge one's fundamental expectations regarding safety and property and the sanctity of covenants. Other pronouncements of an essentially moral nature – honoring God, not coveting what others have, fidelity in monogamous marriage – have traditionally been supported by creeds around which spiritual communities form.

But the globalization of ethics has introduced values with different kinds of significance. Social goals such as diversity and pluralism have become core values in some societies in their own right while remaining suppressed in others. An example of the latter is Japan, which, because of its low birthrate that is insufficient to sustain population, is confronted with a critical shortage of inexpensive labor, and where the emphasis on conformity and homogeneity is so strong that the society appears prepared to endure economic stagnation rather than use immigration to address the problem.

Other global values have fared somewhat better, such as environmentalism or sustainability, where the interests of the planet are placed above the interests of national entities or individual profit. In a world that daily seems more obviously interdependent, issues such as imbalance in the consumption of non-renewable resources or the manner in which despoiling the atmosphere crosses national boundaries become legitimate issues of concern, though, perhaps not surprisingly, the rhetoric has often run ahead of law and

---

[10] The rights enumerated in this paragraph and portions of their description are taken from the United Nations' 1948 Universal Declaration of Human Rights (Appendix A).

policy even in those societies that have most aggressively championed these causes.

So, too, with notions that are often considered parts of liberal democracy, such as opportunities for political participation, transparency of government decision making, restrictions on entrepreneurship, freedom of travel and employment, and so on. Generally, as societies have become more complex, with ever greater volumes of transactions, individuals have become increasingly practiced in negotiating these environments. Accompanying this newly found competence has been an increased confidence in individual determinism and agency, with consequences for how one balances the interests of the individual with the collective interest of large groups.

From this point of view, it appears that if Buddhism cannot be said to have won the competition for numbers when reckoning the world's spiritual allegiance, it has in substantial measure already seen many of its core teachings and principles emerge as central to the newly globalized ethics. Buddhism appeals to the altruism of modernity, while at the same time honoring the sovereignty over self so characteristic of post-modernity. Its emphasis on compassion and conquest through the force of ideas and not arms is integral to the professed values of any global order discernible on the horizon, just as Buddhism's confidence in karmic retribution allows for the promise of social justice without an extra-terrestrial social legislator.

To be sure, Buddhism cannot make exclusive claims to some of the truths that we've been examining. For example, if Buddhism makes claims regarding what constitute appropriate responses to a world of change, then so did King Solomon when he opined that all is meaningless or recognized that there is a time for everything (Eccl. 1:2, 3:1); and if Buddhism warns of the dangers of attachment to the self, then so did Jesus when he exhorted his followers to deny themselves in order to find the truth (Matt. 16:24–25); and again if Buddhism counsels us regarding our responsibilities to others, then so did Mohammed when he alerts us to our responsibilities to orphans and beggars (Koran, 93rd Surah). It is thus not the case that Buddhism can make exclusive or hegemonic claims on any number of values likely to figure prominently in any emergent global ethic, but it does appear that it can legitimately claim more of these values as its own than any other major religious tradition.

On the second day of his 2004 visit to the University of British Columbia, and in his roundtable dialog with fellow Nobel Prize laureates and other spiritual leaders, the Dalai Lama spoke of his conviction that moral ethics, as represented in a value like altruism, can exist independent of religious faith. He further stressed that even though religious faith can strengthen ethical and moral behavior in some individuals, secular society today needs to learn how to develop ethical values and teachings – "secular ethics" without religious faith. He clearly struck a resonant chord among many sympathizers when he opined that without religion, one could still be a good warm-hearted person. And what exactly are the notes that comprise that chord? Though others will surely wish to add to or edit my list, I would suggest the following three: remarkable faith in science and technology, hostility toward religious partisanship, and a hunger for community and rootedness.

If I understand the trajectory of the globalization of ethics correctly, Buddhism will fare well in the future as many individuals continue to seek belief and symbol systems that may have roots in religion but which suppress their "religious" (read "superstitious") character. Buddhism's traditional concern with compassion can thus serve as a foundational value in a newly globalized system of ethics, using the same rationale as classical Buddhism itself – that is, the interdependence of all creatures and interconnectedness of all phenomena, but without explicitly drawing Buddhism into the dialogue. In this sense, Buddhism may be even more allied with the proponents of globalized ethics than any of the Abrahamic traditions, and, with Buddhism's universalized principles and history of accommodation, it may enjoy an advantage in this respect over teachings such as the situational ethics of Confucianism, with which it would otherwise share much.

6

Muslim Perspectives on Global Ethics

Muhammad Khalid Masud

It was probably in 1996 that Professor Riffat Hassan first introduced me to the debate on Global Ethics. The idea was attractive, but I felt reluctant to participate for two reasons. These same two reasons continue to inhibit my enthusiasm for the subject even today. First, I find it problematic to represent Islam or Muslims because no one can speak on behalf of all Muslims or can authoritatively represent Muslims or Islam. This problem is apparent in inter-faith dialogue. Dialogues between Muslims and other religious communities falter because while the other religious communities may be represented by their institutional authorities (Sunni) Muslims have no equivalent institution-alized or official religious authority. Muslim religious scholars (Ulama), who are often considered as religious authorities, enjoy no such official position in fact. Various modern organizations, such as Islamic Councils, which also claim to be representatives of Islam, have no official position.

Furthermore, it is not only a question of the absence of institutionalized religious authority, but also one of representation. Genuine representation is not feasible because there is such a wide range of diversity present in religious beliefs and practices among Muslims for example, between the Shi'a and the Sunnis, the two main sects in Islam. There is also such a plurality of opinions among Muslim thinkers and intellectuals on current issues that no one person or group can truly claim to represent the range of Muslim thought and opin-ion and negotiate on behalf of the community as a monolithic body. I do not consider this situation as a weakness, but rather illustrative of the strength of Muslim intellectual tradition. In my view, the term "global ethics" reflects the universality of ethical principles in terms of their general acceptability in pop-ular public discourse, and not merely in academic circles. It cannot, therefore, be decided by religious scholars, experts, and philosophers alone, however authoritative they may claim to be. This universality fits in well with the situ-ation I have just described because it prevents a monopoly of representation or interpretation by a single Muslim body or person.

Second, the definition of the term "global" has been problematic for me, and has become increasingly so in recent years. I used to understand the terms "universal" and "global" as ethical and philosophical terms that refer to values and practices that are universally shared by all human beings. Recent terms such as Globalization, New World Order, WTO, and Turbo Capitalism have transformed the semantics of the terms "global" and "universal" such that particular "local" interests are propagated as "global" values and "ethical" is defined in terms of expediency.

Recent events in world history defy my current understanding of "global." I see a new meaning emerging, which is difficult for me to grasp because I see gross inconsistencies in how it is defined and justified. For example, when the clash of particular local and economic interests with the rest of the world is termed as "clash of civilizations," and when "Western" countries begin to justify regime change, target killings, and sub-human treatment of the accused and prisoners in the name of national security and globalization, I am very disturbed. The same crimes are ostensibly condemned as a violation of human rights on one side of the globe, and at the same time justified in the name of globalization and national security on the other side. Possession of weapons of mass destruction is deemed a cognizable offence with reference to some nations, but not for others. This difficult situation compels me to speak about the need for global ethics, though I am no longer sure if the way I understand the term "global" is relevant anymore.

This chapter is an analysis of Muslim perspectives on global ethics. Since I believe that I do not and cannot represent Muslims, I am describing how recent Muslim publications have dealt with questions relating to gender relations, democracy, and corporal punishment, which are currently debated as problems of "global ethic/s." I describe these perspectives as Muslim because the writers are very consciously presenting these views as specifically Muslim perspectives. I will also explore whether the ethical principles that form the basis of these issues are propagated as universal/global principles, or not. If global, two other questions arise: are they disseminated as alternative systems of ethics, and is the focus on uniformity or diversity? The chapter is divided into three parts. Part 1 offers an analysis of Muslim responses to human rights and to two recent declarations on "global ethics." Part 2 reviews a selection of recent Muslim writings on the aforementioned three issues. My concluding remarks in the Part 3 explore the contested meanings of "global/universal" and "globalization."

1 Declarations on Human Rights and Global Ethics

I am taking human rights as a point of departure, because Muslim attempts to define these rights provide a very significant perspective on global ethics as well. I will begin by comparing two Muslim documents on human rights with the Universal Declaration of Human Rights (UDHR) of 1948. These two documents are: (1) The Universal Islamic Declaration of Human Rights (UIDHR) 1981, and (2) the Cairo Declaration of Human Rights in Islam (CDHRI), 1990. In Part 2, I analyze Muslim responses to two declarations on Global Ethics by Hans Küng and Leonard Swidler.

Human Rights

The UIDHR was issued in 1981 to mark the fifteenth century of the Islamic Era by the Islamic Council, a non-governmental Muslim organization based in London. The Islamic Council was largely constituted of Islamist groups who either belonged to opposition political parties in the Middle East and had migrated to Europe, or who lived in countries such as Sudan, Pakistan, Iran, and Saudi Arabia, where the process of Islamization had already begun. As opposition political parties, these groups were often targeted by the ruling regimes in their countries of origin. Given this history, they were, quite logically, critical of the widespread violation of fundamental rights by Muslim states. The literature produced by these groups focused on the idea of freedom, and insisted that this was a fundamental right given by God and that no one could take it away from a human being.[1] They were also critical of the Universal Declaration of Human Rights for its neglect of cultural and religious contexts present in Muslim societies.

The Islamic Council felt the need for a human rights document that would secure the fundamental rights of these political groups and would be "Islamic" in its perspective. To achieve this goal, the Council held an International Conference on the Prophet Muhammad and His Message in London April 12–15, 1980, and proclaimed the Universal Islamic Declaration in 1981.

Salem Azzam, the Secretary General of the Islamic Council, explained in his foreword to this document that it was "compiled by eminent Muslim scholars, jurists and representatives of Islamic movements and thought." Justifying the proclamation, he commented that "It is unfortunate that human rights are trampled upon with impunity in many countries of the world, including some Muslim countries. Such violations are a matter of serious concern and [arouse] the conscience of more and more people throughout the world." The foreword does not refer to the 1948 Declaration of Human Rights. Instead, Azzam claims that "Human rights in Islam are an integral part of the overall Islamic order and it is obligatory on all Muslim governments and organs of society to implement them in letter and spirit within the framework of that order."

The second document, the CDHRI, was prepared by the Secretariat of the Organization of the Islamic Conference (OIC) and was adopted by forty-five countries at the Nineteenth Islamic Conference of Foreign Ministers of

---

[1] This point was stressed by Abu'l A'la Mawdudi in *Human Rights in Islam* (Leicester, 1976, p. 14). The Islamist writers underscore this characteristic Islamic approach to human rights frequently; see for instance, Muqtedar Khan (2006), "Syed Qutb – John Locke of the Islamic World."

the OIC in Cairo on August 5, 1990. Support for the CDHRI was recently reiterated at the 32nd Session (June 28–30, 2005) of the Islamic Conference of Foreign Ministers of the OIC held in Sana'a, Yemen, in its Resolution of Human Rights (No. 1/32-LEG).

I am not referring to these documents as official Muslim documents, nor do I claim that they have been ratified by all Muslim countries. I am using them to illustrate two Muslim perspectives on human rights. Both documents show a basic concern for human rights, as well as for defining them from a Muslim perspective. While the UIDHR takes a non-state Muslim perspective, the CDHRI presents a state perspective. They are not mutually contradictory, and the CDHRI is not meant to denounce the UIDHR or to replace it. Both were proclaimed in response to different needs. The UIDHR seems to be part of the Islamization movements that emerged with the advent of the fifteenth century of the Islamic Era, which corresponds to 1979 and onwards in the Gregorian calendar. The CDHRI seems to respond to several international pressures that Muslim countries, especially the Organization of Islamic Countries, felt during this period.

Technically, it is quite difficult to compare these documents with each other or with the UDHR, because of their different styles and focuses. I do not, therefore, claim this analysis to be complete. My purpose is to compare similarities and differences in general terms with the Universal Declaration.

In this brief comparative analysis[2] (see Table 6.1), I find that the similarities between the Muslim documents and the UDHR are greater than the differences. The two documents share the twentieth and fourteenth themes respectively (expressed as rights) with those mentioned in the UDHR. It is also significant that the Universal Islamic Declaration, which is a non-state declaration, has more in common with the UDHR than the Cairo Declaration, which is a state document. In 1999, the Cairo Institute for Human Rights Studies organized a conference of Arab intellectuals to discuss human rights charters. The conference termed the Cairo Declaration as "insulting to Islam" and called for discarding the Arab Charter of Human Rights as well as the Cairo Declaration of Human Rights in Islam.[3]

The Muslim documents differ with the UDHR on the following themes: freedom of thought and expression, protection of life, penal laws, marriage,

---

[2] In this table, I have examined the two documents, UIDHR and CDHRI, indicating them respectively as * and #. I use these symbols twice if the theme mentioned in the UDHR is included, and only once if the theme is restricted or qualified in these documents. I consider the theme restricted when the Muslim documents use phrases such as "in accordance with Law," "subject to Law," and "as provided by the Law." As explained by the documents, "Law" in such phrases means Islamic law. Absence of these symbols indicates that the theme or the value mentioned in the relevant article of the UDHR is not included in the Muslim document.

[3] Bahey el-Din Hassan, *Arabs Caught between Domestic Oppression and Foreign Injustice* (Cairo: Cairo Institute of Human Rights Studies, 2001), p. 10.

TABLE 6.1. *Human Rights Declarations Compared*

UDHR	General theme	UDHR	CDHRI
Article no.		Article no.	Article no.
I	Freedom	* II a	## 11
2	Freedom	** II b	
3	Life, liberty, security	* Ia, IIa	# 2, ## 18
4	No slavery	** Preamble giii	## 11
5	Torture	* Ia, ** IIa	
6	Protection of law	** IIIa, VI	## 19a
7	Equality before law	** IIIa Vi	## 19 a
8	Right to justice	** IV Va	## 19b
9	No arbitrary arrest	** XXIIIb, V	## 20
10	Fair trial	** V	
11	Innocence, penalty	** V	## 19c
12	Privacy	** VI, VIII, XXII	## 4, 18b
13	Movement	** XXIII	# 12
14	Asylum	** IX a	# 12
15	Nationality		
16	Marriage	* XIXa, XIX i	## 5, 5a
17	Ownership of property	** XVc, XVI	## 15
18	Freedom of thought	* XII	
19	Freedom of expression	* XIId	# 22a
20	Assembly	**	# 22a
21	Political participation	**	# 23
22	Public office	* XIa, XI b	# 23b
23	Free development of personality	** XVIII	
24	Employment	** IIIb,c, XVII	## 13 # 14
25	Right to rest	** XVII	
26	Standard life	** XVIII	## 17
27	Education	** XXI	## 9b
28	Cultural life		
29	International order		
30	Protection of rights		
31	Interpretation of the Declaration		

Note: * and #. Used twice if the theme mentioned in the UDHR is included, and only once if the theme is restricted or qualified in these documents.

and holding public office. Both documents are silent on the right to nationality, cultural life, and international order. In addition, the Cairo Declaration is also silent on some aspects of freedom: torture, free trial, freedom of thought, and free development of personality. Examining the differences, while the UDHR defines human rights within the framework of a nation-state, the two documents focus on an intra-Muslim state context.

The Muslim documents rarely repeat the wording in the UDHR; they use a different vocabulary and a different order of arrangement in enumerating these rights. Sometimes the Muslim documents are more expansive than the Universal Declaration. There is a difference in style and emphasis between the two Muslim documents as well. As noted earlier, the Universal Islamic Declaration, as a non-state document, is more open and shares more themes with the UDHR. The CDHRI is more restrictive and uses more religious language. The Universal Islamic Declaration demonstrates a greater emphasis on human rights, compared with the CDHRI, in the areas of freedom, torture, fair trial, development of personality, right to rest, and freedom of thought. The CDHRI is either silent or restrictive on these points.

Pending deeper analysis, the non-state UIDHR is more concerned with political freedom, while the CDHRI, as a state document, has security concerns, and is apprehensive of these freedoms. The reason is that the UIDHR was proposed by Muslim groups that belonged to opposition political parties and organizations in Muslim countries. They were more concerned with political freedoms than other rights.

On the whole, there is an attempt in both documents to come closer to the global community. The same trend is reflected in numerous Muslim writings on human rights that stress common perspectives among them.[4] They suggest uniformity with an emphasis on diversity. In other words, diversity in these writings stresses the possibility of localizing the universals. For example, universal rights are expressed in language drawn from a uniquely Muslim perspective, but also often claiming that Islam is the first religion to award these human rights to everyone.

From the Muslim perspective, the major obstacle in the universal application of human rights is the fear that powerful Western countries are using human rights to sustain their hegemonic power. A section of the resolution[5] (1997)[6] of the Islamic Summit conference on the fiftieth anniversary

---

[4] I would like to mention the following two books written respectively from traditional and liberal perspectives: Abd al-Wahhab Abd al-Aziz al-Shishani, Huquq al-insan wa hurriyatihu al-asasiyya fi al-nizam al-Islami wa al-nuzum al-mu'asara (*Rights of Man and his Basic Freedoms in the Islamic System and Contemporary Systems*, Riyadh: al-Jam'iyyat al-Ilmiyya al-malikiyya, 1980); Ali Abd al-Wahid Wafi, Huquq al-Insan fi'l Islam (*Human Rights in Islam*, Cairo: Nahda Misr, 1999, sixth edition).

[5] Resolutions Concerning Political, Muslim Minorities and Communities, Legal and Information Affairs Adopted by The Eighth Session of the Islamic Summit Conference (Session of Dignity, Dialogue, Participation), Tehran, Islamic Republic Of Iran, 9–11 Sha'aban, 1418h (9–11 December, 1997); Resolution No. 56/8-P (Is) on Contribution of the Organization of the Islamic Conference on the Occasion of the Fiftieth Anniversary of the Universal Declaration of Human Rights.

[6] This fear is more clearly pronounced in the aforementioned OIC Resolution no. 1/32-LEG 2005. The resolution, among other things, calls for "abstaining from using the universality of human rights as a pretext to interfere in the states' internal affairs and undermine their national sovereignty."

of the UDHR illustrates this fear. It acknowledges Muslim approval of human rights in general, but expresses serious reservations about the undermining of national sovereignty and regional particularities. The resolution calls for serious discussion on these issues among the member states.

> ...[R]eiterating the necessity of taking advantage of the occasion of the Fiftieth Anniversary of the Universal Declaration of Human Rights to highlight the lofty human values brought in by Islam long before any positive covenants:
>
> 1. Calls upon members of the international community in commemorating the Fiftieth Anniversary of Universal Declaration of Human Rights to reiterate their commitments to respect the universally accepted principles as follows:
>   - (a) The international community must treat human rights in a fair and equal manner. To this end, the significance of national and regional particularities and various historical, cultural and religious backgrounds must be respected;
>   - (b) The right to development and decent living is a universal and inalienable right and an integral part of fundamental human rights, which should be promoted and fully realized through the international cooperation and the creation of favorable economic international environment without hegemony or the imposition of policies of coercion or starvation on Member States;
>   - (c) The exploitation of human rights for political and economic objectives is contrary to the purposes and principles of the Charter of Untied Nations, in particular recognition of and full respect for non-violability of the sovereignty of nations, their independence and non-interference in their internal affairs as well as to the very spirit and objectives of Universal Declaration of Human Rights;
>   - (d) The principles of objectivity, non-selectivity, and transparency, in the promotion of Human Rights, are of utmost importance;
>   - (e) The enhancement of international cooperation and consensus building through genuine dialogue instead of confrontation is essential for the effective promotion and protection of all human rights;
>   - (f) Recognition and full respect for the principal legal systems of the world including the Islamic jurisprudence is essential for the promotion of the comprehensive understanding of and the universality of the Universal Declaration of Human Rights; ...[7]

The claim by Muslim scholars that human rights originate in Islam, and their subsequent emphasis on regional, religious, and cultural particularities, is often criticized by Western scholars. This position is sometimes described

---

[7] http://www.president.ir/oic/oicpol.html.

as "mimicry," and frequently termed "apologetics."[8] I find this critique problematic.

For the successful application of any idea within a community, it is essential that people come to own that idea. An academic discussion of whether human rights originated in the West or in Islam is not so important if Muslim societies do not violate them. I do not find the strategy of expressing human rights in Islamic language mimicking or apologetic; I consider it a serious attempt by Muslims to internalize an understanding and application of human rights.

Another criticism that is often leveled at Muslims is that Islamic modernist thought is also "apologetic" or defensive about Islam with regard to human rights. In my view, it is West-centrism that blurs the sense of direction in this dynamic. Instead of the perception that Muslims are defending Islam to Westerners, it is possible that this dynamic is directed towards the Muslim community. In other words, it may very well be a defense of human rights and justification of their compatibility with Islam directed towards conservative Muslim traditionalists who object to human rights as an essentially Western construct. The Western critique of Muslims weakens the adoption of human rights and endorses the position of Muslim conservatives who oppose these ideas because they are perceived as Western.

Western writers also dislike the use of religious language by Muslims because they believe that human rights are secular and must not be expressed in religious language. I see this perception of secularism as problematic. I will come back to this point later.

The real problem lies in what Ann Elizabeth Mayer rightly observes as "the lack of any explicit methodology" in deriving such "rights" from "Islamic sources." At times, she seems to suggest the impossibility of such a methodology, but nevertheless often refers to the points where Muslim perspectives on human rights differ with those of others. I agree with Mayer that it is a challenge of methodology, but it is not only for Muslims. It is a challenge to define and apply human rights as truly universal principles, and not as an instrument for cultural, economic, and political hegemony of the powerful. For this reason, human rights have to be rooted in universal ethics.

In my view, it is this essential point – the ethical aspect of human rights – which has been lacking in debates on Islam and human rights. A movement for global ethics hopes to fill this gap. I believe Muslim anxieties emerge from concerns about national sovereignty and security on one level, and from religious and cultural perspectives on another. In many cases, human rights are restricted or violated by Muslim governments in the name of national security, and these countries object to international criticism as a violation of their national sovereignty. Concern for national security cannot justify violation of

---

[8] See, for instance, Ann E. Mayer (1991), *Islam and Human Rights,* and Christian Moe (2002) "Islamic Human Rights Thought in Bosnia," especially his section on 'A Critical Survey of Islamic Human Rights Literature' from http://folk.uio.no/chrismoe/research/docproj.htm.

the freedom and dignity of man, but this needs to be applicable in all countries, not just Muslim ones. For example, the U.S., Britain, and Israel, to name a few, also violate human rights and justify them in the name of national security. The UDHR document is quite ambivalent in addressing this situation; it stresses both the universality of human rights and the principle of national sovereignty.

Global Ethics

Since 1993, there has been a steady movement towards defining and understanding global ethics. The Parliament of World Religions in Chicago adopted a "Declaration toward a Global Ethic,"[9] drafted by Hans Küng,[10] a professor at Tübingen University in Germany. Another document, "Toward A Universal Declaration of A Global Ethic," written by Leonard Swidler of Temple University, was analyzed and discussed in the following conferences: the "International Scholars' Annual Trialogue – ISAT" (Jewish-Christian-Muslim) in Graz, Austria (1993); "First International Conference on Universalism," Warsaw (1993); American Academy of Religion Washington D.C (1993); the sixth "International Scholars' Annual Trialogue" (1994); "International Association of Asian Philosophy and Religion–IAAPR" Seoul, Korea (1994); the "World Conference on Religion and Peace–WCRP" (1994); World Assembly in Rome (1994), Italy; "Fiftieth Anniversary of the Founding of the United Nations," San Francisco (1995). Both the Commission on Global Governance and the World Commission on Culture and Development in 1995 called, respectively, for "global civic ethics" and "global ethical standards."[11] Several institutions are engaged in serious work on global ethics.[12]

The movement for global ethics does not specifically connect to the human rights movement, but it shares several common concerns. It is not necessary here to review the entirety of the global ethics movement. I am interested only in looking at Muslim responses to it. The following is a brief summary of the comments by Khalid Duran, a well-known Muslim intellectual, and Riffat Hassan, a professor at Louisville University, on these two documents by Hans Küng and Leonard Swidler. Duran and Hassan both acknowledge the need for global ethics and agree generally with the universal principles propounded in these documents. However, they raise some very essential questions from the Muslim perspective, though they vary on questions of methodology.

---

9 See, for text and explanations, http://astro.temple.edu/~dialogue/Antho/kung.htm, "Explanatory Remarks Concerning a "Declaration of the Religions for a Global Ethic" "A Universal Declaration of Global Ethic" (Appendix 4).

10 See http://astro.temple.edu/~dialogue/Center/kung.htm.

11 See http://www.unesco.org/opi2/philosophyandethics/pronpro.htm for the UNESCO Universal Ethics Project.

12 For instance, Ethikon Institute, California; Institute for Global Ethics, Camden, ME; Center for Global Ethics, and Global Dialogue Institute, Philadelphia.

Khalid Duran[13] raises the question of universality and specificity with reference to ethics. He stresses that Islam is a religion, as well as a culture, and thus its diversity expresses itself in cultural specificities. Islam as culture has developed the concept of Akhlaq (ethics) in addition to Shari'a (law). Both philosophers and Sufis propagate ethics as universal and Shari'a as specific. Focusing on the specific over the universal poses a problem for the universality of ethics. Gender relations and democracy are examples in this regard. According to Khalid Duran, some Muslim groups that are marginal in Muslim societies disregard the principles of ethics in such matters and insist on specific legal aspects. In fact, there is currently an intensive debate throughout the Muslim world on whether Shari'a is applicable to all human beings or only to Muslims. There is also a debate about whether a global ethics is possible.

Duran finds that these discussions are related to some methodological issues. First is the issue of balancing universality and particularity. If a particular global and universal ethic is defined very broadly only in universal terms, while neglecting the particularities, it may create a ready consensus, but it will not be able to achieve the goal. Pressure groups in Muslim societies may use a cultural specificity argument to defeat the purpose of global ethics. According to Duran, the issue is much more complex. He questions the supposition that cultures really differ from each other, in the sense that people in different cultures think in different thought categories. If that is true, as the fundamentalists in Islam and in the West claim, then universality is not possible. One important example of this situation is how the "Other" is culturally defined. Is it because cultures have different assumptions of the "Other" or because their thought categories differ? Duran's question is provocative, yet very basic. It can be argued that creating a uniform perception of the "Other" in a particular community is a social process. It is not something inherent in the culture, because the perceptions change. If that is true, global standards are also possible, but as a process of social change, not by legislation alone.

Duran refers to cross-cultural trends within the Islamic philosophical and intellectual tradition, which has continuously interacted with other cultures throughout history. The Muslim philosopher's story of Hayy bin Yaqzan (The Living One Son of the Awake) describes how a human child who grows up away from humans, among the animals, reaches the same ethical conclusions in his reasoning as those taught by revealed religion. Muslim philosophers used this story to dismiss the claims of conflict between reason and revelation and to argue that by nature humans share the same universal moral values.[14]

Riffat Hassan views "global ethics" as connected with human rights, which she finds problematic from her particular Muslim perspective. She describes

---

[13] Khalid Duran, "Leonard Swidler's Draft of a Global Ethic: A Muslim Perspective," http://astro.temple.edu/~dialogue/Antho/duran.htm.

[14] I have analyzed these different trends in the history of Islam in my essay " The Scope of Pluralism in Islamic Moral Traditions" (Masud, 2003).

human rights as Western and secular and therefore cause for Muslim opposition to them. According to her, Muslims are foremost in resisting global ethics for the same reason. However, she welcomes the global ethics movement as a move toward religion. She calls it a major paradigm shift. This is in contrast to Hans Küng, who still finds religion problematic as a thought category, because not all religions agree on basic concepts, such as the existence of God. Leonard Swidler, on the other hand, finds religion crucial in the universality of ethics. He refers to certain golden rules that all religious traditions agree upon, and hence that could serve as a common point of departure in global ethics.

Riffat Hassan argues that secularism (and humanism), which gives supremacy to reason over revelation, is unacceptable to Muslims.[15] She also disagrees with those who insist that global ethics is possible only with reason, not with revelation. Like Swidler, who seeks common ethical principles in religious scriptures, she finds universal principles of ethics enunciated in the Qur'an. Methodologically, she suggests that a global ethical consensus among Muslims on these universal values is inevitable. Muslims will not adopt ethical standards that are not supported by the Qur'an, according to her argument. She does not find this situation difficult, because the Qur'an already calls for such standards.

Riffat Hassan finds the general Muslim view on gender relations problematic. But, according to her, a new hermeneutical approach to the study of the Qur'an can clarify the fact that over time, cultural assumptions have obscured the original meanings of the Qur'an.

Riffat Hassan questions the universality of the proposed global ethics in the declarations mentioned. She observes that "[T]heir fundamental presuppositions are a priori. They are not the products of an internal dialogue within each religion regarding its central ethical concerns and principles, widening into a dialogue with other religions on the same matters." This observation suggests that the West and a type of democratic process have developed a particular concept and process of consensus that proceeds from the top down. The idea is conceived, drafted, discussed, and agreed upon by the "experts," and signed and legislated by the governments. There is no dialogue or discussion at the grassroots level. These drafts on global ethics are not products of internal dialogues. Hassan is particularly conscious of the fact that despite a shift toward religion in societies all over the world, the documents on human rights and global ethics insist on secularism as a global value.

Duran also refers to the fact that some of the values propagated as global are not really rooted in all cultures across the globe. The ambivalence in the use of terms like "democracy" and "freedom of the press" during the Cold War is a good example of this lack of universality. Most governments, including Muslim dictatorial regimes, use the terms more in a rhetorical than practical

---

[15] Riffat Hassan, "A Muslim's Reflections on a New Global Ethics and Cultural Diversity," http://kvc.minbuza.nl/uk/archive/amsterdam/ukverslag_hassan.html.

sense; elections are often held ritually. It is therefore not surprising that some Muslim thinkers argue that there is no place for democracy in Islam. The underlying reason for this ambivalence is that these concepts and institutions are not internalized indigenously. Therefore, it is not possible to expect Muslim societies to support these concepts as a priori values.

2 Three Trends in Islamic Jurisprudence

Let me now turn to an analysis of recent Muslim works on the specific issues of gender relations, democracy, and penal laws. A comprehensive analysis of Muslim perspectives on these issues is not possible here, not only because there is a wide range of diversity of thought among Muslim scholars, but also because this diversity is informed by a complex understanding of tradition and change that defies easy categorization. Attempts to divide Muslims into "modernists" and "traditionalists," for example, ignore this complexity. For the sake of convenience, I discuss three major trends in Muslim jurisprudence. I focus on these trends because they have tried to develop their own methodologies in order to deal with the three issues. I have not included the extreme ends of this complex spectrum – which we might consider the most Westernized, liberal secular Muslim perspective on the one end, and the most conservative traditional views in Muslim legal thought on the other – as both are already well known, if only as caricatures and stereotypes. My focus, rather, is on the more creative recent developments within Islamic legal and ethical thought.

Neo-conservative

This group has been described as "fundamentalist," "political Muslim," and "Islamist," but I prefer to call them "neo-conservative." I borrow this term from Kecia Ali,[16] a senior researcher at Brandies University, who observes the differences between the way conservatives and neo-conservatives define gender relations in Islamic laws. According to Ali, "neo-conservatives" are a new group that shares the same patriarchal and restrictive positions on gender relations as traditionalists, but who use a distinctly modern diction. Instead of relying only on traditional sources, and the Qur'an and Sunna, they refer to modern authors of books on social sciences. They use current thought categories to support traditional views. Ali gives examples of these types of works by Abdul Rahman Doi,[17] former Director of the Centre for Islamic Legal Studies in Zaria, Nigeria; Muhammad Abdul-Rauf,[18] formerly Director of the

---

[16] Kecia Ali, "Progressive Muslims and Islamic Jurisprudence: The Necessity for Critical Engagement with Marriage and Divorce Law," in Omid Safi (ed), *Progressive Muslims: On Justice, Gender and Pluralism,* Oxford: Oneworld, 2003, pp. 183–189.

[17] Abdul Rahman Doi, *Women in Shari'ah* (Islamic Law) (London: Ta-Ha, 1994).

[18] Muhammad Abdul-Rauf, *Marriage in Islam: A Manual* (Alexandria, VA: Al-Saadawi, 2000, reprint of 1972 edition).

Islamic Center in Washington; and Saalih ibn Ghanim al-Sadlaan,[19] a professor from the College of Shari'ah at Muhammad ibn Saud Islamic University in Riyadh. I have chosen to focus on another professor from the same university, Abdul Wahhab Abdul Aziz al-Shishani, who has written a substantial volume on human rights in Islam.[20] Before delving into this work, it is important to contextualize it by examining the rise of this trend.

Neo-conservative jurists differ from the traditional conservatives in methodology and jurisprudence, but they agree with them in substance on essential issues. To clarify, let me compare the two groups. Neo-conservative Muslim groups such as the Muslim Brotherhood, known as al-Ikhwan al-Muslimun in Arabic, which was founded in Egypt by Hasan al-Banna in 1928, and the Jama'at Islami, which was founded by Mawlana Mawdudi in 1943 in India, often distinguish themselves from the Tablighi Jama'at, whom they regard as typically conservative. The Tablighi Jama'at was founded by Mawlana Muhammad Ilyas in 1930[21] in Mewat, India, and is now operating in more than eighty countries. This group is particularly concerned with the rise of materialism and modernization in Muslim societies. These are also the concerns of the neo-conservative Muslims. The Jama'at takes a very conservative view on issues relating to the position of women, progress and development, modernity, and Westernization. The Jama'at Islami and the Ikhwan also share the conservatism of the Tablighi Jama'at on most of these issues, including, for instance, veiling and seclusion of women, polygamy, and patriarchal family structure.

They differ, however, in their proposed methods of reform in Muslim societies. The Tablighi Jama'at insists on preserving social and moral values by reviving the Islamic concept and institution of hisbah, "commanding good and forbidding evil." It also supports the traditional view of separation between religion and politics. While the conservatives justify their views with reference to Islamic law and history, the neo-conservatives refer more frequently to Western thinkers and history to support their view. The neo-conservatives thus attract followers more among the educated classes than among the masses. While the Tablighi Jama'at remains apolitical and aims at moral and personal reform, the neo-conservative groups accuse the Tablighi Jama'at of neglecting the most essential Islamic obligation of jihad, which they define as a struggle

---

[19] Saalih ibn Ghanim al-Sadlaan, *Marital Discord (al-Nushooz): Its Definition, Cases, Causes, Means of Protection from It, and Its Remedy from the Qur'an and Sunnah,* transl. Jamaal al-Din M. Zarabozo (Boulder: Al-Basheer, 1996).

[20] Abd al-Wahhab Abd al-Aziz al-Shishani, Huquq al-insan wa al-hurriyat al-asasiyya fi al-nizam al-Islami wa al-nuzum al-mu'asara (*Rights of Man and His Basic Freedoms in the Islamic System and Contemporary Systems,* Riyadh: al-Jam'iyyat al-'Ilmiyya al-malikiyya, 1980).

[21] See, for this critique, Muhammad Khalid Masud (editor), *Travelers in Faith:* Studies on *Tablighi Jama'at as a Transnational Movement for the Renewal of Faith* (Brill, Leiden, 2000), chapter 4 on "Ideology and Legitimacy," particularly, pp. 90–94.

for the revival of the political power of Islam. The neo-conservative groups criticize adherence to the traditional schools of Islamic law and Sufism that have led to neglect of the fundamentals of Islam in their view – the establishment of an Islamic state and the sovereignty of God.

Neo-conservative ideology and jurisprudence is articulated in the context of modernity, which neo-conservatives define as a clash between civilization and paganism. Sayyid Qutb (d. 1966) and Mawlana Mawdudi (d. 1979) both speak about the modern state of ignorance and paganism (linked to the pre-Islamic social conditions termed jahiliyya), which denies the sovereignty (Hakimiyya) of God. Qutb developed an elaborate critique of the West and modernity as a type of paganism clashing with the civilization of Islam. Mawlana Abu'l Hasan Ali Nadwi (d. 1999), one of the ideologues of the Tablighi Jama'at, recognizes the conflict, but does not suggest the separation of Muslims from the West as a response.[22] Nadwi favors selective adoption of Western sciences. Qutb and Mawdudi, on the other hand, regard Islamic revival as the only way to save humanity from this paganism.

Sayyid Qutb's jurisprudence is a product of his critique of Western thought on materialism, democracy, humanism, secularism, and morality. He distinguishes Islamic society from others because it is based on the permanent foundations of Shari'a. He defines Shari'a as a Divine law that is natural, immutable, and comprehensive. He insists on the purity of Islamic thought and law and argues that the real damage was caused in Islam when faith was mixed with the methods of philosophy. This attempt to combine the facts of Islamic faith with the confusing ideas of metaphysics produced the so-called Islamic philosophy (Qutb, 1980, pp. 12–13).

The neo-conservative jurisprudence that developed under the influence of Sayyid Qutb's thought distinguishes Shari'a from Fiqh (traditional Islamic jurisprudence). Shari'a is divine and immutable, while the Fiqh is of human origin, historical and changeable (Qutb, 1988, pp. 47–50). Neo-conservative jurisprudence believes that the Shari'a is the only expression of Divine sovereignty. According to Qutb (1988), there are four possible situations in a Shari'a ruling in a given case: (1) Shari'a ruling is clear and explicit, (2) Shari'a ruling is not clear, (3) Shari'a ruling is general, not specific, and (4) Shari'a is silent. There is no role for Ijtihad, or independent legal reasoning, in the first situation, but it is certainly required in the second and third situations, and absolutely imperative in the fourth (p. 57–58).

Sayyid Qutb suggests going back directly to the permanent and immutable Shari'a and disregarding the importance of Fiqh. His dismissal of jurisprudence leaves a jurist at a loss. He regards Shari'a as immutable and permanent, but he also argues that society is continuously changing. He recognizes the need

---

[22] See Abu'l Hasan Ali Nadwi (1976, 1982), Muslim Mamalik men Islamiyyat awr Maghrabiyyat ki Kashmakash; and Western Civilization: Islam and Muslims.

for Ijtihad, but rejects the tradition of Fiqh and its methods of legal reasoning. He gives a very idealistic view of Shari'a and Islamic society, but supports the traditional view on gender relations, democracy, and penal laws. He claims that while other societies are not based on permanent principles, and hence change continuously and aimlessly, Islamic society is based on permanent principles of Shari'a, and despite some deviations and changes has always stayed close to the Shari'a (Qutb, 1988, p. 68). He offers a very complex view of Shari'a and Islamic society and therefore a very complicated set of legal views.

Sayyid Qutb did not write specifically on human rights or global ethics, but there is another author whose work can offer some perspectives on this issue. Abdul Wahhab Abdul Aziz al-Shishani's work on human rights in Islam, although little known in the West, is extremely important because it illustrates an aspect of neo-conservative Islamic jurisprudence.[23]

Shishani calls attention to the major paradigm shift in the concept of state in the modern period. A modern state's purpose is defined as protecting the rights of the individual (Shishani, 1980, p. 5). The centrality of the state with reference to Islamic law (Shari'a) calls for an examination of classical jurisprudence, especially its doctrine of the sources of law. Traditionally, the Qur'an, the Sunna (the rulings and practice of Prophet Muhammad), Qiyas (analogies from these two), and Ijma' (consensus of the jurists) are regarded as the four authoritative sources of Islamic law. Shishani adds six more to this list, explaining that this inclusion is still debatable.[24]

Following the model articulated in traditional jurisprudence, Shishani divides rights into two groups: the rights of God and the rights of humans. Rights of God include acts of worship and rituals, as well as penalties outlined in the Shari'a that are aimed at protecting life, property, reason, and family. They are also public rights. These rights of God cannot be abolished or amended (Shishani, 1980, p. 300).

Among the rights of humans, freedom and equality are basic rights, according to Shishani. Freedom of belief is derived from freedom of thought and reason (Shishani, 1980, p. 495). It includes freedom to worship and to discuss religious matters. Islam regards protection of this freedom as an individual as well as a collective obligation. Traditionally, freedom of belief does not include disavowal of Islam; apostasy is punishable by death. Shishani agrees with this traditional view and explains that apostasy is a threat to the essence of freedom. Since there is no compulsion to accept Islam, and a person embraces

---

[23] See Abdul Wahhab Abd al-Aziz al-Shishani (1980), Huquq al-insan wa hurriyatihu al-asasiyya fi al-nizam al-Islami wa al-nuzum al-mu'asara (*Rights of Man and His Basic Freedoms in Islamic System and Contemporary Systems*.

[24] They are the following: Istihsan (preference on the basis of common good), masalih (common interest), istishab (precedent), urf (custom), madhhab sahabi (opinion and practice of the companions of the Prophet Muhammad), and shar' min qabalina (revealed laws before the Prophet Muhammad).

Islam by exercising his freedom to choose, apostasy challenges this freedom, because it challenges a belief in Islam (Shishani, 1980, p. 558). It deserves the most severe penalty in order to protect public interest. Similarly, freedom of expression is also restricted in order to maintain public interest, prevention of evil and social disruption and falsehood and to protect the honor and integrity of people against abusive and derogatory remarks (Shishani, 1980, p. 571).

Regarding democracy, Shishani argues that the source of political authority in Islam is the umma (Muslim people) [(Shishani, 1980, p. 607)]. This argument appears to challenge the idea of the sovereignty of God expounded by Mawdudi and Qutb. Shishani explains that the people have a right to choose and depose the ruler, according to Islamic teachings. Shura, or mutual consultation, is the basic principle in the political process (Shishani, 1980, p. 617). A caliph, Muslim head of state, is elected in three phases: first, there is a proposal for nomination; second, the proposal is deliberated and voted upon by eligible voters; and third, a general vote of allegiance (bay'a) is given. Agreement is defined in terms of the will of the majority (Shishani, 1980, p. 624). Shishani's explanation makes democracy more compatible with Islamic teachings than the ideas proposed by Mawdudi and Qutb.

The value of equality, according to Shishani, has several dimensions: equality before the law, equality in judicial process, and equality in economic opportunity and equality in holding public office. Women and non-Muslims are not allowed absolute equality. Non-Muslims have full freedom and equality in the practice of their religion, and their personal laws. However, this freedom is restricted when it is in conflict with the freedom of Muslims or when it is harmful to them (Shishani, 1980, p. 667). That is also the reason why a non-Muslim cannot hold public offices that have an impact on the practice of Islam. Here, Sishani cites Mawdudi, explaining that an Islamic state is an ideological state, and a person who is hostile or does not share the belief in that ideology cannot be allowed to hold a public office (Shishani, 1980, p. 671).

According to Sishani, the equality of women in political matters is not an Islamic issue. It is a Western problem. The absence of this equality does not harm the objectives of Islam, in his opinion. Furthermore, he argues that women differ from men physically, mentally, and in their natural abilities, and therefore scientists have explained that women have no interest in public office (Shishani, 1980, p. 687). He agrees with classical jurists who have unanimously ruled that a woman cannot hold a public office, especially that of the head of state, because women have no ability to deal with such matters (Shishani, 1980, p. 697).

This brief analysis of the neo-conservative trend is sufficient to indicate that, despite its criticism of traditional jurisprudence, neo-conservative jurisprudence is focused on preserving conservative views on gender relations, penal laws, and democracy, and seeks to buttress them by adding a global, political perspective to the doctrines of traditional fiqh.

Islamic Modernist

In contrast to the conservatives, Islamic modernists believe that modernity is compatible with Islam. Like Neo-conservatives, they stress Ijtihad (independent reasoning) as opposed to strict adherence to the Islamic legal tradition, but they define it as "reinterpretation" or "reconstruction."[25] They believe that the classical legal doctrines were products of historical and social contexts, and therefore there is a need for reform in the contemporary context. During the period between 1950 and 1970, most Muslim countries were able to introduce reforms in family[26] and constitutional laws with the help of Islamic modernists. This group believes that modern challenges call for the reinterpretation of Islam, because Islam has been always responsive to the needs of the time. Their methodology consists of explaining the historical and social contexts of the basic Islamic texts, including the Qur'an and Hadith, and reinterpreting them in view of modern needs. To illustrate this trend here, I have selected the proceedings of an international conference on "Islamic Laws and Women in the Modern World," held in Islamabad in 1995.[27] Prominent jurists and thinkers from Bangladesh, Egypt, India, Indonesia, Iran, Malaysia, Pakistan, Tunisia, and Turkey participated in this conference. The conference deliberated on the following issues relating to gender relations: age at marriage, divorce, polygamy, inheritance, women's legal testimony, and Hudud laws.

The conference found the issue of age at marriage interlinked with the concept of the patriarchal family. Legally, this issue raised questions about the consent of spouses to marriage, definition of adulthood, and the role and authority of parents and others as marriage guardians. Islamic law defines marriage as a contract that requires the consent of the individuals, who must have legal capacity to enter into a contract. However, Islamic traditional law also allows child marriage, and justifies it as a social need to protect the interest of minors. The institution of marriage guardians exists for this reason, and guardians can and do frequently intervene in marriage between adults if they find it contrary to their interest. Islamic legal tradition defines puberty as the criterion for adulthood.

The Islamic modernists disagree with the definition of adulthood and the justification for marriages of minors and call for reforms on account of medical, legal and social grounds and reinterpretation of the Qur'an. The conference reported that, according to recent reforms, the legal age of marriage in Iran is set at $14\frac{1}{2}$ years for males, and $8\frac{1}{2}$ for females; in other countries, the laws

---

[25] For instance, Muhammad Iqbal (d. 1938), a Muslim thinker who influenced Muslim thinking in the subcontinent, used the term "reconstruction." See Muhammad Khalid Masud (2003a), *Iqbal's Reconstruction of Ijtihad* (2nd edition).

[26] For a comprehensive study of reforms in family laws, see Tahir Mahmood (1972), *Family Law Reform in the Muslim World.*

[27] Giant Forum, International Conference on Islamic Laws and Women in the Modern World (Islamabad: Giant Forum, 1996).

have been reformed to set the legal age at marriage between 17 and 21 years for males and between 15 and 18 years for females. During the discussion, the participants observed that legal reforms have not been able to change the common practice of child marriage in Muslim societies. Some members who supported child marriage argued that these reforms do not take into consideration the sexual needs of teenagers, which are best channelled into a marriage.

Regarding the issue of polygamy, the Qur'an permits it under the condition of justice between the wives. Islamic modernists call for the abolition or reduction of this practice. The presence of social, financial, and international pressures has drastically reduced the practice of polygamy. With reference to legal reforms, Turkey and Tunisia forbid polygamy, Iran allows it, and other countries restrict it by subjecting the second marriage to the permission of the first wife. The participants generally observed that polygamy deprives women of their basic rights, and that merely stipulating that the first wife has a right to permit or prevent polygamy, as provided for in some reformed family laws, was not an adequate solution. The husband either disregarded this stipulation or coerced the first wife into giving this permission. Some participants argued that absolute prohibition was not in the public interest because there could be circumstances, such as a war-affected society, where men could be outnumbered by women, therefore making marriage a justifiable way to protect women in society.

With reference to divorce, it is claimed that Islamic law provides a husband with an unlimited right to divorce. The wife's right to divorce is debatable. Islamic modernists insist on the equality of men and women and explore Islamic legal provisions that allow women the right to divorce. Islamic modernists find support for their position in the Muslim legal tradition in three ways: according to the doctrines of (1) Khul' (a wife can negotiate divorce with her husband by returning some property given to her by the husband), (2) Tafwid Talaq (stipulating a clause in the marriage contract that a wife can divorce her husband under certain conditions), and (3) Tafriq (the doctrine of judicial divorce). Accordingly, divorce laws were reformed in several Muslim countries. Egypt and Iran retained an Islamic legal provision to give the husband a unilateral right to divorce his wife. Turkey and Tunisia provided equal rights for husband and wife to divorce each other. Pakistan, Malaysia, and Bangladesh extended to Muslim wives the right of judicial and delegated divorce.

The conference observed that these reforms have not been able to change social thinking about the stigma of divorce. The law has also not taken into consideration the social and financial impact of divorce, particularly on children. The problem of the custody of children also prevents women from opting for divorce.

The issue of women appearing as legal witnesses in court is connected to the principle of equality between men and women. In general, Islamic law allows women to appear as witnesses in most lawsuits, except in criminal law cases. Traditional Islamic law defines the testimony of a female witness as the equivalent of half a man's testimony, and therefore it must be corroborated by a male witness in order to make it completely valid. Islamic modernists disagree with this interpretation and call for equality between men and women's testimonies as witnesses. The difference in interpretations has resulted in varying law reforms. Bangladesh, Tunisia, and Turkey maintain the equality of men and women as witnesses in court, while Pakistan, Egypt, Iran, and Malaysia have recently restricted this equality, disallowing female witness in some cases and calling for additional male witness in other cases. The participants found such restrictions discriminatory because such laws suggest that women are inferior to men.

The Qur'an prescribes corporal punishments for certain offences such as theft, homicide, fornication, and adultery. Islamic modernists argue that they are severe punishments. In view of these severe punishments, Muslim jurists built around them a complex set of legal conditions, which appear to be impossible to fulfill in most cases. Generally, however, even the Islamic modernists find it difficult to reform these penal laws. These laws were heavily reformed by colonial rulers, and in many cases, Muslim countries have continued to apply these reformed criminal laws. Some Muslim countries have revised the colonial laws in favor of Islamic laws. In Iran and Pakistan, the Hudud laws, based on the traditional Fiqh, were introduced in the 1980s. The application of these laws has exposed the weaknesses of the juristic constructions of these laws, which have generally harmed women. The parallel existence of Islamic and Western criminal laws often results in compounded punishments.

Islamic modernist jurisprudence has offered sound Islamic grounds for reform in Islamic law on gender relations, penal laws, and democracy. This jurisprudence was successful until the 1980s, when re-Islamization of laws by the neo-conservatives challenged their reforms. However, most of the reforms in personal laws remain in force, and the principle of democracy goes unchallenged.

Progressive Muslims

Progressive Muslims describe themselves as distinct from the conservative and the liberals, including Islamic modernists, because they believe that Muslim liberals have relativised Islamic values and that they operate in a framework informed by the Western impact. Omid Safi of Colgate University defines the choice of this self-identification and the interests of this group[28] as a commitment to three basic issues: social justice, pluralism, and gender justice.[29] A progressive Muslim engages with tradition in the light of modernity, but at the same is critical of the arrogance of modernity. Progressive Muslims are

---

[28] Omid Safi (ed.), *Progressive Muslims* (Oxford: Oneworld, 2003).
[29] Safi, 2.

contesting injustice, exposing violations of human rights and freedom, standing up to the increasingly hegemonic Western political, economic, and intellectual structures that perpetuate an unequal distribution of resources around the world. They are also challenging the policies of the United States and other countries that put profit before human rights and "strategic interests" before the dignity of every human being.[30] They are critical of "globalization that works to the exclusive benefits of multi-national corporations to the detriment of ordinary citizens." Safi gives as an example "the drug companies who clutch their patents of HIV drugs while untold millions die of AIDS in Africa and elsewhere."[31]

Progressive Muslims distinguish themselves from the conservative Muslims who adhere to the authority of the schools of law. They also set themselves apart from the neo-conservatives, whom Safi describes as a reactionary theological movement based on a trivial ideology.[32] On the other hand, progressive Muslims also differentiate themselves from secularists and "modernists," who look to the prevalent notion of Western modernity as something to be imitated and duplicated in toto. The modernists in this critique are different from the Islamic modernists who do not regard modernity as essentially Western.

Progressive Muslims have developed a methodology, which they call "multiple critique," because it is critical of both tradition and modernity simultaneously. Sa'diyya Shaikh, from the University of Cape Town in South Africa, explains this methodology with reference to gender relations. "Some Western feminists, who would otherwise be sensitized to questions of diversity, persist on making sweeping claims about Muslim women or Islam without engaging the necessary levels of complexity and specificity. . . . Such Western discourses on Muslim women are predicated on unquestioned cultural and social assumptions that do not allow for the engagement of specific Muslim societies in their own terms" (Shaikh, 2003, p. 151).

She argues that, in many Western feminist discourses, the standards of First World women are used as superior norms, and these cultural ideas are imposed on women who come from very different religious and cultural traditions. She also argues that Western feminist paradigms construct women as a priori victims, and hence, as powerless. This approach is not based on an examination of particular material conditions and ideological frameworks that generate a certain context of disempowerment for a specific group of women. Instead, examples of a few disempowered women are used to prove the general thesis. The crucial fact that social categories of women are constituted through the processes and structures of social relations is obscured."[33]

---

[30] Safi, 2–3.
[31] Safi, 10.
[32] Safi, 27 fn 3.
[33] Shaikh, 152.

For example, veiling, or hijab, is not indicative of subjugation of women in all cases (Shaikh, 2003, pp. 151–154). In most cases, veiling is accepted as a strategy of negotiating the right to work. "In Iran and Egypt, for example, as in other parts of the Muslim world, the wearing of the hijab has neutralized public space for many traditional families, thus making it more acceptable for women to occupy such space" (Shaikh, 2003, p. 153).[34]

Shaikh identifies three trends in contemporary Islamic feminism. Azizah al-Hibri,[35] a U.S. Muslim jurist, exemplifies the first trend that maintains that patriarchal interpretations of Islamic teachings are products of social contexts. The second trend, represented by Riffat Hassan and Amina Wadud,[36] takes a theological view. They adhere to the primacy of egalitarianism, in spite of the tension between patriarchy and egalitarianism. They insist on reading the Qur'an as a primary and comprehensive source. The third trend, exemplified by Fatima Mernissi[37] and Leila Ahmed,[38] takes a critical, historical view of Islamic tradition on gender relations. The methodology developed by progressive Muslims allows them to make a deeper analysis of Islamic tradition and to explore the thought categories in that tradition, as a way of dealing with the challenging issues of modern times.

3 Globalization of Ethics: Concluding Remarks

I have shown in the preceding pages the diversity of Muslim perspectives, not only on specific issues, but also in methodology and jurisprudence. Muslims are discussing these global issues seriously, but they are committed to exploring solutions within their own traditions. There is a common concern that the West is not taking regional and cultural specificities, especially the Muslim ones, seriously. This is evident from recent declarations and debates on Human Rights and Global Ethics. Invitations to dialogue and debate are on values that are defined as global values, a priori. The fear is that if these values are applied to all societies, without taking the specific cultural understandings of these values into serious consideration, these global values will be too general to be applied effectively.

A related concern, expressed by many Muslim perspectives, is that Western debates over global ethics neglect the fact that law and ethics operate

---

[34] Shaikh. 153, citing Ziba Mir-Hosseini.
[35] Azizah al-Hibri, "Islamic Law," Alison M. Jaggar and Iris M. Young (eds.), *A Companion to Feminist Philosophy* (Oxford: Blackwell, 1998), 541–9. Also "Karamah: Muslim Women Lawyers for Human Rights," http://www.karamah.org.
[36] Amina Wadud, *Qur'an and Women: Reading the Sacred Text from a Woman's Perspective* (New York: Oxford University Press, 1998).
[37] Fatima Mernissi, *The Veil and the Male Elite* (Bloomington: Indiana University Press, 1987).
[38] Leila Ahmed, *Women and Gender in Islam: Historical Roots of Modern Debate* (New York: Yale University Press, 1992).

in different ways. In this respect, the global ethics movement is following in the footsteps of the human rights movement by drafting ethical values in the form of laws and declarations and seeking formal agreement by experts and representatives. In fact, discussion about global ethics needs to be part of a universal discourse, what Jürgen Habermas calls "communicative action," aimed at mutual understanding, rather than as strategic or instrumental action aimed at compelling behavior.

It is important to point out an ambiguity between law and ethics, particularly in the Islamic tradition, which affects the current debates. The issues of morality and doctrines of ethics were expressed more systematically in 'ilm al-akhlaq (the science of morality/ethics) in the Islamic tradition of learning than in 'ilm al-fiqh (the science of law). The science of ethics in Islam developed as a part of the discipline of philosophy. The authors of the texts on 'ilm al-akhlaq – for example, Miskawayh (d. 1031), Jalal al-Din Dawwani (d. 1501), and Nasir al-Din Tusi (d.1274) relied on Greek texts on ethics. It was not counted as a religious science.

Ethics derived its validity from human reason and experience, while Islamic law derived from divine commands. Although some Muslim scholars tried to reconcile law and ethics by arguing that divine laws were not contrary to human reason, generally, ethics was distinguished from law because of volition, whereas law was coercive. Law in Muslim societies developed in two forms: Fiqh and Qanun, both prescribing penalties in case of disobedience. Fiqh doctrines, articulated by the jurists, conceived law also as rights; rights of God and rights of men were distinguished from each other in terms of who can claim and who can forgive these rights. The traditional law abhorred any interference in Shari'a, even by codification and legislation. Fiqh appears as a "doctrine of duties," but in fact it is voluntary. The aversion to the power of the state (kings, caliphs, or sultans) resulted from the repressive laws enforced by the state. These state laws were known as Qanun. Since the authority of the state was broader than that of Fiqh, Qanun had more scope and jurisdiction than Fiqh. Jurists did not regard these laws as part of Shari'a. This ambiguity was perpetuated in the colonial period, as the distinction between the state law and Fiqh became more pronounced. The application of Fiqh continued as a private religious law. The fact that this duality was recognized in the domain of personal and customary laws by the colonial legal systems further pushed Fiqh into the realm of ethics. This ambiguity still continues in Muslim societies in the modern period.

One consequence of this ambiguity is that in case of a conflict between the state law and Fiqh, people feel more at ease in following Fiqh because the law is imposed by the state and Fiqh is applied voluntarily. Human rights are seen more and more as a law imposed on Muslims from the outside. It is also easier to discuss human rights issues on an abstract level and to share cultural and ethical values. Muslim thinkers usually express their anxiety about the coercive measures in which human rights are introduced. They also point to the contents of these human rights declarations, which do not include the ethical and cultural concerns of Muslims. Before they are put into declarations or laws, these "rights" must be discussed and negotiated on an abstract level. Once their common underpinning as ethical values is uniformly accepted, these rights can be expressed in a suitable legal language.

Since the experience of globalization differs from culture to culture, it is not practical to assume that global values in one culture are defined in the same way in another culture. I find Leonard Swidler's explanation of globalization quite useful in pointing to the paradigm shifts and epistemological revolutions in Western cultures and civilizations. He sees a movement from monologue to dialogue to a global dialogue, but I do not see this happening in the cultures that I know. He observes that a revolution in the way people understood their reality began in the West in the eighteenth century, and ultimately spread more and more throughout the whole world. The limitations of all statements about the meaning of things began to dawn on isolated thinkers, and then increasingly spread to the middle and even grass-roots levels. This change in perceptions of reality came through the following series of epistemological revolutions: historicism, pragmatism, sociology of knowledge, language analysis, hermeneutics, and finally dialogue.[39]

These revolutions are not happening yet in the Muslim world. I believe that Swidler's sense of globalization has been essentialized in the Western experience. Thus, his following conclusion might read more like a prediction. "Now that it is more and more understood that the Muslim, Christian, secularist, Buddhist, etc. perception of the meaning of things is necessarily limited, the Muslim, Christian, secularist, etc. increasingly feels not only no longer driven to replace, or at least dominate, all other religions, ideologies, cultures, but even drawn to enter into dialogue with them, so as to expand, deepen, enrich each of their necessarily limited perceptions of the meaning of things."[40] No doubt, some thinkers in the Muslim world are under the effect of these global changes, but they do not correspond with the paradigm shifts and epistemological changes occurring within the Muslim tradition.

Globalization has been taking place within Muslim societies since the eighteenth century, but it differs from the Western experience in very significant ways. For example, unlike European nationalism, religion played a very significant role in nationalist struggles in the Muslim world. Concepts of the nation-state, democracy, and legal, judicial, and economic systems based on the Western model have not brought the prosperity and stability that provides Europeans a sense of trust and security in globalism.

Analyzing globalization in Asian societies, Vervoorn argues that, in a very general sense, globalization refers to the way in which individuals and communities are caught up in larger and larger entities. In that sense, globalization

---

[39] Leonard Swidler, as cited earlier.
[40] Ibid.

is becoming inevitable and isolation in the sense of disregarding linkages with others is no longer practical. For the West, 1945 marks the beginning of the contemporary era: a time of peace and international cooperation. However, 1945 did not mark a time of peace for the rest of the world: The U.S. occupation of Japan lasted until 1952, civil war and revolution in China ended only in 1949, and the communist regime in the country was not recognized until 1970. Wars between India and Pakistan began in 1948 and continued until 1971. The situation in the Middle East was not different from that in other parts of the world. Struggles for the right of self determination began in Kashmir, the Palestinian Territories, Algeria, and elsewhere, and international institutions failed to end violence and to bring peace. Egypt and other countries were attacked by European allied forces, and Western countries supported local armies to effect regime changes in Asia, Africa, and South America.

No doubt, non-Western societies feel the need for global ethics, but not because they see globalization as a welcome alternative to their local situation. They are critical of globalization and international organizations for the lack of ethical standards that could ensure equal opportunities for them also.

7

Confucianism

Ethical Uniformity and Diversity

Richard Madsen

"Confucianism" (a Western term for what the Chinese today simply call the "thought of the scholars") is a broad, multilayered tradition of thought, full of debates, institutionalized in different ways at different periods of history, and commingled at various times with external traditions, including Buddhism, Daoism, and, recently, even Western philosophies.

Following the contemporary Confucian scholar Tu Wei-ming, we can roughly distinguish three major historical phases of the Confucian tradition: *classical Confucianism*, which began with Confucius (551–472 BCE), became institutionalized as a state ideology in the Han Dynasty and ended with the disintegration of the Han in the third century CE; *neo-Confucianism*, developed through an integration of Confucian ideas about ethics with Buddhist ideas about cosmology during the Song Dynasty (960–1279 CE) and disseminated throughout East Asia until the end of the nineteenth century; and *new Confucianism*, an ongoing series of efforts to adapt Confucian ideas to the challenges of modernity in the twentieth century.[1] According to Tu Wei-ming, "The difference between Classical Confucianism and Neo-Confucianism is arguably more pronounced than the difference between Catholicism and Protestantism and, mainly because of the impact of the West, the rupture between Neo-Confucianism and the New Confucianism of the twentieth century is perhaps more radical than that between traditional Christology and the contemporary 'God is dead' theology."[2]

Many Christians would of course deny that "God is dead" theology is Christian at all. Not a few scholars of Confucianism would likewise deny that "new Confucianism" is more than a collection of Confucian terms that have ceased to have any meaningful connection to a coherent ethical system. But

---

[1] Tu Wei-ming, "Multiple Modernities – Implications of the Rise of 'Confucian' East Asia" in Karl-Heinz Pohl and Anselm W. Muller, ed., *Chinese Ethics in a Global Context* (Leiden: Brill, 2002), 55–56.
[2] Tu, op. cit., 55.

there is no "pope" of Confucianism, no definitive authority to determine what ideas and practices constitute true or false interpretations of the Confucian tradition. Nor are there any clearly bounded Confucian sects, membership within which could identify one as a particular kind of Confucian. According to Roger Ames, "*Any particular doctrinal commitment or set of values that we might associate with Confucianism needs to be qualified by its resolutely porous nature, absorbing into itself, especially in periods of disunity, whatever it needs* to thrive within its particular historical moment."

What unity Confucianism has today comes from common reference to the writings of certain exemplary classical scholars – Confucius, first of all, but also Mencius and Xunzi, from critical engagement with later "neo-Confucian" thinkers such as Zhu Xi and Wang Yangming, and from common discussion of contemporary thinkers such as Tang Junyi and Tu Wei-ming. Especially for a chapter like this, which seeks to discuss the form of a global ethic in a world fundamentally different from that in which the classical Confucian scholars lived, it would seem fruitless to try to recover some pure essence of classical Confucianism. Yet for all its fluidity, the Confucian tradition is not infinitely diverse and elastic. In all its various guises, the "Confucian persuasion" represents a distinctive way of thinking about the basic values that underlie a good society.

I will base my discussion on some common moral assumptions and some forms of thinking that are found throughout virtually all versions of the Confucian tradition – and I will suggest how these assumptions and forms of thinking might lead to an approach that is somewhat different from, though perhaps complementary to, the other traditions presented in this volume.

The Confucian tradition is not radically different in its basic values from the major world religions and even most modern secular philosophies. Central to Confucius's own teaching in the *Analects* is a version of the Golden Rule – "Do not impose upon others what you yourself do not desire" (Analects 12.2) – surely a value that is almost universally shared among world civilizations. Other basic Confucian values – the preference for persuasion rather than force in achieving social order, loyalty to family members, superiors and friends, the importance of generalized reciprocity – are also widely shared across cultures.[3] Where the Confucian tradition may diverge from other ethical systems is not at the level of such basic values, but in the tradition's understanding of how to realize such values under concrete social and political circumstances – how to cultivate habits of mind and heart that will enable people to pursue such values, how to undertake the moral reasoning that would enable one to apply the values to ambiguous situations, how to reconcile conflicts between values, and how to create institutions that will embody these values. Confucianism is more of an ethical program than a system of values, not so much a vision of

---

3 Stephen F. Teiser, "The Spirits of Chinese Religion" in Donald S. Lopez, ed., *Religions of Asia in Practice* (Princeton: Princeton University Press, 2002), 296.

the good as a way of seeking the good. What are some of the main elements in this way of seeking the good, how does this differ from that of other religious and philosophical traditions, and how would this lead to a distinctive way of seeking the global good in the modern world?

Confucian Themes

The Confucian view of human nature is radically social. As Herbert Fingarette put it, "For Confucius, unless there are at least two human beings, there are no human beings."[4] The character for the primary Confucian virtue, *ren*, variously translated as "human benevolence" or "humanity at its best," consists of the Chinese character for "person" combined with the character for "two." It is the virtue of "being-in-relationship." To be a good person, one must learn to recognize the different relationships that constitute one's identity and one must develop the interior capacities necessary to sustain and deepen them.

The main relationships are familial: between parent and child, husband and wife, older and younger siblings. These relationships entail hierarchies of deference: the child should defer to the parent, wife to husband, and younger sibling to older. But they also require mutual responsibility: for example, the parent ought to promote the best interests of the child, and the child needs to help the parent become a good parent, if necessary by "gently remonstrating" with the parent if he or she is doing something wrong.

Relationships outside of the family are modeled after the basic family relationships. The relationship between ruler and subject is like the relationship between parent and child. The ruler has a responsibility to promote the welfare of the subject (which is not necessarily the same as giving the subject what he or she wants or thinks he or she wants at any given time) and the subject has the responsibility of making the ruler act in the best interests of the people, if necessary by criticizing the ruler if the ruler is doing something wrong. Relationships between friends also take on something of the quality of family relationships: they are supposed to be based on loyalty, deference to seniority, and attention to gender differences.

In this way of thinking, there is not a clear distinction between public and private relationships. Most Western philosophical traditions hold that a proper understanding of the public good is achieved by stepping outside of the family, so that one can see the family's interest in the light of a higher reality. Hegel even claimed that the beginnings of Western civilization were to be found in the story of Abraham, who left behind his extended family and followed the call of God to a new land.[5] Confucian philosophies, on the other hand, try to see one's responsibilities to the larger world from the point of view of someone who stays home, while using healthy family relations to achieve

---

4 Herbert Fingarette, *Confucius – the Secular as Sacred* (New York: Harper and Row, 1972).
5 See Heath Chamberlain, in *Modern China*.

a generous view of larger realities. Confucians have a hard time imagining a principled conflict between responsibilities to one's family and responsibilities to a wider public order. And if there is a conflict, the family comes first. In the Analects, Confucius criticizes a man who gave evidence against his father, who had stolen a sheep. Confucius argued that fathers should "cover up for their sons, and sons cover up for their fathers." (13:8)

Fidelity to family relationships does not subordinate public life to private; it is the necessary condition for the proper practice of the relationship between ruler and subject, and therefore the foundation for public life. "Only when families are regulated are states governed." (*Great Learning*)

There is a dynamic quality to these relationships. For example, the nature of a child's responsibility to its parents differs over the course of a lifetime. When the child is young, he or she has to accept the parent's authoritative guidance. When the child is grown up and the parent is old, the child may have to care for the parent as if the parent were a child. Similarly, the ruler-subject relationship can change with transformations in the overall political context. One can know the specific content of one's responsibilities only by a deep understanding of the whole situation within which one is embedded.

Confucianism thus represents a holistic moral perspective that is at variance with modern Western philosophies, especially the liberal tradition, which sees society as made up of individuals, rather than the other way around, and which posits a sharp distinction between public and private life.

At the same time, certain aspects of Confucianism seem curiously modern, or even post-modern. One such aspect is the emphasis on language as constitutive of social reality. Confucius was concerned with the "rectification of names," by which he meant using the right words to denominate the social roles that constituted a social identity: who one was dependent on, what one was named – for example, father, husband, ruler. One had to live up the meanings embedded in these names (which in turn got their meanings from a larger system of discourse) and one had to relate to others on the basis of their appropriate names. Thus, a subject should not defy (as opposed to remonstrate with) a ruler. But if a political leader ceased caring for the welfare of the people and ruled in an arbitrary, self-serving way, he was no longer a ruler but a tyrant; and it was morally right to overthrow a tyrant.[6] (Mencius 1B: 8)

The system of names, and the relationships they at once expressed and brought into being, was made powerfully alive through the practice of ritual. The notion of ritual is central to the Confucian worldview. Rituals are actions that follow certain specific rules – such as those delineated in the *Classic of Rites*. Rituals express the distinctions between different social roles and enact the forms of deference and responsibility that occupants of one role owe the

---

[6] See Peter Nosco, "Confucian Perspectives on Civil Society and Government," in Nancy L. Rosenblum and Robert C. Post, eds., *Civil Society and Government* (Princeton, NJ: Princeton University Press, 2002), 343–4.

other. By symbolically enacting the essential features of these relationships, rituals strengthen an interior commitment to the relationships.

Effective rituals are a balance of external form and internal intention. For Confucius, it was not enough that one simply had an interior attitude of benevolence toward others. Such attitudes needed to be given shape and substance through rituals. But rituals that were purely formal and external, without any genuine intentions behind them, could not be effective. Many generations of Confucian scholars have struggled to articulate how the exterior form and internal intentions of rituals should be reconciled and balanced.

Within the Confucian tradition, rituals referred to much more than the ceremonies marking major life-cycle events or communal occasions. Rituals also included what we would call rules of etiquette, and in traditional Asian cultures, such rules were densely woven throughout the whole fabric of ordinary life. According to David Hall and Roger Ames, "*li* requires the utmost attention in every detail of what one does at every moment that one is doing it, from the drama of the high court to the posture one assumes in going to sleep, from the reception of different guests to the proper way to comport oneself when alone; from how one behaves in formal dining situations to appropriate extemporaneous gestures."[7]

The purpose of *li* is not to routinize experience but to enliven it. As Hall and Ames put it, "*li* are intended as means of enchanting the everyday and inspiring the ordinary. Appropriately performed, *li* elevate the commonplace and customary into something elegant and profoundly meaningful. The focus on the familiar is an attempt to optimize the creative possibilities of the human community and to transform the patterns of everyday living into profoundly socioreligious practices."[8]

In the Confucian tradition, rituals were much more important than any framework of laws for maintaining good social order. In the Chinese Legalist tradition, "laws" (*fa*) were simply written regulations backed up by explicit rewards and punishments. Confucians thought that, no matter how strong the rewards and punishments, such rules could not be effective unless people were deeply socialized to follow them.

In opposition to philosophers in the Legalist tradition, Confucian scholars insisted that political order had to be based on moral persuasion rather than coercion. This moral education took place though teaching, example, and especially through the proper practice of ritual. Laws, at least as the Legalists understood them, could not provide this education for ordinary people, nor could they effectively constrain rulers. Indeed, in the Legalist tradition, law did not have any transcendent standing. Rulers did not stand under the judgment

---

[7] David L. Hall and Roger T. Ames, "A Pragmatist Understanding of Confucian Democracy," in Daniel A. Bell and Hahm Chaibong, eds., *Confucianism for the Modern World* (Cambridge, UK: Cambridge University Press, 2003), 150.

[8] Hall and Ames, op. cit., 150.

of the law; they used law to control their subjects, and could change the laws if this suited their purposes. But even rulers were enmeshed in rituals, and to be good rulers they had to conform to rituals. Mencius gave the example of the legendary emperor Shun, who accepted his brother back into his family even after the brother had tried to assassinate him. (Mencius V: A, 2–3) Maintaining and repairing the proper rituals of family relationships was more important than seeking justice or even being primarily concerned for political security.

A proper moral education leads to the cultivation of virtues (*de*). Good rulership is based on virtues, which are capacities to act flexibly in ways sensitive to one's total context to realize certain goods. Among the most important of the political goods are harmony (*he*) and righteousness (*yi*). Harmony is to be achieved not by obliterating opposition but by making the compromises necessary to maintain the relationships expressed through ritual. Righteousness is not the justice that gives every individual his or her due, but a principle that places everyone in a proper position within a web of relationships.

We can see a contemporary example of how harmony is pursued within a Confucian tradition by considering the mediating work of Venerable Master Hsing Yun, founder of the Buddha's Light Mountain monastic order in Taiwan. Hsing Yun has acquired something of a reputation as a "political monk," and his involvement in politics can be seen to be based as much on Confucian values as upon Buddhist ones. In 1967, Hsing Yun was asked by Nationalist Party (KMT) leaders in Taiwan's Ilan County to mediate a dispute between a Mrs. Yu and the Nationalist Party establishment. Mrs. Yu got the majority of votes in a local election, but the Nationalist Party at that time did not want women in its legislative assembly, so it declared her rival the winner. Mrs. Yu wanted to take her case to a law court. Hsing Yun was asked to help resolve the dispute "for the sake of national and local stability." Hsing Yun did not try to achieve a harmony based on some notion of strict justice. He used his extensive network of friends to fashion a solution that preserved the delicate web of relationships maintaining a workable harmony in Ilan. The solution was to persuade a friend of his to step down from the directorship of a large charitable foundation and to give the job to Mrs. Yu, who then agreed to bow out of the political contest. Hsing Yun recounts this incident in his biographical writings, which are meant to provide life lessons for his followers.[9] Following Confucian principles, a harmony based on the rituals of proper relationships was maintained, even if Western principles of justice were not.

The Confucian moral approach is opposed to any form of justice that would obliterate ritual distinctions among people. The philosopher Mozi, a rival of Mencius's during the warring states period (5th century to 221 BCE), argued that the good person should love everyone equally. Mencius argued that if one tried to love everyone in the same way that he loved his father, he would

---

[9] Venerable Master Hsing Yun, *Where There is Dharma, There is a Way* (Taipei: Foguang Cultural Enterprise, 2001), 149–150.

love his father in the same way as he loved everyone. One should love one's father differently from others. One should treat one's parents, siblings, friends, and rulers in different ways appropriate to their roles. One should not apply impersonal standards of justice. (Mencius III:B, 9)

Confucian tradition has been filled with debates about the proper moral responses to novel social and political challenges, but the debates virtually all take for granted the embeddedness of individuals within society, the centrality of the family as the model for all other social institutions, and the overriding importance of ritual – all broad areas of contrast with major Western philosophic traditions. There are also broad contrasts with Western philosophies in the patterns of discourse Confucian scholars have used to make moral judgments in complex circumstances.

Much of Western moral philosophy seems to seek a set of abstract principles – whether based in a revelation of the will of God or in principles of Reason itself – that transcend any particular context. Then it uses a kind of casuistry to apply these principles to particular situations. In the Confucian perspective, however, moral principles are not derived from abstract ideas but from the concrete rituals of ordinary life. The moral task involves an effort to understand these concrete rituals in the widest possible context. Western philosophy tends to proceed through a kind of linguistic evolution – metaphor is replaced by precisely defined concepts, poetry gives way to logic. Much of Confucian philosophy tends to proceed through linguistic involution. Metaphors are deepened and stretched. Thus family relationships provide metaphors for relationships with the wider community, with the Empire, even with the cosmos.

If someone reasoned in this way and was committed to the basic assumptions I have outlined here, how might such a person answer the modern questions about the globalization of ethics that are discussed in this volume? Could these answers be plausible under modern conditions? How would these answers conflict with those of other ethical systems?

Alternatives: A Uniform or Pluralistic Planetary Ethic?

Confucius saw himself as transmitting values that had universal validity. He stated that he would be willing to teach these values to anyone who expressed a desire to learn. In principle he excluded no one from the possibility of becoming a "superior person" (*junzi* – which has also been translated as "humanity at its best"). However, Confucius recognized that not everyone was willing to cultivate a high degree of moral virtue, and that not everyone who tried would succeed. In practice, Confucius seemed to believe that only a minority would succeed in attaining moral superiority, and that he should concentrate his effort on enabling such a moral elite to become good leaders of the rest.

This moral elitism became a mainstay of the Confucian tradition, intensified (and perhaps distorted) by the use of the Confucian canon as the curriculum for aspiring government officials. If applied to the development of a modern global ethic, such an approach would accept the inevitably of different levels of moral attainment around the world, but it would try to cultivate a moral elite that could persuade others to improve themselves by following the virtues of the superior person.

However tolerant of diversity, this approach assumes a universal hierarchy of moral goodness, and as such is contrary to a liberal democratic ethos that makes morality a private matter, refuses to give public privilege to any particular version of the good, and is wary of any kind of condescending elitism.

If one goes beyond the classical tradition to the neo-Confucian tradition, it becomes even more difficult to make a case for Confucian standards of excellence that would be plausible under modern circumstances. The neo-Confucian tradition naturalizes the hierarchy of moral excellence, making it part of a comprehensive cosmology. Since the hierarchy of goodness is a part of the nature of things, of the Overriding Principle that governs all spheres of life, there is no way to challenge it and no way to confront a modern world in which different spheres of life – economic, political, aesthetic, scientific – seem to develop their own standards of excellence and criteria of success. In the analysis of Maruyama Masao, the great twentieth-century Japanese social theorist, Japan began to move toward a modern, critical historical consciousness only when intellectuals of the early Tokugawa period began to undermine the Japanese version of neo-Confucianism.[10] In recent years, the dissident Chinese intellectual Jin Guantao has followed Maruyama in seeing the neo-Confucian legacy as an impediment to a modern consciousness that could support a commitment to democracy, cosmopolitanism, and scientific innovation.[11]

In view of such problems with the Confucian tradition, many East Asian intellectuals have advocated a wholesale rejection of the Confucian legacy. But many others, especially in the past quarter of a century, have sought ways to revive and adapt the legacy to modern conditions. One feature of such attempts is a democratization of Confucianism through an emphasis on the idea (already present in the writings of Confucius himself) that anyone can become a superior person (*junzi*). Confucian teachings about benevolence, concern for parents and relatives, and respect for authority are disseminated through elementary and high school textbooks, sometimes with pedagogical techniques that encourage critical discussion and role playing.[12] Attempts are made to render Confucian values compatible with modern economic activity

---

[10] See Robert N. Bellah, *Imagining Japan* (Berkeley: University of California Press, 2003), "Notes on Maruyama Masao," pp. 140–146.

[11] Jin Guantao, *Zai Lishi Biaoxiangde Beihou* (Sichuan Renminchubanshe, 1983).

[12] An example would be the curricula for "life education" in Taiwan elementary schools developed by the Buddhist Compassion Relief Society (Tz'u-chu). Although these materials are put out by a Buddhist organization, they have been written so as to be acceptable to Taiwanese of all religious faiths, and the basic virtues for family life are Confucian.

(by seeing economic development as a means to achieve a healthy family life) and the relatively egalitarian relations of the modern nuclear family (by stressing interdependent reciprocity rather than submission to patriarchal authority). It remains difficult on the basis of classic Confucian texts and the practices of 2,500 years of Confucian tradition to justify complete equality between men and women. But some new Confucians are trying to extend the tradition in ways that would allow for such equality.[13]

Another feature of the attempt to create a "new Confuciansm" is a jettisoning of the metaphysics of neo-Confucianism. In the twentieth and twenty-first centuries, Confucian notions of moral excellence are being based on sociology and ecology. It is argued that the Confucian virtues are good because they promote social trust and facilitate the social transactions necessary for the harmonious functioning of an interdependent world.

Such attempts to modernize Confucianism can actually take away some of the ethical pluralism of traditional East Asian societies. In the past, the well-cultivated Confucian gentleman might look with bemused tolerance at the customs of ordinary people. Now everyone is supposed to display Confucian values. Confucianism, as Tu Wei-ming puts it, becomes a "new way of conceptualizing the form of life, the habits of the heart, or the social praxis of those societies that have been under the influence of Confucian education for centuries."[14]

Seen this way, Confucianism can come to be seen not as an ethic for superior persons but for a superior region – it is that distinctive part of East Asian cultures that makes them superior to Western or Middle Eastern cultures. From the Confucian point of view, however, such ethical superiority does not have to lead to a "clash of civilizations." The moral principles of Western civilizations can be seen as inferior but tolerable. An important Confucian moral principle is that differences should be reconciled if at all possible through mediation rather than confrontation, persuasion rather than coercion. The Confucian can coexist with and even learn from other civilizations, as long as proponents of other philosophies do not try to attack the foundations of Confucian civilization. The Confucian approach toward the globalization of ethics would be one of global accommodation of conflicting ethical differences, with the expectation that adherents to other ethical traditions would eventually be persuaded to accept key Confucian values because of their manifest moral superiority. Indeed, the possibility of a true global peace would ultimately involve a broad acceptance of Confucian principles, or at least of values that were compatible with those principles – a "thick universalism." This indeed was the path that Confucians traditionally followed in building a peaceful environment for the Chinese empire in Asia.

---

[13] Chan Sin Yee, "The Confucian Conception of Gender in the Twenty First Century" in Bell and Hahm, op. cit., 312–333.
[14] Tu, *Multiple Modernities*, 74.

Diversity and the Limits of Toleration

There is no evidence of a "crusader mentality" in the Confucian tradition. Confucian scholars argued that social order had to be based on moral persuasion rather than political coercion. They were happy to disseminate their teachings as widely as possible, and, as we have noted, during the neo-Confucian era they did indeed spread their ideas and practices throughout East Asia. But they showed no desire to use force to change customs of distant "barbarians." Today, self-described proponents of Confucian values in Asia, like Singapore's Lee Kuan Yew, are not above lecturing Western societies about the dangers of moral decadence, but they make no effort to put political pressure on other cultures to change their values.[15] The primary posture of even relatively assertive Confucians is defensive. They argue that powerful outsiders should not try to impose foreign standards on them.

In an interdependent modern world, however, it is impossible to stand completely apart from the moral practices of others. There are international regimes for trade, institutionalized in the WTO (World Trade Organization) and global standards for human rights, and these regimes and standards correspond better with individualistic Western philosophies than with ethical practices based on the Confucian tradition. The WTO, for example, tries to establish a global economy in which the prices of commodities are set solely by laws of supply and demand and all parties to commercial transactions are treated on a completely equal basis. This contradicts a Confucian principle that relatives and friends should be treated differently from outsiders. Moreover, international human rights standards seek to protect the autonomy of individuals, whereas Confucian ethics emphasizes the responsibility of the individual to a larger community.

Asian countries such as China and Japan may, with some success, avoid complying with international norms for trade and human rights, and leaders of such countries may rationalize such non-compliance by saying that the norms are at odds with Confucian principles. But they do not at present have the power to challenge the validity of the international norms themselves. As Asian countries gain more power, they may someday try to change the norms of international economic and political institutions. Insofar as they were to do this on the basis of Confucian ethical principle (rather than simply realpolitik), what kind of changes might they make?

They would probably insist on the legitimacy of a loose form of economic protectionism. By the logic of Confucian ethics, they would insist that families, on the one hand, and nations, on the other, have a primary responsibility to ensure the overall welfare of their members. Free trade would in principle be subordinated to this principle. Even by Confucian principles, this could

---

[15] See Lee Kuan Yew, *The Singapore Story: Memoirs of Lee Kuan Yew* (New York: Prentice Hall, 1998).

lead to an enormous amount of free trade in practice, but such trade should in principle be limited if it threatened the general economic prosperity and social solidarity of particular nations.

As for human rights, leaders acting on the basis of Confucian principles would have to affirm the dignity of individual persons, and on this basis they would have to support international norms against arbitrary arrest, torture, religious or ethnic discrimination, and freedom of peaceful expression. However, they would probably demand that societies in principle should be able to seek ways of protecting individual autonomy that would be consistent with the needs of social harmony and maintenance of right relationships within family and community. Ways of doing this would be context-specific, so that different societies in different circumstances would have different ways of striking the proper balance. The result would be a principled affirmation of a global pluralism of political systems but with an overlapping consensus on the need to protect the basic integrity of the person.[16]

Mix: Which Practices Should be Universally Accepted and Which Particular?

In Confucian thinking, the dignity of the individual comes not from the capacity to act independently of other members of society but from the capacity to be a part of an interdependent whole. The primary social institution is, of course, the family, seen as a system of interlocking social roles, each with different responsibilities for the good of the whole. The individual's capacity to live out these roles properly depends on his or her capacity to learn. Learning requires voluntary action, so any form of coercion that would keep an individual from becoming an active learner would be contrary to the dignity of that person. Therefore, individuals should be protected from all forms of physical harm that might keep them from actively learning their proper social roles. Moreover, since we now have a stronger understanding of the psychological conditions that facilitate social learning, we might assume that a Confucian perspective would hold that individuals should be protected against forms of psychological manipulation (including being subjected to self-serving political propaganda) that would keep them from making a sincere moral commitment to their roles. These considerations would lead to a universal disapproval of all forms of political totalitarianism, although the moral logic behind such disapproval would be different from that of philosophical liberalism.[17]

---

[16] William Theodore de Bary, *Asian Values and Human Rights: a Confucian Communitarian Perspective* (Cambridge, MA: Harvard University Press, 1998). William Theodore de Bary and Tu Weiming, eds., *Confucianism and Human Rights* (New York: Columbia University Press, 1997).

[17] Geir Helgesen, "The Case for Moral Education," in Bell and Hahm, op. cit., 161–177.

The Confucian moral logic would, however, allow and indeed encourage governmental paternalism – the role of the ruler is, after all, modeled on the role of the paterfamilias. In East Asian countries that have been at least partially influenced by Confucian thought, governments (with the approval of most citizens) undertake to educate citizens in proper morality by mandating moral education in the schools, trying to promote strong family life by discouraging divorce, and mandating care of aged parents. Liberal theorists might worry that such communitarian paternalism could slide into a coercive authoritarianism. Confucians might argue that a concern for the common good might stave off the social atomization that has all too often also led to authoritarianism.

Confucians would not, however, try to resolve such arguments by force. As long as a society did not violate the fundamental dignity of its members, and as long as it did not try to force its values on Confucians, Confucians would adopt a live-and-let-live posture. The guiding principle here is that differences should be resolved through education and persuasion rather than coercion. The only intolerable differences are those that would shut off all possibilities for creative moral agency.

Propagation

Because moral development is so dependent on education, and education depends on open channels of communication, Confucians would advocate a free flow of ideas around the world. They would insist especially strongly on having the opportunity to teach their understanding of the good to anyone willing to listen. Insofar as they are convinced that theirs is a superior way of life, and that its superiority should be apparent to reasonable persons, they would be confident that enlightened people everywhere would over time be persuaded to follow them.

Throughout history, however, Confucian thinkers have been concerned about protecting people from misleading, seductive ideas – ideas that might beguile or blind good people from following the correct path to moral cultivation. As we said, the role of the teacher is partially modeled after the paterfamilias, and it includes morally shaping the student, not just presenting information that the student is free to accept or reject.[18]

Historically, such concerns about protecting the less well-educated from heterodox ideas have been more pronounced when Confucian societies found themselves politically vulnerable and on the defensive. In Confucian thought, it is also part of the paternalistic role of government to protect citizens from unhealthy influences. This attitude is apparent in the contemporary People's Republic of China, which periodically launches campaigns against "spiritual

---

[18] Ibid. Also, Gerhold K. Becker, "Moral Education in China and the 'West': Ideals and Reality in Cross-Cultural Perspective," in Pohl and Muller, op. cit., 245–278.

pollution" and censors the media to eliminate subversive political ideas and morally offensive imagery, such as pornography.

There is therefore an asymmetry to the Confucian approach to propagating values. In principle, Confucians would want to be able to propagate their values as freely and effectively as possible, because they regard their basic values as superior to all others. But they would out of principle be wary of unrestricted exposure to non-Confucian values. Sometimes this principle has led to a rigid closing of Asian societies to outside influences. More often, especially in the recent past, it has allowed a considerable degree of openness to the outside, justified partly by the notion that such participation in a two-way street is necessary for Confucians to be able to spread the benefits of their moral superiority widely. But the openness is always contingent, never grounded in an absolute principle.

Law

In both the classical and neo-Confucian variants of the Confucian tradition, Confucians advocated a rule by virtue rather than by law. Laws can enforce only external compliance, not the interior consent that is the basis of a harmonious society. Laws also produce a rigidity within social policy that makes it difficult for rulers to find the proper balance of policies within particular situations. By themselves, laws that protect individual rights encourage people to act in selfish ways, and by themselves such laws cannot generate the sense of social responsibility necessary to bring people into right relationship. Leaders of high moral character, on the other hand, can bring vitality to the rites of solidarity and deference that create a moral consensus in favor of good order among the common people. Such virtuous leaders can better find the best balanced mix of social policies to fit a particular situation if the leaders are not hampered by a rigid framework of fixed laws.[19]

In line with this attitude, modern Confucians would be skeptical of the capacity of international laws to create the foundations for global peace. They would probably put greater emphasis on personal negotiations among well-cultivated elites. But they would want to protect the ability of virtuous leaders to respond to their particular national circumstances, so they would welcome international laws that would protect the prerogative of national sovereignties.

This concern for protecting the discretion of national authorities, on the other hand, could lead to a reluctance to promote international laws protecting the rights of individuals. As we have seen, Confucians could agree with the substance of all of the articles in the International Declaration of Human Rights. Any honest reading of the classics of the Confucian tradition would support opposition to arbitrary imprisonment, torture, racial discrimination,

---

[19] Albert H.Y. Chen, "Mediation, Litigation, and Justice: Confucian Reflections in a Modern Liberal Society," in Bell and Hahm, op. cit., 257–287.

and religious persecution. Confucians would also accept the substance of laws protecting rights to free expression and free political assembly, although they would worry that, pursued without regard to context, such laws could undermine proper deference to authority. Confucians would, however, be skeptical of the ability of such laws actually to guarantee humane respect for individuals' integrity. And they would be worried that a rigid reliance on such laws might substitute litigious procedure for the moral consensus necessary to protect individual dignity, and especially concerned that such laws could be used as justification for international actors to undermine the efforts of virtuous national leaders to protect human dignity in a balanced way under complicated circumstances.

Prospects

What are the prospects that such Confucian principles could actually become part of a global ethic, and how might this happen? Unlike other religious and philosophical ethical systems presented in this volume, Confucianism does not have a well-institutionalized base for influencing the development of a global ethic. There are no official organizations for disseminating Confucianism, no authoritative spokespersons. It can be argued that Confucian values exert a broad, subtle influence on East Asian societies. Confucianism has an influence on major social institutions and is a part of major public philosophies. But in all East Asian societies, Confucian values are amalgamated with a great many other cultural influences. When leaders (political, cultural, religious) of such societies enter into dialogues in international forums, they rarely make a reflexive, explicit case for Confucian values, even though at some level, they may have been deeply influenced by such values.

Moreover, such influences can lead in different directions, and Confucianism can be coopted for different purposes. Some ideologues in the People's Republic of China have been promoting Confucianism to support political dictatorship.[20] The government of Singapore calls on Confucianism to justify its brand of authoritarianism. Meanwhile, leaders in South Korea invoke Confucian principles to legitimize a form of democracy. Some political and cultural leaders in Taiwan do the same. And in Hong Kong, public debates have been raging about whether the Confucian heritage requires submission to the established government or democratic dissent.[21] In contemporary East Asia, Confucianism serves more as a basis for domestic controversies than a unified agenda for international dialogue.[22]

---

[20] See, for example, Sun Chuanwei, "Scholar Kang Xiaoguang: China's Democratization Means a Calamitous Choice for the Country and the People," Singapore Lianhe Zaobao, November 8, 2004.

[21] Victoria Hui, "Confucius and Patriotism: Speak from the Heart," *South China Morning Post*, February 14, 2004.

[22] Kenneth Christie and Denny Rou, *The Politics of Human Rights in East Asia* (London: Pluto Press, 2001).

Yet, throughout East Asia, there is rising unease at the prospects of becoming engulfed in a global monoculture based on an American version of liberalism. Many Asians are concerned that the mix of rights-based individualism and globalized commercial capitalism promoted by the United States in the name of the supposedly universal values of Western liberalism will lead to widening gaps between rich and poor, to economic and political instability, and to a breakdown of social solidarity. Confucian ways of thinking influence Asian expressions of such concern.

For a concrete example of a Confucian-influenced response to Western liberalism, we can consider the Bangkok Declaration on Human Rights, which was issued in April 1993 by representatives of thirty Asian and Middle Eastern states in preparation for the 1993 UN World Conference on Human Rights.[23] In no way is this straightforwardly a Confucian document. The signatories come out of many different cultural and religious traditions, including Islam, Christianity, Buddhism, and Hinduism, as well as Confucianism. Moreover, besides being influenced by culture and religion, the document is a reaction to common recent historical experiences, especially the experience of Western colonialism. Yet one can certainly see echoes of Confucian ethical preoccupations and Confucian reasoning in the Bangkok Declaration – as much as one is likely to see in any important political document from Asia.

The Bangkok Declaration accepts all of the principles of the Universal Declaration of Human Rights, and it indeed affirms the "universality, objectivity, and non-selectivity of all human rights."[24] It rejects attempts, however, to use human rights as an "instrument of political pressure."[25] This is an implicit objection to attempts by Western governments, especially the United States, to put political pressure on countries that allegedly do not conform to Western interpretations of basic human rights. In the Declaration's rhetoric, one can see an echo of the Confucian notion that basic human values should be propagated through persuasion, not imposed through force. The document also stresses that "while human rights are universal in nature, they must be considered in the context of a dynamic and evolving process of international norm-setting, bearing in mind the significance of national and regional particularities and various historical, cultural, and religious backgrounds."[26] Here, too, are echoes of a Confucian insistence on the need for sensitivity to an overall social context when implementing moral principles. An important part of that context for Asian countries is the need for economic development. The Bangkok Declaration does not in principle subordinate civil and political rights to economic rights, but it affirms "that poverty is one of the major obstacles hindering the enjoyment of human rights"[27] and it gives more emphasis to economic and

---

[23] Bangkok Declaration (United Nations High Commission for Human Rights, 1993).
[24] Bangkok Declaration, article 7.
[25] Bangkok Declaration, article 5.
[26] Bangkok Declaration, article 8.
[27] Bangkok Declaration, article 19.

social rights than most Western documents have done. This again resonates with Confucian-inspired traditions of government paternalism. In its various "White Papers" on human rights issued during the past decade, the government of the People's Republic of China (which played a major role in getting the Bangkok Document drafted) repeatedly cites the need to maintain the "social stability" necessary for the basic right of economic development as a justification for its authoritarian rule.

But the political paternalism suggested by the Bangkok Declaration is not the only Confucian-influenced statement about human rights in Asia. A more populist declaration is the "Asian Human Rights Charter: A People's Charter" issued in 1998 on the occasion of the fiftieth anniversary of the Universal Declaration of Human Rights.[28] This human rights charter was drafted by the Asian Human Rights Commission, a grassroots organization based in Hong Kong, with input from a large number of non-governmental organizations and "people's organizations." Like the Bangkok Declaration, this document declares that rights are universal and indivisible, yet "the enjoyment and salience of rights depend on social, economic, and cultural contexts."[29] Also, like the Bangkok Declaration, this document emphasizes the 'primary need to eliminate poverty."[30] Yet the document vehemently rejects all forms of authoritarian paternalism. "Authoritarianism has in many [Asian] states been raised to the level of national ideology, with the deprivation of the rights and freedoms of their citizens, which are denounced as foreign ideas inappropriate to the religious and cultural traditions of Asia. Instead there is the exhortation of spurious theories of 'Asian values' which are a thin disguise for their authoritarianism."[31] The Charter calls not only for democratic and accountable governments within nation states but for the "radical transformation and democratization of the world order."[32]

The drafters of the Asian Human Rights Charter come from the full spectrum of faith traditions in Asia, although Christians are represented more heavily than in the Bangkok Declaration.[33] Contributors to the Charter did not include any self-consciously Confucian organization, and the echoes of Confucian discourse are fainter than in the Bangkok Declaration. Yet one can detect Confucian styles of argument, not only in the document's moralism (which could also come from the other religious traditions that shaped it), but in the Charter's insistence that "rights need to be seen in a holistic manner and that individual rights are best pursued through a broader

---

[28] *Asian Human Rights Charter: A People's Charter* (Hong Kong: Asian Human Rights Commission).

[29] *Asian Human Rights Charter*, article 2.3.

[30] *Asian Human Rights Charter*, article 2.4.

[31] *Asian Human Rights Charter*, article 1.5.

[32] *Asian Human Rights Charter*, article 2.6.

[33] See list of contributors in *Asian Human Rights Charter*, appendix A.

conceptualization. . . . "[34] Although the document calls on Asian peoples to "eliminate those features in our cultures that are contrary to the universal principles of human rights"[35] – especially patriarchal traditions that would support gender inequality – it does not embrace the individualism of a Western liberal conception of rights. Although "we must stop practices which sacrifice the individual to the collectivity," the goal of this liberation of the individual is to "renew our communal and national solidarity."[36]

Thus, although there has not been any purely Confucian position in Asian debates about the ethical basis for a global order, there are strands of Confucian thinking running through opposing sides of the debates. As time goes on, the pressures of such debates may stimulate more systematic, articulate expressions of the Confucian heritage. If the rise of new centers of wealth and power in East Asia then leads to a multipolar world that can accommodate a diversity of ethical perspectives, then the Confucian tradition may well make an important contribution to a global ethic.

[34] Asian Human Rights Charter, article 3.1.
[35] Asian Human Rights Charter, article 6.2.
[36] Asian Human Rights Charter, article 6.2.

8

Natural Law, Common Morality, and Particularity

Mark C. Murphy

What a Natural Law Theory Claims

My aim here is to provide an account of how an adherent of the natural law tradition should approach the topic of the desirability of a uniform planetary ethic.

The term 'natural law theory' is notoriously slippery, and there are uses of it that are so broad as to fail to distinguish it from a variety of moral views (for example, utilitarianism, Kantianism) with which it is customarily taken to compete. While much is controversial about the definition of 'natural law theory,' it is not controversial that Thomas Aquinas is the paradigmatic natural law theorist, and that there are certain general features of Aquinas's view that structure his ethical thought. So I will take these features of Aquinas's view to be what distinguishes natural law theory from other moral views. What are those features?

For Aquinas, natural law can be examined from the 'God's eye' and the 'human's eye' points of view. When we focus on God's role as the giver of the natural law, the natural law is just one aspect of divine providence. When we focus on the human's role as recipient of the natural law, the natural law constitutes the principles of practical rationality, those principles by which human action is to be judged as reasonable or unreasonable.

I will here put to the side Aquinas's emphasis that the natural law is tied to divine providence, instead focusing on the natural law as the basis of practical reasoning. The notion that the natural law constitutes the basic principles of practical rationality implies, for Aquinas, both that the precepts of the natural law are authoritative by nature[1] and that the precepts of the natural law are knowable by nature.[2]

The precepts of the natural law are authoritative by nature: no beings could share our human nature yet fail to be bound by the precepts of the natural

---

[1] Thomas Aquinas, *Summa Theologiae*, IaIIae Q. 94, A. 4. Hereafter cited as ST by part, question, and article number.

[2] ST IaIIae 94, 4; 94, 6.

law. This is so because these precepts direct us toward those goods that are perfective of us given the nature that we share.[3] And the precepts of the natural law are knowable by nature: all human beings possess a basic knowledge of the principles of the natural law.[4] This knowledge is exhibited in our intrinsic directedness toward the various goods, and we can, when necessary and when equipped with the analytical skills to do so, make this implicit awareness explicit through reflection.[5]

The universal authority and knowability of the basic principles of practical rationality are two of the formal features emphasized within the natural law tradition. Is there anything distinctive about the normative *substance* of the natural law position? On this view, we know immediately that there are a variety of things that count as good, and thus to be pursued – Aquinas mentions by way of example, life, procreation, knowledge, society, and reasonable conduct.[6] The good is, on Aquinas's view, prior to the right. But on Aquinas's view we are, somehow, able to reason from these principles about goods to guidelines about how these goods are to be pursued. Aquinas's thoughts are along the following lines: first, there are certain ways of acting in response to the basic human goods that are intrinsically flawed; and second, for an act to be right, or reasonable, is for it to be an act that is in no way intrinsically flawed.[7]

Aquinas indicates various ways in which acts can be intrinsically flawed, and relates these ways to the various features that individuate human actions, such as their objects,[8] their ends,[9] their circumstances,[10] and so forth. An act might be flawed through a mismatch of object and end – that is, between the immediate aim of the action and its more distant point. If one were, for example, to regulate one's pursuit of a greater good in light of a lesser good – if, for example, one were to seek friendship with God for the sake of mere bodily survival rather than vice versa – that would count as an unreasonable act. An act might be flawed through the circumstances: while one is bound to profess one's belief in God, there are certain circumstances in which it is inappropriate to do so.[11] An act might be flawed merely through its intention: to direct oneself against a good – as in murder,[12] and lying,[13] and blasphemy[14] – is always to act in an unfitting way. On Aquinas's view, killing of the innocent

---

3　ST IaIIae 94, 2; ST Ia 5, 1.
4　ST IaIIae 94, 4.
5　ST IaIIae 94, 6.
6　ST IaIIae 94, 2; 94, 3.
7　ST IaIIae 18, 1.
8　ST IaIIae 18, 2.
9　ST IaIIae 18, 3.
10　ST IaIIae 18, 4.
11　ST IIaIIae 3, 2.
12　ST IIaIIae 64, 6.
13　ST IIaIIae 110, 3.
14　ST IIaIIae 13, 2.

is always wrong, as is lying, adultery, sodomy, and blasphemy, and that they are always wrong is a matter of natural law. (These are only examples, not an exhaustive list of absolutely forbidden actions.)[15]

While some take there to be a tension between a 'natural rights' and a 'natural law' approach to moral matters, it is a straightforward conclusion from standard natural law theories, including Aquinas's, that there are certain immunities from others' action to which humans are naturally entitled, and thus there is no strain in saying that there are natural rights to be treated in certain ways. Because it is by nature unreasonable for me to murder, assault, or lie to you, and because the reason that this is unreasonable is that it is an intentional attack on your good, we can say that by nature you ought to be immune from these sorts of harms at my hands. What's more, not only can I have a natural right not to be *treated* in certain ways, I can have a natural right to be *considered* in certain ways in deliberation. Because your good is a reason for action, your good ought to be adequately taken into account in decisions that affect you, and to disregard or to devalue your good in those decisions is to violate your rights. And so even if a policy, plan, or rule does not involve intentionally causing you harm, it can be unjust and unreasonable insofar as that policy's (etc.) execution results in deprivation and that policy (etc.) was formed in disregard of your good.

To repeat: there is some disagreement as to how to understand the form and substance of the natural law view. But I will take Aquinas's view to define the central theses of the tradition, which is followed by contemporary defenders of the natural law view such as MacIntyre,[16] Grisez,[17] Finnis,[18] Hittinger,[19] Gomez-Lobo,[20] Chappell,[21] and myself,[22] regardless of the differences among contemporary defenders of the view. It is this picture of morality that I have

---

[15] For further description of the natural law view, see my "The Natural Law Tradition in Ethics," *The Stanford Encyclopedia of Philosophy (Winter 2002 Edition)*, Edward N. Zalta (ed.), URL = http://plato.stanford.edu/archives/win2002/entries/natural-law-ethics.

[16] Alasdair MacIntyre, *Dependent Rational Animals* (Chicago: Open Court, 1999).

[17] The writings here are numerous. For a summary account, see Germain Grisez, *The Way of the Lord Jesus, Volume 1: Christian Moral Principles* (Chicago: Franciscan Herald Press, 1983), pp. 97–274.

[18] John Finnis, *Natural Law and Natural Rights* (Oxford: Oxford University Press, 1980) (hereafter cited as *Natural Law*); *Fundamentals of Ethics* (Oxford University Press, 1983); *Moral Absolutes: Tradition, Revision, and Truth* (Washington, DC: Catholic University of America Press, 1991).

[19] Russell Hittinger, *The First Grace: Rediscovering the Natural Law in a Post-Christian World* (Wilmington: ISI Books, 2003).

[20] Alfonso Gomez-Lobo, *Morality and the Human Goods* (Washington, DC: Georgetown University Press, 2002).

[21] Timothy Chappell, *Understanding Human Goods* (Edinburgh: Edinburgh University Press, 1998).

[22] Mark C. Murphy, *Natural Law and Practical Rationality* (New York: Cambridge University Press, 2001) (hereafted cited as *Practical Rationality*).

in mind when I ask about the desirability of a universal planetary ethic from the point of view of the natural law tradition.

Two Senses of 'Uniform Planetary Ethic'

There are two senses in which one can ask about the desirability of a common moral system for humanity, or a 'uniform planetary ethic,' from the point of view of the natural law tradition. In one sense of the question, the desirability of the existence of a common moral system for humanity is simply beside the point. For to be a natural law theorist is just to hold that, given what human beings essentially are, there are some things that are good for them and other things that are bad for them, and that given these natural goods and these natural evils, there are certain ways of responding to these goods and evils that are within reason and ways of responding to these goods and evils that are not. The propositions describing what things are necessarily good or bad for human beings, and the propositions describing how one may reasonably act in light of these goods, are the natural law. Since these propositions are not merely a disconnected crowd but are organized in virtue of the features of human nature and its fulfillment, they form a system. So there is, on the natural law view, a set of authoritative normative truths binding all human beings, and this as a matter of necessity. It is thus just as idle to worry about the desirability of a common moral system, in this sense, from the point of view of natural law thought as it is to worry about the desirability of water's being H$_2$0. Both are a matter of necessity, and one should not spend too much time worrying about whether it is good that p when it is necessary that p. One might respond, rightly, that sometimes our grasp of the human good can be improved by reflecting on cases that are necessarily contrary-to-fact: we might learn something about our good by asking whether, for example, it would be good for us (unaided) to know God's essence. But even granting the point of such reflections, we cannot say that it is thereby worthwhile to reflect on whether it is a good thing for us to be under the natural law. For even if one wanted to ask about the desirability of there being a natural law, there is no point of view from which one can ask the question except from within the natural law, for the natural law tells us what is good and bad for human beings, and thus sets the standard for desirability.

If this were the only sense in which one could ask about the desirability of a common moral system for humanity, then the contribution to the question of the globalization of ethics from the natural law perspective would be blessedly brief. Unfortunately, there is a second perfectly good sense to the question. We can think of a moral system as the set of de facto norms of some community. The status of such norms as norms is a conventional matter – that is, it is their *use* as standards for regulating one's own conduct and for criticizing one's own and others' conduct, their use as guidelines for education of the young, and so forth, that *constitutes* those norms' having their status within that community and that *identifies* those norms as the moral system in place within that community.[23] That the status of a de facto moral system as such is due to the general acceptance of its norms is not to say that de facto moral systems cannot be authoritative – that is, giving genuine reasons for action for those that live under them. But the natural law view would hold that whether they are authoritative is a contingent matter.

Contingent on what? The most obvious point on which de facto moral systems might depend with respect to their authority is on the content of those norms. Because there is a standard external to the de facto moral systems of communities, a standard that puts forward all of the natural reasons for action that persons have and that sets the limits of all potentially eligible action, a de facto moral system may lack authority, in whole or in part, due to the fact that some of its norms are contrary to the natural law. There may be other ways in which a de facto moral system can fail to have authority. It might lack authority in virtue of its mode of origin: if a de facto moral system has the character that it has, not in virtue of the free acceptance of those norms by members of that community, but in virtue of its imposition by some dominant class, it might be that the norms of that community lack, of themselves, authority. (Compare this with the case of positive law: it might fail to be authoritative either on account of the defectiveness of its content or because it originated in the wrong way, that is, by persons acting outside of their jurisdiction or by a process somehow unfair.)[24] In what follows, though, I will consider only the content of a de facto moral system in its assessment.

So I will call the uniform planetary ethic that holds as a matter of necessity, given the nature of human beings, *the natural law*; I will call the particular systems of morals in force in various communities *de facto moral systems*. At present, there is a tremendous variety of these de facto moral systems in the world, even though there is but one natural law. Thus we can sensibly ask the questions: would it be good, from the point of view of natural law ethics, for there to be convergence among these de facto moral systems, so that there would be greater or even complete agreement in the content of those systems' norms? And if it would be good, or to the extent that it is good, what steps (if any) could be reasonably taken in pursuit of this sort of convergence?

The Massive Unattractiveness of Complete Convergence

One might think that there is a straightforward answer to the question of the desirability of complete convergence of de facto moral systems. For on the natural law view, there is a single natural law, a single set of authoritative moral norms that hold for all human beings in virtue of their common human nature.

---

[23] In conceiving de facto moral systems in these terms, I follow H. L. A. Hart, *The Concept of Law*, 2nd edition (Oxford: Clarendon Press, 1994), pp. 168–184.
[24] ST IaIIae 96, 4.

Thus all people living under all of these de facto moral systems are bound by the natural law. Given the massive variations in de facto moral systems and the single natural law, it is bound to be the case that these de facto moral systems include norms that are contrary to the natural law, requiring folks to do what is wrong. To avoid this result, these moral systems would have to be revised so that they fall in line with the true natural law. The outcome of the revisions of these de facto moral systems into compliance with the natural law would be complete convergence. Thus complete convergence – at least complete convergence of a particular sort, convergence on the true natural law – is desirable indeed.

This argument for the desirability of complete convergence displays a confusion about the character of the natural law. The mistake is manifest in the move from the claim that it is desirable for de facto moral systems to be revised so that they fall in line with the natural law to the claim that the outcome is complete convergence. This is only true if the natural law fixes in detail what the content of a de facto moral system should be, and that this content is the same for all communities. But both of these claims are false, and it is important to see why both are false.

Suppose, for the sake of argument, that the natural law did fix in detail what the content of each community's de facto moral system should be. There is no reason to think that this content would be the same in detail for each community. For, after all, the precepts of the natural law surely include in their content provisions the satisfaction of which depend on the local conditions that obtain. For example: the natural law surely prescribes (something like) the norm that one should not use for trivial purposes what is needed to secure the essential good of another. But what counts as 'wasting what is needed' surely depends on the local conditions that obtain. In one community, where water is plentiful, this norm of the natural law may forbid relatively little with respect to the use of water: one might use it to wash one's car, wash the dog, water one's lawn, and so forth. Where water is scarce, this norm may forbid all of these things, taking them to be a waste of water that is needed for the sake of others' good. If the de facto moral systems of these communities fell into line with the natural law with respect to this norm, the result would be divergence in their norms regarding water usage: the former community might fail to forbid using water to wash one's dog, whereas the latter community might forbid it, and indeed treat it as a grave moral failing.

So even if we thought that the natural law managed to fix the details of what the de facto moral systems of the various world communities ought to be, we would still lack a basis to think that falling in line with the natural law's prescriptions would result in convergence among these de facto moral systems. But the characteristic natural law view has not even been that the natural law, in conjunction with the local conditions that obtain, fixes the details of the de facto norms that ought to be established. Rather, on the characteristic natural law position, the natural law displays a great deal of *normative openness*, a lack of fixity as to how its precepts are to be fulfilled in concrete circumstances. (This is not to say that there is no substantial determinacy to the natural law, nor is it to say that there are not substantial moral absolutes included in the natural law, as I noted earlier.) Aquinas discusses this normative openness in a very influential passage of the so-called 'Treatise on Law' in which he is considering the relationship between natural law and positive law.[25] When asking whether positive law (at least the best, positive law in worthwhile legal systems) is derived from the natural law, the answer is (like many of Aquinas's answers) yes and no. It is not derived from natural law in the sense of 'wholly deducible from it' – so that, for each rule included in a (defensible) system of positive law, there is a chain of valid deductive reasoning linking the norms of the positive law with the norms of the natural law along with an exhaustive description of the local circumstances. It is, on the other hand, true that the positive law is based on the natural law in the sense that the positive laws, if not deducible from the natural law proper, nevertheless 'fill in the gaps' or 'make concrete' the gappy or vague provisions of the natural law. Aquinas's example is punishment: while the natural law prescribes that persons who commit offenses be punished, it does not provide the fine details of what those punishments should be, but leaves that open to the discretion of the community, either through its customs or through the decisions made by authoritative lawmakers.[26]

There is another source of openness apart from the looseness of the norms of the natural law that require determination to be made specific. That is the multiplicity of the human goods that are the basis for all natural law precepts. As I noted earlier, Aquinas notes a variety of human goods, including life, procreation, society, knowledge, and reasonable agency. Other natural law theorists have suggested additions to this list: aesthetic experience and play, for example.[27] Further openness is generated in the natural law if we allow, as has recently been insisted upon, that these goods are irreducible and incommensurable, and thus that there is no hierarchy of intrinsic value among them. Thus, as a matter of natural reasonableness, there are no hierarchies of intrinsic value among the basic goods that must be respected, and reasonable agents might emphasize different of these goods in their overall scheme of priorities.[28]

So arguments of the form 'one natural law, therefore one defensible type of de facto moral system' are bound to be mistaken. We should say something on the positive side about the sorts of variations that seem possible in de facto moral systems that seem perfectly justifiable, and about why the loss of these variations would be massively undesirable. Then we can turn back and ask what sort of commonality is desirable in the face of these variations.

[25] ST IaIIae 95, 2.
[26] ST IaIIae 95, 2.
[27] Finnis, *Natural Law*, pp. 87–88.
[28] See, for example, Finnis, *Natural Law*, pp. 92–95, and Murphy, *Practical Rationality*, pp. 190–198.

The first source of variation among de facto moral systems that seems perfectly justifiable is that arising from differences in local circumstances. I mentioned one such case, that having to do with the scarcity of water and the norms regarding its use. Let me mention another. Consider the norms regarding punishment in two societies, one of which possesses the techniques to confine those who commit the most heinous offenses against the common good, and one that does not. Aquinas argued that the killing of 'sinners' – that is, those who violate authoritative norms within some community – by the public authority can be justified if those sinners pose a danger to the common good that cannot be countered except through execution.[29] (Aquinas compares it to cutting away a diseased member from the body.) While one might raise some questions about the conditional character of this natural law view of capital punishment (and on both sides),[30] if we do hold to Aquinas's view, then it is clear that the de facto moral systems at different stages in the development and employment of penological technique would be justified in having different norms regarding the use of death as a punishment.

The second source of variation is the normative openness of the natural law. Again, there is much that the natural law requires, but there is much that is vague or gappy about it. And there is good reason to make the natural law less vague and gappy through the devices of de facto morality. The natural law may require care for those contributors to the common good who no longer are able to support themselves, and it may require that those persons who no fault of their own are unable to contribute nevertheless receive what they need.[31] There are, however, a variety of ways to bring these ends about. And it is not as if it would be a good idea simply to leave the details up to each individual person in that community: for how one person goes about doing his or her share for those who cannot care for themselves depends on how others go about doing their shares. It is a coordination problem, not just with respect to bringing about the proper end results but with respect to knowing what sorts of criticism and demands one party can bring to bear on another. So these duties can be specified by laying the burdens on relatives, more or less closely kin to the party to whom care is due, or by laying the burdens on 'the village' more generally, or by laying the burdens on religious or political institutions. While there are of course innumerable ways of concretizing these duties that would be simply unreasonable, there are a number of distinct possibilities that are within reason, and de facto moral systems might incorporate different determinations of these general natural law norms without any of them being in error or being at all subject to rational criticism.

---

[29] ST IIaIIae 64, 2.

[30] That is, one might wonder both about whether defense of the community is a necessary condition on justified execution (as recent Catholic Church pronouncements seem to presuppose) and about whether the necessity for defense would be sufficient to justify it.

[31] See, for a discussion, MacIntyre, *Dependent Rational Animals*, pp. 119–128.

There is a third source of noncriticizable variation among de facto moral systems. The first two sources of noncriticizable variation deal exclusively with the relation between the content of the norms of de facto moral systems and the norms of the natural law: two distinct de facto moral systems can both be justifiable if the difference between the content of their norms is the result of application of the natural law to distinct local circumstances or is the result of free choice concerning how to make the natural law more specific for the sake of a common standard of action. The third source has to do with the very existence of certain norms within the de facto moral system. The idea is this: it can be justifiable for one de facto moral system to contain a natural law norm (or a deduction or determination of it) while another de facto moral system omits it. That is to say: one de facto moral system might include some natural law rule that some other system does not.

One might find this strange, but it seems a perfectly straightforward extension of the natural law thought that not all natural law norms need to be recapitulated in positive law, for there may be little reason to do so, and strong reason not to. (Natural lawyers tend to hold fairly subtle views about the extent to which 'morals legislation' is justifiable, and there is hardly consensus among them.)[32] Some norms might be costly to enforce; their legislation might make imperfect people even more resistant to the more pressing demands that a legal system needs to make, and so forth.[33] Now, the reasons for refraining from legally prohibiting some action that is contrary to the natural law are not the very same as the reasons for refraining from including that prohibition in a de facto moral system. But there are similar types of cost that are here worth noting. The more a de facto morality includes, the more folks have to be willing to criticize each other and impose 'social sanctions' for that conduct, and this involves a certain nosiness and judgmentalism that is, all things being equal, a bit of a bother, and can strain social relationships. Given the level of community exhibited in some place, higher or lower levels of this sort of nosiness can be tolerable, and thus there might be various levels at which the de facto moral system in place should aspire to include comprehensively the norms of the natural law and derivations of it.

It should also be noted that just because it can be permissible to omit certain natural law norms from the de facto moral system of a community, it does not follow that there are no precepts of the natural law that demand a place in every de facto moral system. It could be that there are certain de facto norms that must be in place for certain natural law immunities to be adequately honored, and so justice demands that these natural law norms be taken up into the de facto moral systems of each community. It would, for example,

---

[32] See, for example, Robert George, *Making Men Moral* (New York: Oxford University Press, 1998), and John Finnis, "Legal Enforcement of 'Duties to Oneself': Kant v. Neo-Kantians," *Columbia Law Review* 87 (1987), pp. 433–456.

[33] ST IaIIae 96, 2.

be hard to imagine by what justification a de facto moral system might refuse to include a prohibition of some sort on murder or other gross violations of bodily integrity, especially with respect to the most vulnerable members of society.

Now, I have claimed that there are at least three sources of legitimate variation among de facto moral systems: differences in applications of the natural law to local circumstances, differences in free determinations of the natural law, and differences in the extent to which natural law norms are incorporated into the de facto moral system. One might wish to add a fourth: that there can be legitimate variation in the extent to which norms that are contrary to the natural law are included in the de facto moral system. One might think that it is appropriate in some cases for a de facto moral system not merely to fail to include what the natural law requires, but also to include what the natural law forbids. This might seem obviously wrongheaded, and I do think that the natural law view rejects it. But it is important to be clear on the reason for rejecting it. One might argue, in favor of such variation, in the following way: Recall the considerations that showed that it could be a good idea to fail to include all natural law norms and their general implications in the de facto moral system. To try to include all such norms would involve a lot of confidence in the detailed knowability of these particular norms and a great deal of nosiness in using them as a basis for criticism and demands, and that would be bad on the natural law view. But it could be for the best for a de facto moral system to include a norm that requires what the natural law forbids. It could be that, in some places and in some conditions, people actually end up following the natural law better if the de facto moral system runs contrary to it at some points. For example: given humans' natural tendency to favor their own, and even to an unreasonable extent, folks might more closely approximate compliance with the actual demands of the natural law if their de facto moral systems hold them to excessive demands – demands that, were they followed, would lead them to neglect their special obligations.[34]

There is some plausibility to this argument, but nevertheless there could not be a defensible de facto moral system that included norms requiring what the natural law forbids. To see why, one needs to bring back to mind what is involved in there being a de facto moral system. What makes it the case that a de facto moral system is in place is that people are using the rules of that system as a basis for making demands on each other and for criticizing each other. To endorse there being a norm in a de facto moral system that requires what the natural law forbids is to endorse people's demanding of each other that they violate the natural law. But it is wrong, contrary to the natural law, to make such demands on each other: it is violating our nature as rational beings

---

[34] This is not an unfamiliar phenomenon. Who among us has not been told to arrive for an appointment by a certain time in advance of the actual time at which one is needed, simply in order to take into account the foreseeable effects of tardiness?

to be ordered to do what reason forbids. So while de facto moral systems can legitimately refrain from including some natural law norms within themselves, they cannot legitimately include norms that are contrary to the natural law. (Again, compare with natural law thought on law: while defenders of the natural law view tend to affirm the claim that not everything contrary to the natural law need be contrary to the positive law,[35] no positive law can be suffered adherence to that would require one to violate the natural law).[36]

I have argued thus far that the natural law insistence on a single natural law does not give us any reason to think that the existence of a tremendous variety of de facto moral systems shows that any of those systems must constitute a departure from what a justifiable de facto moral system would be like. So the existence of variation does not show that any individual de facto moral system is defective. But that still leaves another question. Even if nothing can be said against a single de facto moral system simply in virtue of the fact that it differs from others, might there not be some reason to think it desirable that there be coincidence in the demands of de facto moral systems? Might it not provide a basis for easier intercommunity dealings and fewer intercultural misunderstandings if there were not widespread variation, even if it is of the legitimate sorts that I just outlined? Perhaps. But there are other grounds that lead pretty straightforwardly to the conclusion that full convergence would be massively undesirable.

First, given the fact that de facto moral systems might include norms that are deducible from the natural law in conjunction with facts about local conditions, for all de facto moral systems to converge would require some communities either to adopt unjustifiable norms into their de facto moral systems or to thin themselves to an unfortunate extent. Consider again the different communities that, in virtue of their distinct water supplies, have distinct norms concerning the use of water. For them to have the same norms it would be necessary either for them to have the same norms regarding water usage – which means either that in one community water is wasted that is needed for survival or that water is saved that is far more than is needed – or for them to refrain from having any specific norms about water usage at all – thus leaving it to individual judgment as to how the general principles of the natural law bear on water usage. In any of these cases, the de facto moral systems are stripped of their capacity to adopt the specific derivative norms of the natural law that are best for guiding the action of the people living under those norms in a helpful way. So seeking convergence with respect to such norms seems contrary to the very idea of natural law thinking, which is that norms are for the sake of guiding conduct in an appropriately reasonable way.

It is also a bad idea to want convergence with respect to those de facto norms that are free determinations of general natural law principles. For the

---

[35] ST IaIIae 96, 2.
[36] ST IaIIae 96, 4.

determination of general natural law principles in their space of normative openness is a creative act, a chance for a culture to set for itself a certain pattern of concern, to choose to realize one distinctive cultural possibility rather than another. It would be bad to straitjacket cultural options where the natural law does not do so: it would deprive the members of that culture from freely setting their course, for realizing a common life with one set of sensibilities rather than another; and it would deprive outsiders of the opportunity to see a rich, distinctive, fully reasonable alternative way of life realized.[37]

We thus reach a mixed conclusion on the natural law view's stance on the prospect of a uniform planetary ethic. From the natural law standpoint, complete uniformity of de facto moral codes is massively undesirable, and thus there would be no reason to foster the conditions – legal or extralegal, coercive or noncoercive – under which movement toward uniformity would be achieved. But there is a limited commonality that is desirable: no de facto moral system should include provisions that require those living under it to violate the natural law, and no de facto moral system should fail to include provisions that protect those to whom immunity from certain harms is accorded them by the natural law. Every de facto moral system should not require those under it to do wrong, and it should recognize some set of basic rights for those living under it.

That the de facto moral systems of the world not mandate wrongdoing and protect basic rights is the ideal. Where ideals are realized, we can be thankful. But this ideal surely is not.

Intervention into De Facto Moral Systems

An intervention into a de facto moral system occurs when some agent, whether a person or an organization, acts with the intention of bringing about some change in the content of that de facto moral system, whether to revise some of its norms, introduce new norms, or eradicate existing norms.[38] Interventions can be of various sorts: legislation, military invasion, missionary activity, educational measures, revolution. Interventions can be internal, carried out by agents within that de facto moral system, or external, carried out by outsiders, or they can be some hybrid of the two. Here I take as the focus of our question

---

[37] For an argument along the lines that equal respect requires the presumption that cultural differences have something important to say to all human beings – to which the natural law view, with its emphasis on a variety of human goods and the normative openness of their pursuit, is amenable – see Charles Taylor, *Multiculturalism and the "Politics of Recognition"* (Princeton: Princeton University Press, 1992), p. 66.

[38] Note here that I am not asking about what we usually have in mind when we think about humanitarian interventions. Humanitarian interventions usually aim simply to protect people from unjustified violence; whether the intervention itself contributes in any way to a changing of anyone's moral views is, if not entirely beside the point, not the purpose of the intervention.

external interventions. Under what conditions should some agent carry out an external intervention into a de facto moral system?

There is a very quick answer to the question. The quick answer is that an agent should carry out an external intervention into a de facto moral system if the natural law sanctions that external intervention. The natural law sanctions an external intervention only if that external intervention is effective and is not otherwise excluded by its precepts. Whether the 'effectiveness' clause is satisfied is not an issue that moral philosophers have any special competence to discuss: whether a particular intervention is likely to effect a greater approximation to the normative ideal of a de facto moral system is just a matter of empirical fact to be settled, if at all, by the usual methods. The 'not otherwise excluded' clause does require discussion, for what its inclusion suggests is that there are ways of carrying out external interventions that are either forbidden by the natural law or, at least, face a very high burden of proof if they are to be employed.

I will mention several such constraints that have been recognized within the natural law tradition, but let me first note briefly one putative constraint that the natural law tradition should not affirm. The natural law view should *not* affirm the constraint that any de facto moral norm that justifies an intervention must involve injustice – that is, a wrong perpetrated by one party with respect to some other party. If we allow that departures from the natural law might be not unjust but rather instances of some other vice – consider intemperance, for example, and the varieties of ways that a de facto moral system might fail to adequately respond to the ways that human life can be made worse through it – then the defender of the natural law viewpoint faces a real question about the extent to which interventions might be justified not because a norm in some de facto moral system involves doing injury to others but because that norm involves baseness or corruption of the agent acting in accordance with the norm, or because there are insufficient norms directing agents away from such baseness and corruption. Since agents can harm themselves through their violations of the natural law, there is no prima facie reason to think that the only interventions that are justified are those that involve harm to others.

What, then, are the constraints that the natural law view does recognize? The first is that any external interventions must be compatible with existing just law that governs both the community living under the de facto moral system and the agents that propose to intervene into that system. What comes to mind immediately is international law, but we should of course keep in mind that one nation can be inhabited by a number of distinct moral communities with their own de facto moral systems, and thus typical municipal law can be relevant as well.

I put to the side here the question of what, specifically, makes law authoritative (as I have put to the side the question of what makes de facto moral systems authoritative). Assuming that such norms can be authoritative, it is important not to overestimate or underestimate the help that is given in determining the appropriate conditions for external intervention. With respect to overestimating: it needs to be kept in mind that one constraint relevant here is that the law in question be just – that is, within the range of reasonable norms that might be imposed on the subject-matter in question. So a norm of international law that simply declared that no external interventions of any sort into some community's de facto moral system are permissible would be an unjust norm, given the depth of wrong to innocents that de facto moral systems can be implicated in and the draconian character of the limits on contact between members of distinct communities that would be needed to make the norm effective. It is not, then, that recognizing the force of law solves the problem of external interventions for us; one would have to ask in a given case whether the norms in question were just. And whether these norms are just will depend on whether they are acceptable determinations of natural law precepts bearing on intercommunity conduct, and to see whether they are acceptable determinations of such precepts we would need to have an adequate understanding of what those precepts are. These reflections should not, however, lead to the view that the existence of such laws is irrelevant to the question of whether external intervention is permissible. For there are likely to be a wide range of at least minimally acceptable norms regarding intercommunity conduct that might be enacted into law, and the existence of some particular set of laws will settle which of these norms is actually binding. In short, the natural law requires agents to defer to the positive law when the positive law is at least minimally reasonable. (We should also note that the existence of unjust law might be relevant as well, even if not authoritative: for the existence of such law will make a difference as to how it is prudent – both in the narrowly self-interested and the wider 'all-reasons-considered' sense – to proceed).[39]

Positive law governing intercommunity interventions are, if just, reasonable determinations of natural law considerations bearing on such interventions. One such natural law consideration concerns efficiency. It is of course a constraint on rational external intervention that such intervention be plausibly effective, otherwise the intervention would be pointless. But a further constraint on such intervention is that, ceteris paribus, more plausibly effective interventions are to be preferred to less plausibly effective interventions, and plausibly more effective interventions are to be preferred to plausibly less effective interventions. Those interventions with a greater chance of success are to be selected, other things being equal, and those interventions with a chance of greater success are to be selected, other things being equal.

The natural law tradition also professes a preference for noncoercive rather than coercive methods of intervention. An analogy to the natural law just war doctrine seems to the point here. The just war doctrine includes within its *jus ad bellum* provisions the constraint that war is to be waged only when means short of war are bound to be ineffective. Similarly, noncoercive external

---

[39] ST IaIIae 96, 4.

interventions are to be preferred to coercive ones, so that an agent should resort to coercive means only when noncoercive means – exhortation, education, example – have been ineffective and are likely to continue to be ineffective, or when coercive means seem prima facie most promising and the depth of injustice embodied in the de facto moral system is such as to preclude a gradual escalation of means until the injustice is eradicated.

What is the basis for this preference? It is not merely a recapitulation of the claim that the most efficient means are to be used, along with the empirical claim that communities tend to be resistant to coercive measures and coercive measures have costs associated with them that noncoercive methods do not. Sometimes it might be pretty clear that coercive methods can very quickly bring about changes in a de facto moral system in a way that would bring about few unwanted bad consequences. Nor is it simply that coercion is prima facie unjust, that people have a right not to be coerced. The immunity from coercion affirmed by the natural law view is characteristically conditional, conditional on one's being mature, of sound mind, not posing a threat to others, not pursuing an intended evil aim, and so forth. But ex hypothesi, these are cases in which a community is sustaining a moral system that is in some way depriving members of that community of a share in natural human goods, and perhaps rather severely. So it is not a general prima facie duty not to coerce that is the basis of this preference.

Rather, the preference is based in an ideal of social relations. Human beings are rational animals, and it is an ideal of interaction among humans that such interaction be carried out on a rational basis – that is, a basis of giving reasons for transforming one's patterns of conduct. We should not understand 'reason-giving' in too limited a way. It does not mean simply giving arguments, as if the ideal of external interventions would be sending over philosophers to give seminars in natural law theory. The reasons for transformation can be shown rather than said, exhibited in the character of moral missionaries, illustrated in stories, and so forth. The preference for noncoercive over coercive means is, then, rooted in a preference for rational over nonrational interaction with our fellow rational animals.

Here is another in-principle preference: the natural law tradition would favor less extensive external interventions to more extensive external interventions. I have no precise way of saying what counts as a more extensive intervention, but what I have in mind is roughly this. If we imagine two plans of action for transforming the de facto moral system of some community so that it is more closely in line with what the natural law requires, and describe these plans of action finely so we are imagining precisely how the requisite changes will occur, one plan of action is 'more extensive' than another to the extent that the actions of the external agent occur more prominently or more frequently in that plan than in the other. By definition, every external intervention involves an agent's poking his or her or its nose into the affairs of some moral community. But 'poking one's nose into the affairs of another' admits of degrees, and the idea here is that the less one pokes one's nose into the other's affairs, the better.

Again, this is not merely an empirical specification of the general requirements of efficiency. But neither is it simply a basic community right of privacy, where a community can do what it like in its own affairs. While communities may enjoy some such sovereignty, it does not hold where, ex hypothesi, its members' goods are being violated by the de facto moral norms that are being propagated and socially enforced. Consider the principle of subsidiarity: the view that higher-level organizations should not take over activities that can be carried out by lower-level organizations; rather, higher-level organizations should provide help (*subsidium*) for them to carry out these activities on their own, fostering the conditions so that they can do these jobs for themselves. Subsidiarity appears most prominently in Catholic social thought,[40] but it has been defended as a natural law principle on the supposition that the formulating of intelligent, creative responses to practical problems is itself a human good of which persons should not be deprived.[41] The case of external intervention is not the sort of case to which the principle of subsidiarity is customarily taken to apply, for the relationship between the external agent and the community living under a defective de facto moral system is not one of higher-level and lower-level organizations. But nevertheless the good at stake – that of dealing with one's own problems in a fruitful and clever way – is the good that is at stake in subsidiarity cases, and thus external agents have the same principled reason for restraint.

I have mentioned three principles that, in addition to the constraint of just law, can help to determine when an external intervention is justifiable. But all three of these principles – efficiency, anti-coercion, and pro-subsidiarity principles – are defeasible, *ceteris paribus* principles. To these we may add a requirement of impartiality, the Golden-Rule-like requirement that any decision on the correctness of an external intervention that one reaches must be one that can be affirmed for all similar situations. There are various ways to model such impartiality – Rawls's 'original position' being perhaps the best-worked-out[42] – but the point is that a judgment that an external intervention is justified must be one that would hold even for those cases in which one belongs to the intervened-in moral community rather than in which one is the prospective intervening agent.

---

[40] See Pope Pius XI's *Quadragesimo Anno* (1931), §79.

[41] See John Finnis, "Natural Law Theory and Limited Government," in Robert George, ed. *Natural Law, Liberalism, and Morality* (New York: Oxford University Press, 1996), and Christopher Wolfe, "Subsidiarity: The 'Other' Ground of Limited Government," in Kenneth Grasso et al., eds., *Catholicism, Liberalism, and Communitarianism* (Lanham: Rowman and Littlefield, 1995).

[42] See John Rawls, *A Theory of Justice*, revised ed. (Cambridge: Harvard University Press, 1999b), pp. 102–168.

The natural law tradition thus affirms some substantive constraints on the licitness of external interventions into defective de facto moral systems. We can imagine some egregious violations of these principles, and so it is clear that the natural law view is not toothless in condemning certain ways of carrying out such external interventions. But most of the cases that we will ever have to concern ourselves with are not egregious. The hard fact here is that the application to these principles in harder cases requires not just a straightforward ability to apply rules to cases but a sensitivity to the point of those rules, the goods that those rules mean to promote and the evils that those rules mean to avoid. Thus Aquinas writes that

There is still more uncertainty if one wishes to descend further to the resolution of particular cases. For this subject is not subsumed under art or tradition, because the causes of particular actions are infinitely diversified. Hence, the judgment of particular cases is left to each person's prudence. One who employs prudence aims to consider the things that should be done at the present time, having considered all the particular circumstances.[43]

The most complete proximate standard for the correctness of such decisions is prudence, the capacity to judge rightly in concrete cases. But even where "the judgment depends on perception,"[44] prudence is not an 'unmeasured measure'; it aspires to a standard of correctness that is independent of it. That standard of correctness is the natural law.

[43] Thomas Aquinas, *Commentary on the Nicomachean Ethics*, Book II, Lectio 2, §259.
[44] Aristotle, *Nicomachean Ethics*, trans. Terence Irwin (Indianapolis: Hackett, 1999), 1109b23.

9

Liberalism and the Globalization of Ethics

Chris Brown

Introduction: Many Liberalisms

When the words 'liberal' and 'liberalism' entered the broad political discourse of Europe in the first quarter of the nineteenth century, it was as terms of abuse; the association was with libertinism – when Don Giovanni gives the toast 'Viva la libertà' in the Finale to Act I of Mozart's opera it seems unlikely he had any specifically *political* principle in mind. Soon, as is often the way, the terms came to be accepted by those who advocated a programme of personal freedom that encompassed civil and political rights for the individual instead of, or sometimes perhaps as well as, the liberation from conventional sexual mores toasted by the Don. This programme remains the core of the liberal conception of the world. In the helpful formulation of Will Kymlicka:

Liberals demand a substantial realm of personal freedom – including freedom of conscience, speech, association, occupation, and, more recently, sexuality – which the state should not intrude upon except to protect others from harm.[1]

In pursuit of this realm of personal freedom, liberals generally favour constitutional forms of government, the separation of powers and the rule of law, with representative, but not usually direct, democracy, and are broadly sceptical of accounts of politics that are based around the promotion of any particular conception of the Good (except that conception of the Good that involves not having an overriding conception of the Good). It is this latter position that distinguishes liberalism from the 'civic republican' tradition that, in many respects, it otherwise resembles – civic republicans also favour constitutionalism and the rule of law, but are broadly sympathetic to the idea that the state has a duty to promote the Good in the form of republican virtue.[2]

---

[1] 'Liberalism,' in *The Oxford Companion to Philosophy* (Oxford: Oxford University Press, 1995) p. 483.

[2] For civic republicanism see, for example, J. G. A. Pocock, *The Machiavellian Moment: Florentine Political Thought and the Atlantic Republican Tradition* (Princeton: Princeton University

Although most liberals would accept something like this short summary description of their political position, the status of liberalism as the dominant political philosophy of capitalist democracy, a status that has developed over the past two centuries, surviving the challenges of Marxism and fascism in the process, has inevitably led to its differentiation into a number of quite radically different sub-ideologies, reflecting different national traditions and circumstances. To further complicate matters, these core divisions do not necessarily map neatly onto liberal thought on the globalisation of ethics. Thus, before addressing the themes identified as central to the latter topic, a certain amount of under-labouring is necessary in order to distinguish broad schools of thought within liberalism. To oversimplify somewhat, we can distinguish between Anglo-American and Continental liberalism, and between cosmopolitan and pluralist liberalism.

The first of these distinctions revolves around the role of the state vis-à-vis the economy, or, perhaps more generally, around what is involved in 'protecting others from harm,' to return to Kymlicka's formulation. A central proposition for Continental liberals is that the state should provide the context within which economic activity can take place, but should not attempt to regulate that activity unduly, and, in particular, should not intervene in order to try to ensure that the operation of the free market brings about any allegedly desirable outcome. From this perspective, liberal individualism precludes notions of distributive justice – the distribution of goods (in the broadest sense) produced by the market is neither just nor unjust, and attempts to make this distribution 'just' involve improper interference with personal freedom in the name of exactly the kind of conception of the Good that liberals deny exist. In any event, such attempts are doomed to failure since, as the failure of central planning demonstrates, human agency is unable to replicate the impersonal information-processing capacity of the market. This tradition of liberalism can trace its descent from the Hobbesian and Lockean notion that freedom exists where the law is silent and the eighteenth-century notion – somewhat tendentiously associated with Adam Smith – of the 'night-watchman state.' Its most important modern intellectual is probably the Austrian economist Friedrich von Hayek (a conservative in institutional terms, but devoted to liberty and the free economy) and it is the underlying position of modern Continental European Liberal parties such as the German Free Democrats, and of the Thatcherite tendency within the British Conservative Party.

In the U.S. context, such a position would be thought of as 'libertarian' rather than liberal. In American political discourse, a liberal is a progressive, left-leaning figure with a propensity to favour state intervention to right the wrongs done by the market and other agents of inequality. Rather than Hayek, the key figure here is John Rawls, whose *A Theory of Justice* is generically liberal

Press, 1975), and Quentin Skinner, *Liberty before Liberalism* (Cambridge: Cambridge University Press, 1998).

insofar as it asserts that that the first principle of justice is that 'each person is to have an equal right to the most extensive scheme of equal basic liberties compatible with a similar scheme of liberties for others.'[3] Rawls, however, argues that there is a second principle of justice that is concerned with outcomes: a society is just only if positions within it are distributed in accordance with 'fair' equality of opportunity, where the influence of social circumstances such as class and family wealth are eliminated, and inequalities of outcome are acceptable only if they can reasonably be expected to be to everyone's advantage – that is to say, only if they work to the benefit of the least advantaged members of society. By no means all American liberals are Rawlsians, and, as we will see, Rawlsians themselves differ on a number of key issues, but the association of liberalism with state action to 'correct' the workings of the free market is a standard feature of the American idea of the discourse. From a Continental perspective, this version of 'liberalism' is actually much closer to what Europeans would regard as Social Democratic (or Democratic Socialist) politics – and it is indeed the case that Rawlsian thinking has been quite influential in the British Labour Party and, to a lesser extent, with German Social Democrats.[4]

Between the thoughts of von Hayek and Rawls, there is an extraordinarily wide gap, but the situation gets even more complicated when the global dimension of liberal thought is factored into the equation. Again there is a major divide to be mapped out, but this divide does not correspond to that which separates American from Continental liberalism. There is, initially, one point upon which all liberals can agree – namely, that the *ultimate* reference point for a global ethics is the individual, as opposed, for example, to God in any of his/her many manifestations, or to social class, or gender, or the state – but this consensus breaks down as soon as any of the hard questions about global ethics are asked. Liberals can agree that state and society exist ultimately to serve the individual, and not vice versa, but this does not help to resolve any of the key questions of global ethics, which revolve around the comparative importance to be placed on the interests of fellow citizens as opposed to the population of the world as a whole. Is it justified, for example, to restrict the benefits of a welfare state to fellow citizens, assuming, of course, that a welfare state can itself be justified in liberal terms? Can restrictions on the free movement of individuals be justified?

In principle, 'cosmopolitan' liberals answer this kind of question in the negative, although they may acknowledge that there are practical problems involved in, for example, a policy of open borders. From a cosmopolitan viewpoint, national identities are always secondary to one's identity as a 'citizen of the world,' and one should extend to one's fellow global citizens as many

---

3 John Rawls, *A Theory of Justice*, revised ed. (Cambridge, MA: Harvard University Press, 1999) p. 52.
4 Likewise with the British Liberal Party, whose ideology, where discernable, is broadly social democratic.

political and civil rights as is practicable. Liberal communitarians or pluralist liberals or liberal nationalists – there is no agreed terminology here, and these terms will be used as synonyms – on the other hand, argue that one of the key rights possessed by individuals is the right to govern themselves and to pursue collective projects in discreet societies, which implies that, for example, control of membership in these societies is of critical importance.[5] From this perspective, we have duties towards our fellow citizens (and, for that matter, claims upon them) that are qualitatively different from our duties to humanity as a whole – but, it should be noted, no liberal denies that we have such duties to all our fellow human beings; the issue is simply, but importantly, how extensive such duties are.

It might be thought that cosmopolitan liberals would tend to be Continental while liberal nationalists would tend to be Anglo-American, since the latter have a far more positive approach to national welfare systems than the former. However, things are not that simple. Some libertarians are indeed cosmopolitan insofar as they believe in free (but, of course, wholly unassisted) movement of peoples between states (which, in any event, ought to be as weak as possible), but other Continental liberals believe that although the state ought to interfere as little as possible in the operation of the market, this need not imply that national identification should be weak or that national societies do not have the right to determine their own membership and constitutional arrangements.[6] Similar divides can be found in Anglo-American liberalism: figures such as John Rawls, Michael Walzer, and David Miller focus on national societies as the only plausible containers for liberal, social democratic, welfarist politics, while cosmopolitans such as Charles Beitz and Brian Barry look to the emergence of a kind of redistributive global welfare state.[7]

What this means is that in order to address the six questions around which this volume is oriented from a liberal perspective, it will be necessary very frequently to give multiple alternative answers – often there will be four different positions on each question that could with equal plausibility claim to be liberal. Since it would be excessively tedious actually to present four answers to each question, matters will be simplified by focusing most of the time on just two of these positions. The Anglo-American school of liberalism will be one focus,

---

[5] This position shades into the civic republicanism mentioned earlier; to help others judge the fairness of the account of liberalism presented here, it should be noted that it is on this borderline that the author would situate himself.

[6] For a libertarian defence of free movement, see Hillel Steiner, 'Libertarianism and the Transnational Migration of People,' in Brian Barry and Robert Goodin, eds., *Free Movement* (Hemel Hempstead: Harvester Wheatsheaf, 1992).

[7] John Rawls, *The Law of Peoples* (Cambridge MA: Harvard University Press, 1999); David Miller and Michael Walzer, eds., *Pluralism, Justice and Equality* (Oxford: Oxford University Press, 1995); Charles Beitz, *Political Theory and International Relations*, 2nd ed (Princeton NJ: Princeton University Press, 2000); Brian Barry, 'International Society from a Cosmopolitan Perspective,' in David Mapel and Terry Nardin, eds., *International Society* (Princeton NJ: Princeton University Press, 1998).

introducing libertarian thinking only occasionally into the dominant 'global welfare state' version of cosmopolitanism, while the Rawls/Walzer/J. S. Mill account of liberal nationalism will be treated as the basic alternative to liberal cosmopolitanism.

A Uniform Planetary Ethic?

Is a uniform planetary ethic the ideal, or should liberals accept a global accommodation of difference or some mixture of uniformity and particularism? Would each of these positions be morally acceptable or, at least, tolerable? To answer these questions, it is necessary to explore what liberals understand by the notion of a conception of the Good, and, in particular what it means to say that liberals privilege no particular conception of the Good. Do liberals in fact privilege a conception of the Good that says that no conception of the Good should be privileged? Is liberal neutrality genuinely neutral? This is a key issue, which needs to be explored at length both in general and with respect to cosmopolitan as opposed to pluralist varieties of liberalism – examining the matter now, in the context of this set of questions on alternatives, will make it easier to answer the next three sets.

The core liberal position is that the priority of personal freedom as a value entails that whatever conception of the Good an individual holds should be a matter of individual choice and not foisted upon him or her by any external force, be the latter the state, a religion, or pressures emanating from society at large. The actual content of such conceptions of the Good is, from a liberal perspective, not crucially important as long as they are freely chosen and do not impose duties on others that others are not prepared to accept, although most liberals value freedom for its own sake and thus would hold that there are some rights that are unalienable – for example, individuals ought not to be allowed to sell themselves into slavery even if this represents a free choice on their part. In short, to borrow out of context some terminology from John Rawls, liberalism is a political doctrine not a metaphysical doctrine, and in a liberal society there is room for a plurality of reasonable comprehensive doctrines (that is, what I have been calling conceptions of the Good).[8] In so far as such a society could be said to have an ethic, it would be based on an overlapping consensus amongst such reasonable doctrines.

On the face of it, this position would seem to allow plenty of room for divergent ethical perspectives; any 'planetary ethic' would be uniform only insofar as it provided a framework within which diverse comprehensive doctrines could flourish – there is space for a plurality of reasonable doctrines, and toleration is a key liberal virtue. A multicultural version of liberalism is easy to design upon these lines. However, predictably, things are not that simple. When we look closer, there are a number of serious problems with liberal neutrality and tolerance, which liberal cosmopolitans and liberal nationalists

---

[8] John Rawls, *Political Liberalism* (Cambridge MA: Harvard University Press, 1995).

handle in quite different ways. Consider first the notion of a reasonable comprehensive doctrine, which, for the sake of exposition, we can think of here as
a religious creed that provides the individual with answers to the great questions thrown up by human existence. There clearly are a great many modern
religious believers (Christians, Jews, and perhaps Muslims – I am less clear
of the implications of the position for non-theist religions) who regard their
beliefs as essentially life-style choices, although they usually do not put it that
way. Such modern believers would not wish to impose their beliefs on others and would be content with the freedom to practice their own religion in
their own way. Liberal toleration works well for them, most of the time; there
might be the occasional problem thrown up when, for example, dietary rules
go against community standards vis-à-vis the treatment of animals (kosher and
halal butchery) and the education of the children of believers may pose problems, but there is no reason to think that such difficulties cannot be handled
smoothly given goodwill on all sides.

Still, even such tolerant modern believers may well have sticking points
that cannot be dealt with so easily. To take an obvious example of great significance in the United States – they may hold that abortion is not simply
an option that they themselves would never consider as a personal choice,
but something that is wrong in itself and should not be available to anyone,
regardless of their beliefs. Does this position mean that the comprehensive
doctrine on which it is based is not 'reasonable' and ought not to be tolerated
in a liberal society? Or, putting the issue the other way round, is a liberal
society abandoning liberal neutrality if it enacts laws that enforce a woman's
right to choose when many people believe that no one should possess such a
right? The situation is, of course, much more problematic when we move away
from 'modern' believers and shift to those for whom it is not so much a matter
of an occasional sticking point, but of a root and branch disjuncture between
liberal neutrality and a whole way of life. Many religious believers reject the
separation of church and state (or mosque and state) upon which liberalism
is founded, and wish to impose religious uniformity where they are able to do
so. This position is clearly incompatible with liberal neutrality and cannot to
be tolerated by liberals – but what kind of steps may liberals take to prevent
such theocracies from emerging? If the members of a society freely choose
to adopt a state religion, should their free choice be overridden in the name
of liberal values? In order to prevent the emergence of a theocracy, a number of Muslim-majority societies (for example, Turkey and Tunisia) interfere
with personal freedom by banning the wearing of the veil; is this a legitimate
interference with personal freedom or an affront to liberal values?[9] Looking

---

[9] The recent French ban on the *hijab* in schools is different; it applies only to the wearing of the
veil in a public institution, not in private or on the street – in any event, the French tradition
of civic republicanism is explicitly non-liberal in its desire to promote a particular conception
of what it is to be French.

at the matter from another angle, is it necessarily the case that, for a liberal, a society that is based on a particular comprehensive doctrine is by definition unjust and not to be tolerated, regardless of the content of that doctrine?

There are clearly tricky problems to be handled here, and different liberals handle them in different ways. In essence, the more cosmopolitan the liberalism, the less tolerance for difference can be expected. Thus, cosmopolitan liberals are, in principle, committed to the full package of political, civil, and economic rights set out in the contemporary international human rights regime – the Universal Declaration of Human Rights of 1948, the two International Covenants of 1966, the Convention on the Elimination of Discrimination Against Women of 1979, and so on.[10] This regime sets out a very comprehensive account of the rights that individuals ought to possess, and provides the basis for a liberal 'uniform planetary ethic.' The liberal conception of human flourishing is not exhaustively defined by the international rights regime – and indeed existed before that regime came into existence – but, as a rough approximation, the Universal Declaration and subsequent elaborations thereof can serve as a practical summary of what is entailed by cosmopolitan liberalism. Ethical differences can only be accommodated if they concern practices that are not subject to this international standard-setting. Only those conceptions of the Good/comprehensive doctrines that are compatible with the internationally-agreed body of human rights law are to be regarded as 'reasonable.'

There are, of course, a great many issues that divide cosmopolitan liberals. Are the personal freedoms guaranteed by the 1966 International Covenant on Civil and Political Rights compatible with the economic, social, and cultural rights laid out in the companion Covenant? Libertarian cosmopolitans deny that the latter are actually rights at all, while writers such as Thomas Pogge justify wholesale incursions into individual freedom in the name of combating world poverty.[11] However, such divisions do not take away from the basic point that the drive for uniformity is a feature of cosmopolitanism. The scope for legitimate variation is not something that can be determined locally; for example, if capital punishment is wrong, it is wrong not simply in Western Europe but also in Iran, China, Singapore, and Texas, and, similarly, women's rights do not vary according to climate, latitude, or longitude. There is basically one standard for international legitimacy, and all national societies have to be judged in accordance with where they stand in relation to it; non-liberal societies are by definition illegitimate, albeit to varying degrees.

Liberal nationalists approach this matter rather differently. John Rawls, for example, in his *The Law of Peoples*, outlines a category of non-liberal but

---

[10] For details, see Ian Brownlie, *Basic Instruments on Human Rights*, 5th ed (Oxford: Clarendon Press, 2002) for the texts of these treaties.

[11] Thomas Pogge, *World Poverty and Human Rights* (Cambridge, UK: Polity Press, 2002).

'decent' peoples who ought to be tolerated and accepted by liberals.[12] The basic institutions of decent peoples must meet certain standards – his account of decent hierarchical peoples mandates that they respect a minimal set of basic human rights, including political freedoms and subsistence rights, they live under something like the rule of law, they are un-aggressive with respect to the rest of the world and, at a minimum, they have some form of mechanism for consultation. However, and crucially, they are not liberal societies because they privilege a particular comprehensive doctrine – religious or political – and non-adherents to this doctrine are not accorded the same rights as adherents (although they do possess the minimum rights, which include, for example, freedom of speech and religion). Such societies/peoples are, for Rawls, to be regarded as members in good standing of a Society of Peoples along with liberal societies, although the text is somewhat ambiguous as to whether non-liberal but decent peoples are to be regarded as co-owners of the Law of Peoples or whether their presence in the Society of Peoples is because they are tolerated by liberal peoples.

Rawls's *Law of Peoples* has come under heavy fire from cosmopolitan liberals who accuse him of abandoning the universalism of *A Theory of Justice*, but it might equally be thought that his account of decent peoples makes them so similar to liberal peoples that what we have here is a distinction without too much of a difference.[13] Certainly his account of a fictional Muslim society (Kazanistan) is so far away from any past and present actually existing Muslim society as to be wholly implausible – but then again, really existing liberal societies do not bear much resemblance to Rawls's model either. A much stronger critique of cosmopolitan liberalism comes from those who argue that the rights of individuals crucially entail the right to chose their own forms of government. That communal autonomy is intrinsically valuable (and to be meaningful, such autonomy must, of course, include the right to be different) is, on this account, a principle that can be derived from and defended in accordance with, a notion of personal freedom that is essentially liberal. A key figure here is Michael Walzer. Many cosmopolitans would resist the description of Walzer as a liberal at all, on the principle that he is far too wedded to the idea of communal autonomy – but it seems to me that that his core argument, articulated in *Just and Unjust Wars* nearly thirty years ago, makes it clear that communal autonomy is only to be justified on grounds that are essentially liberal, thus '[the] moral standing of any particular state depends on the reality

---

[12] *Law of Peoples*, p. 60. For reasons of space, Rawls's somewhat esoteric distinction between a people and a society will be disregarded here; this and other matters are discussed in Chris Brown, 'The Construction of a Realistic Utopia: John Rawls and International Political Theory,' *Review of International Studies*, Vol. 28, No. 1, 2002.

[13] For critics, see Charles Beitz 'Rawls's 'Law of Peoples'' and Allen Buchanan, 'Rawls's 'Law of Peoples': Rules for a Vanished Westphalian World,' both *Ethics*, Vol. 110, No. 4, 2000, Andrew Kuper, 'Rawlsian Global Justice: Beyond the Law of Peoples to a Cosmopolitan Law of Persons,' *Political Theory*, Vol. 28, No. 5, 2000.

of the common life it protects and the extent to which the sacrifices required by that protection are willingly accepted and thought worthwhile.'[14]

There is, of course, an issue here about the position of particular individuals who are not prepared willingly to accept the necessary sacrifices – for many cosmopolitan liberals, the whole point of a uniform planetary ethic is to protect the individual who does not want to go along with local mores – but this liberal communitarianism is far more accommodating of conflicting ethical systems than its cosmopolitan alternative, and offers a useful corrective to the moral imperialism of much cosmopolitan thought. Liberal communitarians understand the idea of a global ethic as based on a plurality of autonomous political communities relating to each other in an international legal framework that is based on self-determination, non-aggression, and non-intervention – this is not inconsistent with the idea of international standard-setting via a human rights regime as long as such a regime is understood as declaratory rather than authoritative. The kind of authoritative global institutions favoured by some cosmopolitan liberals are regarded with deep suspicion by liberal pluralists, who do not believe that such institutions would be either viable or desirable.[15] Instead, the kind of international society favoured by Rawls and Walzer bears a family resemblance to both the liberal internationalism of Woodrow Wilson and to the account of the International Society associated with the 'English School' of International Relations theory.[16] All these distinctions will return, and be developed further, in connection with many of the issues to be discussed next.

Competing Universalisms

Intellectually, liberalism in all its forms is the product of one family of societies – namely, those of the 'West'; for the last century and a half, liberalism has been the dominant ideology of industrial society, which itself developed in the West. In the West, those political ideologies that were not liberal in origin – such as socialism – have either failed, or survived by coming to an understanding with liberalism, as has been the case with social democracy, which, as noted earlier, is now very close to Anglo-American liberalism. The human rights regime that is the most obvious concrete expression of liberal individualism in the contemporary world is equally Western in origin; the committee chaired by Eleanor Roosevelt that drafted the Universal Declaration

---

[14] Michael Walzer, *Just and Unjust Wars* (New York: Basic Books, 1992) p. 54. Moreover, excluding Walzer from the liberal canon would also involve excluding J. S Mill, which would be absurd.

[15] For such institutional schemes, see Daniele Archibugi, David Held, and Mathias Köhler (eds.), *Re-Imagining Political Community: Studies in Cosmopolitan Democracy* (Cambridge, UK: Polity Press, 1998).

[16] For brief accounts of both Wilsonianism and the English School, see Chris Brown *Understanding International Relations*, 2nd ed. (Basingstoke: Palgrave, 2001), and for an exploration of the connections between IR theory and international political theory, see Brown, *Sovereignty, Rights, and Justice* (Cambridge: Polity Press, 2002).

of Human Rights contained representatives from many cultures, and dutifully attempted to draw on as many sources as possible, but the resulting document is clearly inspired by the political thought of the West – just as it was made necessary by the appalling failures of Western polities in the 1930s and 1940s. Other cultures and civilisations have developed their own ways of checking the power of over-mighty rulers, but the emphasis on personal freedom and individual rights is distinctively Western.

In this historical sense at least, the *uniform moral code* promoted by liberalism is indeed that of a particular system, that of the modern West – although what is actually meant by the term 'West' is clearly open to interpretation.[17] On the other hand, all strands of liberalism would deny that it is particularist in the substantive sense. Liberalism is based on a universalist account of human flourishing that stresses individualism and personal freedoms and is considered valid for all times and places. 'Man in general has always been what he is,' remarks Voltaire, and when John Rawls approvingly quotes Rousseau's formula of taking 'men as they are and laws as they might be,' he echoes the thought, assuming that human beings have a particular nature (specifically that they are rationally self-interested but capable of taking into account the interests of others) and that political institutions have to be created around that nature rather than by attempting to change it (which, from a liberal perspective, is a cardinal error of Marxism).[18] The gendered nature of this kind of statement has not gone unnoticed, and Susan Moller Okin and Carole Pateman have shown that classical liberal contract theory usually assumes that the contractor is a male head of a family speaking on its behalf without its warrant – but the general point remains.[19] Liberals do not think that different kinds of societies produce different kinds of human beings, and therefore they do not believe that liberalism is restricted in scope to one particular society – indeed, this is one of the points that distinguishes liberal communitarians from those who believe that different societies produce different kinds of human beings and different moral codes, which is why a figure such as Michael Walzer draws inspiration from J. S Mill rather than G. W. F Hegel.

An appropriate universal moral code need not therefore be based on some kind of synthesis of existing moral systems, and the particularistic origins of liberalism need not be seen as an embarrassment. As for the role of alternative 'universal moral codes' – such as those associated with the proselytising religions – this is precisely the issue that has been discussed here in the context of liberal neutrality. Essentially, liberals hold that individuals ought to be free to adhere to whatever moral codes they favour, as long as they do not try to

---

[17] Jacinta O'Hagan, *Conceptualising the West in International Relations: From Spengler to Said* (Basingstoke: Palgrave, 2002) is an interesting recent discussion of this issue.

[18] Voltaire, cited from the Introduction to F. M. Barnard (ed.), *J. G. Herder on Social and Political Culture* (Cambridge: Cambridge University Press, 1969), p. 35: Rawls *Law of Peoples*, p. 13.

[19] Susan Moller Okin, *Justice, Gender, and the Family* (New York: Basic Books, 1991), Carole Pateman, *The Sexual Contract* (Cambridge, UK: Polity Press, 1988).

foist their beliefs on others, but, as noted, this is problematic because, very frequently, the adherents of universal codes do indeed believe that they should be applied, as the designation suggests, universally. From a liberal perspective, this is unacceptable. Liberal toleration has its limits; those who would take away the personal freedoms upon which liberalism is based ought not to be allowed to do so, although exactly what restrictions on personal freedoms are acceptable in the interests of frustrating their desire is controversial. In short, liberalism judges other 'uniform moral codes' from a perspective that privileges itself – as indeed do all such moral codes, the difference being that liberals do not wish to impose a substantive conception of the Good on others.

Accommodating Diversity

As will be apparent from this discussion, liberals have no particular difficulty in principle in accommodating all sorts of diverse practices and social arrangements, assuming that they are freely chosen and that the cost of the practices in question are borne by the individuals who have made the choice. Thus, for example, liberals ought to have no difficulty in accommodating whatever sexual activities consenting adults might get up to in private even if these involve, for example, sado-masochistic practices or other fetishes that harm no one other than the participants. There are, of course, difficulties involved in applying this principle, difficulties that were touched upon earlier. There are very few activities that actually have no implications for others, and in some cases, private choices may come up against legitimately imposed communal standards. Suppose, for example, the practice of following a particular dietary regime involves the slaughtering of animals under conditions that are regarded by most people as cruel, or suppose the practice of wearing of a particular item of clothing contravenes some reasonable safety regulations – and these are, of course, examples drawn from life – should these practices be tolerated in the name of support for the personal freedom of the individuals involved? In practice, many societies, in pursuit of a quiet life, make exceptions to general rules to allow kosher/halal butchery or exempt Sikhs from motor-cycle helmet regulations, but some liberals would resist this compromise, on the grounds that if it is legitimate for the state to make this kind of rule in the first place, there is no good reason to tolerate exceptions. Jews, Muslims, and Sikhs would not be suffering religious persecution thereby since there is nothing in their religions that preclude vegetarianism or mandate motor-cycle riding; specialist diets and turban wearing are akin to 'expensive tastes,' choices that society as a whole is under no obligation to underwrite.[20] Needless to say, most individuals do not regard their religious obligations in this light, which is why so many societies accommodate rather than confront such different practices.

---

[20] The strongest expression of this position is Brian Barry, *Culture and Equality* (Cambridge, UK: Polity Press, 2000).

Rather more serious is the question of who is entitled to make choices on behalf of children. Consider, for an extreme case, the practice of female genital mutilation (FGM); it has been held that it would be acceptable for a mature woman to make the choice of undergoing FGM as a kind of signal that she was gracefully and willingly moving into matronhood and leaving her sexual life behind, and it would be difficult for a liberal to argue against the right to make such a free choice.[21] On the other hand, the vast majority of cases of FGM are carried out on girls under any reasonable age of consent, and here a liberal need have no difficulty in refusing to extend tolerance to the practice of destroying such an important part of any individual's identity. The same issue arises, less dramatically, in the case of the education of the children of members of highly restrictive religions or cults. A liberal ought to tolerate the decision of an adult to become a Scientologist or remain Amish, but the key issue is whether it is tolerable that the children of such believers should receive an education that predisposes them to follow their parents in the faith, and, perhaps, ill-equips them for dealing with society at large. This is a tricky question – it is not immediately clear why, say, a Catholic education should be tolerable while an education in Scientology might not be; having been around for nearly two millennia longer hardly seems an adequately rational way of making this distinction, and defending the proposition that Catholicism is a much richer way of life than Scientology would take liberals somewhere they ought not to go as a matter of principle, even though privately they may find it difficult to disagree that this is so.

These are serious problems, but the issue of toleration is raised even more sharply when it concerns social arrangements that are highly illiberal but are based on a moral code that seems to be widely accepted in a particular society. If such arrangements do not violate basic rights, then at least the more pluralist wing of liberalism may be prepared to be tolerant, but this may well not be the case. A great many social arrangements clearly do violate the personal freedom of their members. The issue of so-called 'Asian values' comes to mind here, as does the position of women within most Muslim-majority societies, and especially in those societies that adopt a specifically Islamic constitution.[22] It may well be the case, as is often argued, that the idea that there are specifically Asian values centred on the family and the community rather than the individual is a self-serving notion promoted by authoritarian Asian elites, but such a notion would have little clout at home if it did not resonate somewhat with local populations, and, similarly, although it is not the custom of Islamic

[21] See Bikhu Parekh, *Rethinking Multiculturalism* (Basingstoke: Macmillan, 2000) and some of the critics of Susan Moller Okin in Joshua Cohen et al., eds., *Is Multiculturalism Bad for Women* (Princeton NJ: Princeton University Press, 1999).

[22] The best collection here is Joanne Bauer and Daniel Bell, eds., *The East Asian Challenge for Human Rights* (Cambridge: Cambridge University Press, 1999). See also Daniel Bell, *East Meets West: Human Rights and Democracy in East Asia* (Princeton: Princeton University Press, 2000).

societies to ask women whether, for example, they wish to be obliged to be enfolded in modesty garments, it is not immediately clear that all women in such societies regard such restrictions as oppressive, even though, from a liberal perspective, they clearly are. However, clearly some women so regard these, just as many Asians demand the same human rights as everyone else, and the position of liberals of all varieties would be generally supportive of their right to resist illiberal restrictions on their freedom.

Are such restrictions 'intolerable'? Possibly some Asian-values-oriented states may actually respect basic rights – though some clearly do not – but radical gender inequality is clearly incompatible with the most basic account of liberal freedoms. So, yes, they are intolerable in the sense that they ought not to be tolerated, but to describe something as intolerable is usually understood to imply that one ought actually to do something about it, and here divisions arise amongst liberals, with the more communitarian-minded liberals arguing against the ability of outsiders to intervene effectively in other societies – and indeed against the ability of outsiders truly to comprehend the social arrangement of societies alien to their own. This raises the issue of the appropriate way in which liberal values might be propagated, which is discussed next.

The Appropriate Mix of Particular and Universal Norms

In the light of what has already been established, what is an appropriate mix is a simple question for liberals to answer. Cosmopolitan liberals will hold that the international human rights regime can serve as a rough approximation of the package of norms and practices that ought to be universally observed. Some libertarian cosmopolitans may well hold that this package is unduly restrictive of the freedom of the individual, while universal welfare state cosmopolitans will hold that it does not go far enough, but this is a debate that revolves around a quite extensive set of universals. Beyond that set (however defined), in areas where the international rights regime does not reach, where the law is silent, different societies (or, more accurately, the individuals who make up those societies) are entitled to follow whatever norms, engage in whatever practices, they please.

Given the detailed scope of current human rights treaties, this position does not allow a great deal of room for particularistic norms to exist, and communitarian liberals will argue (following Rawls's argument set out earlier) that there is within the human rights regime a core of basic rights, but that beyond that, core societies ought to be able to engage in distinctive particularist practices. These liberals may not approve of such practices as that of privileging a particular comprehensive doctrine, but they will tolerate them, assuming that basic rights are observed. For both cosmopolitan and national liberals, the basic criteria for distinguishing those areas of social and individual life where universal norms apply from those where particularism may rule are linked to somewhat different accounts of what is involved in personal freedom.

For communitarian liberals, basic rights provide the basis for an irreducible account of freedom, for cosmopolitans, only the full package will do.

Propagating Liberalism

Ought liberals, or a liberal society, engage in proselytising for liberalism in non-liberal societies, and, if so, what methods are appropriate? This is perhaps the single most important issue in global ethics, not simply for liberalism but for all universalist creeds. It is one thing to have a distinctive conception of the moral world; it is another to attempt to foist such a conception on others, uninvited – but unless one's conception of the world is explicitly particularistic in the sense that it does not claim to set standards for all (the case, I think, with Judaism and Hinduism), some kind of missionary enterprise is more or less inevitable. In the case of liberalism the situation is complicated somewhat by the notion of liberal neutrality; whereas, say, Christians and Muslims have a clear conception of the Good which they wish others to adopt, liberals promote an account of the moral world that suggests that doctrines such as Christianity and Islam ought to be matters of private belief rather than for public consumption. In some respects, this makes things easier for liberals; liberal values of personal freedom and individualism can be promoted without requiring a conversion experience – liberals do not ask others to abandon their particular conception of the Good altogether, 'only' to relegate it to the public sphere. But only is placed in scare-quotes here because, of course, many non-liberals would regard such a step as (literally) anathema. As noted earlier, for example, Catholics do not believe that abortion is wrong for Catholics, but wrong period; similarly, Islamic notions of the difference between genders are designed to operate in the public sphere and not simply in the private life of Muslims. In short, the fact that liberals claim not to be promoting a particular comprehensive doctrine is not going to help them when it comes to missionary work.

What kind of methods may properly be employed by liberals as individuals, or liberal societies, to promote liberal values in non-liberal societies? This question needs to be simplified. First, let a distinction be drawn between those proselytising activities conducted by non-state actors in liberal societies – private individuals, non-state organisations such as Amnesty International (AI), and the like – and those conducted by liberal state authorities. In the first category are to be found activities such as subscribing to AI, writing letters to one's Congressman, MP, or other representative, writing letters to foreign governments, financing and conducting observations of elections in non-liberal countries, engaging in cultural, sporting, or economic boycotts of oppressive regimes, boycotting companies that trade with such regimes, and so on. There are all sorts of pragmatic questions concerning such activities – most basically, are they likely to do more harm than good, will they target accurately the oppressors rather than the oppressed, do the latter welcome these activities and so on – but it is difficult to see any reason why liberals would oppose *in principle* such activities. If I choose to exercise my personal freedom not to consume apartheid-era South African oranges, or to refuse to buy petrol from an oil company that trades in contemporary Myanmar (Burma), it might well be argued that I was mistaken in my belief that I was helping the people I was trying to help, that I was simply engaging in gesture politics, but it would be difficult for a liberal to argue that I was wrong in principle to try to intervene in the affairs of others in this way. Difficult, but probably not impossible, to make this argument – still, far more compelling issues are raised in the context of official as opposed to private action, and the rest of this section will concentrate on the promotion of liberal values by liberal states.[23]

Official action can also take the form of negative and positive sanctions – sticks and carrots. Governments can make official development aid conditional on respect for human rights, and can orient such aid towards democracy-promotion, and liberal governments may use their influence on international organisations such as the IMF, the World Bank, and the Commonwealth to introduce such conditionality into multilateral aid. Governments may institute official economic and financial sanctions in response to human rights violations, and may actually engage in the physical coercion of oppressive regimes – so-called 'humanitarian interventions.'[24] All of these activities go beyond simple persuasion; each involves, albeit to different degrees, actual interventions in the political and social life of non-liberal societies, and, in the extreme case, may involve suppressing that life, at least temporarily. Which, if any, of these activities can be justified by liberals? Cosmopolitans and liberal nationalists will have different answers in principle to this question – although whether they differ much in practice is another matter.

In the latter camp, Michael Walzer has thought longest and to most effect about this issue.[25] From his perspective, for outsiders to intervene in the public life of a society – especially forcibly – is a very grave step that should only be undertaken in very limited circumstances; more generally, the international norm of non-intervention ought to be respected as reflecting the legitimate right of political communities to autonomy. Outsiders are not in a position to

---

[23] 'Liberal states' here is shorthand for 'really-existing liberalism' – that is, for states that are in their basic institutions and practices more-or-less liberal

[24] 'So-called' because those interventions that are actually carried out invariably, and quite properly, involve other motives in addition to humanitarianism; the term humanitarian intervention conjures up the wholly implausible notion of a completely altruistic act. Moreover, as the record of U.S. involvement in Somalia in 1992–93 illustrates, on those rare occasions when altruism dominates, the result is usually disastrous because states without concrete interests lack the will to carry interventions through to a satisfactory conclusion. Still, I will continue to use the term here because it is part of the current vocabulary of international relations.

[25] The following account draws on Walzer, *Just and Unjust Wars*, reinforced by later essays such as *Interpretation and Social Criticism* (Cambridge, MA: Harvard University Press, 1987) and *Thick and Thin: Moral Argument at Home and Abroad* (Notre Dame, IN: University of Notre Dame Press, 1994).

grasp the shared understandings of a society, and the basic assumption is that it is up to citizens of apparently oppressive regimes to struggle arduously to liberate themselves. For outsiders to intervene would be to violate the common life of the society in question, and this is legitimate only if there is good reason to believe that this common life has already broken down – outsiders can presume that this is the case when a regime resorts to enslavement or massacre in order to stay in power, but otherwise intervention would be presumptively illegitimate. If the conditions for legitimate intervention are met, then once having intervened, outsiders should leave as soon as possible and allow the locals to reconstruct their common life as they see fit. Arguably this position overstates both the extent to which there is a 'common life' at all in a great many modern states and the extent to which individuals can now struggle successfully against determined oppressors – things may have been easier for rebels when Mill first put forward the argument in the mid nineteenth century – but it does provide a coherent account of the proper role of outsiders in propagating liberal values. The same cannot be said of cosmopolitan approaches to this problem.[26]

Cosmopolitan liberals are bitterly critical of those who stress the importance of communal autonomy and the rights of political community; they see no principled reason to endorse a general international norm of non-intervention – such a norm is inappropriate because it protects states rather than people.[27] Liberals are entitled to ask that non-liberal societies change their way of life to provide the classic freedoms to their own people – and, by the same token, cosmopolitan advocates of a global welfare state and global environmental change demand that the citizens of wealthy liberal states change *their* way of life, devoting more resources to the eradication of global poverty and ceasing to pollute the planet.[28] Libertarian cosmopolitans do not sign up for this part of the package but share the rejection of the idea that communal autonomy is valuable in its own terms. In principle, cosmopolitan liberals have no problem with the idea that liberal values ought to be propagated. On the other hand, cosmopolitans recognise that there are severe practical problems involved in ignoring the international norm of non-intervention, and are highly sensitive to the charge of imperialism.[29] More generally, cosmopolitan liberals are temperamentally disinclined to support coercion in international relations, and usually place a high value on international co-operation and multilateralism; in this respect, they follow the main thrust of Wilsonian liberal international-ism, with its stress on the rule of law and international organisation (although

[26] Or of Rawls's account in *Law of Peoples*, where the distinctive problems posed by oppressive and predatory regimes are run together in a confusing way.
[27] See, for example, David Luban's critique of Walzer, 'The Romance of the Nation State' and sources cited in fn. 13.
[28] Pogge, *World Poverty and Human Rights*.
[29] See Part II of Beitz *Political Theory and International Relations*.

they do not follow its statism). The problem is that these practical concerns almost always tell against an active policy of promoting liberal values in the world; it is very rare that the 'international community' unites around a cause that is even vaguely liberal – the anti-apartheid campaign comes to mind as an exception to this generalisation – and the relatively few actual examples of humanitarian interventions in the last decade, such as the Kosovo campaign of 1999, have not been based on an international consensus.[30]

The problem for cosmopolitan liberals is that they lack a conceptual framework within which principles and practice can be reconciled. The recent rise in US political discourse of 'neo-conservatism' illustrates the point. The neo-conservatives are, for the most part, liberal internationalists in origins, but as Max Boot has helpfully argued, they are 'hard Wilsonians' as opposed to the 'soft Wilsonianism' of conventional multilateralist liberals.[31] Their readiness to use American power, and their contempt for the restrictions multilateralism imposes on US policy makes their position anathema to the vast majority of cosmopolitan liberals. The latter would (presumably) like to see liberal democratic institutions and respect for human rights in, say, Iraq but are vehemently opposed to the means adopted by neo-conservatives to bring this state of affairs about.[32] But what alternative means do they offer? My anti-war colleagues at the London School of Economics marched last year under a banner reading 'No to War, No to Saddam' – and one of my more subversive graduate students remarked that they should have added, 'Yes, to an Act of God to Get Rid of Him.' She had a point.

Actual physical coercion is, of course, an extreme method of propagating a value system, but the dilemmas involved in such interventions differ only by degree from those posed by less dramatic methods of democracy promotion and human rights advocacy. The employment of economic sanctions against oppressive regimes (including the withdrawal of development assistance) is sometimes supported as an alternative to the use of military force – but the record of economic sanctions suggests that they almost invariably hurt the weakest members of society – the poor, women, and children – and the idea that this is more morally acceptable than the use of military force is simply an illustration of how confused liberal thinking can be on these matters. Once the means employed to promote liberal values move beyond simply advocacy and persuasion, we enter a realm where both communitarian liberals and neo-conservatives – in very different ways – have coherent accounts of the proper behaviour of liberal state authorities, but cosmopolitan liberals face unresolved, and possibly irresolvable, dilemmas.

[30] Humanitarian interventions are an extreme example of ways of propagating liberalism, but illustrate the general point.

[31] Max Boot "What the Heck is a 'Neocon'? Neoconservatives Believe in Using American Might to Promote American Ideals Abroad," *Wall Street Journal* Online, 30 December 2002.

[32] There were, of course, other reasons for the Iraq War of 2003. See fn. 24.

It might be thought that this discussion is, in some respects, unnecessary for liberals to engage in – that the forces of History with a capital 'H' are working in favour of liberal values and that globalisation and, in particular, the spread of global mass media mostly based in really existing liberal societies and spreading values that are essentially liberal will make the role of state authorities in promoting liberalism redundant. This 'liberal expectancy,' to use Daniel P. Moynihan's term, was given its most dramatic expression in Francis Fukuyama's account of the 'end of history,' but it can be found in many of the more sober accounts of globalisation.[33] This is too big a topic to address properly here, but there are a number of reasons to resist this argument, beginning with disbelief in the capitalisation of history and ending with scepticism that figures such as Rupert Murdoch are actually propagating liberal values in the world. More to the point perhaps, the history of the last ten years suggests that globalisation produces its own anti-bodies, resistance movements that are by no means liberal, and that there are ways of being modern that are profoundly anti-liberal – one need look no further than the ultra-modern figure of Osama Bid Laden to make the point.[34]

Liberalism, Global Ethics, and Law

Liberalism has always been associated with the rule of law both domestically and internationally, although liberal thinkers have rarely made a fetish of law, and are open to the suggestion that unjust laws need not be obeyed. This point is of particular relevance when it comes to conventional international law, with its statist bias. When, for example, the Independent International Commission on Kosovo declared the 1999 war to be illegal but not illegitimate, this conclusion upset many international lawyers but posed no conceptual difficulties for liberals, of whom the Commission was largely composed.[35] The idea that it may sometimes be necessary to break the law in the interests of human freedom is very much part of the liberal tradition – which is not to say, of course, that all liberals agreed with the Kosovo War.

As noted earlier, the current international human rights regime is very much the product of liberal thought. There is a great deal of room for disagreement between liberals over the content of the regime – with Continental and libertarian liberals resisting the extension of the idea of rights from the political and the civil to the social and economic – but the general idea of international

---

[33] Moynihan, *Pandemonium* (Oxford: Oxford University Press, 1993); Francis Fukuyama, 'The End Of History,' *The National Interest,* No. 16, 1989; David Held *et al.*; *Global Transformations* (Cambridge, UK: Polity Press, 1999).

[34] See Chris Brown, 'Narratives of Religion, Civilisation and Modernity,' in Ken Booth and Tim Dunne, eds., *Worlds in Collision: Terror and the Future Global Order* (Basingstoke: Palgrave, 2002).

[35] Independent International Commission on Kosovo: *The Kosovo Report* (Oxford: Oxford University Press, 2000).

standard-setting as such is relatively uncontroversial. Post-modern bourgeois liberals such as Richard Rorty may challenge the ontological status of rights, but they do not challenge the regime as such – indeed, Rorty's notion of a 'human rights culture' is a particularly powerful expression of the idea of universal rights, even if his account of how those rights should be defined is somewhat controversial.[36]

More controversial is a recent development in international law towards universal jurisdiction – the idea that certain crimes can be prosecuted anywhere, regardless of where the alleged offence was committed – and the holding of individuals (including national political leaders) personally responsible for breaches of the newly emerging body of international criminal law. These developments have quite a long pre-history – pre-dating, for example, the post-World War II Nuremburg Tribunal – but recent high-profile cases such as the trial of Slobodan Milosevic at the International Criminal Tribunal for Former Yugoslavia for offences allegedly committed when he was head of the Yugoslav government, the Pinochet extradition hearings in London, and the coming into force of the Rome Statute of 1998 with the establishment of an International Criminal Court in 2002 have given them added salience. Cosmopolitan liberals are more or less wholly in favour of such developments, and deplore the unwillingness of the US to ratify the Rome Statute.[37] Those who favour communal autonomy are rather less certain that these developments are to be welcomed, partly because of their likely impact on domestic political processes. It is often said that after the Pinochet decision, the travel plans of former dictators will be much amended; they will be obliged in future to forgo the delights of most European capitals and watering-places.[38] This may be so, but it is also the case that dictators contemplating giving up power on the basis of a negotiated amnesty for past misdeeds may be disinclined to do so. Consider, for example, the transition to majority rule in South Africa; it is clear that, in the end, this took place relatively peacefully because it was understood that there would be no legal sanctions directed against the old regime – the latter would be required to confess past misdeeds to a Truth and Reconciliation Commission but would then receive amnesty. Many people felt that this did not serve the ends of justice, but it is difficult to argue with the political decision taken by the new rulers that the price paid for retribution, however justified, would be too high; the latter would not have been best pleased if this political judgement had been challenged in a British court by, for example, the arrest of former President de Clerk on a visit to London. Cosmopolitan

---

[36] Richard Rorty, 'Human Rights, Rationality, and Sentimentality', in Stephen Shute and Susan Hurley, eds., *On Human Rights* (New York: Basic Book, 1993).

[37] President Clinton signed the Rome Statute on his last day in office, Jan 31, 2001; President Bush 'unsigned' it later in the year, whatever that means.

[38] Marc Weller, 'On the Hazards of Foreign Travel for Dictators and Other Criminals, *International Affairs*, vol. 75, 1999.

liberals might wish to argue that it is not in the power of national polities to forgive crimes against humanity, but communitarian liberals would be more sensitive to the rights of national communities to make their own decisions in matters of this kind.

Conclusion

Because of the importance of liberalism as a political doctrine, and because of the divisions amongst liberals, it has been necessary to range widely in this chapter, and to cover many issues from almost diametrically opposed points of view. The contrast between the different approaches of cosmopolitan and communitarian liberals has been at times striking, and it might be thought appropriate finally to address the issue of whether in fact it makes sense to treat these two positions as coming from the same basic source. Certainly some cosmopolitan liberals seem to feel that all liberals ought to be cosmopolitan; even a cursory examination of the various liberal condemnations of Rawls's *Law of Peoples* reveals this attitude. Figures such as Beitz and Buchanan have, in effect, read Rawls's final book out of the liberal canon because it explicitly rejects the cosmopolitan concern with the well-being of individuals globally in favour of an emphasis on a just and stable order governing liberal and decent peoples.[39] However, the same cosmopolitan liberals are also opposed to Continental liberals and libertarians who, although cosmopolitan in other respects, wish to envisage the freedom of the individual in terms of political and civic rights as opposed to economic and social rights – perhaps it is welfare-state cosmopolitan intolerance that is the problem here, rather than back-sliding by figures such as John Rawls?

For all these disagreements, there is still a great deal of common ground as between all the varieties of liberalism when it comes to global ethics. None of the writers discussed here would deny the central importance of political freedom, although they might differ as to whether this freedom is best guaranteed by global, as opposed to national, law and institutions. All of them would resist the idea that individuals should be obliged against their will to subscribe to some particular conception of the good, although they might differ as to the right of outsiders to judge whether such an imposition is taking place in any particular society. These points, taken together, go a long way towards distinguishing liberal thought from other systems of global ethics.

[39] See fn. 13 and Rawls *Law of Peoples* p. 120.

10

Feminist Perspectives on a Planetary Ethic

Kimberly Hutchings

Introduction: Feminism as an Ethical Tradition

Feminism is not easily categorized either in singular terms (as *one* way of looking at the world) or in terms that are purely ethical. The label 'feminism' acts as an umbrella term covering a variety of ideologically distinct normative positions and a vast array of political struggles.[1] Moreover, it is a label that is more readily defined in terms of *political* than of *moral* ideals.[2] Feminists are concerned with understanding and addressing the ways in which gendered relations of power work to systematically oppress, subordinate, or exclude women's needs and interests. But the interpretations and critiques of gendered relations of power, and the ideas of women's needs and interests within feminism, are so varied that they cannot be said to reflect a unitary set of moral values.[3] It might be claimed that all forms of feminism aim for equality, justice, and freedom for women. However, for some feminists, this aim is legitimated by a deontological liberal morality, whereas for others, for example, it is legitimated by the primacy of 'feminine' moral values of nurture and care. Moreover, the meaning of equality, justice, and freedom for women ranges in feminist thought from adjustments of current practice within liberal states to the wholesale transformation of the world as we currently know it. This makes for considerable difficulty in offering a coherent

---

[1] See A. Basu (ed.), *The Challenge of Local Feminisms: Women's Movements in Global Perspective* (Boulder, CO: Westview Press, 1995).

[2] See I. Whelan, Modern *Feminist Thought: From the Second Wave to 'Post-Feminism'* (Edinburgh: Edinburgh University Press, 1995); J. Squires, *Gender in Political Theory* (Cambridge, UK: Polity Press, 1999).

[3] The range of views within feminist ethics can be gauged from the following collections: E. Frazer, J. Hornsby, & S. Lovibond (eds.), *Ethics: A Feminist Reader* (Oxford: Blackwell, 1992); E. Browning Cole & S. Coultrap-McQuin (eds.), *Explorations in Feminist Ethics: Theory and Practice* (Bloomington & Indianapolis: Indiana University Press, 1992); D. Shogan (ed.), *A Reader in Feminist Ethics* (Toronto: Canadian Scholars' Press, 1993); P. DesAutels & J. Waugh (eds.), *Feminists Doing Ethics* (Lanham: Rowman & Littlefield, 2001).

response to the question of what a global ethics might look like from a feminist perspective.

The difficulty of articulating a feminist global ethics is compounded by the ways in which existing moral codes and values are bound up with gendered relations of power. This is most obvious in the case of those aspects of morality tied up with sex, sexuality, reproduction, and family, but it is also true of the moral legitimacy of forms of violence and killing. In all societies and contexts, the licence to kill (and the licence to inflict physical hurt on other adults) has belonged predominantly to men. The ways in which killing has been legitimated have been tied up with a gendered division of labour and gendered ideologies, often resting on the invocation of man as protector and woman as 'protectee,' which confirm the pattern of women's subordination.[4] Feminists are committed to the abolition of gendered divisions of labour and gendered ideologies that perpetuate women's subordination. Since the latter provides a major resource for how we currently make sense of who may kill and under what circumstances, then it is a massive task to attempt to reformulate norms to govern the morality of killing beyond gender. In addition, as feminist critics have been pointing out for many decades, in thinking about moral values from a feminist perspective, both official and actual versions have to be borne in mind. Some moral viewpoints officially sanction the beating or raping of wives by husbands, but most do not, and in many countries, the former is illegal as is the latter in some. Most moralities disapprove of having sexual relations with young children and of prostitution, whether of children or adults, and in most countries, such activities are subject to legal sanctions of some kind. Yet in most parts of the world, domestic violence, sexual assault, child abuse, and prostitution are commonplace. Feminists are concerned with dealing not just with the official story of what may or may not be legitimate within a particular culture, but with the mores that legitimate what happens in actuality. To the extent that moral codes have traditionally happily coexisted with the abuse of women, feminists are disinclined to take them at face value.

In this chapter, I first analyse the ethical implications of different forms of feminism for the questions about the globalization of ethics around which this book is organized. In order to do this, I categorise feminism into three broad normative traditions under the headings enlightenment feminism, care feminism, and postcolonial feminism. The categories refer to the ethical commitments associated with three different traditions of feminist political struggle. This categorization necessarily oversimplifies both feminist theory and the actuality of the myriad political struggles in which feminists around the world are engaged. However, I hope it may do some justice to what makes feminism both distinctive and useful in addressing the theory and practice of ethical universalism. I will begin by contextualising each of these categories in relation to different forms of feminist politics, and sketching out their key features as

---

[4] See J. S. Goldstein, *War and Gender* (Cambridge: Cambridge University Press, 2001).

an ethical standpoint. In the second, third, and fourth sections of the chapter, I will examine each of these feminist ethical standpoints in terms of their moral goals and the means considered legitimate in pursuit of those goals. In the final section, I will draw out the extent to which we can find common ground within the different forms of feminist ethics, and consider what that tells us about the possibility of a global ethics from a feminist perspective.

Enlightenment Feminism

When feminism first manifested itself as a political movement in emerging liberal/social democratic states in the nineteenth century, it was mainly concerned with arguing for women's equality with men. Political struggles were focused on gaining the vote, reforming property rights, abolishing patriarchal privilege in marriage, and opening up opportunities for education and professional work to women. This kind of feminist politics, inspired by egalitarianism, continues to flourish to the present day.[5] It reflects the ideals of the European Enlightenment and the French Revolution, and the socio-political and economic conditions of liberalism and capitalism.[6] Enlightenment feminism is intertwined, historically and ideologically, with two other egalitarian ideologies that took root in Europe in the nineteenth century, liberalism and socialism, and it is fundamentally humanist and ethically universalist. The key message of enlightenment feminism is that 'women are human too.' That is to say, that they are entitled to the same rights and freedoms as men, whether those rights and freedoms are understood negatively or positively, individualistically or collectively. Thus liberal enlightenment feminisms argue that the same rights to bodily integrity, property, citizenship, and opportunities for work and education that are extended to men within liberal states should also be extended to women. Socialist enlightenment feminists argue similarly that women's exploitation as both workers (paid labour) and reproducers (of the labour force) of capital should be recognized in the same way as men's exploitation is recognized, and that women should participate in revolutionary struggle in the same way as men, and benefit equally from the socialist

---

[5] See Chapters 1 and 2 in Whelan, *Feminist Thought*.

[6] The founding text of enlightenment feminism is generally seen as Mary Wollstonecraft's *Vindication of the Rights of Women*, originally published in 1792 (Harmondsworth: Penguin, 1975). The twentieth-century classic text in enlightenment feminism is Simone de Beauvoir's *The Second Sex* (London: Jonathan Cape, 1953). Liberal feminism is exemplified in the works of Betty Friedan, *The Feminine Mystique* (Harmondsworth: Penguin, 1965); Janice Radcliffe Richards, *The Sceptical Feminist: A Philosphical Inquiry* (Harmondsworth: Penguin, 1982); and Susan Moller Okin *Justice, Gender and the Family* (New York: Basic Books, 1991). Marxist feminism has its ideological origins in Friedrich Engels' *The Origin of the Family, Private Property and the State*, originally published in 1884 (Harmondsworth: Penguin, 1985). Contemporary works in this tradition include: S. Rowbotham, *Woman's Consciousness/Man's World* (Harmondsworth: Penguin, 1973); N. Hartsock, *Money, Sex and Power: Towards a Feminist Historical Materialism* (New York: Longman, 1983); and M. Barrett, *Women's Oppression Today: Problems in Marxist Feminist Analysis* (London: Verso, 1988).

economy and polity that is to be created. Enlightenment feminism argues that there are blind-spots in mainstream liberal and socialist theorizing, but it does not depart significantly from the ethical ideals of liberalism or socialism, or from the conviction that these ideals are rationally apprehensible and of universal validity. The aim of enlightenment feminism is to create a world in which being male or female is immaterial to the capacity of human beings to flourish as human beings. Examples of feminist theorists working through the normative implications of enlightenment feminism in a global context are thinkers such as Martha Nussbaum and Seyla Benhabib.[7] Unsurprisingly in the post-Cold War context, liberal feminism has become the predominant version of enlightenment feminism within the global arena, and in the discussion that follows, I will focus on liberal feminism as the exemplar of enlightenment feminism. The hegemonic language within which liberal feminist activists conduct debates around ethical priorities for peace and development in the contemporary world is that of women's human rights.[8]

Care Feminism

Egalitarian feminist politics was the primary mode of feminist struggles in Europe, North America, and Australasia in the nineteenth and twentieth centuries, but since the 1970s, has been under challenge. Radical feminist politics, which came to prominence in the 1970s and 1980s, is less concerned with the question of equality for women in terms of their formal entitlements and opportunities, and more with the reasons why women continue to be subject to particular kinds of disadvantage and discrimination even when they have attained formal equality (as in certain liberal and socialist states in the 1980s). This kind of feminist politics is focused on challenging assumptions about women's inferiority that are seen to underpin control of women's reproductive capacities, practices of rape, domestic violence, and pornography. The political campaigns of radical feminists are less about equality and more about recognising the particular needs and vulnerabilities of women within a patriarchal order as well as attacking the ideologies that sustain that order.[9] Moreover, radical feminists contest the idea that traditional value hierarchies in which the feminine is denigrated in relation to the masculine should be accepted. On the contrary, they argue for a revaluation of values traditionally associated with femininity, such as care and peace. In focusing on the specificities of women's position, radical feminism connects with a 'maternalist' strand of feminism, which stresses the *difference* of women's identity and role

---

[7] M. Nussbaum, *Women and Human Development* (Cambridge: Cambridge University Press, 2000); S. Benhabib, *The Claims of Culture: Equality and Diversity in the Global Era* (Princeton: Princeton University Press, 2002).

[8] See G. Ashworth, 'The Silencing of Women,' in T. Dunne & N. Wheeler (eds.), *Human Rights in Global Politics* (Cambridge: Cambridge University Press, 1999).

[9] See Chapter 3 in Whelan, *Feminist Thought*.

from that of men, and suggests that a feminist politics premised on *sameness* between men and women will fail to address the sources of women's disadvantage.

I am using the label 'care feminism' to capture those strands in feminist ideology and practice that lay claim to a distinctive and authoritative feminine voice within ethics.[10] Care feminism departs from enlightenment feminism insofar as it rejects what it argues to be the subsumption of women under a *male* norm, in which male characteristics are taken as the model for, amongst other things, moral values and modes of moral reasoning.[11] A characteristic feature of care feminism is a revaluation of the value hierarchies inherent in enlightenment thought, in which reason is valued over passion, universality over particularity, mind over matter, and in each case, the former term is associated with masculinity and the latter with femininity. Care feminists invert these familiar (within Western thought) hierarchies and assert the significance of feeling, contextuality, embodiment, and therefore of femininity for moral agency and judgment. This argument takes many different forms. In some cases, it is grounded in an account of biological sexual difference; more commonly it is grounded in arguments about the different psycho-social practices through which masculinity and femininity are produced in male and female children.[12] The nature of the claims made for the moral significance of femininity also differ, but they often take the form of an ethics more oriented to virtue, responsibility, and contextual sensitivity than to one of universal principle. In contrast to enlightenment feminism, which is wedded to a moral vocabulary of universal equality, the moral vocabulary of care feminism is one of nurture. It is more oriented to ethics as a practice than ethics as the pursuit of overarching ends, and it puts much emphasis on the importance of context and the dangers of moral abstraction.[13] Examples of feminist theorists thinking through the ethical implications of care feminism in a global arena are Sarah Ruddick and

---

[10] Care feminism is most closely associated with radical and maternalist strands of contemporary feminist politics. For representatives of radical feminism, see M. Daly, *Gyn/Ecology: The Metaethics of Radical Feminism* (London: The Women's Press, 1979) and C. MacKinnon, *Towards a Feminist Theory of the State* (Cambridge MA: Harvard University Press, 1989). For examples of thinkers drawing out the idea of a distinctive feminist care ethic, see C. Gilligan, *In A Different Voice: Psychological Theory and Women's Development* (Cambridge MA: Harvard University Press, 1992); and N. Noddings, *Caring: A Feminist Approach to Ethics* (Berkeley: University of California Press, 1984).

[11] Gilligan, *In A Different Voice*, Chapter 6.

[12] See N. Chodorow, *The Reproduction of Mothering* (Berkeley: University of California Press, 1978).

[13] There is now a considerable literature debating the feminist ethic of care. See J. Tronto, *Moral Boundaries: A Political Argument for an Ethic of Care* (London: Routledge, 1993); V. Held, *Feminist Morality: Transforming Culture, Society, and Politics* (Chicago: Chicago University Press, 1993); G. Clement, *Care, Autonomy, and Justice: Feminism and the Ethic of Care* (Boulder, CO: Westview Press, 1996); and D. Koehn, *Rethinking Feminist Ethics: Care, Trust, and Empathy* (London: Routledge, 1998).

Fiona Robinson.[14] In terms of feminist practice, it is in the areas of peace and ecological activism that care feminism has had most influence.[15]

Postcolonial Feminism

The third form of feminist politics involves a challenge to the assumed homogeneity of women's position in both egalitarian and radical feminisms. Since the 1980s, the voices of black, lesbian, and third-world women have been increasingly raised within the feminist movement in condemning the assumptions of earlier generations of primarily white, middle-class, heterosexual Western feminists that feminist struggle is a singular struggle on behalf of women as such with a common set of goals. The point repeatedly made is that not only do feminists have different political priorities in different contexts, but also that there are power relations between women, along lines of race, class, and sexuality, that are insufficiently acknowledged by the egalitarian and radical feminist traditions. In particular, in the context of global issues such as international human rights and economic development, Western feminists have been accused of imposing a political agenda that reflects their view of women's priorities rather than those of women in the developing world.[16] The undermining of the idea that women share a common interest upon which feminist politics must be based supports a trend within feminism as a transnational movement towards localised, contextually specific political movements, which may coalesce around common objectives, but which are fundamentally grounded in the needs and interests of particular constituencies of women.[17]

I am using the label 'postcolonial' to cover forms of feminist theory and practice that challenge the generalisability of the values and prescriptions of both enlightenment and care feminisms.[18] In the case of enlightenment feminism, postcolonial feminists argue that the humanism underlying both liberal and socialist feminisms universalises a eurocentric, historically specific idea of the individual and society, which excludes alternative cultural and ethical

---

[14] S. Ruddick, *Maternal Thinking: Towards a Politics of Peace* (London: The Women's Press, 1989); F. Robinson, *Globalizing Care: Ethics, Feminist Theory, and International Relations* (Boulder, CO: Westview Press, 1999).

[15] See A. Harris & Y. King (eds.), *Rocking the Ship of State: Towards a Feminist Peace Politics* (Boulder, CO: Westview Press, 1989); V. Plumwood, *Feminism and the Mastery of Nature* (London and New York: Routledge, 1993).

[16] J. Steans, *Gender and International Relations: An Introduction* (Cambridge, UK: Polity, 1998): p. 164.

[17] See Chapters 4–6 in Whelan, *Feminist Thought*.

[18] Exemplary postcolonial feminist texts include B. Hooks, *Ain't I a Woman: Black Women and Feminism* (London: Pluto Press, 1982); D. Fuss, *Essentially Speaking: Feminism, Nature, and Difference* (London: Routledge, 1989); J. Butler, *Gender Trouble: Feminism and the Subversion of Identity* (London: Routledge, 1990); C. T. Mohanty, A Russo, & L. Torres (eds.), *Third World Women and the Politics of Feminism* (Bloomington & Indianapolis: Indiana University Press, 1991); C. Moraga, G. Anzalda, & T. C. Bambara (eds.), *This Bridge Called My Back: Writings by Radical Women of Color* (Berkeley, CA: Third Woman Press, 2001).

modes of being human. In particular, the universalisation of human rights dis-courses is argued to confirm the global hegemony of liberal-capitalist social, economic, and political relations. This is a hegemony that is inseparable from the legacies of centuries of European imperialism, exploitation, and racism (within which white European women were situated very differently from all other women). In the case of care feminism, postcolonial feminists argue that the notion of a specifically feminine set of virtues associated with nurture and care is a false generalisation from the experience of a particular sub-category of women to all women. The notion of a feminine mode of ethical reasoning, it is argued, arises out of the context of the public/private divide in modern liberal states and is specifically relevant only to women of a particular culture, sexuality, and class. Rural, working class, black, and lesbian women were never the 'angels of the hearth' or 'beautiful souls.'[19]

The ethical claims of postcolonial feminism focus on both 'difference' and 'power.' In relation to difference, postcolonial feminists insist on the ethical significance of the fact that all women are not the same, either in virtue of being human or in virtue of being women. This means that they are suspicious of general recipes for women's emancipation or flourishing, and indeed of top-down theorizing/legislating for women in general. Instead they celebrate grass roots activism and the importance of listening to what different women them-selves see as their ethical and political priorities and solidarities in practice. However, postcolonial feminism is not simply a feminist version of multicultur-alism, since postcolonial feminists are also deeply concerned about relations of power, in their different manifestations between men and women, men and men, women and women, within and across cultural and political boundaries. This complexity of power relations prevents postcolonial feminists from iden-tifying all women as part of the same oppressed class by virtue of being women. However, it also prevents them from taking any marker of identity (such as nationality, sexuality, ethnicity, or culture) as an automatic moral 'trump' in debates over moral values. In the Anglophone world, postcolonial feminist theory is exemplified in the work of feminists such as Chandra Mohanty and Gayatri Spivak.[20] In practice, it is exemplified in the ways in which feminist movements in Africa, India, and South America, and amongst minority (of all kinds) communities in the affluent North and West, have linked their fem-inism to struggles against political, economic, and cultural imperialism in all its forms.[21]

---

[19] See J. Elshtain, *Women and War* (Chicago & London: Chicago University Press, 1995), Chapter 4.

[20] C. T. Mohanty, *Feminism Without Borders: Decolonising Theory, Practicing Solidarity* (Durham & London: Duke University Press, 2003); G. C. Spivak, *A Critique of Postcolonial Reason: Toward a History of the Vanishing Present* (Princeton: Princeton University Press, 1990).

[21] A. Basu, *The Challenge*; M. H. Marchand & J. Parpart (eds.), *Feminism, Postmodernism, Development* (London & New York: Routledge, 1995).

Enlightenment Feminism and the Globalization of Ethics

The Moral Ends of Enlightenment Feminism

Enlightenment feminism is inherently universalist. Ideally, any version of enlightenment feminism would like to see a world organised according to the particular interpretation of the values of equality, freedom, and justice that it favours (liberal or socialist). From the enlightenment feminist point of view, a global accommodation of existing conflicting ethical differences would undoubtedly permit the continuation of practices that harm and discriminate against women, and that also perpetuate power structures in which women are oppressed, subordinated, and excluded. Liberal feminists point to ethical views around sex, reproduction, marriage, and family, which legitimate a range of outcomes and practices, from the exclusion of women from education to female genital mutilation and selective abortion of female foetuses. Socialist feminists point to the way in which existing ethical views across the world legitimate the unpaid labour of women that underpins capitalism. However, enlightenment feminists are aware of the magnitude of the task of unravelling all of the moral beliefs and commitments that sustain women's oppression. In the post-Cold War global climate, enlightenment feminists have been most concerned, along with other cosmopolitan theorists, to establish those 'bottom line' values that must be globally uniform as opposed to those ethical differences that may be tolerated.[22]

For the purposes of this argument (and given that insofar as an enlightenment feminist voice is heard at all in the formulation of global norms and the conduct of global governance, it is a liberal feminist voice), I will focus on liberal feminism to exemplify the ethical implications of the enlightenment feminist tradition. For liberal feminism, the ethical bottom line, as for other variants of liberalism, is to be found in the idea of basic human rights. Basic human rights are most often identified with rights to bodily integrity and legal, civil, and political rights, rather than with positive socio-economic rights. Unsurprisingly, therefore, liberal feminism is in agreement with liberalism more generally in supporting the development of liberal democratic states as the ideal political structure, and is opposed to punishments that maim, torture, or inflict pain on offenders, though not necessarily to the death penalty. For feminists, however, the right to bodily integrity is most important as an ethical bottom line in relation to women because of the prevalence of gender-based violence in all societies, rather than the institutionalisation of cruel and unusual punishments in some. The recognition of gender-based violence as the most common way in which women's bodily integrity is violated – in domestic

---

[22] Nussbaum attempts to do this through the specification of 'capabilities' necessary for human flourishing (Nussbaum, *Women and Human Development*: 4–15); Benhabib, in contrast, follows the path of Habermasian discourse ethics (Benhabib, *The Claims of Culture*: 36–39).

violence, in genital mutilation, in rape and sexual assault – has made possible the institutionalisation (even if not the implementation) in domestic and international law of the unacceptability of certain practices under the rubric of human rights. For liberal feminists, the border of intolerability is crossed where values are not only explicitly linked to the denigration of women but also work to legitimate the violation of basic human rights. Here we are on familiar liberal ground, in which the state does not seek to legislate the details of personal moralities, but takes certain values as foundational both to the possibility of moral latitude in the first place and as staking out the limits to that latitude.

A liberal feminist moral code, therefore, would operate with something like the distinction Habermas draws between 'morality' and 'ethics.'[23] Morality concerns those ethical principles that are inherently universal and cannot be compromised by the claims of particular interest or customary practice. For Habermas, the archetypal moral principles are those that forbid the institution of slavery or the practice of torture. Both of these principles concern the violation of individual autonomy, which is arguably the supreme moral value from a liberal point of view. For liberal feminists, the archetypal moral principle is that which proclaims women's equal rights with those of men, a principle that rests on the claim that women are autonomous human beings in the same way as men. In keeping with a liberal understanding of rights, this kind of equality constrains what it may be possible to do to others, and in some circumstances, what it may be possible to proclaim publicly. However, it still leaves considerable room for a variety of moral codes to flourish in terms of people's conduct in private life and civil society. The values of ethical life must not directly clash with the principles enshrined in morality, which means that choice and consent become crucial to the possibility of a mixed mode of universal and particular moral codes within a liberal feminist framework. Thus, it is perfectly compatible with liberal feminism for some people to see abortion as a profound moral wrong and others to see it as morally permissible. But it would not be compatible with liberal feminism for the wrongness/permissibility of abortion to be institutionalised in such as way as to force women to have terminations or prevent them from having them if that is what they choose (at least, for most liberal feminists) within certain hotly debated limits.[24] Morally, from a liberal feminist point of view, women as a matter of principle have the right to control their own bodies and fertility. The way in which this right is exercised will vary according to the moral convictions of different women, but morality requires that the right be

---

[23] See J. Habermas, *Moral Consciousness and Communicative Action* (Cambridge, UK: Polity Press, 1990).

[24] See E. Porter, *Feminist Perspectives on Ethics* (London & New York: Longman, 1999), Chapter 6.

universally enshrined. Liberal feminism may tolerate the presence of moral codes that, in their view, work to the detriment of women. However, they could not tolerate a situation in which such codes were imposed on women. The necessity of meaningful choice within the liberal feminist framework means that in practice, anti-feminist moral codes with pretensions to universal validity should not be enforced either through limits on education or through the law.

The Relations Between Ends and Means in Enlightenment Feminism

Liberal feminism, as the British suffragette movement demonstrated, has sometimes been associated with political militancy. As with most other branches of feminism, it also has a history of using various forms of political campaigning and propaganda in the pursuit of its goals. Even within liberal cultures, feminism has had to push its way onto the political agenda and find instruments for coercing reluctant publics into changing behaviour according to feminist principles. In other words, if feminism had waited for an invitation, it would never have made headway even in the cultures in which it initially came to prominence. Of all the branches of feminism, liberal feminism is the one that has made the law the most important means for achieving its moral demands, though this has tended to be in the context of states where legislation emerges out of political lobbying and debate rather than dictatorial fiat or revolutionary struggle. This means that although coercion is perfectly compatible with liberal feminist goals, persuasion is just as important in legitimating the changes that give legal force to the normative requirements of feminist equality of right.

Whether straightforward coercion is compatible with liberal feminism, for instance through the violent imposition of a new constitution on a particular state, is less easy to determine. The suffragettes were happy to destroy property in pursuit of the vote, and some liberal feminists have approved of the violent destruction of regimes inimical to women's rights, such as that of the Taliban, but there is clearly a paradox involved in violating rights in order to enshrine them. For liberal feminism, it is conceivable that the ends of feminism might justify undemocratic coercion (that is to say coercion not legitimated through processes of democratic legislation) and maybe even violence, but this would be exceptional. Liberal feminists are necessarily committed to altering the patterns of gender relations in their own as well as other societies. They are also committed to the promotion of liberal democratic political regimes and, on grounds of basic human rights, the abolition of extreme punishments. However, in general, liberal feminists' conviction as to the rightness and rationality of their beliefs is allied to the conviction that rational and right-minded people will eventually be convinced of the justice of their cause. Along with John Stuart Mill, liberal feminists will always be likely to favour the airing of their views across all possible boundaries as the most effective means by which, in the end, their moral vision will triumph.

Care Feminism and the Globalization of Ethics

The Moral Ends of Care Feminism

Enlightenment feminisms are characterised by the endorsement of a range of principles and values that ought to govern the conduct of individuals and of communities. The substantive prescriptions of care feminism are less easy to grasp, largely because care feminism eschews the articulation of moral norms in the abstract. Nevertheless, I would argue that care feminism does put forward recommendations for ethics that are taken to be universally applicable and that imply certain uniform ethical requirements for all people and peoples. Care feminism requires that the overriding values that orient moral conduct should be those inherent in the practice of care, a practice often exemplified by the relation of mother to child. The practice of care includes the responsibility to attend to the specific, contextually located physical and spiritual needs of others, those who are recognised as dependent beings as opposed to autonomous beings. But the requirements of care go beyond this to demand that the carer takes responsibility for enabling the physical and spiritual growth and flourishing of those in her or his care, so that they themselves emerge as capable of taking responsibility for the care of themselves and others.[25] The generalisation of an ethic of care would involve the mutual recognition of all human beings as needy and dependent creatures and would be antithetical to the institutionalisation of any beliefs or practices that judged some human beings a priori as more worthy of (or worthy of more) care than others. For this reason, a morality of care is clearly not compatible with values that legitimate the denigration, subordination, or straightforward expendability of any group of human individuals. However, it is less clear what this might imply in terms of ethical uniformity and diversity in practice.

Unlike enlightenment feminisms, care feminism has no tradition of positing an ideal in abstraction from existing moral realities. This is not to say that care feminism does not embody ideals, but these ideals are always located in existing relations and practices, and moral values and conduct are seen as necessarily and rightly embedded in specific contexts. This means that it is open to care feminists to argue that what is right for particular individuals can and does vary according to circumstances, and that the generalisation of specific moral norms, or the idea of a unitary moral code or rule book, is therefore always likely to pose problems for the practice of care. In this sense, care ethics has more in common with consequentialist approaches than with deontological approaches to ethics, in that the same answer may be morally appropriate in some contexts but not in others, according to an overarching commitment to the value and practice of care.

Having said this however, certain, generally applicable, moral prescriptions and prohibitions can be extrapolated from the standpoint of an ethic of care.

---

[25] See Ruddick, *Maternal Thinking*, Chapter 2; Robinson *Globalizing Care*, Chapter 2.

As a moral approach, it is oriented towards the meeting of needs and against the use of violence. A society governed by an ethic of care would have to be one in which bodily integrity and the meeting of basic needs were guaranteed. An ethic of care is incompatible with a world in which it is legitimate for bodies to be broken or malnourished, or where there is no support for the education and health of all. This implies that a care-based society would be one in which mutual respect was entrenched, personal security was protected, and distributive justice was taken for granted as a collective responsibility. Such universal protections and entitlements, however, will not necessarily be interpreted as meaning the same for men as for women, or indeed for all men and all women. Insofar as actual distributions of responsibility and vulnerability are different for different men and women, then the meaning of security and justice may also be different.

The clearest example within care feminisms of a universal moral prohibition is its delegitimation of all forms of systematic violence – that is to say, violence that is based on the recognition of some specified groups of people as unworthy of care. A society organised according to the ethic of care would be one in which not only all forms of sexual violence, but also the practice of war, would be delegitimated. If the ethical bottom line of liberal feminism is in the notion of basic human rights, then for care feminism, it is in a fundamental commitment to non-violence and to a non-instrumental conception of human relations. For instance, whereas in the case of liberal feminism, a legitimate version of the practice of prostitution, based on principles of consent and contract, could be envisaged, it is difficult to see how any such practice could be legitimate within the terms of care feminism, regardless of the consent of the participants or the fairness of the contractual terms.

As with all forms of feminism, care ethics is committed to altering gendered relations of power in which women are systematically devalued and disadvantaged. However, in contrast to liberal feminism, this does not necessarily mean the abolition of a sexual division of labour. For care feminism, what needs to change is the ways in which traditionally women's work and women's moral skills are valued. Similarly, care ethics does not involve a clear commitment to the overturning of particular political systems. This is partly because of care feminism's lack of faith in political and legal structures to embody and apply contextually sensitive principles of care, and partly because care takes its starting point from how things are rather than how they might be. Nevertheless, principles of care imply that both democracy and welfare are required in any polity that will support the practice of care, and that coercive systems of rule are in tension with care practices. Much more clear cut is the rejection by care feminism of modes of punishment that inflict suffering, not only on the body but also on the spirit. Care feminism is more closely allied with restorative than with retributive conceptions of justice, and would see most judicial sanctions as they are currently employed by states as morally inadequate.

The Relation between Ends and Means in Care Feminism

The generalisation of an ethic of care could not permit the expendability of one individual's welfare in the pursuit of some greater end, though it might permit the constraining of an individual's autonomy for her own good as well as that of others. It is therefore possible that care feminism could permit the coercion of the less vulnerable in the interests of the more vulnerable, though not at the expense of the capacity of the less vulnerable for virtue. However, just as it is antithetical to an ethic of care to categorise any group as more or less worthy of care, so is it antithetical to care feminism to force the uprooting of existing attachments to people and values, even where those attachments might embody discrimination for or against a particular group, including women. The ethic of care is obliged to work through example and persuasion rather than through legislation or more direct coercion. But precisely because it sees care as a practice that is universally present across different cultures, it does not see care as something outside that needs to be brought in to transform moral cultures. Rather it sees care as the ever-present denigrated other of dominant codified and customary morality, which is usually confined to the sphere of 'women's work,' and which provides a distinctively feminine contribution to ethics. An ethic of care would seek to work with the grain of existing relations of care, and highlight the inconsistencies between the values inherent in care and those implicit in mainstream moral practices in order to bring about a revaluation of those practices. Moreover, it would be more concerned to transform the values of the powerful than of the vulnerable, given the much greater potential of the former to violate duties of care to others.

Although the ethic of care sees law as an imperfect ethical tool, it would nevertheless be likely to support the entrenchment of certain principles in international law, including protection against pain and suffering, and entitlement to the meeting of basic needs (food, water, shelter, health, education). For care feminists, however, the language of rights would be less likely to be emphasised than the language of duty and responsibility. The ethical implications of care feminism are in some respects more conservative than those of liberal feminism and in other respects, more radical. They are more conservative, in that they ground their claims in what is argued to be a universally present but subordinated ethic, which already has purchase across cultures in care practices that are traditionally women's work. Care feminism does not push for the immediate overturning of existing social and political relations, it wants to work immanently and be sensitive to specificities of context. However, care feminism is more radical than liberal feminism in terms of some of its specific ethical prescriptions: it espouses an ethic of non-violence, it supports principles of distributive justice, and it directs attention not to the rights of the vulnerable but to the duties of the powerful. Whereas liberal feminism endorses principles that are already entrenched within international law, care feminism points to a different kind of world altogether.

Postcolonial Feminism and the Globalization of Ethics

The Ends of Morality in Postcolonial Feminism

Liberal feminism is committed to the ideal of a legally entrenched universal moral code, within which women's human rights are enshrined. Care feminists are more sceptical about the moral salience of codes or rule books, but nevertheless also hold to the claim that there are certain moral priorities that ought to be embedded in the conduct of all people and all nations. In contrast, postcolonial feminists are extremely suspicious of the notion of a 'uniform planetary ethic,' at least in the context of the world as it is presently constituted. This is not because postcolonial feminists are moral relativists or moral particularists in any straightforward sense. In the same way they are suspicious of the project of uniformity, so too are they suspicious of the alternative 'global accommodation of conflicting ethical differences,' which would leave in place and legitimate all kinds of values that underpin gendered practices inimical to both men and women. The problem for postcolonial feminists is that the question of morality is always already posed as a choice between a universalist and a particularist language. From the postcolonialist feminist point of view, the former is not only inadequate to capture the meaning of morality, but also helps to reproduce the deep diversity in the ways in which women and men are placed within gendered relations of power. However, the latter, which gives moral priority to different cultural, ideological, or religious traditions, also entrenches gendered relations of power within the particular moral codes and values peculiar to those traditions.[26]

The dangers of moral universalism can be illustrated in relation to the issue of women's control over their fertility. According to liberal feminism, women's right to control their own bodies is sacrosanct, and includes the right of control over fertility. However, the context in which this right is exercised makes all the difference in postcolonial feminist terms to the moral significance of the right. Something that affirms the freedom of an individual woman and perpetuates the equality of women more generally in the context of a developed liberal capitalist state becomes the means by which to selectively abort female foetuses in cultures in which the birth of a daughter is an economic disaster, something that seems neither to increase the freedom of individual women nor to enforce the equality of women more generally. The dangers of moral particularism are perhaps more obvious, since every culture incorporates values that make women particularly vulnerable to sexual exploitation and violence and less likely than men to achieve political power and voice.

The message of postcolonial feminism is that the question of moral universalism versus moral particularism cannot be considered in abstraction from politics, because the moral significance of the answer only emerges within

---

[26] See Mohanty's critiques of both Western universalism (Mohanty, *Feminism Without Borders*, Chapter 1) and multiculturalism (Mohanty, *Feminism Without Borders*, Chapters 4 and 8).

contemporary relations of power in which, to borrow Mohanty's phrase, 'racialized gender' is key to the legitimation of moral positions.[27] We see this as much in the West's utilisation of the abuse of women's rights under the Taliban to legitimate its intervention in Afghanistan post 9/11, as in the reassumption of the veil by women in the Iranian revolution, or President Bush's desire to eliminate the possibility of gay marriage. For postcolonial feminism, therefore, though there is clearly a very strong ethical impulse underlying its critique of both universalist and particularist positions, there is a sense in which specific questions about what moral values should guide human conduct cannot properly be answered until the world has changed in such a way that those currently most excluded from moral debate can be heard. In the meantime, the moral priority is to support the different ways in which women struggle for change in different parts of the world, and for Western, middle-class feminists not to assume that they always already know what the vast majority of women should and do want or need. The touchstone for moral intolerability in the case of postcolonial feminists therefore is neither basic human rights nor the principles of care. Instead, it is principles of respect for difference and the value of an inclusive democracy. To the extent that a particular moral norm, within a particular context of culture and power enhances the capacity of the globally disenfranchised to control their own lives and formulate their own views, then it can be seen as a good thing. To the extent that such a norm pre-empts or closes down democratic engagement, then it can be seen as a bad thing. The same norm may have different implications in different contexts.

Like the other two normative trajectories within feminism (both of which emanate predominantly from Western feminist movements), postcolonial feminism is committed to the alteration of gender relations not simply in 'other' societies but in all societies. However, for postcolonial feminists, the posing of the question as to what attitude to take to 'other' traditions, which are antithetical to feminist moral goals, is itself enmeshed in problematic political and sociological assumptions. In the first place, to ask what should be done about the 'other' easily falls into the familiar position of enlightened 'West' versus backward 'rest.' In the second place, the invocation of 'other' traditions suggests a degree of uniformity and homogeneity of gender relations within cultures. The political effect of the former is to legitimate the view that most peoples in the world are morally backward and incapable of developing a just society without outside help. The political effect of the latter is to legitimate ideas about culture that sustain the power of conservative groups, or help build the power of radical right-wing (ethnic-nationalist, fascist) groups within all cultural contexts. Postcolonial feminists favour radical change in most contemporary political and legal-judicial regimes, but they argue that such change can only be successfully accomplished from within, or at least with the explicit consent and co-operation of those that the change is supposed to advantage. Thus,

---

[27] Mohanty, *Feminism Without Borders*, Chapter 9.

postcolonial feminist movements may be happy to act in alliance with 'outside' feminist movements to bring about change in practices such as female genital mutilation or the use of extreme punishments against women, but they are hostile to interventions in feminist causes that ignore or marginalize feminist activists on the ground.

The Relation between Ends and Means in Postcolonial Feminism

The notion of an inside/outside distinction between societies implies a kind of homogeneity 'inside.' Postcolonial feminism rejects the idea that societies or cultures are singular and homogenous, since cultural traditions of all kinds are invariably internally contested and indigenous feminist movements are invariably in tension with at least some aspects of dominant cultural norms. They also reject the idea that there is a clear inside/outside distinction in a world in which imperialism, colonialism, mass migration, and various forms of economic and political interference across borders (from war to WTO regulations) have been commonplace in most places for a couple of centuries. Nevertheless, postcolonial feminism is committed to the rejection of the imposition of norms from the top down, which is seen as perpetuating relations of dependence and inferiority on the part of the powerless, and preventing the emergence of locally grounded answers to moral and political questions. In particular, postcolonial feminisms object to the globalization of Western norms via the globalization of capitalism, and to the dominance of the global media by one set of normative messages, which ignore or discount the moral agency of those to whom the messages are addressed. A common complaint of postcolonial feminists is the way in which Western liberals in general, including liberal feminists, construct women in the developing world as passive victims in need of 'rescue' from the patriarchal darkness they inhabit.[28] This does not mean that postcolonial feminists favour censorship, but, it does mean that they favour the full opening up of the exchange of cultural values so as to be inclusive of all potential participants. In this sense, postcolonial feminism has something in common with care feminism in that it emphasises the importance of context and the likely inadequacy of abstractly derived universal norms imposed without understanding of the local situation. Unlike care feminism, however, postcolonial feminism puts emphasis on political struggle, as opposed to the practice of care, as the key to changing the world for the better. As with liberal feminism, postcolonial feminism does not necessarily discount violence as a means to morally important ends, though in the case of postcolonial feminism, the archetypal just war is the struggle of national liberation against colonial rule rather than, for instance, humanitarian intervention. In relation to law

---

[28] Mohanty, *Feminism Without Borders*: Chapters 1 and 9; Spivak, 'Cultural Talks in the Hot Peace: Revisiting the "Global Village,"' in P. Cheah & B. Robbins (eds.), *Cosmopolitics: Thinking and Feeling Beyond the Nation* (Minneapolis: University of Minnesota Press, 1998).

as the mechanism for enforcing moral norms, there is nothing in postcolonial feminism to suggest an antithesis in principle to law or the idea of human rights. However, as should be clear from our discussion, postcolonial feminists would see the international inscription of definitive universal norms at present as premature, given the absence of the vast majority of people, men and women, in the processes through which these norms are articulated in the contemporary context.

Conclusion: Feminism as an Ethical Tradition Revisited

Our discussion has characterized feminism as an ethical tradition in terms of its division into three distinct trajectories. In this final section of the chapter, I will argue that, in spite of the differences between feminist viewpoints, there are some shared implications of different forms of feminism for questions about the form and substance of morality. And although these commonalities do not permit the precise specification of a global moral code, they do suggest the overarching moral values by which individual and collective behaviour should be oriented, and they do prohibit the idea that all forms of morality, or all modes of institutionalising morality, are equally legitimate.

When it comes to the question of the *form* morality takes – that is to say, whether it is understood in universal or particular terms – then feminism is clearly closer to the universal than the particular end of the continuum. All forms of feminism are inherently cosmopolitan in that they do not take the boundaries of particular tradition, whether national, cultural or religious, as having any intrinsic moral value separately from what it means to be a man or a woman within that tradition. In general, it is hard to reconcile any form of feminism with status-based moralities, in which the moral superiority or inferiority (capacity for moral agency or moral feeling) of particular categories of persons is assumed a priori. Even within the framework of care feminism, which has been accused of essentialising the moral superiority of the feminine, the point is to universalise that feminine ethic, not to give more status or power to those held to embody feminine characteristics by nature.

Having said this, however, feminism does not rule out space for moral diversity. The fact that traditions do not gain moral status simply by virtue of being traditions does not mean that there may not be a variety of moral codes compatible with gender relations that do not discriminate against or devalue women. The implication of all the forms of feminism we have discussed is that whilst the differences between people's situations and beliefs are as deep as they are at present, then some kind of mix of uniformity and diversity would be appropriate in any global ethic. However, the ultimate aim would be to limit diversity in such a way that ethical values that legitimate and perpetuate gendered relations of power are prohibited. In this sense, feminism in all its forms is a modern ideology, like liberalism, that is committed to change. It is therefore difficult to reconcile feminism with conservative, religious traditions in which gender-specific roles and hierarchies of power are enshrincd.

It is more difficult to draw out substantive than formal commonalities from the moral claims of the different versions of feminism and, to the extent to which this is possible, these substantive claims do not amount to a moral code. Nevertheless, there are certain foundational moral values that cut across different forms feminism. I suggest that these values centre on the moral significance of pain, of need, and of power. Feminists of all kinds attach enormous moral weight to the ways in which women suffer because they are categorised in such a way that it is legitimate for them to be hurt. Sexual violence, domestic violence, female genital mutilation, under-nourishment of women and girls where resources are scarce are all matters given high priority on feminist agendas. It would be highly counter-intuitive for any feminist ethic to favour moral codes that glorified or legitimated the deliberate infliction of pain and suffering in terms of a vocabulary of retributive justice, whether at the individual or collective level. By and large, across the spectrum of feminist politics, feminists have campaigned against the use of violence in disciplining children and against corporal and capital punishments in the judicial system. In relation to need, although different forms of feminism emphasise different means to the end of meeting women's needs, they share common ground in seeing the global exclusion of women from equal access to economic goods as a profound injustice. Feminists typically refer with moral indignation to the famous statistic about women doing two-thirds of the world's work and owning less than one-tenth of its property. This implies a common understanding that the meeting of socio-economic needs is a crucial good, and that any worthwhile moral code will inscribe a commitment to addressing the socio-economic needs of all on an equal basis (whether this is through equal access to the labour market and equality of property rights or through the overthrow of global capitalism). In relation to power, although it is again true that different forms of feminism address inequities of power differently, it is nevertheless the case that systematic inequalities of power based on class or status cannot be justified from a feminist point of view. This implies that any acceptable moral code, for feminists, would have to be compatible with democratic norms, in which all people, including women, could meaningfully participate.

As a political movement that has always been defined in terms of a commitment to change the status quo, feminism has always been confronted with the question of what means it might be permissible to employ in this endeavour. This question has split the movement at various points in feminism's past, and is moot concerning the encounters between different forms of feminism in contemporary debates about women in development and women's human rights at a global level. In general, feminist movements have been antithetical to the use of violence to attain feminist ends per se, and have most often endorsed violence where feminist ends have been linked to broader political agendas such as the pursuit of national liberation, the prevention of genocide, or the ending of oppressive regimes. Feminist reluctance to endorse the use of violence for feminist ends is at least in part a response to their perception that the moral significance of ends cannot easily be detached from that of means and vice versa. In the case of the Natural Law just war tradition, or of the liberal nationalist endorsement of the principle of national self-determination, there are occasions when the use of violence is understood in a clinical and technical sense as a necessary procedure to restore the health of the international community. For feminists, however, the notion that the ends served by violence sanitize the means of violence is questionable. The end of securing rights for women in Afghanistan under the Taliban could certainly be seen as a just cause. But for feminists, particularly in the light of postcolonial feminist critiques of Western imperialism and paternalism, to use bombing as a means towards this end is to further corrupt the already hierarchical relations between women in different parts of the world.

The use of violence requires certainties of many kinds: certain knowledge about the situation in which one wants to interfere; certainty about the rightness of the cause; certainty that the outcome, in which both the perpetrator and victim of violence will be affected in manifold ways, will be worth it. The history of feminism as a trans-national movement is littered with well-meaning attempts to enforce changes for the better that have foundered because what were thought to be certainties turned out to be unfounded. It is perhaps for this reason that of all the non-pacifist traditions considered in this volume, feminism is the most reluctant to see the use of violence as legitimate.

Non-violent protest, persuasion, and the law have been the favoured means by which different feminist movements have campaigned on feminist issues. What is common to feminists in general is that they do not support the closing down of channels of communication on grounds of the vulnerability of traditions in which their ideas might be unwelcome. In addition, they accept that given the ways in which the status quo works to the advantage of some, it is unlikely that changes to the status quo will be able to be implemented entirely consensually. This does not mean, however, that any kind of imposition of feminist policies is acceptable, or will be effective. The power structures that feminism wants to change are highly complex and deeply rooted, and so are the values that sustain and legitimate those structures. This necessitates a pragmatic sensitivity to context and a willingness to be flexible and to listen to those feminists best placed to understand whether and how feminist initiatives might work at a particular place and time.

In many ways, feminism can be seen as a microcosm that offers a model for the difficulties and possibilities of globalizing ethics. Because feminism is a world-wide phenomenon and because within feminism, world-wide differences of identity, culture, and power are replicated, the question of normative universalism versus particularism has been immanent in feminist debate for many decades, as was demonstrated in the great UN-sponsored conferences for women of the 1980s and 1990s.[29] The lessons that feminism provides for the questions with which this volume is concerned are not unambiguous. On the one hand, the different strands of feminism seem to point to the impossibility of agreement on moral values. On the other hand, however, the mere existence of feminisms that are mutually recognisable as feminisms from all different parts of the globe testifies to a shared capacity for moral outrage and moral commitment that hinges on the value attached to the minimisation of pain, the meeting of needs, and the empowerment of the powerless.

---

[29] UN World Conferences for Women were held at the beginning and end of the UN decade for Women (1975–1985) in Mexico and Nairobi, and again in Beijing in 1995. These conferences demonstrated both the capacity of feminists from many different national and cultural contexts to forge networks and alliances across boundaries of tradition and the profound difficulties in attaining consensus about the ethical values to which feminists should give priority (see J. Steans, *Gender and International Relations*, pp. 146–157).

11

Ethical Universalism and Particularism

A Comparison of Outlooks

William M. Sullivan

The chapters in this volume represent an experiment in dialogue among a group of the ethical traditions that shape the contemporary world. Reporting in their several voices, the authors provide notable essays in moral imagination for our time. While they speak from quite different perspectives, the authors meet within a common, if complex, space of discourse. All the contributors have developed their thinking against the backdrop of intensified interaction among various peoples and parts of the globe, rooted in today's expanding technological webs of communication and economic interdependence. These circuits of interaction and awareness provide the material basis for the much-discussed phenomenon of globalization.

Only a decade ago, proponents of globalization, especially in the United States, were hailing the arrival of a new era of worldwide security and prosperity sustained by a global economy and the rule of law. Since then, however, a series of conflicts, including catastrophic violence and savage warfare, have made all too plain the naiveté of that premature celebration. The contributors to this volume are committed to dialogue in the search for ways to strengthen the fragile global web of human solidarity, but they are fully aware of the harsh realities and moral precariousness of the present. They acknowledge the plurality not only of material interests but of moral values and aspirations as well.

Ethical principles are related in complex ways to social institutions. Principles can be used to justify or rationalize an existing social-political order by showing how institutions embody or approximate ethical ideals. Or, in sharp contrast, the universal claims of moral theory can be invoked as a lever to effect political or social change and then as a blueprint for institution-building. In this way, for example, the Eighteenth Century revolutionaries in France and America invoked moral theories of natural right to legitimate the drastic overthrow of existing governments. In the primacy it gives to a theoretical concept of uniform normative order demanding practical implementation, today's "human rights regime," like the "global economy," shares a similar if less cataclysmic bent toward changing institutions to better reflect what are held to be universal moral ideals.

Many parts of the world are today caught up in efforts to change both political structures and social patterns, including gender relations and cultural or religious identities. The sources of these changes are multiple. Perhaps just as importantly, they are seen quite differently by various groups. Since World War II and the founding of the United Nations, efforts to establish a global moral and legal order, sometimes called the "human rights regime," have gained considerable ground. But they have by no means achieved universal consensus. For example, "humanitarian" military interventions by international agencies and various powers into the lives of states are today often legitimated by their supporters as efforts to enforce "human rights." However, these extreme measures can also be viewed not as legitimate efforts to defend individuals but as exercises of hegemonic power to suppress rightful efforts at national liberation or self-definition. How to view and respond to these efforts remains a highly contentious issue. The contributors' reports amply demonstrate how uncertain and contentious it is to attempt to achieve agreement on these matters.

The role that traditions of ethical thought play in the contemporary global context is both important and multifaceted. A range of questions that are at issue today – including the status of women, tolerance for various religious and political options, legal procedures and punishments, patterns of family life, and political governance and political participation – is deeply intertwined with the evident pluralism of ethical commitments embraced by the world's peoples. The very power of moral commitment can strengthen conflict when it arises out of rival perceptions of the good and right. This is especially apparent when groups perceive themselves as the targets of the efforts of others to propagate their notions of the proper social or moral order. The potential for such conflicts is exacerbated in an era when media of communication have brought the values and viewpoints of many others literally into the homes of peoples everywhere. On the other hand, efforts by countries or groups to isolate themselves from influences their authorities deem subversive or immoral can in turn encourage negative stereotypes among outsiders, further discouraging contact and increasing suspicion and animosity between communities.

The authors of this volume were asked to take this context of deep pluralism of moral commitment as the explicit context for their thinking. Their aim has been to identify points of agreement and disagreement across traditions, to expand consensus where that seems feasible, and to imagine ways to diffuse the potential for conflict among differences that remain intractable. They have been asked to address some fundamental questions about how to proceed in the coming era. Speaking from various traditions of moral understanding, does the solution or management of ethically driven conflict demand general adherence to a uniform planetary ethic? Or can conflict be reduced better through ongoing accommodation of moral differences? One of the insights that emerges from the chapters is that tolerance of diversity – even diversity among moral commitments – can be expanded by global communication and serious dialogue. It would be naïve to underestimate the liabilities attendant on global moral diversity. But it would be equally mistaken to discount the potential of expanded dialogue among traditions for easing dangerous tensions that threaten our collective future.

The value of these chapters lies in their invitation to the reader to explore with the writers the complexity of the issues posed by ethical pluralism on a global scale. Dialogue becomes possible only by learning to see from the other's point of view. It is sustained when the other's point of view becomes something of importance, even a source of possible enrichment of one's own. The contributors have sought to foster dialogue by opening up areas of possible conversation that could produce insight and greater mutual understanding across differences among ways of ethical thinking. In doing so, these authors also demonstrate a positive potential of globalization: they enable the reader to appreciate the scope and possibilities for moral dialogue made possible by increased contact among societies and ethical traditions.

Organization and Assumptions

What sort of conversation, then, is this? Each of the authors speaks to the common topic as self-conscious reporters for specific traditions of ethical reflection. The first assumption underlying this approach is an understanding that all ethical thinking takes place on the basis of traditions of thought that have been shaped by their histories within specific social contexts. However, ethical theories also seek to present moral ideas in general language in order to gain some purchase on the fine-grained quality of lived experience. The first section of this overview chapter will explore some of the implications for the topic of this contrast between the density of "thick" contexts of actual life and the "thin" formulations of principles found in contemporary international law and much ethical theory.

The overview's second assumption is that ethical traditions lead us to perceive situations in characteristic "frames" that highlight particular aspects of situations as morally salient. However, these perceptions can change over time as traditions engage in internal argument over the meaning of their core moral perceptions. Globalization is proving to be a major stimulus of such reconsideration, as the authors show by a series of examples, including the contemporary salience of gender as an area of ethical attention. Traditions can learn from each other, and reformulate important aspects of their thinking as a result. At the same time, differences remain, or may develop as a result of interaction among traditions. This is clear in contrasts between Western liberalism and East Asian moral thought over the meaning of freedom and social responsibility. There also are important differences between the vision of a "uniform planetary ethic" put forward in international law and those religious traditions, including the Abrahamic monotheistic religions, that advance denser, more substantive conceptions of the good life and good person. The Overview ends with consideration of how these tensions might be addressed through efforts to develop mutual comprehension and viable communication among traditions, a project understood as a robust form of institutionalized practical rationality.

The Themes of the Conversation: Thin Principles but Thick Identities

In their chapters, each contributor has struggled with a vital, but as yet unresolved issue at the heart of discussions of globalization. At least since the signing of the 1948 United Nations' Universal Declaration of Human Rights, efforts have been underway through an expanding series of similar treaties and international covenants to construct an "international human rights regime" to protect individuals. This project of international law is probably the most visible effort to provide a reasoned legal framework that aims to encompass a wide range of different moral commitments. As Daniel Philpott describes it in his chapter, "Global Ethics and the International Law Tradition," the strategy behind these developments has been to constrain the shape and functioning of states by their subscription to a growing set of common principles of international conduct. These efforts were initiated by Western governments, especially in the wake of World War II, though they have arguably been taken up by many other states as well as international bodies. Conceived as freestanding principles that could compel assent outside of particular moral traditions, these principles were from the beginning decidedly "constructivist" in intent. Their history includes a fifty-year long effort to secure a stable global economic regime through institutions ranging from the International Monetary Fund and World Bank to the relatively new World Trade Organization.

The whole set of institutional arrangements is premised upon a theory of individual rights. It remains an open question as to whether this idea can really fulfill the aspirations of its proponents in the post-World War II era to resolve international conflict by peaceful means. Is it too identified with specifically Western ethical and religious views to be universally acceptable? Should we imagine this international human rights regime as the basis of an emerging world order organized around a universal moral consensus? Or is the current situation, as well as any possible future, fated to remain, at best, coexistence among diverse peoples shaped by many cultural and ethnic particularities that have deep and poorly understood historical roots? As Philpott and other contributors point out, the end of the Cold War has allowed space for significant challenges to the universality of the norms guiding the "international human rights regime." The 1993 Bangkok Declaration registered explicit dissent on the part of a number of Asian, Middle Eastern, and African governments to the use of this ethic as an "instrument of political pressure," presumably directed at them. The advance of Western models of development, and of direct Western interventions elsewhere in the world, seems to have called out more violent counter-trends, including unprecedented stateless, global terrorism. These unsettling outcomes raise serious questions about how "thick" any possible global consensus might be, especially if the latter is to justify forms of intervention that intrude upon national sovereignty. The recent defection of the United States from a number of international treaties and jurisdictions underlines the precariousness of the intended universality.

If this rather chastened view is closer to the truth than expectations of an advancing universality, then how can we best contribute toward improving today's decidedly shaky interdependence in the interests of human welfare? Is a genuine pluralism of civilizations compatible with the universal ethical aspirations manifest in current formulations of international law? What contributions should traditions other than human rights liberalism be expected to make to a future global ethical consensus? What forms of dialogue are possible to bridge differences in the interests of preserving peace and expanding solidarity?

In an anthropological sense, we all live "thick" and particular lives within specific networks of relationship, among certain people but not others, particular communities with which we share understandings of the world. Here we often cultivate identities that are enmeshed in relationships of loyalty, piety, and deference in which individual flourishing requires a nuanced balancing of often competing goods. At the same time, international competition in the economic, cultural, religious, and sometimes military spheres is spurring greater mutual awareness and, often, invidious comparison among nations and within societies. This presents another challenge for the contributors: to explore ways of thinking and speaking that can enable such diverse groups to cooperate to strengthen planetary interdependence – and at the same time be morally acceptable to all. The terms of general agreement are typically "thin," and emphasize the most general level of moral understanding, often glossing over the density of "thick" particularistic loyalties. Mediating these two opposing tendencies – the differentiation of multiple identities on the ground versus the reach for high-level theories, principles, procedures, and discourse to manage the resulting social complexity – is one of the great, enduring problems of modern politics. How might conversations that are self-consciously informed by ethical traditions help address these issues?

The Defining Frame: A Dialogue among Traditions

While this volume represents a dialogue among contemporary thinkers, each author has attempted to address the questions under discussion from the perspective and particular viewpoint of one recognized body of ethical discourse. The emphasis upon traditions is noteworthy. It requires each author to frame the universality-particularity problem in a way consonant with a given tradition's inherited perspective. Such a requirement has the virtue of forcing into clarity those features of the contemporary situation that are morally salient for a particular tradition. At the same time, making the ethical traditions into dialogue partners also requires the writers to think consciously within a field of deep moral pluralism.

Much philosophical argument is carried on in a supposed medium of reason divorced from history and social context. Speaking consciously about modes of ethical thinking as traditions undercuts that presumption. The conversation presented in this volume is premised instead on awareness that all forms of thinking are marked by their particular location in the social and historical world. So, these authors do not speak from a position of self-evident reason-ableness. They do not invoke a contrast between "reason" (usually the supple way the writer thinks) and "tradition" (often caricatured as a conservative, monolithic repository of frozen opinion). Nor, however, do they assume a facile and self-defeating relativism of values.

The point is rather that all reasoning takes place within traditions: opinions and patterns of thinking that have been handed on from previous discussions and debates about a particular topic. Like individual identities, perceptions and opinions develop within ongoing conversations which unfold as narratives. A tradition, then, is a dynamic, and historically contingent, process of dialogue and argument. In Alasdair MacIntyre's (1981) useful formulation, "A living tradition ... is a historically extended, socially embodied argument, and an argument precisely in part about the good which constitute that tradition" (p. 207). Reason, whether in its scientific or ethical forms, develops within tra-ditions of articulation and argument whose distinctive aspects receive expres-sion in characteristic framing metaphors and styles of argument.

In intellectual life, as in practical affairs, it is often breakdowns, such as fail-ures in attempts to communicate, that spur the effort to articulate the usually taken-for-granted assumptions that underlie a particular practice – or to find new, more effective practices of discourse. Something like this seems to be the case regarding the self-conscious awareness of tradition. For triumphant nineteenth-century Europeans, and many Westerners in the twentieth century as well, it seemed evident that the world was advancing toward a universal civilization based upon not only a uniform science and technology but upon converging moral and political systems. The recurrent wreckage of various forms of those utopian hopes has sustained a search for alternative, more cir-cumspect ways of understanding our situation. Not for everyone, to be sure, but for many it is now apparent that all thinking, including that very aspira-tion to a universal and progressive moral order, represents at best a partial view, a perspective and mode of perceiving. It can always benefit from corrob-oration and correction from dialogue with alternative efforts at articulation. The kinds of thinking employed by the authors of this volume stem from that understanding. They have sought points of contact across traditions while reflecting on the historically conditioned nature of the traditions for which they are reporting. This viewpoint is not relativistic. But it does demand that all claims for the universality of particular values must be argued for rather than assumed.

Moral Salience, Ethical Framing, and Resonance

For example, when reporting on modern liberalism, Chris Brown begins his chapter, "Liberalism and the Globalization of Ethics," with an important observation. He points out that while liberalism stands today as the dominant political philosophy of industrial, Western nations, it has in fact developed through several centuries both of external conflict, some of it violent with opponents such as fascism and communism, and of intense internal debate. Brown continues with the further point, an important correlative of MacIntrye's assertion that traditions of thinking are always in part "arguments about the goods constitutive of that tradition." Liberalism, Brown points out, is better described as a family of viewpoints that share a core emphasis upon the dignity and freedom of the individual, rather than a single viewpoint.

Individual autonomy, then, would be the "constitutive good" of the liberal tradition. But liberals continue to argue over what this good entails. As Brown points out, liberals are internally divided over the question of how best to support and extend the core good of individual freedom. Does this good demand an insistence on universal standards of fairness that are everywhere applicable? Or is it best nourished within particular political communities such as nations with strong identities? Because liberalism is hegemonic today among the globe's currently dominant societies, it inclines easily toward assuming its own universal validity. This has been especially true for exponents of what Brown describes as "cosmopolitan" liberalism that insists upon the priority of universal principles over particular custom. It is this tendency within liberalism that has most often given theoretical sanction to active international intervention to enforce liberal norms. However, the divergences among liberal thinkers suggest a tradition more open to the claims of the particular than it might at first appear. As Brown points out, liberalism's "nationalist" or "communitarian" forms are far more sympathetic to the values of national self-determination and ethnic diversity that are being strongly endorsed by other, non-liberal ethical traditions. These forms of liberalism tend to reject external intervention except under the most pressing circumstances, and then only as temporary measures.

This essential pluralism of voices within traditions – the "extended argument" that constitutes their vitality – thus opens the possibility of meaningful dialogue across traditions as well as within them. Consider, for example, Michael Walzer's chapter, "Morality and Universality in Jewish Thought." There, Walzer presents that ancient tradition of ethical thinking as having long struggled with the tension between affirming universal moral demands, attendant upon monotheism, while also defending the integrity of a particular moral code rooted in an historical ethnicity. In the modern West, Walzer shows, many Jews have felt a strong affinity with liberalism's assertion of universal human dignity for all persons regardless of national or religious identity. But the very universality of liberal ideals has in turned helped Jews to see in their own tradition as a "mix" between uniform moral standards and particular loyalties that has potential value for others: a framework for reconciling a universal morality with the claims of peoplehood.

Islam and Christianity, the other monotheistic religions represented, also approach such questions with an emphasis on universal moral demands. Unlike Judaism, however, they have not typically thought of themselves as particular communities so much as the normative cores of universal civilizations. That this traditional way of understanding themselves is today in flux is an insight common to the chapters by Muhammad Masud, "Muslim Perspectives on Global Ethics," Max Stackhouse, "Globalization and Christian Ethics," and Mark Murphy, "Natural Law, Common Morality, and Particularism." In as much as global realities have forced an awareness of moral pluralism upon both of these monotheistic world religions, these scholars all call attention to resources within their respective traditions for balancing the affirmation of a particularistic identity with the affirmation of norms that both shape and yet transcend that identity.

On the other hand, the East Asian universalisms of Buddhism and Confucianism seem likely to develop other ways of responding to their contemporary situation. Like the monotheistic Abrahamic faiths, both these traditions are products of the "axial age" of human history identified by Karl Jaspers. As such, they too give a certain primacy to individual conscience and moral responsibility. In "Buddhism and the Globalization of Ethics," Peter Nosco reports that in principle, Buddhism's distinctive emphasis upon freeing individuals from ignorance or delusion as the source of suffering, because it engenders an ethic of compassion, provides a relatively tolerant perspective, universalistic though not dogmatic. However, its historical record is mixed and not free of examples to the contrary. By contrast, in "Confucianism: Ethical Uniformity and Diversity," Richard Madsen argues that Confucianism has preferred to think that the moral perfection of the person-in-particular social relationships is best achieved through paternalistic government by moral elites, thereby placing the tradition in strong tension with a universal ethic that presumes autonomous individuals operating under common laws as the legitimate social context. This is most dramatically clear in contemporary China.

In all these cases, however divergent in content and however different their current relationship to globalizing trends, certain common features of moral traditions as such stand out. Moral traditions are theoretical enterprises, intellectual frameworks through which it is possible to describe the morally salient features of situations, interpret their significance, and deliberate about appropriate responses. However, they also represent patterns of understanding that are socially embedded and more deeply rooted in collective and individual identity than their theoretical articulations. Moral understanding is an important facet of identity. It stems from habits and dispositions formed through shared language and participation in shared practices, including patterns of moral discussion and decision-making. Growth or change in moral understanding grows out of an expansion of conversation, often through the improvisation of new practices of discourse or of new sites of dialogue.

The traditions the authors are reporting upon all represent moral traditions in this deep sense. They provide – and shape – characteristic ways of perceiving and interpreting morally salient aspects of a situation. Moral traditions determine what a person sees as morally significant. In "Feminist Perspectives on a Planetary Ethic," Kimberly Hutchings illustrates this powerfully in her chapter on the historically young politics of feminism. In a relatively short period of time, feminism in its several varieties has placed gender relations into an unprecedented salience in many political contexts. Hutchings argues that feminism has to date functioned more as a political movement than an ethics, presenting feminism as a set of moral insights that await and spur ethical elaboration.

This elaboration, however, is already proceeding in several not wholly compatible voices. Feminists do not agree about how much the discourse of individual rights should frame discussions of gender equality. Some argue instead that questions of gender equity require framing social relationships in terms of responsibility and care. Yet other feminists, those Hutchings names Postcolonial, insist that attending to inequalities in power in local contexts is necessary in order to do justice not only to the situation of women but to the question of equity itself. Each of these tendencies within feminist politics represents an incipient ethics, all with universal implications, while they differ strongly as to how that universalizing of concern with gender equality should be carried out. These tendencies, in turn, resonate with similar concerns in other traditions – Enlightenment feminism with cosmopolitan liberalism, or care feminism with communitarian liberalism and perhaps with the salience given to compassion by several religious ethics, for example – while maintaining their distinctiveness as articulations of moral salience.

Contemporary moral disputes put this potential for resonance to the test. Thus, for a Confucian understanding, it is the individual in a holistic context of social relationships, particular familial ties that constitutes the immediately important moral fact. By contrast, most liberals would focus upon a very different aspect of a situation. For them, it is the individual's degree of freedom and discretion and how well-equipped the person is to exercise freedom of decision that stand out. These moral interpretations, then, determine how one perceives, describes, and analyzes the moral relevance of situations. So, while liberals have long framed conflicts over gender equality in public life not as a matter of social roles but as a collision between the values of equality and paternalism, someone formed by a Confucian ethic could, with equal accuracy, describe the situation as confusion about identity and right relationship. Each framing, of course, holds a very different implication for how one would deliberate and respond, as Madsen shows with the example of the resolution of "Mrs. Yu's" contested election in Taiwan. For their part, feminists might approach the issue differently depending upon their angle of vision, but the feminist tradition as a whole would support the liberal perception of the dispute as requiring the elimination of gender-restricted access to public office.

How we interpret, and how we deliberate about, moral situations, then, are both significantly shaped, at a more profound level than the theoretical, by the distinctive ethical tradition in which we have been formed. In contemporary conditions, however, no moral identity is self-contained or uninfluenced by the constant exchange of perspective globalization brings in its wake. In particular, the volume of global "flows" of people, commodities, and information push all traditions to reach for their most general expressions in order to give individuals and groups tools and resources for making sense of new situations. This emphasis upon the more general, "thin" modes of discourse also heightens possibilities for finding resonance across traditions.

Peter Nosco explores some of the implications of this push toward the general and the thin in his discussion of what he describes as Buddhism's relative success in the "competition for hearts and minds, the dueling propositions represented by the globalization of ethics." Nosco notes Buddhism's long history of accommodating its core teachings, especially its path of spiritual cultivation of essential "realization" with a variety of regimes and its flexible incorporation or acceptance of local customs. In today's global context, these habits serve the tradition well. They have allowed Buddhists to represent their teachings, and therefore to proselytize, by veiling many of its pre-modern devotional manifestations in favor of an emphasis upon its core metaphysical or philosophical ideas concerning the transience and interdependence of all things. The traditional Buddhist ethic of compassion has also been rearticulated in ways that appeal to many beyond traditional Buddhist lands, as the remarkable world influence of the Dalai Lama shows.

On the other hand, Buddhism has at various periods been an important support of monarchical regimes that would make a bad fit with today's global ethic of democracy and development. However, in this context, the universal quality of the core Buddhist message, as scholars can reconstruct its emergence two millennia ago, provides contemporary Buddhists with important moral resources with which to address issues such as environmental stewardship. They also permit accommodation with many if not all of the key values of the U.N.'s Universal Declaration on Universal Human Rights. While Buddhism historically subordinated women to men in the ontological hierarchy (for instance, by requiring women to be reborn as males in their progress toward full realization), Buddhism's core doctrine, that salvation from suffering is available to all by taking control of one's thinking, resonates with those aspects of feminism emphasizing care as a primary human virtue. Buddhism may be the prime example of an ancient religious tradition that has been able to articulate its core values in ways that are already contributing to the global consensus. It also seems peculiarly able to affirm many of the ethical claims of the other world religions. These features make it a potential source of moral resources for groups concerned to bridge traditions or to find means for moral navigation of pluralistic modernity.

Contrasting Universalisms: East versus West?

We can perhaps gain further insight into the possibilities for dialogue across moral pluralism by noting how conflicting moral interpretations of the current human rights regime and global economic integration also reveal thematic resonances across differences. Both Daniel Philpott and Richard Madsen, reporting from the vantage points of international law and Confucianism, note the importance of the so-called Bangkok Declaration of 1993. Then, in preparation for a meeting of the U.N. Conference on Human Rights in Vienna, a group of thirty Asian and Middle Eastern states first met in Bangkok to issue a dissenting document. The nature of their dissent was not to the "universal principles of human rights" as such. Rather, their objection was to attempts by Western states to pressure other nations to conform to Western interpretations of those rights. As Philpott points out, from the perspective of liberal international lawyers this was a significant setback. On the other hand, Madsen shows that, even excepting its anti-colonial overtones, the document also revealed a possible alternative lens for viewing the contemporary world.

The Bangkok Declaration, in Madsen's telling, embodied a number of classic Confucian notions about statecraft and the good society. It stressed the importance of persuasion in affairs among states, in effect appealing to moral example as a force in itself. It spoke about the need for sensitivity to the overall context when implementing moral principles, "bearing in mind the significance of national and regional peculiarities and various historical, cultural, and religious backgrounds." Finally, the Declaration emphasized the need to give priority to overcoming mass poverty through rapid economic growth, in effect justifying state paternalism, if not outright authoritarian rule, as a needed instrument in many societies. It stressed, in other words, the importance of a moral elite at the summit of decision-making to balance the typical Western emphasis upon individual rights and economic liberty.

Madsen notes that the Bangkok Declaration was an agreement among states, many of them authoritarian or at least non-democratic in nature, including the People's Republic of China. However, in 1998, on the fiftieth anniversary of the U.N.'s Universal Declaration of Human Rights, a grassroots Asian Human Rights Commission gathered in Hong Kong a very different representation of the emerging civil society of East Asia to issue the "Asian Human Rights Charter: A People's Charter." This document also emphasized the priority of fighting mass poverty and key Confucian themes such as the importance of particular contexts. However, unlike the Bangkok Declaration, the Charter strongly assailed authoritarian government and "spurious theories of

"Asian Values.'" It called for democratically accountable governments. Finally, it advocated an international agenda of cultural change to allow for the full implementation of universal human rights within Asian nations, especially the dismantling of patriarchal restrictions on gender equality. In these ways, it was broadly compatible with the hopes of the international lawyers. As Madsen notes, however, its central message emphasizes a moral salience that is distinctively (though not exclusively) East Asian, ultimately Confucian. The Charter stresses the need to stop "practices which sacrifice the individual to the collectivity" not simply to liberate the individual but "to renew our communal and national solidarity." So, modern human rights and equality are here understood as the moral basis for a new kind of social trust and reciprocity, themes deeply resonant with Confucian tradition.

The thinking embodied in the Asian Human Rights Charter suggests a distinctive way of understanding not just Asia's struggles for development but the travails of other modernizing societies as well. The implicit narrative behind the Charter starts with traditional societies, in which it alleges that individuals, particularly women and the young, are routinely "sacrificed to the collectivity." Modernity means multiple, dynamic, and conflicting social spheres with their own logics. These free individuals from traditional controls. But they also threaten widespread social atomization and conflict. From this perspective, the alternative paths are, essentially, just three: (1) a descent into anarchy and breakdown; (2) an authoritarian imposition of "stability" from above to prevent breakdown amid growth, as in the contemporary PRC; or (3), the Charter's preferred alternative of a new democratic order built on human rights seen as conditions for true moral development and hence of social trust and solidarity.

This vision of a socially responsible kind of freedom obviously has resonances with important themes in Western thought. From Hegel and Durkheim to various forms of "communitarian" or social liberalism, a number of Western thinkers have sought to reintegrate individual rights and market dynamism with social solidarity. In the liberal rights tradition, however, these themes have not been the dominant focus. In contrast, the moral framework of the Charter places human rights within specific cultural and historical contexts that stress the values of solidarity and moral improvement. It thereby provides a framing for national projects of democracy and economic development that gives salience to just those values that much of the liberal rights tradition tends to assume as background.

What emerges from these alternative framings of the same event is an illuminating incongruity of perspective. The historical virtue of liberalism is to have raised awareness everywhere of the moral dignity of individuals, increasingly pushing that value across distinctions of religion, race or ethnicity, age, gender, nationality, or particular identity. On the other hand, for those societies strongly influenced by the centuries-long spread of Confucianism from China through East Asia, the salient moral aspects of the present can appear rather differently, giving rise to an alternative framing of the challenges and possibilities of our time. Considering things from another's perception of moral salience and thinking within another interpretive frame in this case reveals a plausible moral world that while not wholly congruent with the liberal one, might be able to provide useful resources toward a more ecumenical planetary ethic. As Madsen notes, should this model of democratic modernity take firm root in East Asia, it could contribute importantly to the future balance of individualist and communitarian emphases in any emerging global ethic.

Universals in Context: Islam, Christianity, and Global Liberalism

What, then, of the other universalistic religious traditions? Despite its famous tolerance, liberalism is not without its own moral boundaries. Its core value commitments do make liberals of both cosmopolitan and nationalist stripe advocates of broad tolerance of religious and cultural difference, while leading liberals to oppose the basing of political programs on compulsory consent to some highest good, such as that revealed by divine truth or paradigmatic way of life. This is only intermittently controversial within established liberal societies such as those of the contemporary West. However, Chris Brown points out, such is not the case everywhere and it has certainly not been true in the past anywhere, including early modern Europe. The great monotheistic religions of Judaism, Islam, and Christianity, for example, have been firmly rooted in "perfectionist" visions of the human good that demand adherence. Individuals' adherence to such moral understandings can be tolerated by liberals, but only when they are understood to reflect the choices of individuals – and are not imposed upon other individuals against their will. But this seems to make of them something other than their adherents believe them to be.

Here, then, is a major point of conflict with several other moral traditions. What liberals see as an illegitimate imposition (because it precludes individual quests for the good), even should it be chosen by a majority within a given society, has been historically the accepted understanding of how morality is related to politics for most of the world. Opposition to the political establishment of comprehensive conceptions of the good life functions, we might say, as one principled boundary that defines the liberal perception of the moral world, to which the Christian and Muslim traditions direct attention.

Commenting on the importance of the 1948 U.N. Universal Declaration, in "Muslim Perspectives on Global Ethics," Muhammad Khalid Masud draws attention to two subsequent international declarations in which Muslims have affirmed resonance between the language of universal human rights and their inherited understanding of the human ethical situation. In the 1981 Universal Islamic Declaration of Human Rights, issued by a non-governmental meeting in London, and in the inter-governmental Cairo Declaration of Human Rights in Islam of 1990, there is a striking agreement with most of the points outlined in the U.N. Universal Declaration. The non-state document stresses political freedoms, while the Cairo Declaration is less enthusiastic about these but affirms strongly the right of states to self-determination. Both, Masud argues, nevertheless represent efforts to find common ground with the global community. (The 1993 Bangkok Declaration, as we have seen, opposes external interventions by using the language of international law, justifying this in part by invoking the right of national self-determination against other universal rights.)

Within the multivocal world of Muslim scholarship, a series of efforts have been underway for decades to adapt and update traditional law to the changing circumstances of modernity, including the accommodation of greater autonomy for women. Among states in predominantly Muslim countries, there is no uniform pattern: Kemalist Turkey forbids public invocation of traditional religious law, while Saudi Arabia has officially installed it as its basic law. Indonesia, while overwhelmingly Muslim, permits a kind of "local option" by its diverse national and religious citizenry. As Masud points out, the various modern scholarly efforts build upon a long history of intellectual struggles to balance the universal and the particular in Islamic culture, dating back to the universalism of the Sufis and medieval philosophers in argument with the jurists of traditional religious law. Today, of course, these efforts are more laden with divisive political potential than ever.

However, Masud also notes, the situation of Muslim nations in today's global distribution of wealth and power makes the debates among international lawyers less than adequate. These inequalities have become very clear to many Muslim intellectuals, increasingly their sensitivity to the rhetorical aspects of arguments that may appear to Western thinkers as simple matters of logic and its application. That is, for Muslim intellectuals today, a certain salience attaches to the questions of who is using the language of human rights, in what context, and for what apparent ends? It has, of course, been Western states and international institutions that have spoken in the language of international law. From the perspective of many non-Westerners, the invocation of such principles to support interventions and attacks on non-Western states smacks of inconsistency, to say the least. This is accentuated, as Masud points out, by the often-overlooked historical experience of nations in the formerly colonial world. The period since 1945, or even the end of the Cold War in the early 1990s, has been very different from that of the West, with far less peace, development, or stability among Muslim lands.

As a result, dialogue across these differences is often tense and difficult. On the other hand, a serious effort to listen to and understand those voices opens up potentially important perspectives on what degree of globalization of ethics might be achievable. A number of formerly colonial countries that signed the 1993 Bangkok Declaration seem inclined toward China's resistance to the extension of human rights interventions within their societies. This has been markedly true for a number of predominantly Muslim states, especially around maintenance of gender inequality and, in some cases, extreme forms of punishment allegedly legitimated by holy law. Whether these conflicts will prove susceptible to evolutionary resolution is hard to predict. However, as Masud argues, it is seems likely that sensitivity to historical complexity, sharpened by the salience of social location for the moral credibility of the participants in the international discussion, is a prerequisite for advancing the dialogue.

The situation of Christianity in this discussion is peculiarly complex. As Max Stackhouse reminds us, the modern West, including many of its chief cultural ideals, is the historical heir of Christendom. So, Christian values and thinking, such as the Natural Law tradition that Mark Murphy has described, have been important formative influences on such post-Enlightenment developments as liberalism and international law. Yet, today, most Christians inhabit lands formerly colonial or even outside the Western orbit altogether. There, suspicion about Western intentions is widespread. Formerly colonized peoples are understandably reluctant to accept at face value moral admonitions addressed to them by former colonizers. Nonetheless, globalizing forces have created the need to find language in which to negotiate relationships. For societies with large Christian or nominally Christian populations, the availability of moral resources stemming from Christian ethical traditions is a matter of live interest.

What could those moral resources be? In his chapter, "Globalization and Christian Ethics," Max Stackhouse takes up this question by pointing out that the Western Protestant tradition is today the site of a lively contest about the most appropriate from of moral reasoning for addressing social and political questions. It is also a tradition that has for some time been arguing over the most relevant way of making moral sense of the spread of globalization. For Stackhouse, there are three essential dimensions of any Christian theological response to the issues of globalization. The first is interpretive: what is the religious and moral meaning of the emerging global order? Here, Christians tend to divide into those who see globalization as "Another Fall," essentially unjust and oppressive, a manifestation of human sinfulness, versus those who view it as primarily a matter of "Providential Grace." Both camps, however, agree that Christianity, by postulating a historical Providence, is committed to reading the "signs of the times" as the start of any ethical assessment of the present situation.

Christianity, on this understanding, also brings to bear a second and a third dimension of its ethical standpoint. Like Judaism and Islam, Christianity has tended to see a kind of natural revelation at work in broad principles of morality such as those summarized in the Decalogue. These "Ten Commandments" have long functioned in Christian thinking as a kind of minimal morality binding on all peoples independently of faith or divine revelation. Presumably, these norms can legitimately be enforced, at least within the structure of legitimate states. However, the Christian churches have also gone beyond this

moral code to enunciate a set of ideal ethical aims, as summoned up in the
Beatitudes drawn from the Sermon on the Mount.

Beyond this second dimension, the Gospels depict Jesus as setting out a
set of moral qualities that define an ideal endpoint to history: the reign of
God. These moral norms ("Blessed are those who hunger and thirst for righteousness...Blessed are the peacemakers...") are not rules so much as ideals
and expressions of ethical aspiration. They define a "perfected" humanity. As
such, they do not so much supersede the minimal morality of the Decalogue
as point toward one possible ideal completion. Christian history, of course,
reveals enormous ambiguity about the proper relationship between these two
sets of ethics, as well as about whether the distinctive Christian ethic ought to
be enforced. The very word Crusade, after all, was the invention of medieval
Christendom. In Stackhouse's version, the preference of today's believers in
Providential Grace is toward an essentially peaceful, persuasive effort to ame-
liorate the global order in the direction of the gentler ideals of Christian perfection. Historically, however, Christians have believed themselves enjoined by
divine command to preach the full realization of the ideal ethic of perfection,
while disagreeing about legitimate and appropriate means for propagating
these values.

The Natural Law tradition represents one longstanding effort to sort out
these ambiguities. It descends from medieval times through the social teachings
of today's Roman Catholic Church, including the doctrine of just and unjust
wars. In Mark Murphy's presentation of this tradition, the problem of interpreting the dispensations of divine Providence is subsumed under the rubric
of "practical rationality." As understood by Thomas Aquinas, from whom the
Roman Catholic concept of natural law descends, practical reasoning starts
from premises based in a universally shared human nature knowable by reason. While the basic structure of natural law (to avoid evil and pursue the good)
is rooted in human nature, its concrete application always requires prudential
judgment that takes account of particular situations and their demands. As a
general approach, Murphy shows, natural law moves back and forth between
general norms and concrete situations, imperatives and situational possibilities in a kind of casuistry, seeking to illuminate cases through principles and to
concretize the meaning of rules through their application to particular events.
This has allowed natural law theorists to accommodate an emphasis upon universal aspirations with the recognition of different "sensibilities" embodied
in particular cultures and legal traditions. From this orientation, natural law
theorists evolved the doctrine and casuistry of just war theory.

While it emphasizes flexibility, natural law thinking contains essentially non-
negotiable aspects. These include recognition of the good of impartiality, as in
the Golden Rule, and a general preference for non-coercive forms of moral
intervention due to both the dignity of human persons and the "intrinsic good
of rational community life." Intervention by force can be legitimate, however,
when decided upon by "legitimate authorities" following "established legal

norms," provided that such intervention is done in the most "efficient" and least intrusive way possible, in accord with the principle of subsidiarity, or that action rightly devolves to the governmental entity nearest the persons involved. The determination of when to apply such principles, however, is ultimately always a matter of the "practical wisdom" or prudence exercised by the relevant authority. In this way, natural law thinking shares elements with the Confucian focus upon nurturing intellectual and moral habits of prudence and enlightened judgment. It also overlaps with liberal international law in emphasizing proper procedure. However, while liberalism stresses the protection of human vulnerabilities as its basic legitimizing principle, natural law's Aristotelian roots lead to a greater stress upon the positive support of human capabilities, including community life.

The history of the natural law tradition provides an early example of the "two-level" approach to global ethics described in Will Kymlicka's "Introduction" to the volume. The first level of "self-standing international" discourse seeks to define minimum standards agreeable to all, while this is supplemented and filled out by a variety of particular ethical traditions. As Kymlicka has pointed out, the legal and ethical principles of the sixteenth-century Spanish Empire were designed on this model, with Thomistic natural law ethics providing the international discourse of universal "reason," and Roman Catholicism the fuller account of human flourishing that the Spanish also saw as their mission to assist in propagating. While in practice the two were often conflated (and the natural law brutally flouted), the structural parallel to today's efforts to erect a human rights regime is noteworthy.

The distinctly modern correction is the formal rejection of imperial sovereignty as a legitimate principle of rule. Autonomy and equality among nations and religions as well as among persons has gained prominence in contemporary efforts toward a renewed "two-tier" global ethics. Today's international lawyers aim to find common agreement and, if possible, make common cause with other ethical traditions. Daniel Philpott provides a provocative example of this process in his account of Roman Catholicism's reversal on the question of the legitimacy of religious pluralism since the 1960s. This instance suggests that a convergence toward practical consensus on political norms can develop even when underlying value positions – such as those of liberal conceptions of human nature versus those foundational to the natural law tradition – remain distinct and at least partially at odds.

Critics might object that natural law's emphasis upon practical rationality and prudential judgment is finally too vague to be of help in providing ethical guidance consonant with the aspirations of international law. The international law tradition has sought to build an institutional structure of adjudication not on the basis of prudence but on positive law and covenants among states. This implicit legal positivism enables international lawyers to sidestep questions of the source of legitimacy for the human rights regime, but it also makes its authority more directly subject to the power of states. But as the examples

Philpott adduces show, international law must also rely upon the development of better understanding across states, since the strength of international
agreements depends upon not only world public opinion but the consent of
states.

The Necessity of Practical Rationality

But is there really, in either international law or in liberalism itself, an alternative to reliance upon morally grounded prudence? Chris Brown's chapter,
"Liberalism and the Globalization of Ethics," shows with effect that even a
strong endorsement of principles cannot provide liberals with a "conceptual
framework within which principles and practice can be reconciled" on the
question of intervention. Liberals of both cosmopolitan and communitarian
leanings wish to affirm both individual rights and the values of international cooperation and non-intervention. Within this framework, both the arguments of
American neo-conservatives in favor of unilateral intervention in Iraq as well
as those of liberals opposed to this intervention because of its abandonment
of unilateralism (and just war casuistry), have standing and merit. In this clash
of competing goods, it is not clear that liberals can resolve the issue without
considerations of essentially prudential character, that is without recourse to
practical reason.

I would argue that the idea of practical rationality despite its historical origins in Greek philosophy and the natural law tradition, should not be seen
primarily as a peculiar feature of those traditions. Rather, the very project of
engaging in dialogue across traditions demands recourse to the idea of practical rationality as its enabling intellectual condition. Intellectual efforts to
recover the tradition of practical reasoning as an intellectual resource with
broad import have been in process for the past several decades.[1] These developments hold out valuable potential for the supporting the difficult practice
of dialogue among traditions. This is because practical reasoning, in contrast
to theoretical thinking, always starts out from the aim at some good or value.
As we have seen, ethical theories postulate various ideals and often elaborate
these at length. In practice, however, goods are always encountered in particular situations and contexts. The great problem for practical rationality is
therefore to discover the meaning of these goods and values in the situation,
to discern the limits of both what is ethically demanded and what is possible.
A particular ethical tradition provides a starting sense of moral salience, but
the "interpretive circle" of practical reasoning requires the effort to test that
moral aim against the complexities of the actual situation – and the sometimes
different moral perceptions of others also involved.

---

[1] See, for example, Stephen Toulmin (2000), *Return to Reason*, as well as Albert R. Jonsen and
   Stephen Toulmin (1988), *The Abuse of Casuistry: A History of Moral Reasoning*.

To reason well practically, good faith dialogue with others is important. Here, cognition cannot be severed from the moral stance of the agent. Without a principled openness to understanding the other, practical reason can become locked into a solipsistic circle of reasoning, with destructive consequences. The aim, then, is not to flee all prejudice by denying particularity, but to strive to broaden the sense of moral salience to encompass wider, and so more universal, understandings. As a methodological premise for the project of globalizing ethics, the priority of practical reasoning means the inventive effort at dialogue as opposed to attempts to impose a point of view from without. Vaclav Havel has posed the issue well in speaking about Europe's need to recover a sense of conscience, by which he means responsibility for its own political and social values. What Havel (1996) finds valuable in the European heritage seems applicable as a value for today's multipolar and pluralistic world as well: "universalism, the commandment to think of everyone, to act as everyone should act, and to look for universally acceptable solutions" (p. 41).

Summing Up: Agreement and Divergence

As a summing up, we might note several key areas of converging agreement and then areas of substantive divergence and disagreement. There are three broad propositions to which all the traditions represented in the volume subscribe. First, there is now general repudiation of any natural hierarchies among peoples or societies. This supports a deepening conviction that persuasion rather than coercion is the ethically preferable option for engaging moral difference. Second, all the traditions surveyed would agree that peaceful ethical pluralism can only be sustained in practice provided that there are at least some universally shared values and agreements about what is legitimate and illegitimate in social and political affairs.

Third, in trying to determine those universally shared norms, none of the traditions claims to have a self-standing algorithm through which to make such decisions. All acknowledge the need to weigh multiple, sometimes conflicting goods, such as the claims of individuals against the welfare of communities, or the value of particular cultural understandings against the needs for shared standards for cooperation across difference. As we have seen, this acknowledgement of the perplexities of judgment opens all participants to the imperative of dialogue and learning from others. In itself, however, awareness of the need for judgment and learning through dialogue does not provide an answer to the question of how the problems of moral diversity can be negotiated in the interest of cooperation and mutual respect among diverse peoples and commitments.

Here the differences we have encountered among the traditions count heavily. There are at least three major areas of divergence. First, there are serious substantive differences among the traditions regarding the relative moral salience of individual action, social order, inclusion, and authority. To put the

matter starkly: while conscientious objection to tyranny or gross evil has resonance in all the great traditions, the liberal acceptance of public disagreement
about matters of principle as contributing to moral progress is less congenial
for societies with Confucian sensibilities and for many Islamic traditions. East
Asian countries place much greater importance upon consensus and, often,
authoritative guidance by government than is compatible with the forms of
liberalism now dominant in much of the West. So, for example, the language
of universal rights can stir antagonism rather than compel assent when it is
perceived as threatening social cohesion or undermining collective responsibility. Again, while feminist concerns about women's dignity resonate in
many societies today, feminism can also arouse suspicion or rejection when it
seems to violate values connected to the family, whether Confucian, Islamic, or
Christian.

Second, the porous nature of social boundaries has made the global pluralism of value traditions an increasingly tense matter. As nations and social
movements struggle to gain control of their lives and identities, issues of propagating values, proselytizing for ideas identified with one or another tradition,
even the diffusion of outlooks attendant upon increased communication and
tourism, become areas of potential conflict. The same situation can appear
quite differently to advocates of what they conceive as enlightened, cosmopolitan norms, on the one hand, and adherents of particular substantive values,
on the other. Faced with what is perceived as serious material or moral threat,
the natural impulse is to defend one's moral commitments by questioning the
legitimacy of those who appear to propagate what undermines one's morale
and identity. A kind of East-West divide is evident in this area as well, though
the issue also cuts through the liberal tradition, in the division between cosmopolitan and national liberals. The major lesson here is that considerations
of moral legitimacy cannot be separated from issues of geopolitical power and
the relative autonomy of states and peoples. These divergences often make
reaching moral understanding across traditions a challenge and arriving at
moral agreement an achievement.

Third, and finally, there remains disagreement about the adequacy of the
discourse of universal human rights to provide a "first tier" of moral agreement
on a global basis. Besides the complications entailed by international law's
role in justifying armed interventions, there stands the question of whether
its insistence on the language of "rights" can do justice to ethical norms such
as collective responsibility and environmental concern. From the perspective
of many of the traditions surveyed, "rights talk" is also suspect because the
tradition of international law seems to want to supplant or at least preempt
ethical decisions based upon sensibilities built up over time with presumably
greater sensitivity to "local" social contexts. So, despite its half century of
successes in winning endorsements from much of the world, international law
embodies a paradox. On the one hand, its "free-standing" features enable it to
provide a context for dialogue about a uniform planetary ethics. On the other

hand, the relative thinness of the consensus it represents renders its undeniable achievements precarious. Whatever may be its future, however, the project of international law seems inevitably tied to the question of the conditions under which a fruitful interchange among ethical traditions can go forward.

By giving analogies and examples that try to speak across traditions, the chapters in this volume provide a variety of suggestive essays in the direction of global ethical dialogue. In doing this, they lay the groundwork for further exploration. They suggest an ethical enterprise that is based upon the aim of making our unavoidable interdependence work positively for the global common good.

Appendix

Key Documents on Global Ethics

A. Universal Declaration of Human Rights

Adopted by the United Nations General Assembly, December 10, 1948.

Preamble

Whereas recognition of the inherent dignity and of the equal and inalienable rights of all members of the human family is the foundation of freedom, justice and peace in the world,

Whereas disregard and contempt for human rights have resulted in barbarous acts which have outraged the conscience of mankind, and the advent of a world in which human beings shall enjoy freedom of speech and belief and freedom from fear and want has been proclaimed as the highest aspiration of the common people,

Whereas it is essential, if man is not to be compelled to have recourse, as a last resort, to rebellion against tyranny and oppression, that human rights should be protected by the rule of law,

Whereas it is essential to promote the development of friendly relations between nations,

Whereas the peoples of the United Nations have in the Charter reaffirmed their faith in fundamental human rights, in the dignity and worth of the human person and in the equal rights of men and women and have determined to promote social progress and better standards of life in larger freedom,

Whereas Member States have pledged themselves to achieve, in cooperation with the United Nations, the promotion of universal respect for and observance of human rights and fundamental freedoms,

Whereas a common understanding of these rights and freedoms is of the greatest importance for the full realization of this pledge,

Now, therefore,

The General Assembly,

Proclaims this Universal Declaration of Human Rights as a common standard of achievement for all peoples and all nations, to the end that every individual and every organ of society, keeping this Declaration constantly in mind, shall strive by teaching and education to promote respect for these rights and freedoms and by progressive measures, national and international, to secure their universal and effective recognition and observance, both among the peoples of Member States themselves and among the peoples of territories under their jurisdiction.

Article 1
All human beings are born free and equal in dignity and rights. They are endowed with reason and conscience and should act towards one another in a spirit of brotherhood.

Article 2
Everyone is entitled to all the rights and freedoms set forth in this Declaration, without distinction of any kind, such as race, colour, sex, language, religion, political or other opinion, national or social origin, property, birth or other status.

Furthermore, no distinction shall be made on the basis of the political, jurisdictional or international status of the country or territory to which a person belongs, whether it be independent, trust, non-self-governing or under any other limitation of sovereignty.

Article 3
Everyone has the right to life, liberty and security of person.

Article 4
No one shall be held in slavery or servitude; slavery and the slave trade shall be prohibited in all their forms.

Article 5
No one shall be subjected to torture or to cruel, inhuman or degrading treatment or punishment.

Article 6
Everyone has the right to recognition everywhere as a person before the law.

Article 7
All are equal before the law and are entitled without any discrimination to equal protection of the law. All are entitled to equal protection against any discrimination in violation of this Declaration and against any incitement to such discrimination.

Article 8
Everyone has the right to an effective remedy by the competent national tribunals for acts violating the fundamental rights granted him by the constitution or by law.

Article 9
No one shall be subjected to arbitrary arrest, detention or exile.

Article 10
Everyone is entitled in full equality to a fair and public hearing by an independent and impartial tribunal, in the determination of his rights and obligations and of any criminal charge against him.

Article 11
Everyone charged with a penal offence has the right to be presumed innocent until proved guilty according to law in a public trial at which he has had all the guarantees necessary for his defence.

No one shall be held guilty of any penal offence on account of any act or omission which did not constitute a penal offence, under national or international law, at the time when it was committed. Nor shall a heavier penalty be imposed than the one that was applicable at the time the penal offence was committed.

Article 12
No one shall be subjected to arbitrary interference with his privacy, family, home or correspondence, nor to attacks upon his honour and reputation. Everyone has the right to the protection of the law against such interference or attacks.

Article 13
Everyone has the right to freedom of movement and residence within the borders of each State.

Everyone has the right to leave any country, including his own, and to return to his country.

Article 14
Everyone has the right to seek and to enjoy in other countries asylum from persecution.

This right may not be invoked in the case of prosecutions genuinely arising from non-political crimes or from acts contrary to the purposes and principles of the United Nations.

Article 15
Everyone has the right to a nationality.

No one shall be arbitrarily deprived of his nationality nor denied the right to change his nationality.

Article 16
Men and women of full age, without any limitation due to race, nationality or religion, have the right to marry and to found a family. They are entitled to equal rights as to marriage, during marriage and at its dissolution.

Marriage shall be entered into only with the free and full consent of the intending spouses.

The family is the natural and fundamental group unit of society and is entitled to protection by society and the State.

Article 17
Everyone has the right to own property alone as well as in association with others.

No one shall be arbitrarily deprived of his property.

Article 18
Everyone has the right to freedom of thought, conscience and religion; this right includes freedom to change his religion or belief, and freedom, either alone or in community with others and in public or private, to manifest his religion or belief in teaching, practice, worship and observance.

Article 19
Everyone has the right to freedom of opinion and expression; this right includes freedom to hold opinions without interference and to seek, receive and impart information and ideas through any media and regardless of frontiers.

Article 20
Everyone has the right to freedom of peaceful assembly and association.

No one may be compelled to belong to an association.

Article 21
Everyone has the right to take part in the government of his country, directly or through freely chosen representatives.

Everyone has the right to equal access to public service in his country.

The will of the people shall be the basis of the authority of government; this will shall be expressed in periodic and genuine elections which shall be by universal and equal suffrage and shall be held by secret vote or by equivalent free voting procedures.

Article 22
Everyone, as a member of society, has the right to social security and is entitled to realization, through national effort and international co-operation and in

accordance with the organization and resources of each State, of the economic, social and cultural rights indispensable for his dignity and the free development of his personality.

Article 23
Everyone has the right to work, to free choice of employment, to just and favourable conditions of work and to protection against unemployment.

Everyone, without any discrimination, has the right to equal pay for equal work.

Everyone who works has the right to just and favourable remuneration ensuring for himself and his family an existence worthy of human dignity, and supplemented, if necessary, by other means of social protection.

Everyone has the right to form and to join trade unions for the protection of his interests.

Article 24
Everyone has the right to rest and leisure, including reasonable limitation of working hours and periodic holidays with pay.

Article 25
Everyone has the right to a standard of living adequate for the health and well-being of himself and of his family, including food, clothing, housing and medical care and necessary social services, and the right to security in the event of unemployment, sickness, disability, widowhood, old age or other lack of livelihood in circumstances beyond his control.

Motherhood and childhood are entitled to special care and assistance. All children, whether born in or out of wedlock, shall enjoy the same social protection.

Article 26
Everyone has the right to education. Education shall be free, at least in the elementary and fundamental stages. Elementary education shall be compulsory. Technical and professional education shall be made generally available and higher education shall be equally accessible to all on the basis of merit.

Education shall be directed to the full development of the human personality and to the strengthening of respect for human rights and fundamental freedoms. It shall promote understanding, tolerance and friendship among all nations, racial or religious groups, and shall further the activities of the United Nations for the maintenance of peace.

Parents have a prior right to choose the kind of education that shall be given to their children.

Article 27
Everyone has the right freely to participate in the cultural life of the community, to enjoy the arts and to share in scientific advancement and its benefits.

Everyone has the right to the protection of the moral and material interests resulting from any scientific, literary or artistic production of which he is the author.

Article 28

Everyone is entitled to a social and international order in which the rights and freedoms set forth in this Declaration can be fully realized.

Article 29

Everyone has duties to the community in which alone the free and full development of his personality is possible.

In the exercise of his rights and freedoms, everyone shall be subject only to such limitations as are determined by law solely for the purpose of securing due recognition and respect for the rights and freedoms of others and of meeting the just requirements of morality, public order and the general welfare in a democratic society.

These rights and freedoms may in no case be exercised contrary to the purposes and principles of the United Nations.

Article 30

Nothing in this Declaration may be interpreted as implying for any State, group or person any right to engage in any activity or to perform any act aimed at the destruction of any of the rights and freedoms set forth herein.

B. International Covenant on Civil and Political Rights

Adopted by the United Nations General Assembly, December 16, 1966.

Preamble

The States Parties to the present Covenant,

Considering that, in accordance with the principles proclaimed in the Charter of the United Nations, recognition of the inherent dignity and of the equal and inalienable rights of all members of the human family is the foundation of freedom, justice and peace in the world,

Recognizing that these rights derive from the inherent dignity of the human person,

Recognizing that, in accordance with the Universal Declaration of Human Rights, the ideal of free human beings enjoying civil and political freedom and freedom from fear and want can only be achieved if conditions are created whereby everyone may enjoy his civil and political rights, as well as his economic, social and cultural rights,

Considering the obligation of States under the Charter of the United Nations to promote universal respect for, and observance of, human rights and freedoms,

Realizing that the individual, having duties to other individuals and to the community to which he belongs, is under a responsibility to strive for the promotion and observance of the rights recognized in the present Covenant,

Agree upon the following articles:

PART I

Article 1

1. All peoples have the right of self-determination. By virtue of that right they freely determine their political status and freely pursue their economic, social and cultural development.
2. All peoples may, for their own ends, freely dispose of their natural wealth and resources without prejudice to any obligations arising out of international economic co-operation, based upon the principle of mutual benefit, and international law. In no case may a people be deprived of its own means of subsistence.
3. The States Parties to the present Covenant, including those having responsibility for the administration of Non-Self-Governing and Trust Territories, shall promote the realization of the right of self-determination, and shall respect that right, in conformity with the provisions of the Charter of the United Nations.

PART II

Article 2

1. Each State Party to the present Covenant undertakes to respect and to ensure to all individuals within its territory and subject to its jurisdiction the rights recognized in the present Covenant, without distinction of any kind, such as race, colour, sex, language, religion, political or other opinion, national or social origin, property, birth or other status.

2. Where not already provided for by existing legislative or other measures, each State Party to the present Covenant undertakes to take the necessary steps, in accordance with its constitutional processes and with the provisions of the present Covenant, to adopt such legislative or other measures as may be necessary to give effect to the rights recognized in the present Covenant.

3. Each State Party to the present Covenant undertakes:
    (a) To ensure that any person whose rights or freedoms as herein recognized are violated shall have an effective remedy, notwithstanding that the violation has been committed by persons acting in an official capacity;
    (b) To ensure that any person claiming such a remedy shall have his right thereto determined by competent judicial, administrative or legislative authorities, or by any other competent authority provided for by the legal system of the State, and to develop the possibilities of judicial remedy;
    (c) To ensure that the competent authorities shall enforce such remedies when granted.

Article 3

The States Parties to the present Covenant undertake to ensure the equal right of men and women to the enjoyment of all civil and political rights set forth in the present Covenant.

Article 4

1. In time of public emergency which threatens the life of the nation and the existence of which is officially proclaimed, the States Parties to the present Covenant may take measures derogating from their obligations under the present Covenant to the extent strictly required by the exigencies of the situation, provided that such measures are not inconsistent with their other obligations under international law and do not involve discrimination solely on the ground of race, colour, sex, language, religion or social origin.

2. No derogation from articles 6, 7, 8 (paragraphs I and 2), 11, 15, 16 and 18 may be made under this provision.

3. Any State Party to the present Covenant availing itself of the right of derogation shall immediately inform the other States Parties to the present Covenant, through the intermediary of the Secretary-General of the United Nations, of the provisions from which it has derogated and of the reasons by which it was actuated. A further communication shall be made, through the same intermediary, on the date on which it terminates such derogation.

Article 5

1. Nothing in the present Covenant may be interpreted as implying for any State, group or person any right to engage in any activity or perform any act aimed at the destruction of any of the rights and freedoms recognized herein or at their limitation to a greater extent than is provided for in the present Covenant.
2. There shall be no restriction upon or derogation from any of the fundamental human rights recognized or existing in any State Party to the present Covenant pursuant to law, conventions, regulations or custom on the pretext that the present Covenant does not recognize such rights or that it recognizes them to a lesser extent.

PART III

Article 6

1. Every human being has the inherent right to life. This right shall be protected by law. No one shall be arbitrarily deprived of his life.
2. In countries which have not abolished the death penalty, sentence of death may be imposed only for the most serious crimes in accordance with the law in force at the time of the commission of the crime and not contrary to the provisions of the present Covenant and to the Convention on the Prevention and Punishment of the Crime of Genocide. This penalty can only be carried out pursuant to a final judgement rendered by a competent court.
3. When deprivation of life constitutes the crime of genocide, it is understood that nothing in this article shall authorize any State Party to the present Covenant to derogate in any way from any obligation assumed under the provisions of the Convention on the Prevention and Punishment of the Crime of Genocide.
4. Anyone sentenced to death shall have the right to seek pardon or commutation of the sentence. Amnesty, pardon or commutation of the sentence of death may be granted in all cases.
5. Sentence of death shall not be imposed for crimes committed by persons below eighteen years of age and shall not be carried out on pregnant women.

6. Nothing in this article shall be invoked to delay or to prevent the abolition of capital punishment by any State Party to the present Covenant.

Article 7
No one shall be subjected to torture or to cruel, inhuman or degrading treatment or punishment. In particular, no one shall be subjected without his free
consent to medical or scientific experimentation.

Article 8
1. No one shall be held in slavery; slavery and the slave-trade in all their
   forms shall be prohibited.
2. No one shall be held in servitude.
3. (a) No one shall be required to perform forced or compulsory labour;
   (b) Paragraph 3 (a) shall not be held to preclude, in countries where
       imprisonment with hard labour may be imposed as a punishment for
       a crime, the performance of hard labour in pursuance of a sentence
       to such punishment by a competent court;
   (c) For the purpose of this paragraph the term "forced or compulsory
       labour" shall not include:
       (i) Any work or service, not referred to in subparagraph (b), nor-
           mally required of a person who is under detention in conse-
           quence of a lawful order of a court, or of a person during con-
           ditional release from such detention;
       (ii) Any service of a military character and, in countries where con-
            scientious objection is recognized, any national service required
            by law of conscientious objectors;
       (iii) Any service exacted in cases of emergency or calamity threat-
             ening the life or well-being of the community;
       (iv) Any work or service which forms part of normal civil obliga-
            tions.

Article 9
1. Everyone has the right to liberty and security of person. No one shall be
   subjected to arbitrary arrest or detention. No one shall be deprived of his
   liberty except on such grounds and in accordance with such procedure
   as are established by law.
2. Anyone who is arrested shall be informed, at the time of arrest, of the
   reasons for his arrest and shall be promptly informed of any charges
   against him.
3. Anyone arrested or detained on a criminal charge shall be brought
   promptly before a judge or other officer authorized by law to exercise
   judicial power and shall be entitled to trial within a reasonable time or
   to release. It shall not be the general rule that persons awaiting trial

shall be detained in custody, but release may be subject to guarantees to appear for trial, at any other stage of the judicial proceedings, and, should occasion arise, for execution of the judgement.

4. Anyone who is deprived of his liberty by arrest or detention shall be entitled to take proceedings before a court, in order that court may decide without delay on the lawfulness of his detention and order his release if the detention is not lawful.

5. Anyone who has been the victim of unlawful arrest or detention shall have an enforceable right to compensation.

Article 10

1. All persons deprived of their liberty shall be treated with humanity and with respect for the inherent dignity of the human person.

2. (a) Accused persons shall, save in exceptional circumstances, be segregated from convicted persons and shall be subject to separate treatment appropriate to their status as unconvicted persons;

   (b) Accused juvenile persons shall be separated from adults and brought as speedily as possible for adjudication.

3. The penitentiary system shall comprise treatment of prisoners the essential aim of which shall be their reformation and social rehabilitation. Juvenile offenders shall be segregated from adults and be accorded treatment appropriate to their age and legal status.

Article 11

No one shall be imprisoned merely on the ground of inability to fulfil a contractual obligation.

Article 12

1. Everyone lawfully within the territory of a State shall, within that territory, have the right to liberty of movement and freedom to choose his residence.

2. Everyone shall be free to leave any country, including his own.

3. The above-mentioned rights shall not be subject to any restrictions except those which are provided by law, are necessary to protect national security, public order (*ordre public*), public health or morals or the rights and freedoms of others, and are consistent with the other rights recognized in the present Covenant.

4. No one shall be arbitrarily deprived of the right to enter his own country.

Article 13

An alien lawfully in the territory of a State Party to the present Covenant may be expelled therefrom only in pursuance of a decision reached in accordance with law and shall, except where compelling reasons of national security otherwise require, be allowed to submit the reasons against his expulsion and to have his case reviewed by, and be represented for the purpose before, the competent authority or a person or persons especially designated by the competent authority.

Article 14

1. All persons shall be equal before the courts and tribunals. In the determination of any criminal charge against him, or of his rights and obligations in a suit at law, everyone shall be entitled to a fair and public hearing by a competent, independent and impartial tribunal established by law. The press and the public may be excluded from all or part of a trial for reasons of morals, public order *(ordre public)* or national security in a democratic society, or when the interest of the private lives of the parties so requires, or to the extent strictly necessary in the opinion of the court in special circumstances where publicity would prejudice the interests of justice; but any judgement rendered in a criminal case or in a suit at law shall be made public except where the interest of juvenile persons otherwise requires or the proceedings concern matrimonial disputes or the guardianship of children.

2. Everyone charged with a criminal offence shall have the right to be presumed innocent until proved guilty according to law.

3. In the determination of any criminal charge against him, everyone shall be entitled to the following minimum guarantees, in full equality:

    (a) To be informed promptly and in detail in a language which he understands of the nature and cause of the charge against him;

    (b) To have adequate time and facilities for the preparation of his defence and to communicate with counsel of his own choosing;

    (c) To be tried without undue delay;

    (d) To be tried in his presence, and to defend himself in person or through legal assistance of his own choosing; to be informed, if he does not have legal assistance, of this right; and to have legal assistance assigned to him, in any case where the interests of justice so require, and without payment by him in any such case if he does not have sufficient means to pay for it;

    (e) To examine, or have examined, the witnesses against him and to obtain the attendance and examination of witnesses on his behalf under the same conditions as witnesses against him;

    (f) To have the free assistance of an interpreter if he cannot understand or speak the language used in court;

    (g) Not to be compelled to testify against himself or to confess guilt.

4. In the case of juvenile persons, the procedure shall be such as will take account of their age and the desirability of promoting their rehabilitation.

5. Everyone convicted of a crime shall have the right to his conviction and sentence being reviewed by a higher tribunal according to law.

6. When a person has by a final decision been convicted of a criminal offence and when subsequently his conviction has been reversed or he has been pardoned on the ground that a new or newly discovered fact shows conclusively that there has been a miscarriage of justice, the person who has suffered punishment as a result of such conviction shall be compensated according to law, unless it is proved that the non-disclosure of the unknown fact in time is wholly or partly attributable to him.

7. No one shall be liable to be tried or punished again for an offence for which he has already been finally convicted or acquitted in accordance with the law and penal procedure of each country.

Article 15

1. No one shall be held guilty of any criminal offence on account of any act or omission which did not constitute a criminal offence, under national or international law, at the time when it was committed. Nor shall a heavier penalty be imposed than the one that was applicable at the time when the criminal offence was committed. If, subsequent to the commission of the offence, provision is made by law for the imposition of the lighter penalty, the offender shall benefit thereby.

2. Nothing in this article shall prejudice the trial and punishment of any person for any act or omission which, at the time when it was committed, was criminal according to the general principles of law recognized by the community of nations.

Article 16

Everyone shall have the right to recognition everywhere as a person before the law.

Article 17

1. No one shall be subjected to arbitrary or unlawful interference with his privacy, family, home or correspondence, nor to unlawful attacks on his honour and reputation.

2. Everyone has the right to the protection of the law against such interference or attacks.

Article 18

1. Everyone shall have the right to freedom of thought, conscience and religion. This right shall include freedom to have or to adopt a religion or belief of his choice, and freedom, either individually or in community with others and in public or private, to manifest his religion or belief in worship, observance, practice and teaching.

2. No one shall be subject to coercion which would impair his freedom to have or to adopt a religion or belief of his choice.
3. Freedom to manifest one's religion or beliefs may be subject only to such limitations as are prescribed by law and are necessary to protect public safety, order, health, or morals or the fundamental rights and freedoms of others.
4. The States parties to the present Covenant undertake to have respect for the liberty of parents and, when applicable, legal guardians to ensure the religious and moral education of their children in conformity with their own convictions.

Article 19
1. Everyone shall have the right to hold opinions without interference.
2. Everyone shall have the right to freedom of expression; this right shall include freedom to seek, receive and impart information and ideas of all kinds, regardless of frontiers, either orally, in writing or in print, in the form of art, or through any other media of his choice.
3. The exercise of the rights provided for in paragraph 2 of this article carries with it special duties and responsibilities. It may therefore be subject to certain restrictions, but these shall only be such as are provided by law and are necessary:
   (a) For respect of the rights or reputations of others;
   (b) For the protection of national security or of public order (*ordre public*), or of public health or morals.

Article 20
1. Any propaganda for war shall be prohibited by law.
2. Any advocacy of national, racial or religious hatred that constitutes incitement to discrimination, hostility or violence shall be prohibited by law.

Article 21
The right of peaceful assembly shall be recognized. No restrictions may be placed on the exercise of this right other than those imposed in conformity with the law and which are necessary in a democratic society in the interests of national security or public safety, public order (*ordre public*), the protection of public health or morals or the protection of the rights and freedoms of others.

Article 22
1. Everyone shall have the right to freedom of association with others, including the right to form and join trade unions for the protection of his interests.
2. No restrictions may be placed on the exercise of this right other than those which are prescribed by law and which are necessary in a

democratic society in the interests of national security or public safety, public order (*ordre public*), the protection of public health or morals or the protection of the rights and freedoms of others. This article shall not prevent the imposition of lawful restrictions on members of the armed forces and of the police in their exercise of this right.

3. Nothing in this article shall authorize States Parties to the International Labour Organisation Convention of 1948 concerning Freedom of Association and Protection of the Right to Organize to take legislative measures which would prejudice, or to apply the law in such a manner as to prejudice, the guarantees provided for in that Convention.

Article 23

1. The family is the natural and fundamental group unit of society and is entitled to protection by society and the State.
2. The right of men and women of marriageable age to marry and to found a family shall be recognized.
3. No marriage shall be entered into without the free and full consent of the intending spouses.
4. States Parties to the present Covenant shall take appropriate steps to ensure equality of rights and responsibilities of spouses as to marriage, during marriage and at its dissolution. In the case of dissolution, provision shall be made for the necessary protection of any children.

Article 24

1. Every child shall have, without any discrimination as to race, colour, sex, language, religion, national or social origin, property or birth, the right to such measures of protection as are required by his status as a minor, on the part of his family, society and the State.
2. Every child shall be registered immediately after birth and shall have a name.
3. Every child has the right to acquire a nationality.

Article 25

Every citizen shall have the right and the opportunity, without any of the distinctions mentioned in article 2 and without unreasonable restrictions:

(a) To take part in the conduct of public affairs, directly or through freely chosen representatives;
(b) To vote and to be elected at genuine periodic elections which shall be by universal and equal suffrage and shall be held by secret ballot, guaranteeing the free expression of the will of the electors;
(c) To have access, on general terms of equality, to public service in his country.

Article 26

All persons are equal before the law and are entitled without any discrimination to the equal protection of the law. In this respect, the law shall prohibit any discrimination and guarantee to all persons equal and effective protection against discrimination on any ground such as race, colour, sex, language, religion, political or other opinion, national or social origin, property, birth or other status.

Article 27

In those States in which ethnic, religious or linguistic minorities exist, persons belonging to such minorities shall not be denied the right, in community with the other members of their group, to enjoy their own culture, to profess and practice their religion, or to use their own language.

C. International Covenant on Social, Economic and Cultural Rights

Adopted by the United Nations General Assembly, December 16, 1966.

Preamble

The States Parties to the present Covenant,

Considering that, in accordance with the principles proclaimed in the Charter of the United Nations, recognition of the inherent dignity and of the equal and inalienable rights of all members of the human family is the foundation of freedom, justice and peace in the world,

Recognizing that these rights derive from the inherent dignity of the human person,

Recognizing that, in accordance with the Universal Declaration of Human Rights, the ideal of free human beings enjoying freedom from fear and want can only be achieved if conditions are created whereby everyone may enjoy his economic, social and cultural rights, as well as his civil and political rights,

Considering the obligation of States under the Charter of the United Nations to promote universal respect for, and observance of, human rights and freedoms,

Realizing that the individual, having duties to other individuals and to the community to which he belongs, is under a responsibility to strive for the promotion and observance of the rights recognized in the present Covenant,

Agree upon the following articles:

PART I

Article 1

1. All peoples have the right of self-determination. By virtue of that right they freely determine their political status and freely pursue their economic, social and cultural development.
2. All peoples may, for their own ends, freely dispose of their natural wealth and resources without prejudice to any obligations arising out of international economic co-operation, based upon the principle of mutual benefit, and international law. In no case may a people be deprived of its own means of subsistence.
3. The States Parties to the present Covenant, including those having responsibility for the administration of Non-Self-Governing and

Trust Territories, shall promote the realization of the right of self-determination, and shall respect that right, in conformity with the provisions of the Charter of the United Nations.

PART II

Article 2

1. Each State Party to the present Covenant undertakes to take steps, individually and through international assistance and co-operation, especially economic and technical, to the maximum of its available resources, with a view to achieving progressively the full realization of the rights recognized in the present Covenant by all appropriate means, including particularly the adoption of legislative measures.

2. The States Parties to the present Covenant undertake to guarantee that the rights enunciated in the present Covenant will be exercised without discrimination of any kind as to race, colour, sex, language, religion, political or other opinion, national or social origin, property, birth or other status.

3. Developing countries, with due regard to human rights and their national economy, may determine to what extent they would guarantee the economic rights recognized in the present Covenant to non-nationals.

Article 3

The States Parties to the present Covenant undertake to ensure the equal right of men and women to the enjoyment of all economic, social and cultural rights set forth in the present Covenant.

Article 4

The States Parties to the present Covenant recognize that, in the enjoyment of those rights provided by the State in conformity with the present Covenant, the State may subject such rights only to such limitations as are determined by law only in so far as this may be compatible with the nature of these rights and solely for the purpose of promoting the general welfare in a democratic society.

Article 5

1. Nothing in the present Covenant may be interpreted as implying for any State, group or person any right to engage in any activity or to perform any act aimed at the destruction of any of the rights or freedoms recognized herein, or at their limitation to a greater extent than is provided for in the present Covenant.

2. No restriction upon or derogation from any of the fundamental human rights recognized or existing in any country in virtue of law, conventions, regulations or custom shall be admitted on the pretext that the present

Covenant does not recognize such rights or that it recognizes them to a lesser extent.

PART III

Article 6
1. The States Parties to the present Covenant recognize the right to work, which includes the right of everyone to the opportunity to gain his living by work which he freely chooses or accepts, and will take appropriate steps to safeguard this right.
2. The steps to be taken by a State Party to the present Covenant to achieve the full realization of this right shall include technical and vocational guidance and training programmes, policies and techniques to achieve steady economic, social and cultural development and full and productive employment under conditions safeguarding fundamental political and economic freedoms to the individual.

Article 7
The States Parties to the present Covenant recognize the right of everyone to the enjoyment of just and favourable conditions of work which ensure, in particular:

(a) Remuneration which provides all workers, as a minimum, with:
  (i) Fair wages and equal remuneration for work of equal value without distinction of any kind, in particular women being guaranteed conditions of work not inferior to those enjoyed by men, with equal pay for equal work;
  (ii) A decent living for themselves and their families in accordance with the provisions of the present Covenant;
(b) Safe and healthy working conditions;
(c) Equal opportunity for everyone to be promoted in his employment to an appropriate higher level, subject to no considerations other than those of seniority and competence;
(d) Rest, leisure and reasonable limitation of working hours and periodic holidays with pay, as well as remuneration for public holidays.

Article 8
1. The States Parties to the present Covenant undertake to ensure:
  (a) The right of everyone to form trade unions and join the trade union of his choice, subject only to the rules of the organization concerned, for the promotion and protection of his economic and social interests. No restrictions may be placed on the exercise of this right other than those prescribed by law and which are necessary in a

democratic society in the interests of national security or public order or for the protection of the rights and freedoms of others;

(b) The right of trade unions to establish national federations or confederations and the right of the latter to form or join international trade-union organizations;

(c) The right of trade unions to function freely subject to no limitations other than those prescribed by law and which are necessary in a democratic society in the interests of national security or public order or for the protection of the rights and freedoms of others;

(d) The right to strike, provided that it is exercised in conformity with the laws of the particular country.

2. This article shall not prevent the imposition of lawful restrictions on the exercise of these rights by members of the armed forces or of the police or of the administration of the State.

3. Nothing in this article shall authorize States Parties to the International Labour Organisation Convention of 1948 concerning Freedom of Association and Protection of the Right to Organize to take legislative measures which would prejudice, or apply the law in such a manner as would prejudice, the guarantees provided for in that Convention.

Article 9
The States Parties to the present Covenant recognize the right of everyone to social security, including social insurance.

Article 10
The States Parties to the present Covenant recognize that:

1. The widest possible protection and assistance should be accorded to the family, which is the natural and fundamental group unit of society, particularly for its establishment and while it is responsible for the care and education of dependent children. Marriage must be entered into with the free consent of the intending spouses.

2. Special protection should be accorded to mothers during a reasonable period before and after childbirth. During such period working mothers should be accorded paid leave or leave with adequate social security benefits.

3. Special measures of protection and assistance should be taken on behalf of all children and young persons without any discrimination for reasons of parentage or other conditions. Children and young persons should be protected from economic and social exploitation. Their employment in work harmful to their morals or health or dangerous to life or likely to hamper their normal development should be punishable by law. States should also set age limits below which the paid employment of child labour should be prohibited and punishable by law.

Article 11

1. The States Parties to the present Covenant recognize the right of everyone to an adequate standard of living for himself and his family, including adequate food, clothing and housing, and to the continuous improvement of living conditions. The States Parties will take appropriate steps to ensure the realization of this right, recognizing to this effect the essential importance of international co-operation based on free consent.

2. The States Parties to the present Covenant, recognizing the fundamental right of everyone to be free from hunger, shall take, individually and through international co-operation, the measures, including specific programmes, which are needed:

   (a) To improve methods of production, conservation and distribution of food by making full use of technical and scientific knowledge, by disseminating knowledge of the principles of nutrition and by developing or reforming agrarian systems in such a way as to achieve the most efficient development and utilization of natural resources;

   (b) Taking into account the problems of both food-importing and food-exporting countries, to ensure an equitable distribution of world food supplies in relation to need.

Article 12

1. The States Parties to the present Covenant recognize the right of everyone to the enjoyment of the highest attainable standard of physical and mental health.

2. The steps to be taken by the States Parties to the present Covenant to achieve the full realization of this right shall include those necessary for:

   (a) The provision for the reduction of the stillbirth-rate and of infant mortality and for the healthy development of the child;

   (b) The improvement of all aspects of environmental and industrial hygiene;

   (c) The prevention, treatment and control of epidemic, endemic, occupational and other diseases;

   (d) The creation of conditions which would assure to all medical service and medical attention in the event of sickness.

Article 13

1. The States Parties to the present Covenant recognize the right of everyone to education. They agree that education shall be directed to the full development of the human personality and the sense of its dignity, and shall strengthen the respect for human rights and fundamental freedoms. They further agree that education shall enable all persons to

participate effectively in a free society, promote understanding, tolerance and friendship among all nations and all racial, ethnic or religious groups, and further the activities of the United Nations for the maintenance of peace.

2. The States Parties to the present Covenant recognize that, with a view to achieving the full realization of this right:

   (a) Primary education shall be compulsory and available free to all;

   (b) Secondary education in its different forms, including technical and vocational secondary education, shall be made generally available and accessible to all by every appropriate means, and in particular by the progressive introduction of free education;

   (c) Higher education shall be made equally accessible to all, on the basis of capacity, by every appropriate means, and in particular by the progressive introduction of free education;

   (d) Fundamental education shall be encouraged or intensified as far as possible for those persons who have not received or completed the whole period of their primary education;

   (e) The development of a system of schools at all levels shall be actively pursued, an adequate fellowship system shall be established, and the material conditions of teaching staff shall be continuously improved.

3. The States Parties to the present Covenant undertake to have respect for the liberty of parents and, when applicable, legal guardians to choose for their children schools, other than those established by the public authorities, which conform to such minimum educational standards as may be laid down or approved by the State and to ensure the religious and moral education of their children in conformity with their own convictions.

4. No part of this article shall be construed so as to interfere with the liberty of individuals and bodies to establish and direct educational institutions, subject always to the observance of the principles set forth in paragraph I of this article and to the requirement that the education given in such institutions shall conform to such minimum standards as may be laid down by the State.

Article 14

Each State Party to the present Covenant which, at the time of becoming a Party, has not been able to secure in its metropolitan territory or other territories under its jurisdiction compulsory primary education, free of charge, undertakes, within two years, to work out and adopt a detailed plan of action for the progressive implementation, within a reasonable number of years, to be fixed in the plan, of the principle of compulsory education free of charge for all.

Article 15

1. The States Parties to the present Covenant recognize the right of every-one:

   (a) To take part in cultural life;
   (b) To enjoy the benefits of scientific progress and its applications;
   (c) To benefit from the protection of the moral and material interests resulting from any scientific, literary or artistic production of which he is the author.

2. The steps to be taken by the States Parties to the present Covenant to achieve the full realization of this right shall include those necessary for the conservation, the development and the diffusion of science and culture.

3. The States Parties to the present Covenant undertake to respect the freedom indispensable for scientific research and creative activity.

4. The States Parties to the present Covenant recognize the benefits to be derived from the encouragement and development of international contacts and co-operation in the scientific and cultural fields.

D. Declaration Toward a Global Ethic

Endorsed by the Parliament of the World's Religions in Chicago, September 4, 1993.

The Principles of a Global Ethic

Our world is experiencing a fundamental crisis: A crisis in global economy, global ecology, and global politics. The lack of a grand vision, the tangle of unresolved problems, political paralysis, mediocre political leadership with little insight or foresight, and in general too little sense for the commonweal are seen everywhere: Too many old answers to new challenges.

Hundreds of millions of human beings on our planet increasingly suffer from unemployment, poverty, hunger, and the destruction of their families. Hope for a lasting peace among nations slips away from us. There are tensions between the sexes and generations. Children die, kill, and are killed. More and more countries are shaken by corruption in politics and business. It is increasingly difficult to live together peacefully in our cities because of social, racial, and ethnic conflicts, the abuse of drugs, organized crime, and even anarchy. Even neighbors often live in fear of one another. Our planet continues to be ruthlessly plundered. A collapse of the ecosystem threatens us.

Time and again we see leaders and members of religions incite aggression, fanaticism, hate, and xenophobia – even inspire and legitimize violent and bloody conflicts. Religion often is misused for purely power-political goals, including war. We are filled with disgust.

We condemn these blights and declare that they need not be. An ethic already exists within the religious teachings of the world which can counter the global distress. Of course this ethic provides no direct solution for all the immense problems of the world, but it does supply the moral foundation for a better individual and global order: A vision which can lead women and men away from despair, and society away from chaos.

We are persons who have committed ourselves to the precepts and practices of the world's religions. We confirm that there is already a consensus among the religions which can be the basis for a global ethic – a minimal fundamental consensus concerning binding values, irrevocable standards, and fundamental moral attitudes.

I. No New Global Order without a New Global Ethic

We women and men of various religions and regions of Earth therefore address all people, religious and non-religious. We wish to express the following convictions which we hold in common:

- We all have a responsibility for a better global order.
- Our involvement for the sake of human rights, freedom, justice, peace, and the preservation of Earth is absolutely necessary.

- Our different religious and cultural traditions must not prevent our common involvement in opposing all forms of inhumanity and working for greater humaneness.
- The principles expressed in this Global Ethic can be affirmed by all persons with ethical convictions, whether religiously grounded or not.
- As religious and spiritual persons we base our lives on an Ultimate Reality, and draw spiritual power and hope therefrom, in trust, in prayer or meditation, in word or silence. We have a special responsibility for the welfare of all humanity and care for the planet Earth. We do not consider ourselves better than other women and men, but we trust that the ancient wisdom of our religions can point the way for the future.

After two world wars and the end of the cold war, the collapse of fascism and nazism, the shaking to the foundations of communism and colonialism, humanity has entered a new phase of its history. Today we possess sufficient economic, cultural, and spiritual resources to introduce a better global order. But old and new ethnic, national, social, economic, and religious tensions threaten the peaceful building of a better world. We have experienced greater technological progress than ever before, yet we see that world-wide poverty, hunger, death of children, unemployment, misery, and the destruction of nature have not diminished but rather have increased. Many peoples are threatened with economic ruin, social disarray, political marginalization, ecological catastrophe, and national collapse.

In such a dramatic global situation humanity needs a vision of peoples living peacefully together, of ethnic and ethical groupings and of religions sharing responsibility for the care of Earth. A vision rests on hopes, goals, ideals, standards. But all over the world these have slipped from our hands. Yet we are convinced that, despite their frequent abuses and failures, it is the communities of faith who bear a responsibility to demonstrate that such hopes, ideals, and standards can be guarded, grounded, and lived. This is especially true in the modern state. Guarantees of freedom of conscience and religion are necessary but they do not substitute for binding values, convictions, and norms which are valid for all humans regardless of their social origin, sex, skin color, language, or religion.

We are convinced of the fundamental unity of the human family on Earth. We recall the 1948 Universal Declaration of Human Rights of the United Nations. What it formally proclaimed on the level of rights we wish to confirm and deepen here from the perspective of an ethic: The full realization of the intrinsic dignity of the human person, the inalienable freedom and equality in principle of all humans, and the necessary solidarity and interdependence of all humans with each other.

On the basis of personal experiences and the burdensome history of our planet we have learned

- that a better global order cannot be created or enforced by laws, prescriptions, and conventions alone;

- that the realization of peace, justice, and the protection of Earth depends on the insight and readiness of men and women to act justly;
- that action in favor of rights and freedoms presumes a consciousness of responsibility and duty, and that therefore both the minds and hearts of women and men must be addressed;
- that rights without morality cannot long endure, and that there will be no better global order without a global ethic.

By a global ethic we do not mean a global ideology or a single unified religion beyond all existing religions, and certainly not the domination of one religion over all others. By a global ethic we mean a fundamental consensus on binding values, irrevocable standards, and personal attitudes. Without such a fundamental consensus on an ethic, sooner or later every community will be threatened by chaos or dictatorship, and individuals will despair.

II. A Fundamental Demand: Every Human Being Must be Treated Humanely

We are all fallible, imperfect men and women with limitations and defects. We know the reality of evil. Precisely because of this, we feel compelled for the sake of global welfare to express what the fundamental elements of a global ethic should be – for individuals as well as for communities and organizations, for states as well as for the religions themselves. We trust that our often millennia-old religious and ethical traditions provide an ethic which is convincing and practicable for all women and men of good will, religious and non-religious.

At the same time we know that our various religious and ethical traditions often offer very different bases for what is helpful and what is unhelpful for men and women, what is right and what is wrong, what is good and what is evil. We do not wish to gloss over or ignore the serious differences among the individual religions. However, they should not hinder us from proclaiming publicly those things which we already hold in common and which we jointly affirm, each on the basis of our own religious or ethical grounds.

We know that religions cannot solve the environmental, economic, political, and social problems of Earth. However they can provide what obviously cannot be attained by economic plans, political programs, or legal regulations alone: A change in the inner orientation, the whole mentality, the "hearts" of people, and a conversion from a false path to a new orientation for life. Humankind urgently needs social and ecological reforms, but it needs spiritual renewal just as urgently. As religious or spiritual persons we commit ourselves to this task. The spiritual powers of the religions can offer a fundamental sense of trust, a ground of meaning, ultimate standards, and a spiritual home. Of course religions are credible only when they eliminate those conflicts which spring from the religions themselves, dismantling mutual arrogance, mistrust, prejudice, and even hostile images, and thus demonstrate respect for the traditions, holy places, feasts, and rituals of people who believe differently.

Now as before, women and men are treated inhumanely all over the world. They are robbed of their opportunities and their freedom; their human rights are trampled underfoot; their dignity is disregarded. But might does not make right! In the face of all inhumanity our religious and ethical convictions demand that every human being must be treated humanely!

This means that every human being without distinction of age, sex, race, skin color, physical or mental ability, language, religion, political view, or national or social origin possesses an inalienable and untouchable dignity, and everyone, the individual as well as the state, is therefore obliged to honor this dignity and protect it. Humans must always be the subjects of rights, must be ends, never mere means, never objects of commercialization and industrialization in economics, politics and media, in research institutes, and industrial corporations. No one stands "above good and evil" – no human being, no social class, no influential interest group, no cartel, no police apparatus, no army, and no state. On the contrary: Possessed of reason and conscience, every human is obliged to behave in a genuinely human fashion, to do good and avoid evil!

It is the intention of this Global Ethic to clarify what this means. In it we wish to recall irrevocable, unconditional ethical norms. These should not be bonds and chains, but helps and supports for people to find and realize once again their lives' direction, values, orientations, and meaning.

There is a principle which is found and has persisted in many religious and ethical traditions of humankind for thousands of years: What you do not wish done to yourself, do not do to others. Or in positive terms: What you wish done to yourself, do to others! This should be the irrevocable, unconditional norm for all areas of life, for families and communities, for races, nations, and religions.

Every form of egoism should be rejected: All selfishness, whether individual or collective, whether in the form of class thinking, racism, nationalism, or sexism. We condemn these because they prevent humans from being authentically human. Self-determination and self-realization are thoroughly legitimate so long as they are not separated from human self-responsibility and global responsibility, that is, from responsibility for fellow humans and for the planet Earth.

This principle implies very concrete standards to which we humans should hold firm. From it arise four broad, ancient guidelines for human behavior which are found in most of the religions of the world.

III. Irrevocable Directives

1. Commitment to a Culture of Non-Violence and Respect for Life
Numberless women and men of all regions and religions strive to lead lives not determined by egoism but by commitment to their fellow humans and to the world around them. Nevertheless, all over the world we find endless hatred,

envy, jealousy, and violence, not only between individuals but also between social and ethnic groups, between classes, races, nations, and religions. The use of violence, drug trafficking and organized crime, often equipped with new technical possibilities, has reached global proportions. Many places still are ruled by terror "from above;" dictators oppress their own people, and institutional violence is widespread. Even in some countries where laws exist to protect individual freedoms, prisoners are tortured, men and women are mutilated, hostages are killed.

A. In the great ancient religious and ethical traditions of humankind we find the directive: You shall not kill! Or in positive terms: Have respect for life! Let us reflect anew on the consequences of this ancient directive: All people have a right to life, safety, and the free development of personality insofar as they do not injure the rights of others. No one has the right physically or psychically to torture, injure, much less kill, any other human being. And no people, no state, no race, no religion has the right to hate, to discriminate against, to "cleanse," to exile, much less to liquidate a "foreign" minority which is different in behavior or holds different beliefs.

B. Of course, wherever there are humans there will be conflicts. Such conflicts, however, should be resolved without violence within a framework of justice. This is true for states as well as for individuals. Persons who hold political power must work within the framework of a just order and commit themselves to the most non-violent, peaceful solutions possible. And they should work for this within an international order of peace which itself has need of protection and defense against perpetrators of violence. Armament is a mistaken path; disarmament is the commandment of the times. Let no one be deceived: There is no survival for humanity without global peace!

C. Young people must learn at home and in school that violence may not be a means of settling differences with others. Only thus can a culture of non-violence be created.

D. A human person is infinitely precious and must be unconditionally protected. But likewise the lives of animals and plants which inhabit this planet with us deserve protection, preservation, and care. Limitless exploitation of the natural foundations of life, ruthless destruction of the biosphere, and militarization of the cosmos are all outrages. As human beings we have a special responsibility – especially with a view to future generations – for Earth and the cosmos, for the air, water, and soil. We are all intertwined together in this cosmos and we are all dependent on each other. Each one of us depends on the welfare of all. Therefore the dominance of humanity over nature and the cosmos must not be encouraged. Instead we must cultivate living in harmony with nature and the cosmos.

E. To be authentically human in the spirit of our great religious and ethical traditions means that in public as well as in private life we must be concerned for others and ready to help. We must never be ruthless and brutal. Every people, every race, every religion must show tolerance and respect – indeed high appreciation – for every other. Minorities need protection and support, whether they be racial, ethnic, or religious.

2. *Commitment to a Culture of Solidarity and a Just Economic Order*

Numberless men and women of all regions and religions strive to live their lives in solidarity with one another and to work for authentic fulfillment of their vocations. Nevertheless, all over the world we find endless hunger, deficiency, and need. Not only individuals, but especially unjust institutions and structures are responsible for these tragedies. Millions of people are without work; millions are exploited by poor wages, forced to the edges of society, with their possibilities for the future destroyed. In many lands the gap between the poor and the rich, between the powerful and the powerless is immense. We live in a world in which totalitarian state socialism as well as unbridled capitalism have hollowed out and destroyed many ethical and spiritual values. A materialistic mentality breeds greed for unlimited profit and a grasping for endless plunder. These demands claim more and more of the community's resources without obliging the individual to contribute more. The cancerous social evil of corruption thrives in the developing countries and in the developed countries alike.

A. In the great ancient religious and ethical traditions of humankind we find the directive: You shall not steal! Or in positive terms: Deal honestly and fairly! Let us reflect anew on the consequences of this ancient directive: No one has the right to rob or dispossess in any way whatsoever any other person or the commonweal. Further, no one has the right to use her or his possessions without concern for the needs of society and Earth.

B. Where extreme poverty reigns, helplessness and despair spread, and theft occurs again and again for the sake of survival. Where power and wealth are accumulated ruthlessly, feelings of envy, resentment, and deadly hatred and rebellion inevitably well up in the disadvantaged and marginalized. This leads to a vicious circle of violence and counter-violence. Let no one be deceived: There is no global peace without global justice!

C. Young people must learn at home and in school that property, limited though it may be, carries with it an obligation, and that its uses should at the same time serve the common good. Only thus can a just economic order be built up.

D. If the plight of the poorest billions of humans on this planet, particularly women and children, is to be improved, the world economy must be structured more justly. Individual good deeds, and assistance projects, indispensable though they be, are insufficient. The participation of all states and the authority of international organizations are needed to build just economic institutions.

A solution which can be supported by all sides must be sought for the debt crisis and the poverty of the dissolving second world, and even more the third world. Of course conflicts of interest are unavoidable. In the developed countries, a distinction must be made between necessary and limitless consumption, between socially beneficial and non-beneficial uses of property, between justified and unjustified uses of natural resources, and between a profit-only and a socially beneficial and ecologically oriented market economy. Even the developing nations must search their national consciences.

Wherever those ruling threaten to repress those ruled, wherever institutions threaten persons, and wherever might oppresses right, we are obligated to resist – whenever possible non-violently.

E. To be authentically human in the spirit of our great religious and ethical traditions means the following:
- We must utilize economic and political power for service to humanity instead of misusing it in ruthless battles for domination. We must develop a spirit of compassion with those who suffer, with special care for the children, the aged, the poor, the disabled, the refugees, and the lonely.
- We must cultivate mutual respect and consideration, so as to reach a reasonable balance of interests, instead of thinking only of unlimited power and unavoidable competitive struggles.
- We must value a sense of moderation and modesty instead of an unquenchable greed for money, prestige, and consumption. In greed humans lose their "souls," their freedom, their composure, their inner peace, and thus that which makes them human.

3. *Commitment to a Culture of Tolerance and a Life of Truthfulness*
Numberless women and men of all regions and religions strive to lead lives of honesty and truthfulness. Nevertheless, all over the world we find endless lies, and deceit, swindling and hypocrisy, ideology and demagoguery:

- Politicians and business people who use lies as a means to success;
- Mass media which spread ideological propaganda instead of accurate reporting, misinformation instead of information, cynical commercial interest instead of loyalty to the truth;
- Scientists and researchers who give themselves over to morally questionable ideological or political programs or to economic interest groups, or who justify research which violates fundamental ethical values;

- Representatives of religions who dismiss other religions as of little value and who preach fanaticism and intolerance instead of respect and understanding.

A. In the great ancient religious and ethical traditions of humankind we find the directive: You shall not lie! Or in positive terms: Speak and act truthfully! Let us reflect anew on the consequences of this ancient directive: No woman or man, no institution, no state or church or religious community has the right to speak lies to other humans.

B. This is especially true:
   - for those who work in the mass media, to whom we entrust the freedom to report for the sake of truth and to whom we thus grant the office of guardian. They do not stand above morality but have the obligation to respect human dignity, human rights, and fundamental values. They are duty-bound to objectivity, fairness, and the preservation of human dignity. They have no right to intrude into individuals' private spheres, to manipulate public opinion, or to distort reality;
   - for artists, writers, and scientists, to whom we entrust artistic and academic freedom. They are not exempt from general ethical standards and must serve the truth;
   - for the leaders of countries, politicians, and political parties, to whom we entrust our own freedoms. When they lie in the faces of their people, when they manipulate the truth, or when they are guilty of venality or ruthlessness in domestic or foreign affairs, they forsake their credibility and deserve to lose their offices and their voters. Conversely, public opinion should support those politicians who dare to speak the truth to the people at all times;
   - finally, for representatives of religion. When they stir up prejudice, hatred, and enmity towards those of different belief, or even incite or legitimize religious wars, they deserve the condemnation of humankind and the loss of their adherents.

   Let no one be deceived: There is no global justice without truthfulness and humaneness!

C. Young people must learn at home and in school to think, speak, and act truthfully. They have a right to information and education to be able to make the decisions that will form their lives. Without an ethical formation they will hardly be able to distinguish the important from the unimportant. In the daily flood of information, ethical standards will help them discern when opinions are portrayed as facts, interests veiled, tendencies exaggerated, and facts twisted.

D. To be authentically human in the spirit of our great religious and ethical traditions means the following:
   - We must not confuse freedom with arbitrariness or pluralism with indifference to truth.

- We must cultivate truthfulness in all our relationships instead of dishonesty, dissembling, and opportunism.
- We must constantly seek truth and incorruptible sincerity instead of spreading ideological or partisan half-truths.
- We must courageously serve the truth and we must remain constant and trustworthy, instead of yielding to opportunistic accommodation to life.

4. Commitment to a Culture of Equal Rights and Partnership between Men and Women

Numberless men and women of all regions and religions strive to live their lives in a spirit of partnership and responsible action in the areas of love, sexuality, and family. Nevertheless, all over the world there are condemnable forms of patriarchy, domination of one sex over the other, exploitation of women, sexual misuse of children, and forced prostitution. Too frequently, social inequities force women and even children into prostitution as a means of survival – particularly in less developed countries.

A. In the great ancient religious and ethical traditions of humankind we find the directive: You shall not commit sexual immorality! Or in positive terms: Respect and love one another! Let us reflect anew on the consequences of this ancient directive: No one has the right to degrade others to mere sex objects, to lead them into or hold them in sexual dependency.

B. We condemn sexual exploitation and sexual discrimination as one of the worst forms of human degradation. We have the duty to resist wherever the domination of one sex over the other is preached – even in the name of religious conviction; wherever sexual exploitation is tolerated, wherever prostitution is fostered or children are misused. Let no one be deceived: There is no authentic humaneness without a living together in partnership!

C. Young people must learn at home and in school that sexuality is not a negative, destructive, or exploitative force, but creative and affirmative. Sexuality as a life-affirming shaper of community can only be effective when partners accept the responsibilities of caring for one another's happiness.

D. The relationship between women and men should be characterized not by patronizing behavior or exploitation, but by love, partnership, and trustworthiness. Human fulfillment is not identical with sexual pleasure. Sexuality should express and reinforce a loving relationship lived by equal partners. Some religious traditions know the ideal of a voluntary renunciation of the full use of sexuality. Voluntary renunciation also can be an expression of identity and meaningful fulfillment.

E. The social institution of marriage, despite all its cultural and religious variety, is characterized by love, loyalty, and permanence. It aims at and should guarantee security and mutual support to husband, wife, and child. It should secure the rights of all family members. All lands and cultures should develop economic and social relationships which will enable marriage and family life worthy of human beings, especially for older people. Children have a right of access to education. Parents should not exploit children, nor children parents. Their relationships should reflect mutual respect, appreciation, and concern.

F. To be authentically human in the spirit of our great religious and ethical traditions means the following:
   - We need mutual respect, partnership, and understanding, instead of patriarchal domination and degradation, which are expressions of violence and engender counter-violence.
   - We need mutual concern, tolerance, readiness for reconciliation, and love, instead of any form of possessive lust or sexual misuse.

Only what has already been experienced in personal and familial relationships can be practiced on the level of nations and religions.

IV. A Transformation of Consciousness

Historical experience demonstrates the following: Earth cannot be changed for the better unless we achieve a transformation in the consciousness of individuals and in public life. The possibilities for transformation have already been glimpsed in areas such as war and peace, economy, and ecology, where in recent decades fundamental changes have taken place. This transformation must also be achieved in the area of ethics and values! Every individual has intrinsic dignity and inalienable rights, and each also has an inescapable responsibility for what she or he does and does not do. All our decisions and deeds, even our omissions and failures, have consequences.

Keeping this sense of responsibility alive, deepening it and passing it on to future generations, is the special task of religions. We are realistic about what we have achieved in this consensus, and so we urge that the following be observed:

1. A universal consensus on many disputed ethical questions (from bio- and sexual ethics through mass media and scientific ethics to economic and political ethics) will be difficult to attain. Nevertheless, even for many controversial questions, suitable solutions should be attainable in the spirit of the fundamental principles we have jointly developed here.

2. In many areas of life a new consciousness of ethical responsibility has already arisen. Therefore we would be pleased if as many professions as possible, such as those of physicians, scientists, business people, journalists, and politicians, would develop up-to-date codes of ethics which would provide specific guidelines for the vexing questions of these particular professions.

3. Above all, we urge the various communities of faith to formulate their very specific ethics: What does each faith tradition have to say for example, about the meaning of life and death, the enduring of suffering and the forgiveness of gult, about selfless sacrifice and the necessity of renunciation, about compassion and joy? These will deepen, and make more specific, the already discernible global ethic.

In conclusion, we appeal to all the inhabitants of this planet. Earth cannot be changed for the better unless the consciousness of individuals is changed. We pledge to work for such transformation in individual and collective consciousness, for the awakening of our spiritual powers through reflection, meditation, prayer, or positive thinking, for a conversion of the heart. Together we can move mountains! Without a willingness to take risks and a readiness to sacrifice there can be no fundamental change in our situation! Therefore we commit ourselves to a common global ethic, to better mutual understanding, as well as to socially beneficial, peace-fostering, and Earth-friendly ways of life.

We invite all men and women, whether religious or not, to do the same!

E. Universal Islamic Declaration of Human Rights

Adopted by the Islamic Council, London, April 15, 1980.

21 Dhul Qaidah 1401, 19 September 1981.

This is a declaration for mankind, a guidance and instruction to those who fear God.

(Al Qur'an, Al-Imran 3:138)

Foreword

Islam gave to mankind an ideal code of human rights fourteen centuries ago. These rights aim at conferring honour and dignity on mankind and eliminating exploitation, oppression and injustice.

Human rights in Islam are firmly rooted in the belief that God, and God alone, is the Law Giver and the Source of all human rights. Due to their Divine origin, no ruler, government, assembly or authority can curtail or violate in any way the human rights conferred by God, nor can they be surrendered.

Human rights in Islam are an integral part of the overall Islamic order and it is obligatory on all Muslim governments and organs of society to implement them in letter and in spirit within the framework of that order.

It is unfortunate that human rights are being trampled upon with impunity in many countries of the world, including some Muslim countries. Such violations are a matter of serious concern and are arousing the conscience of more and more people throughout the world.

I sincerely hope that this *Declaration of Human Rights* will give a powerful impetus to the Muslim peoples to stand firm and defend resolutely and courageously the rights conferred on them by God.

This *Declaration of Human Rights* is the second fundamental document proclaimed by the Islamic Council to mark the beginning of the 15th Century of the Islamic era, the first being the *Universal Islamic Declaration* announced at the International Conference on The Prophet Muhammad (peace and blessings be upon him) and his Message, held in London from 12 to 15 April 1980.

The *Universal Islamic Declaration of Human Rights* is based on the Qur'an and the Sunnah and has been compiled by eminent Muslim scholars, jurists and representatives of Islamic movements and thought. May God reward them all for their efforts and guide us along the right path.

Paris 21 Dhul Qaidah 1401 Salem Azzam

19 September 1981 *Secretary General*

O men! Behold, We have created you all out of a male and a female, and have made you into nations and tribes, so that you might come to know one another. Verily, the noblest of you in the sight of God is the one who is most deeply conscious of Him. Behold, God is all-knowing, all aware. (Al Qur'an, Al-Hujurat 49:13)

Preamble

WHEREAS the age-old human aspiration for a just world order wherein people could live, develop and prosper in an environment free from fear, oppression, exploitation and deprivation, remains largely unfulfilled;

WHEREAS the Divine Mercy unto mankind reflected in its having been endowed with super-abundant economic sustenance is being wasted, or unfairly or unjustly withheld from the inhabitants of the earth;

WHEREAS Allah (God) has given mankind through His revelations in the Holy Qur'an and the Sunnah of His Blessed Prophet Muhammad an abiding legal and moral framework within which to establish and regulate human institutions and relationships;

WHEREAS the human rights decreed by the Divine Law aim at conferring dignity and honour on mankind and are designed to eliminate oppression and injustice;

WHEREAS by virtue of their Divine source and sanction these rights can neither be curtailed, abrogated or disregarded by authorities, assemblies or other institutions, nor can they be surrendered or alienated;

Therefore we, as Muslims, who believe

    a) in God, the Beneficent and Merciful, the Creator, the Sustainer, the Sovereign, the sole Guide of mankind and the Source of all Law;

    b) in the Viceregency (*Khalifah*) of man who has been created to fulfill the Will of God on earth;

    c) in the wisdom of Divine guidance brought by the Prophets, whose mission found its culmination in the final Divine message that was conveyed by the Prophet Muhammad (Peace be upon him) to all mankind;

    d) that rationality by itself without the light of revelation from God can neither be a sure guide in the affairs of mankind nor provide spiritual nourishment to the human soul, and, knowing that the teachings of Islam represent the quintessence of Divine guidance in its final and perfect form, feel duty-bound to remind man of the high status and dignity bestowed on him by God;

e) in inviting all mankind to the message of Islam;

f) that by the terms of our primeval covenant with God our duties and obligations have priority over our rights, and that each one of us is under a bounden duty to spread the teachings of Islam by word, deed, and indeed in all gentle ways, and to make them effective not only in our individual lives but also in the society around us;

g) in our obligation to establish an Islamic order:

   i) wherein all human beings shall be equal and none shall enjoy a privilege or suffer a disadvantage or discrimination by reason of race, colour, sex, origin or language;

   ii) wherein all human beings are born free;

   iii) wherein slavery and forced labour are abhorred;

   iv) wherein conditions shall be established such that the institution of family shall be preserved, protected and honoured as the basis of all social life;

   v) wherein the rulers and the ruled alike are subject to, and equal before, the Law;

   vi) wherein obedience shall be rendered only to those commands that are in consonance with the Law;

   vii) wherein all worldly power shall be considered as a sacred trust, to be exercised within the limits prescribed by the Law and in a manner approved by it, and with due regard for the priorities fixed by it;

   viii) wherein all economic resources shall be treated as Divine blessings bestowed upon mankind, to be enjoyed by all in accordance with the rules and the values set out in the Qur'an and the Sunnah;

   ix) wherein all public affairs shall be determined and conducted, and the authority to administer them shall be exercised after mutual consultation *(Shura)* between the believers qualified to contribute to a decision which would accord well with the Law and the public good;

   x) wherein everyone shall undertake obligations proportionate to his capacity and shall be held responsible pro rata for his deeds;

   xi) wherein everyone shall, in case of an infringement of his rights, be assured of appropriate remedial measures in accordance with the Law;

   xii) wherein no one shall be deprived of the rights assured to him by the Law except by its authority and to the extent permitted by it;

   xiii) wherein every individual shall have the right to bring legal action against anyone who commits a crime against society as a whole or against any of its members;

xiv) wherein every effort shall be made to
  (a) secure unto mankind deliverance from every type of exploita-
      tion, injustice and oppression,
  (b) ensure to everyone security, dignity and liberty in terms set
      out and by methods approved and within the limits set by the
      Law;

*Do hereby, as servants of Allah and as members of the Universal Brotherhood
of Islam, at the beginning of the Fifteenth Century of the Islamic Era, affirm our
commitment to uphold the following inviolable and inalienable human rights
that we consider are enjoined by Islam.*

I Right to Life
a) Human life is sacred and inviolable and every effort shall be made to
   protect it. In particular no one shall be exposed to injury or death, except
   under the authority of the Law.
b) Just as in life, so also after death, the sanctity of a person's body shall
   be inviolable. It is the obligation of believers to see that a deceased
   person's body is handled with due solemnity.

II Right to Freedom
a) Man is born free. No inroads shall be made on his right to liberty except
   under the authority and in due process of the Law.
b) Every individual and every people has the inalienable right to freedom
   in all its forms – physical, cultural, economic and political – and shall be
   entitled to struggle by all available means against any infringement or
   abrogation of this right; and every oppressed individual or people has
   a legitimate claim to the support of other individuals and/or peoples in
   such a struggle.

III Right to Equality and Prohibition Against Impermissible Discrimination
a) All persons are equal before the Law and are entitled to equal opportunities and protection of the Law.
b) All persons shall be entitled to equal wage for equal work.
c) No person shall be denied the opportunity to work or be discriminated
   against in any manner or exposed to greater physical risk by reason of
   religious belief, colour, race, origin, sex or language.

IV Right to Justice
a) Every person has the right to be treated in accordance with the Law,
   and only in accordance with the Law.
b) Every person has not only the right but also the obligation to protest
   against injustice; to recourse to remedies provided by the Law in respect

of any unwarranted personal injury or loss; to self-defence against any charges that are preferred against him and to obtain fair adjudication before an independent judicial tribunal in any dispute with public authorities or any other person.
c) It is the right and duty of every person to defend the rights of any other person and the community in general *(Hisbah)*.
d) No person shall be discriminated against while seeking to defend private and public rights.
e) It is the right and duty of every Muslim to refuse to obey any command which is contrary to the Law, no matter by whom it may be issued.

V   Right to Fair Trial
a) No person shall be adjudged guilty of an offence and made liable to punishment except after proof of his guilt before an independent judicial tribunal.
b) No person shall be adjudged guilty except after a fair trial and after reasonable opportunity for defence has been provided to him.
c) Punishment shall be awarded in accordance with the Law, in proportion to the seriousness of the offence and with due consideration of the circumstances under which it was committed.
d) No act shall be considered a crime unless it is stipulated as such in the clear wording of the Law.
e) Every individual is responsible for his actions. Responsibility for a crime cannot be vicariously extended to other members of his family or group, who are not otherwise directly or indirectly involved in the commission of the crime in question.

VI   Right to Protection Against Abuse of Power
Every person has the right to protection against harassment by official agencies. He is not liable to account for himself except for making a defence to the charges made against him or where he is found in a situation wherein a question regarding suspicion of his involvement in a crime could be *reasonably* raised

VII   Right to Protection Against Torture
No person shall be subjected to torture in mind or body, or degraded, or threatened with injury either to himself or to anyone related to or held dear by him, or forcibly made to confess to the commission of a crime, or forced to consent to an act which is injurious to his interests.

VIII   Right to Protection of Honour and Reputation
Every person has the right to protect his honour and reputation against calumnies, groundless charges or deliberate attempts at defamation and blackmail.

IX   Right to Asylum

a) Every persecuted or oppressed person has the right to seek refuge and asylum. This right is guaranteed to every human being irrespective of race, religion, colour and sex.

b) Al Masjid Al Haram (the sacred house of Allah) in Mecca is a sanctuary for all Muslims.

X   Rights of Minorities

a) The Qur'anic principle "There is no compulsion in religion" shall govern the religious rights of non-Muslim minorities.

b) In a Muslim country religious minorities shall have the choice to be governed in respect of their civil and personal matters by Islamic Law, or by their own laws.

XI   Right and Obligation to Participate in the Conduct and Management of Public Affairs

a) Subject to the Law, every individual in the community *(Ummah)* is entitled to assume public office.

b) Process of free consultation *(Shura)* is the basis of the administrative relationship between the government and the people. People also have the right to choose and remove their rulers in accordance with this principle.

XII   Right to Freedom of Belief, Thought and Speech

a) Every person has the right to express his thoughts and beliefs so long as he remains within the limits prescribed by the Law. No one, however, is entitled to disseminate falsehood or to circulate reports which may outrage public decency, or to indulge in slander, innuendo or to cast defamatory aspersions on other persons.

b) Pursuit of knowledge and search after truth is not only a right but a duty of every Muslim.

c) It is the right and duty of every Muslim to protest and strive (within the limits set out by the Law) against oppression even if it involves challenging the highest authority in the state.

d) There shall be no bar on the dissemination of information provided it does not endanger the security of the society or the state and is confined within the limits imposed by the Law.

e) No one shall hold in contempt or ridicule the religious beliefs of others or incite public hostility against them; respect for the religious feelings of others is obligatory on all Muslims.

XIII   Right to Freedom of Religion

Every person has the right to freedom of conscience and worship in accordance with his religious beliefs.

XIV Right to Free Association
  a) Every person is entitled to participate individually and collectively in the religious, social, cultural and political life of his community and to establish institutions and agencies meant to enjoin what is right *(ma'roof)* and to prevent what is wrong *(munkar)*.
  b) Every person is entitled to strive for the establishment of institutions whereunder an enjoyment of these rights would be made possible. Collectively, the community is obliged to establish conditions so as to allow its members full development of their personalities.

XV The Economic Order and the Rights Evolving Therefrom
  a) In their economic pursuits, all persons are entitled to the full benefits of nature and all its resources. These are blessings bestowed by God for the benefit of mankind as a whole.
  b) All human beings are entitled to earn their living according to the Law.
  c) Every person is entitled to own property individually or in association with others. State ownership of certain economic resources in the public interest is legitimate.
  d) The poor have the right to a prescribed share in the wealth of the rich, as fixed by Zakah, levied and collected in accordance with the Law.
  e) All means of production shall be utilised in the interest of the community *(Ummah)* as a whole, and may not be neglected or misused.
  f) In order to promote the development of a balanced economy and to protect society from exploitation, Islamic Law forbids monopolies, unreasonable restrictive trade practices, usury, the use of coercion in the making of contracts and the publication of misleading advertisements.
  g) All economic activities are permitted provided they are not detrimental to the interests of the community*(Ummah)* and do not violate Islamic laws and values.

XVI Right to Protection of Property
No property may be expropriated except in the public interest and on payment of fair and adequate compensation.

XVII Status and Dignity of Workers
Islam honours work and the worker and enjoins Muslims not only to treat the worker justly but also generously. He is not only to be paid his earned wages promptly, but is also entitled to adequate rest and leisure.

XVIII Right to Social Security
Every person has the right to food, shelter, clothing, education and medical care consistent with the resources of the community. This obligation of the community extends in particular to all individuals who cannot take care of themselves due to some temporary or permanent disability.

XIX Right to Found a Family and Related Matters
  a) Every person is entitled to marry, to found a family and to bring up children in conformity with his religion, traditions and culture. Every spouse is entitled to such rights and privileges and carries such obligations as are stipulated by the Law.
  b) Each of the partners in a marriage is entitled to respect and consideration from the other.
  c) Every husband is obligated to maintain his wife and children according to his means.
  d) Every child has the right to be maintained and properly brought up by its parents, it being forbidden that children are made to work at an early age or that any burden is put on them which would arrest or harm their natural development.
  e) If parents are for some reason unable to discharge their obligations towards a child it becomes the responsibility of the community to fulfill these obligations at public expense.
  f) Every person is entitled to material support, as well as care and protection, from his family during his childhood, old age or incapacity. Parents are entitled to material support as well as care and protection from their children.
  g) Motherhood is entitled to special respect, care and assistance on the part of the family and the public organs of the community *(Ummah)*.
  h) Within the family, men and women are to share in their obligations and responsibilities according to their sex, their natural endowments, talents and inclinations, bearing in mind their common responsibilities toward their progeny and their relatives.
  i) No person may be married against his or her will, or lose or suffer dimunition of legal personality on account of marriage.

XX Rights of Married Women
Every married woman is entitled to:

  a) live in the house in which her husband lives;
  b) receive the means necessary for maintaining a standard of living which is not inferior to that of her spouse, and, in the event of divorce, receive during the statutory period of waiting *(iddah)* means of maintenance commensurate with her husband's resources, for herself as well as for the children she nurses or keeps, irrespective of her own financial status, earnings, or property that she may hold in her own rights;
  c) seek and obtain dissolution of marriage *(Khul'a)* in accordance with the terms of the Law. This right is in addition to her right to seek divorce through the courts.
  d) inherit from her husband, her parents, her children and other relatives according to the Law;

e) strict confidentiality from her spouse, or ex-spouse if divorced, with regard to any information that he may have obtained about her, the disclosure of which could prove detrimental to her interests. A similar responsibility rests upon her in respect of her spouse or ex-spouse.

XXI Right to Education
a) Every person is entitled to receive education in accordance with his natural capabilities.
b) Every person is entitled to a free choice of profession and career and to the opportunity for the full development of his natural endowments.

XXII Right of Privacy
Every person is entitled to the protection of his privacy.

XXIII Right to Freedom of Movement and Residence
a) In view of the fact that the World of Islam is veritably *Ummah Islamia,* every Muslim shall have the right to freely move in and out of any Muslim country.
b) No one shall be forced to leave the country of his residence, or be arbitrarily deported therefrom without recourse to due process of Law.

Explanatory Notes
1. In the above formulation of Human Rights, unless the context provides otherwise:
   a) the term 'person' refers to both the male and female sexes.
   b) the term 'Law' denotes the *Shari'ah*, i.e. the totality of ordinances derived from the Qur'an and the Sunnah and any other laws that are deduced from these two sources by methods considered valid in Islamic jurisprudence.
2. Each one of the Human Rights enunciated in this declaration carries a corresponding duty.
3. In the exercise and enjoyment of the rights referred to above every person shall be subject only to such limitations as are enjoined by the Law for the purpose of securing the due recognition of, and respect for, the rights and the freedom of others and of meeting the just requirements of morality, public order and the general welfare of the Community *(Ummah)*.
4. The Arabic text of this *Declaration* is the original.

Glossary of Arabic Terms
Sunnah – The example or way of life of the Prophet (peace be upon him), embracing what he said, did or agreed to.

Khalifah – The viceregency of man on earth or succession to the Prophet, transliterated into English as the Caliphate.

Hisbah – Public vigilance, an institution of the Islamic State enjoined to observe and facilitate the fulfillment of right norms of public behaviour. The "Hisbah" consists in public vigilance as well as an opportunity to private individuals to seek redress through it.

Ma'roof – Good act.

Munkar – Reprehensible deed.

Zakah – The 'purifying' tax on wealth, one of the five pillars of Islam obligatory on Muslims.

'Iddah – The waiting period of a widowed or divorced woman during which she is not to re-marry.

Khul'a – Divorce a woman obtains at her own request.

Ummah Islamia – World Muslim community.

Shari'ah – Islamic law.

F. Cairo Declaration on Human Rights in Islam

Adopted at the Nineteenth Islamic Conference of Foreign Ministers, Cairo, August 5, 1990.

The Member States of the Organization of the Islamic Conference,

Reaffirming the civilizing and historical role of the Islamic Ummah which God made the best nation that has given mankind a universal and well-balanced civilization in which harmony is established between this life and the hereafter and knowledge is combined with faith; and the role that this Ummah should play to guide a humanity confused by competing trends and ideologies and to provide solutions to the chronic problems of this materialistic civilization;

Wishing to contribute to the efforts of mankind to assert human rights, to protect man from exploitation and persecution, and to affirm his freedom and right to a dignified life in accordance with the Islamic Shari'ah;

Convinced that mankind which has reached an advanced stage in materialistic science is still, and shall remain, in dire need of faith to support its civilization and of a self-motivating force to guard its rights;

Believing that fundamental rights and universal freedoms in Islam are an integral part of the Islamic religion and that no one as a matter of principle has the right to suspend them in whole or in part or violate or ignore them in as much as they are binding divine commandments, which are contained in the Revealed Books of God and were sent through the last of His Prophets to complete the preceding divine messages thereby making their observance an act of worship and their neglect or violation an abominable sin, and accordingly every person is individually responsible – and the Ummah collectively responsible – for their safeguard.

Proceeding from the above-mentioned principles,

Declare the following:

Article 1
    (a) All human beings form one family whose members are united by submission to God and descent from Adam. All men are equal in terms of basic human dignity and basic obligations and responsibilities, without any discrimination on the grounds of race, colour, language, sex, religious belief, political affiliation, social status or other considerations. True faith is the guarantee for enhancing such dignity along the path to human perfection.

(b) All human beings are God's subjects, and the most loved by him are those who are most useful to the rest of His subjects, and no one has superiority over another except on the basis of piety and good deeds.

Article 2

(a) Life is a God-given gift and the right to life is guaranteed to every human being. It is the duty of individuals, societies and states to protect this right from any violation, and it is prohibited to take away life except for a Shari'ah-prescribed reason.

(b) It is forbidden to resort to such means as may result in the genocidal annihilation of mankind.

(c) The preservation of human life throughout the term of time willed by God is a duty prescribed by Shari'ah.

(d) Safety from bodily harm is a guaranteed right. It is the duty of the state to safeguard it, and it is prohibited to breach it without a Shari'ah-prescribed reason.

Article 3

(a) In the event of the use of force and in case of armed conflict, it is not permissible to kill non-belligerents such as old men, women and children. The wounded and the sick shall have the right to medical treatment; and prisoners of war shall have the right to be fed, sheltered and clothed. It is prohibited to mutilate dead bodies. It is a duty to exchange prisoners of war and to arrange visits or reunions of the families separated by the circumstances of war.

(b) It is prohibited to fell trees, to damage crops or livestock, and to destroy the enemy's civilian buildings and installations by shelling, blasting or any other means.

Article 4

Every human being is entitled to inviolability and the protection of his good name and honour during his life and after his death. The state and society shall protect his remains and burial place.

Article 5

(a) The family is the foundation of society, and marriage is the basis of its formation. Men and women have the right to marriage, and no restrictions stemming from race, colour or nationality shall prevent them from enjoying this right.

(b) Society and the State shall remove all obstacles to marriage and shall facilitate marital procedure. They shall ensure family protection and welfare.

Article 6

    (a) Woman is equal to man in human dignity, and has rights to enjoy as well as duties to perform; she has her own civil entity and financial independence, and the right to retain her name and lineage.

    (b) The husband is responsible for the support and welfare of the family.

Article 7

    (a) As of the moment of birth, every child has rights due from the parents, society and the state to be accorded proper nursing, education and material, hygienic and moral care. Both the fetus and the mother must be protected and accorded special care.

    (b) Parents and those in such like capacity have the right to choose the type of education they desire for their children, provided they take into consideration the interest and future of the children in accordance with ethical values and the principles of the Shari'ah.

    (c) Both parents are entitled to certain rights from their children, and relatives are entitled to rights from their kin, in accordance with the tenets of the Shari'ah.

Article 8

Every human being has the right to enjoy his legal capacity in terms of both obligation and commitment. Should this capacity be lost or impaired, he shall be represented by his guardian.

Article 9

    (a) The quest for knowledge is an obligation, and the provision of education is a duty for society and the State. The State shall ensure the availability of ways and means to acquire education and shall guarantee educational diversity in the interest of society so as to enable man to be acquainted with the religion of Islam and the facts of the Universe for the benefit of mankind.

    (b) Every human being has the right to receive both religious and worldly education from the various institutions of education and guidance, including the family, the school, the university, the media, etc., and in such an integrated and balanced manner as to develop his personality, strengthen his faith in God and promote his respect for and defence of both rights and obligations.

Article 10

Islam is the religion of unspoiled nature. It is prohibited to exercise any form of compulsion on man or to exploit his poverty or ignorance in order to convert him to another religion or to atheism.

Article 11

(a) Human beings are born free, and no one has the right to enslave, humiliate, oppress or exploit them, and there can be no subjugation but to God the Most-High.

(b) Colonialism of all types being one of the most evil forms of enslavement is totally prohibited. Peoples suffering from colonialism have the full right to freedom and self-determination. It is the duty of all States and peoples to support the struggle of colonized peoples for the liquidation of all forms of colonialism and occupation, and all States and peoples have the right to preserve their independent identity and exercise control over their wealth and natural resources.

Article 12

Every man shall have the right, within the framework of Shari'ah, to free movement and to select his place of residence whether inside or outside his country and, if persecuted, is entitled to seek asylum in another country. The country of refuge shall ensure his protection until he reaches safety, unless asylum is motivated by an act which Shari'ah regards as a crime.

Article 13

Work is a right guaranteed by the State and Society for each person able to work. Everyone shall be free to choose the work that suits him best and which serves his interests and those of society. The employee shall have the right to safety and security as well as to all other social guarantees. He may neither be assigned work beyond his capacity nor be subjected to compulsion or exploited or harmed in any way. He shall be entitled – without any discrimination between males and females – to fair wages for his work without delay, as well as to the holidays, allowances and promotions which he deserves. For his part, he shall be required to be dedicated and meticulous in his work. Should workers and employers disagree on any matter, the State shall intervene to settle the dispute and have the grievances redressed, the rights confirmed and justice enforced without bias.

Article 14

Everyone shall have the right to legitimate gains without monopolization, deceit or harm to oneself or to others. Usury *(riba)* is absolutely prohibited.

Article 15

(a) Everyone shall have the right to own property acquired in a legitimate way, and shall be entitled to the rights of ownership, without prejudice to oneself, others or to society in general. Expropriation is not permissible except for the requirements of public interest and upon payment of immediate and fair compensation

(b) Confiscation and seizure of property is prohibited except for a necessity dictated by law.

Article 16

Everyone shall have the right to enjoy the fruits of his scientific, literary, artistic or technical production and the right to protect the moral and material interests stemming therefrom, provided that such production is not contrary to the principles of Shari'ah.

Article 17
  (a) Everyone shall have the right to live in a clean environment, away from vice and moral corruption, an environment that would foster his self-development; and it is incumbent upon the State and society in general to afford that right.
  (b) Everyone shall have the right to medical and social care, and to all public amenities provided by society and the State within the limits of their available resources.
  (c) The State shall ensure the right of the individual to a decent living which will enable him to meet all his requirements and those of his dependents, including food, clothing, housing, education, medical care and all other basic needs.

Article 18
  (a) Everyone shall have the right to live in security for himself, his religion, his dependents, his honour and his property.
  (b) Everyone shall have the right to privacy in the conduct of his private affairs, in his home, among his family, with regard to his property and his relationships. It is not permitted to spy on him, to place him under surveillance or to besmirch his good name. The State shall protect him from arbitrary interference.
  (c) A private residence is inviolable in all cases. It will not be entered without permission from its inhabitants or in any unlawful manner, nor shall it be demolished or confiscated and its dwellers evicted.

Article 19
  (a) All individuals are equal before the law, without distinction between the ruler and the ruled.
  (b) The right to resort to justice is guaranteed to everyone.
  (c) Liability is in essence personal.
  (d) There shall be no crime or punishment except as provided for in the Shari'ah.
  (e) A defendant is innocent until his guilt is proven in a fair trial in which he shall be given all the guarantees of defence.

Article 20

It is not permitted without legitimate reason to arrest an individual, or restrict his freedom, to exile or to punish him. It is not permitted to subject him to physical or psychological torture or to any form of humiliation, cruelty or indignity. Nor is it permitted to subject an individual to medical or scientific experimentation without his consent or at the risk of his health or of his life. Nor is it permitted to promulgate emergency laws that would provide executive authority for such actions.

Article 21

Taking hostages under any form or for any purpose is expressly forbidden.

Article 22

  (a) Everyone shall have the right to express his opinion freely in such manner as would not be contrary to the principles of the Shari'ah.

  (b) Everyone shall have the right to advocate what is right, and propagate what is good, and warn against what is wrong and evil according to the norms of Islamic Shari'ah.

  (c) Information is a vital necessity to society. It may not be exploited or misused in such a way as may violate sanctities and the dignity of Prophets, undermine moral and ethical values or disintegrate, corrupt or harm society or weaken its faith.

  (d) It is not permitted to arouse nationalistic or doctrinal hatred or to do anything that may be an incitement to any form of racial discrimination.

Article 23

  (a) Authority is a trust; and abuse or malicious exploitation thereof is absolutely prohibited, so that fundamental human rights may be guaranteed.

  (b) Everyone shall have the right to participate, directly or indirectly in the administration of his country's public affairs. He shall also have the right to assume public office in accordance with the provisions of Shari'ah.

Article 24

All the rights and freedoms stipulated in this Declaration are subject to the Islamic Shari'ah.

Article 25

The Islamic Shari'ah is the only source of reference for the explanation or clarification to any of the articles of this Declaration.

G. The Bangkok Declaration: The Final Declaration of the Regional Meeting for Asia of the World Conference on Human Rights

Adopted by the Ministers and representatives of Asian States, Bangkok, 2 April 1993.

The Ministers and representatives of Asian States, meeting at Bangkok from 29 March to 2 April 1993, pursuant to General Assembly resolution 46/116 of 17 December 1991 in the context of preparations for the World Conference on Human rights,

Adopt this Declaration, to be known as "The Bangkok Declaration," which contains the aspirations and commitments of the Asian region.

Bangkok Declaration

Emphasizing the significance of the World Conference on Human Rights, which provides an invaluable opportunity to review all aspects of human rights and ensure a just and balanced approach thereto,

Recognizing the contribution that can be made to the World Conference by Asian countries with their diverse and rich cultures and traditions,

Welcoming the increased attention being paid to human rights in the international community,

Reaffirming their commitment to principles contained in the Charter of the United Nations and the Universal Declaration on Human Rights,

Recalling that in the Charter of the United Nations the question of universal observance and promotion of human rights and fundamental freedoms has been rightly placed within the context of international cooperation,

Noting the progress made in the codification of human rights instruments, and in the establishment of international human rights mechanisms, while *expressing concern* that these mechanisms relate mainly to one category of rights,

Emphasizing that ratification of international human rights instruments, particularly the International Covenant on Civil and Political Rights and the International Covenant on Economic, Social and Cultural Rights, by all States should be further encouraged,

Reaffirming the principles of respect for national sovereignty, territorial integrity and non-interference in the internal affairs of States,

Stressing the universality, objectivity and non-selectivity of all human rights and the need to avoid the application of double standards in the implementation of human rights and its politicization,

Recognizing that the promotion of human rights should be encouraged by cooperation and consensus, and not through confrontation and the imposition of incompatible values,

Reiterating the interdependence and indivisibility of economic, social, cultural, civil and political rights, and the inherent interrelationship between development, democracy, universal enjoyment of all human rights, and social justice, which must be addressed in an integrated and balanced manner,

Recalling that the Declaration on the Right to Development has recognized the right to development as a universal and inalienable right and an integral part of fundamental human rights,

Emphasizing that endeavours to move towards the creation of uniform international human rights norms must go hand in hand with endeavours to work towards a just and fair world economic order,

Convinced that economic and social progress facilitates the growing trend towards democracy and the promotion and protection of human rights,

Stressing the importance of education and training in human rights at the national, regional and international levels and the need for international cooperation aimed at overcoming the lack of public awareness of human rights,

1. *Reaffirm* their commitment to the principles contained in the Charter of the United Nations and the Universal Declaration on Human Rights as well as the full realization of all human rights throughout the world;
2. *Underline* the essential need to create favourable conditions for effective enjoyment of human rights at both the national and international levels;
3. *Stress* the urgent need to democratize the United Nations system, eliminate selectivity and improve procedures and mechanisms in order to strengthen international cooperation, based on principles of equality and mutual respect, and ensure a positive, balanced and non-confrontational approach in addressing and realizing all aspects of human rights;
4. *Discourage* any attempt to use human rights as a conditionality for extending development assistance;
5. *Emphasize* the principles of respect for national sovereignty and territorial integrity as well as non-interference in the internal affairs of States, and the non-use of human rights as an instrument of political pressure;

6. *Reiterate* that all countries, large and small, have the right to determine their political systems, control and freely utilize their resources, and freely pursue their economic, social and cultural development;
7. *Stress* the universality, objectivity and non-selectivity of all human rights and the need to avoid the application of double standards in the implementation of human rights and its politicization, and that no violation of human rights can be justified;
8. *Recognize* that while human rights are universal in nature, they must be considered in the context of a dynamic and evolving process of international norm-setting, bearing in mind the significance of national and regional particularities and various historical, cultural and religious backgrounds;
9. *Recognize further* that States have the primary responsibility for the promotion and protection of human rights through appropriate infrastructure and mechanisms, and also recognize that remedies must be sought and provided primarily through such mechanisms and procedures;
10. *Reaffirm* the interdependence and indivisibility of economic, social, cultural, civil and political rights, and the need to give equal emphasis to all categories of human rights;
11. *Emphasize* the importance of guaranteeing the human rights and fundamental freedoms of vulnerable groups such as ethnic, national, racial, religious and linguistic minorities, migrant workers, disabled persons, indigenous peoples, refugees and displaced persons;
12. *Reiterate* that self-determination is a principle of international law and a universal right recognized by the United Nations for peoples under alien or colonial domination and foreign occupation, by virtue of which they can freely determine their political status and freely pursue their economic, social and cultural development, and that its denial constitutes a grave violation of human rights;
13. *Stress* that the right to self-determination is applicable to peoples under alien or colonial domination and foreign occupation, and should not be used to undermine the territorial integrity, national sovereignty and political independence of States;
14. *Express concern* over all forms of violation of human rights, including manifestations of racial discrimination, racism, apartheid, colonialism, foreign aggression and occupation, and the establishment of illegal settlements in occupied territories, as well as the recent resurgence of neonazism, xenophobia and ethnic cleansing;
15. *Underline* the need for taking effective international measures in order to guarantee and monitor the implementation of human rights standards and effective and legal protection of people under foreign occupation;
16. *Strongly affirm* their support for the legitimate struggle of the Palestinian people to restore their national and inalienable rights to self-determination and independence, and demand an immediate end to

the grave violations of human rights in the Palestinian, Syrian Golan and other occupied Arab territories including Jerusalem;

17. *Reaffirm* the right to development, as established in the Declaration on the Right to Development, as a universal and inalienable right and an integral part of fundamental human rights, which must be realized through international cooperation, respect for fundamental human rights, the establishment of a monitoring mechanism and the creation of essential international conditions for the realization of such right;

18. *Recognize* that the main obstacles to the realization of the right to development lie at the international macroeconomic level, as reflected in the widening gap between the North and the South, the rich and the poor;

19. *Affirm* that poverty is one of the major obstacles hindering the full enjoyment of human rights;

20. *Affirm also* the need to develop the right of humankind regarding a clean, safe and healthy environment;

21. *Note* that terrorism, in all its forms and manifestations, as distinguished from the legitimate struggle of peoples under colonial or alien domination and foreign occupation, has emerged as one of the most dangerous threats to the enjoyment of human rights and democracy, threatening the territorial integrity and security of States and destabilizing legitimately constituted governments, and that it must be unequivocally condemned by the international community;

22. *Reaffirm* their strong commitment to the promotion and protection of the rights of women through the guarantee of equal participation in the political, social, economic and cultural concerns of society, and the eradication of all forms of discrimination and of gender-based violence against women;

23. *Recognize* the rights of the child to enjoy special protection and to be afforded the opportunities and facilities to develop physically, mentally, morally, spiritually and socially in a healthy and normal manner and in conditions of freedom and dignity;

24. *Welcome* the important role played by national institutions in the genuine and constructive promotion of human rights, and believe that the conceptualization and eventual establishment of such institutions are best left for the States to decide;

25. *Acknowledge* the importance of cooperation and dialogue between governments and non-governmental organizations on the basis of shared values as well as mutual respect and understanding in the promotion of human rights, and encourage the non-governmental organizations in consultative status with the Economic and Social Council to contribute positively to this process in accordance with Council resolution 1296 (XLIV);

26. *Reiterate* the need to explore the possibilities of establishing regional arrangements for the promotion and protection of human rights in Asia;

27. *Reiterate further* the need to explore ways to generate international cooperation and financial support for education and training in the field of human rights at the national level and for the establishment of national infrastructures to promote and protect human rights if requested by States;

28. *Emphasize* the necessity to rationalize the United Nations human rights mechanism in order to enhance its effectiveness and efficiency and the need to ensure avoidance of the duplication of work that exists between the treaty bodies, the Sub-Commission on Prevention of Discrimination and Protection of Minorities and the Commission on Human Rights, as well as the need to avoid the multiplicity of parallel mechanisms;

29. *Stress* the importance of strengthening the United Nations Centre for Human Rights with the necessary resources to enable it to provide a wide range of advisory services and technical assistance programmes in the promotion of human rights to requesting States in a timely and effective manner, as well as to enable it to finance adequately other activities in the field of human rights authorized by competent bodies;

30. *Call for* increased representation of the developing countries in the Centre for Human Rights.

H. Asian Human Rights Charter: A People's Charter

Declared in Kwangju, South Korea, May 14–17, 1998.

Preamble

For long, especially during the colonial period, the peoples of Asia suffered from gross violations of their rights and freedoms. Today large sections of our people continue to be exploited and oppressed and many of our societies are torn apart by hatred and intolerance. Increasingly the people realize that peace and dignity are possible only when the equal and inalienable rights of all persons and groups are recognised and protected. They are determined to secure peace and justice for themselves and the coming generations through the struggle for human rights and freedoms. Towards that end they adopt this Charter as an affirmation of the desire and aspirations of the peoples of Asia to live in peace and dignity.

Background to the Charter

1.1 The Asian struggle for rights and freedoms has deep historical roots, in the fight against oppression in civil society and the political oppression of colonialism, and subsequently for the establishment or restoration of democracy. The reaffirmation of rights is necessary now more than ever before. Asia is passing through a period of rapid change, which affects social structures, political institutions and the economy. Traditional values are under threat from new forms of development and technologies, as well as political authorities and economic organizations that manage these changes.

1.2 In particular the marketization and globalization of economies are changing the balance between the private and the public, the state and the international community, and worsening the situation of the poor and the disadvantaged. These changes threaten many valued aspects of life, the result of the dehumanizing effects of technology, the material orientation of the market, and the destruction of the community. People have decreasing control over their lives and environment, and some communities do not have protection even against eviction from their traditional homes and grounds. There is a massive exploitation of workers, with wages that are frequently inadequate for even bare subsistence and low safety standards that put the lives of workers in constant danger. Even the most elementary of labour rights and laws are seldom enforced.

1.3 Asian development is full of contradictions. There is massive and deepening poverty in the midst of growing affluence of some sections of the people. Levels of health, nutrition and education of large numbers of our people are appalling, denying the dignity of human life. At the same time valuable resources are wasted on armaments, Asia being the largest purchaser of arms of all regions. Our governments claim to be pursuing development directed at increasing levels of production and welfare but our natural resources are being depleted most irresponsibly and the environment is so degraded that the quality of life has worsened immeasurably, even for the better off among us. Building of golf courses has a higher priority than the care of the poor and the disadvantaged.

1.3 Asians have in recent decades suffered from various forms of conflict and violence, arising from ultra-nationalism, perverted ideologies, ethnic differences, and fundamentalism of all religions. Violence emanates from both the state and sections of civil society. For large masses, there is little security of person, property or community. There is massive displacement of communities and there are an increasing number of refugees.

1.4 Governments have arrogated enormous powers to themselves. They have enacted legislation to suppress people's rights and freedoms and colluded with foreign firms and groups in the plunder of national resources. Corruption and nepotism are rampant and there is little accountability of those holding public or private power. Authoritarianism has in many states been raised to the level of national ideology, with the deprivation of the rights and freedoms of their citizens, which are denounced as foreign ideas inappropriate to the religious and cultural traditions of Asia. Instead there is the exhortation of spurious theories of Asian Values. which are a thin disguise for their authoritarianism. Not surprisingly, Asia, of all the major regions of the world, is without a regional official charter or other regional arrangements for the protection of rights and freedoms.

1.4 In contrast to the official disregard or contempt of human rights in many Asian states, there is increasing awareness among their peoples of the importance of rights and freedoms. They realize the connections between their poverty and political powerlessness and the denial to them of these rights and freedoms. They believe that political and economic systems have to operate within a framework of human rights and freedoms to ensure economic justice, political participation and accountability, and social peace. There are many social movements that have taken up the fight to secure for the people their rights and freedoms.

1.5 Our commitment to rights is not due to any abstract ideological reasons. We believe that respect for human rights provides the basis for a just, humane and caring society. A regime of rights is premised on the belief that we are all inherently equal and have an equal right to live in dignity. It is based on our right to determine our destiny through participation in policy making and administration. It enables us to develop and enjoy our culture and to give expression to our artistic impulses. It respects diversity. It recognizes our obligations to future generations and the environment they will inherit. It establishes standards for assessing the worth and legitimacy of our institutions and policies.

General Principles

2.1 It is possible from specific rights and the institutions and procedures for their protection to draw some general principles which underlie these rights and whose acceptance and implementation facilitates their full enjoyment. The principles, which are discussed below, should provide the broad framework for public policies within which we believe rights would be promoted.

Universality and Indivisibility of Rights

2.2 We endorse the Universal Declaration of Human Rights, the International Covenant on Economic, Social and Cultural Rights, the International Covenant on Civil and Political Rights, and other international instruments for the protection of rights and freedoms. We believe that rights are universal, every person being entitled to them by virtue of being a human being. Cultural traditions affect the way in which a society organizes relationships within itself, but they do not detract from the universalism of rights which are primarily concerned with the relationship of citizens with the state and the inherent dignity of persons and groups. We also believe that rights and freedoms are indivisible and it is a fallacy to suppose that some types of rights can be suppressed in the name of other rights.

Human beings have social, cultural and economic needs and aspirations that cannot be fragmented or compartmentalised, but are mutually dependent. Civil, political and cultural rights have little meaning unless there are the economic resources to exercise and enjoy them. Equally, the pursuit and acquisition of material wealth is sterile and self-defeating without political freedoms, the opportunity to develop and express one's personality and to engage in cultural and other discourses.

2.3 Notwithstanding their universality and indivisibility, the enjoyment and the salience of rights depend on social, economic and cultural contexts. Rights are not abstractions, but foundations for action and policy. Consequently we must move from abstract formulations of rights to their concretization in the Asian context by examining the circumstances of specific groups whose situation is defined by massive violations of their rights. It is only by relating rights and their implementation to the specificity of the Asian situation that the enjoyment of rights will be possible. Only in this way will Asia be able to contribute to the world-wide movement for the protection of rights.

2.4 Widespread poverty, even in states which have achieved a high rate of economic development, is a principal cause of the violation of rights. Poverty deprives individuals, families, and communities of their rights and promotes prostitution, child labour, slavery, sale of human organs, and the mutilation of the body to enhance the capacity to beg. A life of dignity is impossible in the midst of poverty. Asian states must direct their development policies towards the elimination of poverty through more equitable forms of development.

The Responsibility for the Protection of Human Rights

2.5 The responsibility for the protection of rights is both international and domestic. The international community has agreed upon norms and institutions that should govern the practice of human rights. The peoples of Asia support international measures for the protection of rights. State sovereignty cannot be used as an excuse to evade international norms or ignore international institutions.

The claim of state sovereignty is justified only when a state fully protects the rights of its citizens.

2.6 On the other hand, international responsibility cannot be used for the selective chastisement or punishment of particular states; or for the privileging of one set of rights over others. Some fundamental causes of the violation of human rights lie in the inequities of the international world economic and political order. The radical transformation and democratization of the world order is a necessary condition for the global enjoyment of human rights. The logic of the universalism and equality of rights is the responsibility of the international community for the social and economic welfare of all people throughout the world, and consequently the obligation to ensure a more equitable distribution of resources and opportunities across the world.

2.7 The primary responsibility for the promotion of human rights rests with states. The rights of states and peoples to just economic, social, political and cultural development must not be negated by global processes. States must establish open political processes in which rights and obligations of different groups are acknowledged and the balance between the interests of individuals and the community is achieved. Democratic and accountable governments are the key to the promotion and protection of rights.

2.8 The capacity of the international community and states to promote and protect rights has been weakened by processes of globalization as more and more power over economic and social policy and activities has moved from states to business corporations. States are increasingly held hostage by financial and other corporations to implement narrow and short sighted economic policies which cause so much misery to so many people, while increasing the wealth of the few. Business corporations are responsible for numerous violations of rights, particularly those of workers, women and indigenous peoples.

It is necessary to strengthen the regime of rights by making corporations liable for the violation of rights.

Sustainable Development and the Protection of the Environment

2.9 Economic development must be sustainable. We must protect the environment against the avarice and depredations of commercial enterprises to ensure that the quality of life does not decline just as the gross national product increases. Technology must liberate, not enslave human beings. Natural resources must be used in a manner consistent with our obligation to future generations. We must never forget that we are merely temporary custodians of the resources of nature. Nor should we forget that these resources are given to all human kind, and consequently we have a joint responsibility for their responsible, fair and equitable use.

Rights

3.1 We endorse all the rights that are contained in international instruments. It is unnecessary to restate them here. We believe that these rights need to be seen in a holistic manner and that individual rights are best pursued through a broader conceptualization which forms the basis of the following section.

The Right to Life

3.2 Foremost among rights is the right to life, from which flow other rights and freedoms. The right to life is not confined to mere physical or animal existence but includes the right to every limb or faculty through which life is enjoyed. It signifies the right to live with basic human dignity, the right to livelihood, the right to a habitat or home, the right to education and the right to a clean and healthy environment for without these there can be no real and effective exercise or enjoyment of the right to life. The state must also take all possible measures to prevent infant mortality, eliminate malnutrition and epidemics, and increase life expectancy through a clean and healthy environment and adequate preventative as well as curative medical facilities. It must make primary education free and compulsory.

3.3 Yet in many parts of Asia, wars, ethnic conflicts, cultural and religious oppression, corruption of politics, environmental pollution, disappearances, torture, state or private terrorism, violence against women, and other acts of mass violence continue to be a scourge to humanity resulting in the loss of thousands of innocent human lives.

3.4 To ensure the right to life, propagation of war or ethnic conflict or incitement to hatred and violence in all spheres of individual or societal or national or international life should be prohibited.

3.5 The state has the responsibility to thoroughly investigate cases of torture, disappearances and custodial deaths, rapes and sexual abuses and to bring culprits to justice.

3.6 There must be no arbitrary deprivation of life. States should take measures not only to prevent and mete out punish for the deprivation of life by criminal acts and terrorist acts but also prevent arbitrary disappearances and killings by their own security forces. The law must strictly control and limit the circumstances in which a person may be deprived of his or her life by state authorities or officials.

3.7 All states must abolish the death penalty. Where it exists, it may be imposed only rarely for the most serious crimes. Before a person can be deprived of life by the imposition of the death penalty, he or she must be ensured a fair trial before an independent and impartial tribunal with full opportunity of legal representation of his or her choice, adequate time for preparation of defence, presumption of innocence and the right to review by a higher tribunal. Execution should never be carried out in public or otherwise exhibited in public.

The Right to Peace

4.1 All persons have the right to live in peace so that they can fully develop all their capacities, physical, intellectual, moral and spiritual, without being the target of any kind of violence. The peoples of Asia have suffered great hardships and tragedies due to wars and civil conflicts which have caused many deaths, mutilation of bodies, external or internal displacement of persons, break up of families, and in general the denial of any prospects of a civilized or peaceful existence. Both the state and civil society have in many countries become heavily militarized in which all scores are settled by force and citizens have no protection against the intimidation and terror of state or private armies.

4.2 The duty of the state to maintain law and order should be conducted under strict restraint on the use of force in accordance with standards established by the international community, including humanitarian law. Every individual and group is entitled to protection against all forms of state violence, including violence perpetrated by its police and military forces.

4.3 The right to live in peace requires that political, economic or social activities of the state, the corporate sector and the civil society should respect the security of all peoples, especially of vulnerable groups. People must be ensured security in relation to the natural environment they live in, the political, economic and social conditions which permit them to satisfy their needs and aspirations without recourse to oppression, exploitation, violence, and without detracting from all that is of value in their society.

4.4 In fighting fascist invasion, colonialism, and neo-colonialism, Asian states played a crucial role in creating conditions for their peoples to live in peace. In this fight, they had justifiably stressed the importance of national integrity and nonintervention by hegemonic powers. However, the demands of national integrity or protection against the threats of foreign domination cannot now be used as a pretext for refusing to the people their right to personal security and peaceful existence any more than the suppression of people's rights can be justified as an excuse to attract foreign investments. Neither can they justify any refusal to inform the international community about the individual security of its people. The right of persons to live in peace can be guaranteed only if the states are accountable to the international community.

4.5 The international community of states has been deeply implicated in wars and civil conflicts in Asia. Foreign states have used Asian groups as surrogates to wage wars and have armed groups and governments engaged in internal conflicts.

They have made huge profits out of the sale of armaments.

The enormous expenditures on arms have diverted public revenues from programmes for the development of the country or the well-being of the people. Military bases and other establishments (often of foreign powers) have threatened the social and physical security of the people who live in their vicinity.

The Right to Democracy

5.1 Colonialism and other modern developments significantly changed the nature of Asian political societies. The traditional systems of accountability and public participation in affairs of state as well as the relationship of citizens to the government were altered fundamentally. Citizens became subjects, while the government became more pervasive and powerful. Colonial laws and authoritarian habits and style of administration persisted after independence. The state has become the source of corruption and the oppression of the people. The democratization and humanization of the state is a pre-condition for the respect for and the protection of rights.

5.2 The state, which claims to have the primary responsibility for the development and well-being of the people, should be humane, open and accountable. The corollary of the respect for human rights is a tolerant and pluralistic system, in which people are free to express their views and to seek to persuade others and in which the rights of minorities are respected. People must participate in public affairs, through the electoral and other decision-making and implementing processes, free from racial, religious or gender discriminations.

The Right to Cultural Identity and the Freedom of Conscience

6.1 The right to life involves not only material but also the moral conditions which permit a person to lead a meaningful existence. This meaning is not only individually determined but is also based on shared living with other human beings.

The Asian traditions stress the importance of common cultural identities. Cultural identities help individuals and communities to cope with the pressures of economic and social change; they give meaning to life in a period of rapid transformation. They are the source of pride and security. There are many vulnerable communities in Asia as elsewhere whose cultures are threatened or derided. Asian peoples and governments must respect the cultures and traditions of its diverse communities.

6.2 The plurality of cultural identities in Asia is not contrary to the universality of human rights but rather as so many cultural manifestations of human dignity enriching universal norms.

At the same time we Asian peoples must eliminate those features in our cultures which are contrary to the universal principles of human rights. We must transcend the traditional concept of the family based on patriarchal traditions so as to retrieve in each of our cultural traditions, the diversity of family norms which guarantee women's human rights. We must be bold in reinterpreting our religious beliefs which support gender inequality. We must also eliminate discriminations based on caste, ethnic origins, occupation, place of origin and others, while enhancing in our respective cultures all values related to mutual tolerance and mutual support. We must stop practices which sacrifice the individual to the collectivity or to the powerful, and thus renew our communal and national solidarity.

6.3 The freedom of religion and conscience is particularly important in Asia where most people are deeply religious.

Religion is a source of comfort and solace in the midst of poverty and oppression. Many find their primary identity in religion. However religious fundamentalism is also a cause of divisions and conflict. Religious tolerance is essential for the enjoyment of the right of conscience of others, which includes the right to change one's belief.

The Right to Development and Social Justice

7.1 Every individual has the right to the basic necessities of life and to protection against abuse and exploitation. We all have the right to literacy and knowledge, to food and clean water, shelter and to medical facilities for a healthy existence. All individuals and human groups are entitled to share the benefits of the progress of technology and of the growth of the world economy.

7.2 Development, for individuals and states, does not mean merely economic development. It means the realization of the full potential of the human person. Consequently they have the right to artistic freedom, freedom of expression and the cultivation of their cultural and spiritual capacities. It means the right to participate in the affairs of the state and the community. It implies that states have the right to determine their own economic, social and cultural policies free from hegemonic pressures and influences.

Rights of Vulnerable Groups

8.1 Asian states should formulate and implement public policies within the above general framework of rights. We believe that in this way we will establish fair and humane conditions for our individual and corporate lives and ensure social justice. However, there are particular groups who for historical or other reasons are weak and vulnerable and consequently require special protection for the equal and effective enjoyment of their human rights. We discuss the situation of several such groups, but we recognize that there are also other groups who suffer from discrimination and oppression. They include people who through civil conflict, government policies or economic hardships are displaced from their homes and seek refuge in other places internally or in foreign lands. Our states and societies have become less tolerant of minorities and indigenous people, whose most basic rights are frequently violated. Many of our societies still discriminate against gays and lesbians, denying them their identity and causing them great anguish and misery. Various economic groups, like peasants and fishing communities, suffer from great deprivation and live in constant fear of threats to their livelihood from landlords and capitalist enterprises. All these groups deserve special attention.

We urge states and communities to give the highest priority to the amelioration of their social and economic conditions.

Women

9.1 In most Asian societies women suffer from discrimination and oppression. The cause of their oppression lies in both history and contemporary social and economic systems.

9.2 The roots of patriarchy are systemic and its structures dominate all institutions, attitudes, social norms and customary laws, religions and values in Asian societies, crossing the boundaries of class, culture, caste and ethnicity. Oppression takes many forms, but is most evident in sexual slavery, domestic violence, trafficking in women and rape. They suffer discrimination in both public and private spheres. The increasing militarization of many societies in Asia has led to the increase of violence against women in situations of armed conflict, including mass rape, forced labour, racism, kidnapping and displacement from their homes. As female victims of armed conflict are often denied justice, rehabilitation, compensation and reparation of the war crimes committed against them, it is important to emphasis that systematic rape is a war crime and a crime against humanity.

9.3 To end discrimination against women in the field of employment and the right to work, women should be given the right to employment opportunities, the free choice of profession, job security, equal remuneration, the right to compensation in respect of domestic work, the right to protection of health and safe working conditions, especially in safeguarding of the function of reproduction and special protection in times of pregnancy from work that may be harmful. Women should be given the full right to control their sexual and reproductive health, free from discrimination or coercion, and be given access to information about sexual and reproductive health care and safe reproductive technology.

9.4 There are few legal provisions to protect women against violations of their rights within the domestic and patriarchal realm. Their rights in public law are seldom observed. Affirmative measures should be taken to ensure full and equal participation of women in the political and public life of the society. A considerable increase in the presence of women in the various institutions of state power and in the fields of business, agriculture and land ownership must be provided for by way of affirmative action. The political, social and economic empowerment of women is essential for the defence of their legal rights.

Children

10.1 As with women, their oppression takes many forms, the most pervasive of which are child labour; sexual slavery; child pornography; the sale and trafficking of children; prostitution; sale of organs; conscription into drug trafficking; the physical, sexual and psychological abuse of children within families; discrimination against children with HIV/AIDS; forced religious conversion of children; the displacement of children with and without their families by armed conflicts; discrimination; and environmental degradation. An increasing number of children are forced to live on the streets of Asian cities and are deprived of the social and economic support of families and communities.

10.2 Widespread poverty, lack of access to education and social dislocation in rural areas are among the causes of the trends which increase the vulnerability of children. Long-established forms of exploitation and abuse, such as bonded labour or the use of children for begging or sexual gratification are rampant. Female infanticide due to patriarchal gender preference and female genital mutilation are widely practised in some Asian countries.

10.3 Asian states have failed dismally to look after children and provide them with even the bare means of subsistence or shelter. We call on Asian states to ratify and implement the Convention on the Rights of the Child. We also call on communities to take the responsibility for monitoring violations of children.s rights and to press for the implementation of the UN Convention in appropriate ways in their own social contexts.

Differently Abled Persons

11.1 Traditionally Asian societies cared for those who were physically or mentally handicapped. Increasingly our communal values and structures, under the pressure of new forms of economic organizations, have become less tolerant of such persons. They suffer enormous discrimination in access to education, employment and housing. They are unable to enjoy many of their human rights due to prejudice against them and the absence of provisions responding to their special demands. Their considerable abilities are not properly recognized and they are forced into jobs which offer low pay and little prospects of promotion. They have the right to provisions which enable them to live in dignity, with security and respect, and to have opportunities to realize their full potential.

11.2 The need to treat such persons with respect for their human rights is apparent in the dismal way Asian states treat those with HIV or AIDS. They are the victims of gross discrimination. A civilized society which respects human rights would recognize their right to live and die with dignity.

It would secure to them the right to adequate medical care and to be protected from prejudice, discrimination or persecution.

Workers

12.1 The rapid industrialization of Asian societies has undermined traditional forms of the subsistence economy and has destroyed possibilities of the livelihood of large sections of the rural people. Increasingly they and other groups are forced into wage employment, often in industry, working under appalling conditions. For the majority of the workers there is little or no protection from unfair labour laws. The fundamental rights to form trade unions and bargain collectively are denied to many. Their wages are grossly inadequate and working conditions are frequently grim and dangerous.

Globalization adds to the pressures on workers as many Asian states seek to reduce the costs of production, often in collusion with foreign corporations and international financial institutions.

12.2 A particularly vulnerable category of workers are migrant workers.

Frequently separated from their families, they are exploited in foreign states whose laws they do not understand and are afraid to invoke. They are often denied rights and conditions which local workers enjoy. They slog without access to adequate accommodation, health care, or legal protection. In many cases migrants suffer racism and xenophobia, and domestic helpers are subjected to humiliation and sometimes, sexual abuse.

Students

13.1 Students in Asia struggled against colonialism and fought for democratization and social justice. As a result of their fearless commitment to social transformation they have often suffered from state violence and repression and remain as one of the key targets for counter-insurgency operations and internal security laws and operations. Students are frequently denied the right to academic freedom and to the freedoms of expression and association.

Prisoners and Political Detainees

14.1 In few areas is there such a massive violation of internationally recognized norms as in relation to prisoners and political detainees.

14.2 Arbitrary arrests, detention, imprisonment, ill-treatment, torture, cruel and inhuman punishment are common occurrences in many parts of Asia. Detainees and prisoners are often forced to live in unhygienic conditions, are denied adequate food and health care and are prevented from having communication with, and support from, their families.

Different kinds of prisoners are frequently mixed in one cell, with men, women and children kept in proximity. Prison cells are normally overcrowded. Deaths in custody are common. Prisoners are frequently denied access to lawyers and the right to fair and speedy trials.

14.3 Asian governments often use executive powers of detention without trial. They use national security legislation to arrest and detain political opponents. It is notable that, in many countries in Asia, freedom of thought, belief and conscience have been restricted by administrative limits on freedom of speech and association.

The Enforcement of Rights

15.1 Many Asian states have guarantees of human rights in their constitutions, and many of them have ratified international instruments on human rights. However, there continues to be a wide gap between rights enshrined in these documents and the abject reality that denies people their rights. Asian states must take urgent action to implement the human rights of their citizens and residents.

Principles for Enforcement

15.2 We believe that systems for the protection of rights should be based on the following principles.

15.2a Human rights are violated by the state, civil society and business corporations. The legal protection for rights has to be extended against violations by all these groups. It is also necessary to reform these groups by strengthening their ethical foundations and values and inculcating in them a sense of their responsibility towards the disadvantaged and the oppressed.

15.2b The promotion and enforcement of rights is the responsibility of all groups in society, although the primary responsibility is that of the state. The enjoyment of many rights, especially social and economic, requires a positive and proactive role of governments. There is a clear and legitimate role for NGOs in raising consciousness of rights, formulating standards, and ensuring their protection by governments and other groups.

Professional groups like lawyers and doctors have special responsibilities connected with the nature of their work to promote the enforcement of rights and prevent abuses of power.

15.2c Since rights are seriously violated in situations of civil strife and are strengthened if there is peace, it is the duty of the state and other organizations to find peaceful ways to resolve social and ethnic conflicts and to promote tolerance and harmony. For the same reasons no state should seek to dominate other states and states should settle their differences peacefully.

15.2d Rights are enhanced if democratic and consensual practices are followed and it is therefore the responsibility of all states and other organisations to promote these practices in their work and in their dealings with others.

15.2e Many individuals and groups in Asia are unable to exercise their rights due to restrictive or oppressive social customs and practices, particularly those related to caste, gender, or religion.

Therefore the immediate reform of these customs and practices is necessary for the protection of rights. The reforms must be enforced with vigour and determination.

15.2f A humane and vigorous civil society is necessary for the promotion and protection of human rights and freedoms, for securing rights within civil society and to act as a check on state institutions. Freedoms of expression and association are necessary for the establishment and functioning of institutions of civil society.

15.2g It is necessary to curb the exploitative practices of business corporations and to ensure that they do not violate rights of workers, consumers and the public.

Strengthening the Framework for Rights

15.3a It is essential to secure the legal framework for rights. All states should include guarantees of rights in their constitutions, which should be constitutionally protected against erosion by legislative amendments. They should also ratify international human rights instruments. They should review their legislation and administrative practices against national and international standards with the aim of repealing provisions which contravene these standards, particularly legislation carried over from the colonial period.

15.3b Knowledge and consciousness of rights should be raised among the general public, and state and civil society institutions.

Awareness of the national and international regime of rights should be promoted. Individuals and groups should be acquainted with legal and administrative procedures whereby they can secure their rights and prevent abuse of authority.

NGOs should be encouraged to become familiar with and deploy mechanisms, both national and inter-national, for monitoring and review of rights. Judicial and administrative decisions on the protection of rights should be widely disseminated, nationally and in the Asian region. Governments, NGOs and educational institutions should co-operate in disseminating information about the importance and content of human rights.

15.3c Numerous violations of rights occur while people are in custody and through other activities of security forces. Sometimes these violations take place because the security forces do not respect the permissible scope of their powers or do not realise that the orders under which they are acting are unlawful. Members of the police, prison services and the armed forces should be provided training in human rights norms.

The Machinery for the Enforcement of Rights

15.4a The judiciary is a major means for the protection of rights. It has the power to receive complaints of the violation of rights, to hear evidence, and to provide redress for violations, including punishment for violators. The judiciary can only perform this function if the legal system is strong and well organized.

The members of the judiciary should be competent, experienced and have a commitment to human rights, dignity and justice. They should be independent of the legislature and the executive by vesting the power of their appointment in a judicial service commission and by constitutional safeguards of their tenure. Judicial institutions should fairly reflect the character of the different sections of the people by religion, region, gender and social class. This means that there must be a restructuring of the judiciary and the investigative machinery. More women, more underprivileged categories and more of the Pariahs of society must by deliberate State action be lifted out of the mire and instilled in judicial positions with necessary training. Only such a measure will command the confidence of the weaker sector whose human rights are ordinarily ignored in the traditional societies of Asia.

15.4b The legal profession should be independent. Legal aid should be provided for those who are unable to afford the services of lawyers or have access to courts, for the protection of their rights. Rules which unduly restrict access to courts should be reformed to provide a broad access. Social and welfare organizations should be authorised to bring legal action on behalf of individuals and groups who are unable to utilize the courts.

15.4c All states should establish Human Rights Commissions and specialized institutions for the protection of rights, particularly of vulnerable members of society. They can provide easy, friendly and inexpensive access to justice for victims of human rights violations. These bodies can supplement the role of the judiciary. They enjoy special advantages: they can help establish standards for the implementation of human rights norms; they can disseminate information about human rights; they can investigate allegations of violation of rights; they can promote conciliation and mediation; and they can seek to enforce human rights through administrative or judicial means. They can act on their own initiative as well on complaints from members of the public.

15.4d Civil society institutions can help to enforce rights through the organization of People's Tribunals, which can touch the conscience of the government and the public. The establishment of People's Tribunals emphasizes that the responsibility for the protection of rights is wide, and not a preserve of the state.

They are not confined to legal rules in their adjudication and can consequently help to uncover the moral and spiritual foundations of human rights.

Regional Institutions for the Protection of Rights

16.1 The protection of human rights should be pursued at all levels, local, national, regional and international. Institutions at each level have their special advantages and skills. The primary responsibility for the protection of rights is that of states, therefore priority should be given to the enhancement of state capacity to fulfil this obligation.

16.2 Asian states should adopt regional or sub-regional institutions for the promotion and protection of rights. There should be an inter-state Convention on Human Rights, formulated in regional forums with the collaboration of national and regional NGOs. The Convention must address the realities of Asia, particularly the obstacles that impede the enjoyment of rights. At the same time it must be fully consistent with international norms and standards. It should cover violations of rights by groups and corporations in addition to state institutions. An independent commission or a court must be established to enforce the Convention. Access to the commission or the court must be open to NGOs and other social organizations.

The Asian Human Rights Charter is a people's charter. It is part of an attempt to create in Asia a popular culture on human rights. Thousands of people from various Asian countries participated in the debates during the three-year period of discussion on this document. In addition, more than 200 non-governmental organizations (NGOs) directly took part in the drafting process, and many other NGOs and people's organizations (POs) have endorsed the document. Several drafts of the document, including some translations, were published widely in newspapers, magazines and NGO newsletters.

This final version of the charter was written by Prof. Yash Ghai under the direction of a committee of which he was a member consisting of Justices Krishna Iyer and P. N. Bhagwati, Prof. Kinhide Mushakoji, Mercedes V. Contreras, Lourdes Indai Sajor and Basil Fernando, Mark Daly and Sanjeewa Liyanage from the Asian Human Rights Commission (AHRC). This charter is presented to deepen the Asian debate on human rights, to present the people's views on human rights as against those of some Asian leaders who claim that human rights are alien to Asia and to promote political, social and legal reforms for ensuring human rights in the countries of the region. While drawing from the cultural wells of the region, it also points to the need for cleaning these wells that have been polluted by millenniums of prejudice, discrimination, inequality and violence.

Bibliography

Abdul-Rauf, M. (2000). *Marriage in Islam: A Manual* (2000 ed.). Alexandria: Al-Saadawi.

Ahmed, L. (1992). *Women and Gender in Islam: Historical Roots of Modern Debate.* New York: Yale University Press.

Aikman, D. (2003). *Jesus in Beijing: How Christianity is Transforming China and Changing the Balance of Power in the World.* New York: Regnery.

al-Hibri, A. (1998). "Islamic Law," in A. M. Jaggar & I. M. Young (eds.), *A Companion to Feminist Philosophy* (pp. 541–549). Oxford: Blackwell.

al-Sadlaan, S. I. G. (1996). *Marital Discord (al-Nushooz): Its Definition, Cases, Causes, Means of Protection from It, and Its Remedy from the Qur'an and Sunnah.* Boulder: Al-Basheer.

Ali, K. (2003). "Progressive Muslims and Islamic Jurisprudence: The Necessity for Critical Engagement with Marriage and Divorce Law," in O. Safi (ed.), q. v. (pp. 183–189). Oxford: Oneworld.

Allenby, B. (2002). *Observations on the Philosophic Implications of Earth Systems Engineering and Managment.* Charlottesville, VA: Batten Institute, University of Virginia.

An-Na'im, A. A. (1987). "Religious Minorities Under Islamic Law and the Limits of Cultural Relativism." *Human Rights Quarterly, 9* (1), 1–18.

An-Na'im, A. A. (1990). *Toward an Islamic Reformation: Civil Liberties, Human Rights, and International Law.* Syracuse: Syracuse University Press.

An-Na'im, A. A., & Deng, F. M. (1990). *Human Rights in Africa: Cross-Cultural Perspectives.* Washington, DC: The Brookings Institution.

Annan, K. (1999). *The Backlash against Globalism. The Futurist,* March 27.

Aquinas, T. *Commentary on the Nicomachean Ethics,* Book II, Lectio 2, §259.

Aquinas, T. *Summa Theologiae,* IaIIae, *Q. 94, A. 4.*

Aquinas, T. *Summa Theologiae* (Vol. I, II, 91).

Archibugi, D., Held, D., & Köhler, M. (eds.). (1998). *Re-Imagining Political Community: Studies in Cosmopolitan Democracy.* Cambridge, UK: Polity Press.

Arend, A. C., & Beck, R. J. (1993). *International Law and the Use of Force: Beyond the UN Charter.* New York: Routledge.

Aristotle. (1999). *Nicomachean Ethics* (T. Irwin, trans.). Indianapolis: Hackett.

Arzt, D. E. (1996). "The Treatment of Religious Dissidents under Classical and Contemporary Islamic Law." In J. John Witte & J. van der Vyver (eds.), *Religious Human Rights in Global Perspective*. Hague: Kluwer Law International.

Ashworth, G. (1999). "The Silencing of Women," in In T. Dunne & N. Wheeler (eds.), *Human Rights in Global Politics*. Cambridge: Cambridge University Press.

Atherton, J. (2000). *Public Theology for Changing Times*. London: SPCK.

Austin, J. (1965). *The Province of Jurisprudence Determined and the Uses of the Study of Jurisprudence*. New York: Humanities Press.

Bangkok Declaration. (1993). United Nations High Commission for Human Rights.

Barnard, F. M. Introduction. (1969). In F. M. Barnard (ed.), *J. G. Herder on Social and Political Culture*. Cambridge: Cambridge University Press.

Barrett, M. (1988). *Women's Oppression Today: Problems in Marxist Feminist Analysis*. London: Verso.

Barry, B. (1998). "International Society from a Cosmopolitan Perspective," in D. Mapel & T. Nardin (eds.), *International Society*. Princeton: Princeton University Press.

Barry, B. (2000). *Culture and Equality*. Cambridge, UK: Polity Press.

Basu, A. (ed.). (1995). *The Challenge of Local Feminisms: Women's Movements in Global Perspective*. Boulder: Westview Press.

Bauer, J., & Bell, D. (eds.). (1999). *The East Asian Challenge for Human Rights*. Cambridge: Cambridge University Press.

Becker, G. K. (2002). "Moral Education in China and the 'West ': Ideals and Reality in Cross-Cultural Perspective," in K.-H. Pohl & A. W. Muller (eds.), *Chinese Ethics in a Global Context* (pp. 245–278). Leiden: Brill.

Beitz, C. (2000). *Political Theory and International Relations* (second ed.). Princeton: Princeton University Press.

Bell, D. (2000). *East Meets West: Human Rights and Democracy in East Asia*. Princeton: Princeton University Press.

Bellah, R. N. (2003). *Imagining Japan*. Berkeley: University of California Press.

Benamozegh, E. (1995). *Israel et l'humanité (Israel and Humanity)* (M. Luria, trans.). New York: Paulist Press.

Benhabib, S. (2002). *The Claims of Culture: Equality and Diversity in the Global Era*. Princeton: Princeton University Press.

Berger, P., & et al. (2002). *Many Globalizations: Cultural Diversity and the Contemporary World*. New York: Oxford University Press.

Berman, H. J. (2003). *Law and Revolution* (vol. 2). Cambridge: Harvard University Press.

Bhagwati, J. (2004). *In Defense of Globalization*. New York: Oxford University Press.

Boff, L. (2005). *Global Civilization: Challenges to Society and Christianity*. London: Equinox Publishers.

Boot, M. (2002). "What the Heck is a 'Neocon'? Neoconservatives Believe in Using American Might to Promote American Ideals Abroad." *Wall Street Journal Online*, December 30, 2002, p. A12.

Braaten, C., & Seitz, C. R. (eds.). (2004). *I Am the Lord Your God: Christian Reflections on the Ten Commandments*. Grand Rapids: Wm. Eerdmans.

Brown, C. (2002a). "The Construction of a Realistic Utopia: John Rawls and International Political Theory." *Review of International Studies, 28* (1).

Brown, C. (2002b). "Narratives of Religion, Civilisation and Modernity," in K. Booth & T. Dunne (eds.), *Worlds in Collision: Terror and the Future Global Order.* Basingstoke: Palgrave.

Brown, C. (2001). *Understanding International Relations* (second ed.). Basingstoke: Palgrave.

Brown, C. (2002c). *Sovereignty*, Rights, and Justice. Cambridge, UK: Polity Press.

BrowningCole, E., & Coultrap-McQuin, S. (eds.). (1992). *Explorations in Feminist Ethics: Theory and Practice.* Bloomington & Indianapolis: Indiana University Press.

Brownlie, I. (2002). *Basic Instruments on Human Rights* (fifth ed.). Oxford: Clarendon Press.

Buchanan, A. (2000). "Rawls' Law of Peoples: Rules for a Vanished Westphalian World." *Ethics, 110* (4), 697–721.

Buchanan, A., & Moore, M. (eds.). (2003). *States, Nations, and Borders: The Ethics of Making Boundaries.* Cambridge: Cambridge University Press.

Butler, J. (1990). *Gender Trouble: Feminism and the Subversion of Identity.* London: Routledge.

Caird, G. B. (1956). *Principalities and Powers.* Oxford: Clarendon Press.

Calvin, John. (1599). *Institutes of the Christian Religion*, vol. II, p. viii.

Carlson, J. D., & Owens, E. C. (eds.). (2003). *The Sacred and the Sovereign.* Washington, DC: Georgetown University Press.

Chambers, S., & Kymlicka, W. (eds.). (2002). *Alternative Conceptions of Civil Society.* Princeton: Princeton University Press.

Chappell, T. (1998). *Understanding Human Goods.* Edinburgh: Edinburgh University Press.

Chen, A. H. Y. (2003). "Mediation, Litigation, and Justice: Confucian Reflections in a Modern Liberal Society," in D. A. Bell & H. Chaibong (eds.), *Confucianism for the Modern World* (pp. 257–287). New York: Columbia University Press.

Chodorow, N. (1978). *The Reproduction of Mothering.* Berkeley: University of California Press.

Chopra, J., & Weiss, T. G. (1992). "Sovereignty Is no Longer Sacrosanct: Codifying Humanitarian Intervention." *Ethics and International Affairs, 6* (1), 95–117.

Christie, K., & Rou, D. (2001). *The Politics of Human Rights in East Asia.* London: Pluto Press.

Chuanwei, S. (2004, November 8). "Scholar Kang Xiaoguang: China's Democratization Means a Calamitous Choice for the Country and the People." *Singapore Lianhe Zaobao.*

Clement, G. (1996). *Care, Autonomy and Justice: Feminism and the Ethic of Care.* Boulder: Westview Press.

Cohen, H. (1995). *Religion of Reason out of the Sources of Judaism* (S. Kaplan, trans.). Atlanta: Scholars Press.

Cromartie, M. (1997). *A Preserving Grace: Protestants, Catholics, and Natural Law.* Grand Rapids: Wm. Eerdmans.

Daly, M. (1979). *Gyn/Ecology: the Metaethics of Radical Feminism.* London: The Women's Press.

Damrosch, L. F. (1993). *Enforcing Restraint: Collective Intervention in Internal Conflicts*. New York: Council on Foreign Relations Press.

de Bary, W. T. (1998). *Asian Values and Human Rights: A Confucian Communitarian Perspective*. Cambridge: Harvard University Press.

de Bary, W. T. (ed.). (1972). *The Buddhist Tradition in India, China, and Japan*. New York: Vintage Books.

de Bary, W. T., & Weiming, T. (eds.). (1997). *Confucianism and Human Rights*. New York: Columbia University Press.

de Beauvoir, Simone. (1953). *The Second Sex*. London: Jonathan Cape.

DesAutels, P., & Waugh, J. (eds.). (2001). *Feminists Doing Ethics*. Lanham: Rowman & Littlefield.

Doi, A. R. (1994). *Women in Shari'ah (Islamic Law)*. London: Ta-Ha.

Duchrow, U. (1987). *Global Economy: A Confessional Issue for the Churches*. Geneva: World Council of Churches.

Duchrow, U. (1995). *Alternatives to Global Capitalism*. Kairos Europa: Heidelberg.

Duncan, C. (Ed.). (2004). *Civilizing the Margins: Southeast Asian Government Policies for the Development of Minorities*. Ithaca: Cornell University Press.

Duran, K. (2006). "The Drafting of a Global Ethic: A Muslim Perspective." At http://astro.temple.edu/~dialogue/Antho/duran.htm.

Eishû, M. (1969). *Fujufuseha no genryû to tenkai*. Kyoto: Heirakuji Shoten.

Elazar, D. J. (1995–200). *The Covenant Tradition in Politics* (vol. 4). New Brunswick: Transaction Press.

Elshtain, J. (1995). *Women and War*. Chicago & London: Chicago University Press.

Engels, F. (1985). *The Origin of the Family, Private Property and the State*. Harmondsworth: Penguin.

Explanatory Remarks Concerning a "Declaration of the Religions for a Global Ethic." (2006). At http://astro.temple.edu/~dialogue/Center/kung.htm.

Fingarette, H. (1972). *Confucius – the Secular as Sacred*. New York: Harper and & Row.

Finnis, J. (1996). "Natural Law Theory and Limited Government," in R. George (ed.), *Natural Law, Liberalism, and Morality*. New York: Oxford University Press.

Finnis, J. (1983). *Fundamentals of Ethics*. Oxford University Press.

Finnis, J. (1987). "Legal Enforcement of 'Duties to Oneself': Kant v. Neo-Kantians." *Columbia Law Review* (87), 433–456.

Finnis, J. (1980). *Natural Law and Natural Rights*. Oxford: Oxford University Press.

Frazer, E., Hornsby, J., & Lovibond, S. (eds.). (1992). *Ethics: A Feminist Reader*. Oxford: Blackwell.

Friedan, B. (1965). *The Feminine Mystique*. Harmondsworth: Penguin.

Fukuyama, F. (1989). "The End Of History." *The National Interest* (16). Summer, pp. 3–18.

Fuss, D. (1989). *Essentially Speaking: Feminism, Nature and Difference*. London: Routledge.

George, R. (1998). *Making Men Moral*. New York: Oxford University Press.

Gilg, C. (2002). *The Dilemma of Promoting Human Rights in a World of Deep Diversity: A Critical Examination of the Approach of John Rawls*. Unpublished thesis, University of Notre Dame, Notre Dame, Indiana.

Gilligan, C. (1992). *In A Different Voice: Psychological Theory and Women's Development*. Cambridge: Harvard University Press.

Glendon, M. A. (2001). *A World Made New: Eleanor Roosevelt and the Universal Declaration of Human Rights*. New York: Random House.

Goldstein, J. S. (1991). *War and Gender*. Cambridge: Cambridge University Press.

Gomez-Lobo, A. (2002). *Morality and the Human Goods*. Washington, DC: Georgetown University Press.

Gordis, R. (1990). *The Dynamics of Judaism: A Study in Jewish Law*. Bloomington: Indiana University Press.

Goudzwaard, B., & et al. (eds.). (2001). *Globalization and the Kingdom of God*. Grand Rapids: Baker Books.

Gourevitch, P. (1998). *We Wish to Inform You that Tomorrow We will be Killed with Our Families: Stories from Rwanda*. New York: Farrar, Straus, and Giroux.

Grisez, G. (1983). *The Way of the Lord Jesus: Christian Moral Principles* (vol. 1). Chicago: Franciscan Herald Press.

Guantao, J. (1983). *Zai Lishi Biaoxiangde Beihou*: Sichuan Renminchubanshe.

Ha-am, A. (1970). "The Transvaluation of Values," in L. Simon (ed.), *Selected Essays of Ahad Ha-Am*. New York: Atheneum.

Habermas, J., & McCarthy. Thomas. (1990). *Moral Consciousness and Communicative Action*. Cambridge, UK: Polity Press.

Hall, D. L., & Ames, R. T. (2003). "A Pragmatist Understanding of Confucian Democracy," in D. A. Bell & H. Chaibong (eds.), *Confucianism for the Modern World*. Cambridge: Cambridge University Press.

Hanke, L. (1965). *The Spanish Struggle for Justice in the Conquest of America*. Boston: Little, Brown.

Harrelson, W. (1997). *The Ten Commandments and Human Rights*. Macon: Mercer University Press.

Harris, A., & King, Y. (eds.). (1989). *Rocking the Ship of State: Towards a Feminist-Peace Politics*. Boulder: Westview Press.

Harrison, L., & et al. (eds.). (2000). *Culture Matters: How Values Shape Human Progress*. New York: Basic Books.

Hart, H. L. A. (1994). *The Concept of Law* (second ed.). Oxford: Clarendon Press.

Hartsock, N. (1983). *Money, Sex and Power: Towards a Feminist Historical Materialism*. New York: Longman.

Hashmi, S., & Lee, S. (eds.). (2004). *Ethics and Weapons of Mass Destruction: Religious and Secular Perspectives*. Cambridge: Cambridge University Press.

Hassan, B.e.-D. (2001). *Arabs Caught between Domestic Oppression and Foreign Injustice*. Cairo: Cairo Institute of Human Rights Studies.

Hassan, R. (2006). A Muslim's Reflections on a New Global Ethics and Cultural Diversity. At http://kvc.minbuza.nl/uk/archive/amsterdam/ukverslag_hassan.html.

Havel, V. (1996). "The Hope for Europe." *The New York Review of Books*, June 20 (vol. 43), 11, pp. 40–41.

Hefner, R. W. (1995). *Conversion to Christianity*. Berkeley: University of California Press.

Heim, M. (1995). *Salvations: Truth and Difference in Religion*. Maryknoll: Orbis Books.

Held, D., et al. (1999). *Global Transformations*. Cambridge, UK: Polity Press.

Held, V. (1993). *Feminist Morality: Transforming Culture, Society, and Politics*. Chicago: Chicago University Press.

Helgesen, G. (2003). "The Case for Moral Education," in D. A. Bell & H. Chaibong (eds.), *Confucianism for the Modern World* (pp. 161–177). New York: Columbia University Press.

Hershman, A. M. (1949). *The Code of Maimonides, Book Fourteen; The Book of Judges,* Yale Judaica Series. New Haven: Yale University Press.

Heslam, P. (ed.). (2004). *Globalization and the Good.* London: SPCK.

Hinkelammert, F. J. (1986). *The Ideological Weapons of Death: A Theological Critique of Capitalism.* Maryknoll: Orbis Books.

Hittinger, R. (2004). *The First Grace: Rediscovering Natural Law in a Post-Christian World.* Willmington: ISI.

Hittinger, R. (2003). *The First Grace: Rediscovering the Natural Law in a Post-Christian World.* Wilmington: ISI Books.

Hobbes, T. (1968). *Leviathan.* Harmondsworth: Penguin.

Hollenbach, D. (2003). *The Global Face of Public Faith: Politics, Human Rights, and Christian Ethics.* Washington, DC: Georgetown University Press.

Hooks, B. (1982). *Ain't I a Woman: Black Women and Feminism.* London: Pluto Press.

Hopkins, J. (ed.). (1992). *The Meaning of Life from a Buddhist Perspective.* Boston: Wisdom Publications.

Huff, T. (1993). *The Rise of Early Modern Science: Islam, China, and the West.* New York: Cambridge University Press.

Hui, V. (2004, February 14). "Confucius and Patriotism: Speak from the Heart." *South China Morning Post.*

Hunter, J. R. (1969). *The Fujufuse Controversy in Nichiren Buddhism: The Debate between Nichiô and Jakushôin Nichiken.* University of Wisconsin, Madison.

International Conference on Islamic Laws and Women in the Modern World, Islamabad. (1996). Paper Presented at Conference.

Interpretation and Social Criticism. (1987). Cambridge: Harvard University Press.

Jenkins, P. (2002). *The Next Christendom: The Coming of Global Christianity.* New York: Oxford University Press.

Jones, D. V. (1989). *Code of Peace: Ethics and Security in the World of Warlord States.* Chicago: Chicago University Press.

Jonsen, A. R., & Toulmin, S. (1988). *The Abuse of Casuistry: A History of Moral Reasoning.* Berkeley and Los Angeles: University of California Press.

Cohen Joshua, et al. (eds.) *Is Multiculturalism Bad for Women.* Princeton: Princeton University Press.

Kaplan, M. M. (1934). *Judaism as a Civilization: Towards a Reconstruction of American-Jewish Life* (1957 ed.). New York: Thomas Yoseloff.

Karamah: Muslim Women Lawyers for Human Rights. (2006). At http://www.karamah.org.

Khan, K. B. (1989). "The World of Islam." Paper presented at the Proceedings of the Third World Congress on Religious Liberty, International Religions Liberty Association.

Khan, M. (2006). Syed Qutb – John Locke of the Islamic World [electronic version]. *The Globalist.* At http://www.brookings.edu/views/articles/fellows/khan20030728.htm.

Kim, Y. (2000). "Prospects for a Universal Ethic," in M. L. Stackhouse & P. J. Paris (eds.), *God and Globalization: Religion and the Powers of the Common Life* (vol. 1). Harrisburg: Trinity Press International.

Koehn, D. (1998). *Rethinking Feminist Ethics: Care, Trust, and Empathy*. London: Routledge.

Korten, D. (1995). *When Corporations Rule the World*. West Hartford, CT: Kumanian Press.

Kosovo, Independent International Commission on. (2000). *The Kosovo Report*. Oxford: Oxford University Press.

Krasner, S. D. (1993). "Westphalia and All That," in J. Goldstein & R. O. Keohane (eds.), *Ideas and Foreign Policy: Beliefs, Institutions, and Political Change*. Ithaca: Cornell University Press.

Krasner, S. D. (1996). Compromising Westphalia. *International Security, 20* (3), 115–151.

Küng, H. (1998). *A Global Ethic for Global Politics and Economics*. New York: Oxford University Press.

Küng, H. (1993). Declaration Toward a Global Ethic: Parliament of the World's Religions. At http://astro.temple.edu/~dialogue/Antho/kung.htm_34k.

Küng, H., & Kuschel, K.-J. (eds.). (1995). *A Global Ethic*. New York: Continuum.

Kuntz, P. G. (2004). *The Ten Commandments in History: Mosaic Paradigms for a Well-Ordered Society*. Grand Rapids: Wm. Eerdmans.

Kuper, A. (2000). "Rawlsian Global Justice: Beyond the Law of Peoples to a Cosmopolitan Law of Persons." *Political Theory 28* (5).

Kymlicka, W. (1995). "Liberalism," in Ted Honderich (ed.), *The Oxford Companion to Philosophy*. Oxford: Oxford University Press.

Kymlicka, W., & He, B. (eds.). (2005). *Multiculturalism in Asia*. Oxford: Oxford University Press.

Landes, D. (1983). *Revolution in Time*. Cambridge, MA: Belknap Press.

Lazarus, M. (1900). *The Ethics of Judaism* (H. Szold, trans.). Philadelphia: Jewish Publication Society.

Leewen, A. T. V. (1964). *Christianity in World History*. London: Edinburgh House.

Lichtenstein, A. (1981). *The Seven Laws of Noah*. New York: Rabbi Jacob Joseph School Press.

Little, D., Kelsay, J., & Sachedina, A. (1988). *Human Rights and the Conflicts of Culture: Western and Islamic Perspectives on Religious Liberty*. Columbia: University of South Carolina Press.

Lugo, L. (ed.). (2000). *Religion, Pluralism, and Public Life*. Grand Rapids: Wm. Eerdmans.

Luther. (1811). The Shorter Catechism.

MacIntyre, A. C. (1981). *After Virtue: A Study in Moral Theory*. Notre Dame: University of Notre Dame Press.

MacIntyre, A. (1999). *Dependent Rational Animals*. Chicago: Open Court.

MacKinnon, C. (1989). *Towards a Feminist Theory of the State*. Cambridge: Harvard University Press.

Madsen, R., & Strong, T. (eds.). (2003). *The Many and the One: Religious and Secular Perspectives on Ethical Pluralism in the Modern World*. Princeton: Princeton University Press.

Mahmood, T. (1972). *Family Law Reform in the Muslim World*. Delhi: Indian Law Institute.

Maland, D. (1966). *Europe in the Seventeenth Century*. London: Macmillan.

Mapel, D., & Nardin, T. (eds.). (1998). *International Society: Diverse Ethical Perspectives*. Princeton: Princeton University Press.

Marchand, M. H., & Parpart, J. (eds.). (1995). *Feminism, Postmodernism, Development*. New York: Routledge.

Martin, D. (1990). *Tongues of Fire: The Explosion of Protestantism in Latin America*. Oxford: Blackwell.

Marty, M., & Appleby, S. (2004). *Fundamentalism Comprehended*. Chicago: University of Chicago.

Masud, M. K. (2003a). *Iqbal's reconstruction of Ijtihad* (second ed.). Lahore: Iqbal Academy.

Masud, M. K. (2003b). "The Scope of Pluralism in Islamic Moral Traditions," in R. Madsen & T. Strong (eds.), *The Many and the One, Religious and Secular Perspectives on Ethical Pluralism* (pp. 180–191). Princeton: Princeton University Press.

Masud, M. K. (2000). "Ideology and Legitimacy," in M. K. Masud (ed.), *Travelers in Faith, Studies on Tablighi Jama'at as a Transnational Movement for the Renewal of Faith*. Leiden: Brill.

Mawdudi, A. A. (1976). *Human Rights in Islam*. Leicester: Islamic Foundation.

Mayer, A. E. (1991). *Islam and Human Rights*. Boulder and London. Westview.

Mayer, A. E. (1990). "Current Muslim Thinking on Human Rights," in A. A. An-Na'im & F. M. Deng (eds.), *Human Rights in Africa: Cross-cultural Perspectives* (pp. 133–158). Washington, DC: The Brookings Institution.

McCann, D., & Miller, P. (eds.). (2005). *In Search of the Common Good*. Harrisburg: Trinity Press International.

McGreevy, J. T. (2003). *Catholicism and American Freedom: A History*. New York: W.W. Norton & Company.

Mernissi, F. (1987). *The Veil and the Male Elite*. Bloomington: Indiana University Press.

Miller, D., & Hashmi, S. (eds.). (2001). *Boundaries and Justice: Diverse Ethical Perspectives*. Princeton: Princeton University Press.

Miller, D., & Walzer, M. (eds.). (1995). *Pluralism, Justice and Equality*. Oxford: Oxford University Press.

Miller, P. D. (1990). *Deuteronomy: A Bible Commentary for Teaching and Preaching*. Louisville: John Knox Press.

Moe, C. (2002). Islamic Human Rights Thought in Bosnia. At http://folk.uio.no/chrismoe/research/docproj.htm.

Mohanty, C. T. (2003). *Feminism without Borders: Decolonising Theory, Practicing Solidarity*. Durham and London: Duke University Press.

Mohanty, C. T., Russo, A., & Torres, L. (eds.). (1991). *Third World Women and the Politics of Feminism*. Bloomington and Indianapolis: Indiana University Press.

Moraga, C., Anzaldua, G., & Bambara, T. C. (eds.). (2001). *This Bridge Called My Back: Writings by Radical Women of Color*. Berkeley: Third Woman Press.

Moynihan, Daniel. (1993). *Pandemonium*. Oxford: Oxford University Press.

Murphy, M. C. (2001). *Natural Law and Practical Rationality*. New York: Cambridge University Press.

Murphy, M. C. (2002). "The Natural Law Tradition in Ethics," in E. N. Zalta (ed.), *The Stanford Encyclopedia of Philosophy* (Winter ed.). Stanford: Stanford University Press.

Nadwi, A. A. (1982). *Western Civilization: Islam and Muslims*. Lucknow: Academy of Islamic Research and Publications.

Nadwi, A. A. (1976). *Muslim Mamalik men Islamiyyat awr Maghrabiyyat ki Kashmakash*. Karachi: Majlis Nashriyat Islam.

Nardin, T. (1998). "Legal Postivism As a Theory of International Society," in D. R. Mapel & T. Nardin (eds.), *International Society: Diverse Ethical Perspectives* (pp. 17–35). Princeton: Princeton University Press.

Nardin, T. (ed.). (1996). *The Ethics of War and Peace: Religious and Secular Perspectives*. Princeton: Princeton University Press.

Niebuhr, H. R. (1963). *The Responsible Self: An Essay in Christian Moral Philosophy*. New York: Harper & Row.

Niebuhr, R. (1939–41). *The Nature and Destiny of Man* (vol. 2). New York: Scribner's Sons.

Noble, D. (1997). *The Religion of Technology: The Divinity of Man and the Spirit of Invention*. New York: Alfred Knopf.

Noddings. (1984). *Caring: A Feminist Approach to Ethics*. Berkeley: University of California Press.

Nosco, P. (1996). "Keeping the Faith: Bakuhan Policy Towards Religions in Seventeenth-Century Japan," in P. F. Kornicki & I. J. McMullen (eds.), *Religion in Japan: Arrows to Heaven and Earth*. New York: Cambridge University Press.

Nosco, P. (2002). "Confucian Perspectives on Civil Society and Government," in N. L. Rosenblum & R. C. Post (eds.), *Civil Society and Government*. Princeton: Princeton University Press.

Novak, D. (2000). *Covenantal Rights: A Study in Jewish Political Theory*. Princeton: Princeton University Press.

Novak, D. (1998). *Natural Law in Judaism*. Cambridge: Cambridge University Press.

Novak, D. (1983). *The Image of the Non-Jew in Judaism: An Historical and Constructive Study of the Noahide Laws* (vol. 14). Toronto: Edwin Mellen Press.

Nurser, J. D. (2005). *For All Peoples and All Nations: The Ecumenical Church and Human Rights*. Washington, DC: Georgetown University Press.

Nussbaum, M. (2000). *Women and Human Development*. Cambridge: Cambridge University Press.

O'Hagan, J. (2002). *Conceptualising the West in International Relations: From Spengler to Said*. Basingstoke: Palgrave.

Obenchain, D. (2002). "The Study of Religion and the Coming Global Generation," in M. L. Stackhouse & D. Obenchain (eds.), *God and Globalization: Christ and the Dominions of Civilization* (vol. 3). Harrisburg: Trinity Press International.

Okin, S. M. (1991). *Justice, Gender and the Family*. New York: Basic Books.

Osiander, A. (1994). *The State System of Europe, 1640–1990*. Oxford: Clarendon Press.

Pachuau, L. et al. (forthcoming). *News of Boundless Riches: Interrogating and Reconstructing Missions in a Global Era*. Publication information not available.

Pagden, A. (1982). *The Fall of Natural Man: The American Indian and the Origins of Comparative Ethnology*. Cambridge: Cambridge University Press.

Parekh, B. (2000). *Rethinking Multiculturalism*. Basingstoke: Macmillan.

Paris, P. J. (2001). "Moral Exemplars in Global Community," in M. L. Stackhouse, D. A. Hicks, & D. S. Browning (eds.), *God and Globalization: The Spirit and the Modern Authorities* (vol. 2). Harrisburg: Trinity Press International.

Pateman, C. (1988). *The Sexual Contract*. Cambridge, UK: Polity Press.

Philpott, D. (2004). "The Catholic Wave." *The Journal of Democracy, 15* (2), 32–46.

Philpott, D. (2001). *Revolutions in Sovereignty*. Princeton, NJ: Princeton University Press.

Plumwood, V. (1993). *Feminism and the Mastery of Nature*. London and New York: Routledge.

Pocock, J. G. A. (1975). *The Machiavellian Moment: Florentine Political Thought and the Atlantic Republican Tradition*. Princeton: Princeton University Press.

Pogge, T. (2002). *World Poverty and Human Rights*. Cambridge, UK: Polity Press.

Polanyi, K. (1944). *The Great Transformation*. Boston: Beacon Press.

Pope John Paul II. (1991). *Centesimus Annus.*

Pope John Paul II. (1993). *Veritatis Splendor.*

Pope John Paul II. (1982). Address to the United Nations General Assembly.

Pope Pius XI. (1931). *Quadragesimo Anno*, §79.

Porter, E. (1999). *Feminist Perspectives on Ethics*. London and New York: Longman.

Porter, J. (1999). *Natural and Divine Law: Reclaiming the Tradition for Christian Ethics*. Grand Rapids: Wm. Eerdmans.

Qutb, S. (1980). *Khasa'is al-tasawwur al-Islami wa muqawwimatihi* (seventh ed.). Cairo: Dar al-Shuruq.

Qutb, S. (1988). *Nahw Mujtama' Islami* (eighth ed.). Cairo: Dar al-Shuruq.

Ramban (Nachmanides). (1971). *Commentary on the Torah: Genesis* (C. B. Chavel, trans.). New York: Shilo.

Rawls, J. (1999a). *The Law of Peoples*. Cambridge: Harvard University Press.

Rawls, J. (1999b). *A Theory of Justice* (revised ed.). Cambridge: Harvard University Press.

Rawls, J. (1995). *Political Liberalism* (p/b). New York: Columbia University Press.

Rawls, J. (1993). *Political Liberalism* (h/b). New York: Columbia University Press.

Rawls, J. (1971). *A Theory of Justice*. Cambridge: Harvard University Press.

Razu, I. J. M. (2001). *Transnational Corporations as Agents of Dehumanization*. New Delhi: SCM Press.

Resolutions Concerning Political, Muslim Minorities and Communities, Legal and Information Affairs, Resolution No. 56/8-P (1997, December). Paper presented at the Eighth Session of the Islamic Summit Conference, Tehran, Islamic Republic of Iran.

Richards, J. R. (1982). *The Sceptical Feminist: A Philosphical Inquiry*. Harmondsworth: Penguin.

Robinson, F. (1999). *Globalizing Care: Ethics, Feminist Theory and International Relations*. Boulder: Westview Press.

Rorty. Richard, "Human Rights," in Stephen Shute and Susan Hurley. (eds.), *On Human Rights* (New York: Basic Book, 1993).

Rosenblum, N., & Post, R. C. (eds.). (2002). *Civil Society and Government*. Princeton: Princeton University Press.

Rowbotham, S. (1973). *Woman's Consciousness/Man's World*. Harmondsworth: Penguin.

Ruddick, S. (1989). *Maternal Thinking: Towards a Politics of Peace*. London: The Women's Press.

Sachedina, A. A. (2001). *The Islamic Roots of Democratic Pluralism*. New York: Oxford University Press.

Safi, O. (ed.). (2003). *Progressive Muslims: On Justice, Gender, and Pluralism*. Oxford: Oneworld.

Scheffer, D. (1992). "Toward a Modern Doctrine of Humanitarian Intervention." *University of Toledo Law Review, 23*, 253–293.

Schweiker, W. (2004). *Theological Ethics and Global Dynamics*. London: Blackwell.

Shaikh, S. (2003). "Transforming Feminisms: Islam, Women, and Gender Justice," in O. Safi (ed.), *Progressive Muslims* (pp. 147–162). Oxford: Oneworld.

al-Shishani, A. W. A. (1980). *Huquq al-insan wa al-hurriyat al-asasiyya fi al-nizam al-Islami wa al-nuzum al-mu'asara* (Rights of Man and His Basic Freedoms in the Islamic System and Contemporary Systems). Riyadh: al-Jam'iyyat al-'Ilmiyya al-malikiyya.

Shogan, D. (Ed.). (1993). *A Reader in Feminist Ethics*. Toronto: Canadian Scholars' Press.

Skillen, J. (2004). *In Pursuit of Justice*. Lanham, MD: Rowman and Littlefield.

Skillen, J., & et al. (1991). *Political Order and the Plural Structure of Society*. Atlanta: Scholars Press.

Skinner, Q. (1998). *Liberty before Liberalism*. Cambridge: Cambridge University Press.

Sōka Gakkai International. At http://www.sgi.org/English/SGI/history.htm.

Spivak, G. C. (1990). *A Critique of Postcolonial Reason: Toward a History of the Vanishing Present*. Princeton: Princeton University Press.

Spivak, G. C., & (1998). "Cultural Talks in the Hot Peace: Revisiting the 'Global Village,'" in P. Cheah & B. Robbins (eds.), *Cosmopolitics: Thinking and Feeling Beyond the Nation*. Minneapolis: University of Minnesota Press.

Squires, J. (1999). *Gender in Political Theory*. Cambridge, UK: Polity Press.

Stackhouse, M. L. (2004). "Vocation," in G. Meilaender (ed.), *Oxford Handbook of Theological Ethics*. London: Oxford University Press.

Stackhouse, M. (ed.). (2000–2002). *God and Globalization* (vols. 1–3). Harrisburg: Trinity Press International.

Stackhouse, M. L. (1993). The Moral Roots of the Corporation. *Theology and Public Policy, V* (1), 29–39.

Stackhouse, M. L. (1984). *Creeds, Society, and Human Rights: A Study in Three Cultures*. Grand Rapids: Eerdmans Publishers.

Stackhouse, M. L., & Stratton, L. (2002). *Capitalism, Civil Society, Religion, and the Poor*. Wilmington, DE: ISI.

Steans, J. (1998). *Gender and International Relations: An Introduction*. Cambridge, UK: Polity Press.

Steiner, H. (1992). "Libertarianism and the Transnational Migration of People," in B. Goodin (ed.), *Free Movement*. Hemel Hempstead: Harvester Wheatsheaf.

Stone, J. (1999). *Original Enlightenment and the Transformation of Medieval Japanese Buddhism*. Honolulu: University of Hawaii Press.

Storrar, W. F., & et al. (eds.). (2004). *Public Theology for the 21st Century*. London: T & T Clark.

Tan, K.-C. (1998). "Liberal Toleration in Rawls's Law of Peoples." *Ethics, 108* (2), 276–295.

Tawney, R. H. (1926). *Religion and the Rise of Capitalism*. New York: Harcourt, Brace & Co.

Taylor, C. (1992). *Multiculturalism and the "Politics of Recognition"*. Princeton: Princeton University Press.

Teiser, S. F. (2002). "The Spirits of Chinese Religion," in D. S. Lopez (ed.), *Religions of Asia in Practice*. Princeton, Princeton University Press.

Thurman, R. A. F. (1996). *Essential Tibetan Buddhism*. New Delhi: Harper Collins Publishers India.

Toulmin, S. (2000). *Return to Reason*. Cambridge: Harvard University Press.

Tu Wei-ming. (2002). "Multiple Modernities – Implications of the Rise of 'Confucian' East Asia," in K.-H. Pohl & A. W. Muller (eds.), *Chinese Ethics in a Global Context* (pp. 55–56). Leiden: Brill.

UNESCO. (2006). The Universal Ethics Project. At http://www.unesco.org/opi2/philosophyandethics/pronpro.htm.

United Nations' 1948 Universal Declaration of Human Rights. At http://www.un.org/Overview/rights.html.

van der Vyver, J. D. (1996). "Introduction," in J. D. van der Vyver & J. Witte Jr. (eds.), *Religious Human Rights in Global Perspective*. The Hague: Martinus Nijhoff Publishers.

van Drimmelen, R. (1998). *Faith in the Global Economy*. Geneva: World Council of Churches.

Vervoorn, Aat. (1998). *Re Orient: Change in Asian Societies*. Hong Kong.

Wadud, A. (1998). *Qur'an and Women: Reading the Sacred Text from a Woman's Perspective*. New York: Oxford University Press.

Wafi, A. A.a.-W. (1999). *Huquq al-Insan fi'l Islam* [Human Rights in Islam] (sixth. ed.). Cairo: Nahda Misr.

Walzer, Michael. (2001). *Universalism and Jewish Values, Twentieth Morgenthau Memorial Lecture*. Paper presented at the Carnegie Council on Ethics and International Affairs, New York.

Walzer, Michael. (1994). *Thick and Thin: Moral Argument at Home and Abroad*. Notre Dame: University of Notre Dame Press.

Walzer, M. (1992). *Just and Unjust Wars*. New York: Basic Books.

Walzer, M., Zohar, N. J., Ackerman, A., Lorberbaum, Y., & Lorberbaum, M. (eds.). (2003). *The Jewish Political Tradition* (vol. 2, *Membership*). New Haven: Yale University Press.

Walzer, M., Zohar, N. J., Ackerman, A., Lorberbaum, Y., & Lorberbaum, M. (eds.). (2000). *The Jewish Political Tradition* (vol. 1, Authority). New Haven: Yale University Press.

Weber, M. (1968). "The City" (G. Roth & C. Wittich, trans.), in *Economy and Society*. New York: Bedminster Press.

Weller, Marc. (1999). "On the Hazards of Foreign Travel for Dictators and Other Criminals," *International Affairs*, vol. 75 (3), pp. 599–617.

Whelan, I. (1995). *Modern Feminist Thought: From the Second Wave to 'Post-Feminism.'* Edinburgh: Edinburgh University Press.

Wink, W. (1992). *Engaging the Powers: Discernment and Resistance in a World of Domination*. Philadelphia: Fortress Press.

Wink, W. (1986). *Unmasking the Powers: The Invisible Forces That Determine Human Existence*. Philadelphia: Fortress Press.

Wink, W. (1984). *Naming the Powers: The Language of Power in the New Testament*. Philadelphia: Fortress Press.

Witte, J. (ed.). (1993). *Christianity & Democracy in Global Context*. Boulder: Westview Press.

Witte, J., & et al. (1999). *Sharing the Book: Religious Perspectives on the Rights and Wrongs of Proselytism*. Maryknoll: Orbis Books.

Wolf, M. (2002). *Why Globalization Works*. New Haven: Yale University Press.

Wolfe, C. (1995). "Subsidiarity: The 'Other' Ground of Limited Government," in K. Grasso & et al. (eds.), *Catholicism, Liberalism, and Communitarianism*. Lanham: Rowman and Littlefield.

Wollstonecraft, M. (1975). *Vindication of the Rights of Women*. Harmondsworth: Penguin.

World Council of Churches. (2006). At http://www.wcc-coe.org/wcc/what/jpc.

Wright, J. W. (ed.). (1997). *The New York Times 1998 Almanac*. New York: Penguin Reference.

Wright, R. (1996). "Islam and Liberal Democracy: Two Visions of Reformation." *Journal of Democracy, 7* (2), 64–75.

(2006). From www.president.ir/oic/oicpol.html.

Yee, C. S. (2003). "The Confucian Conception of Gender in the Twenty-First Century," in D. A. Bell & H. Chaibong. (eds.), *Confucianism for the Modern World* (pp. 312–333). Cambridge: Cambridge University Press.

Yehuda, H. (forthcoming). *Kuzari* (B. Kogan, trans.). New Haven: Yale University Press.

Yew, L. K. (1998). *The Singapore Story: Memoirs of Lee Kuan Yew*. New York: Prentice Hall.

Yong, A., & Heltzel, P. G. (2004). *Theology in a Global Context*. London: T & T Clark.

Yun, V. M. H. (2001). *Where There is Dharma, There is a Way*. Taipei: Foguang Cultural Enterprise.

Zohar, N. J. (1993). "Boycott, Crime, and Sin: Ethical and Talmudic Responses to Injustice Abroad." *Ethics and International Affairs, 7* (1), 39–53.

Index